WHEN YOU PAINT

A complete guide for practicing artists

OUR CANVASES ARE THE MILESTONES OF MAN — FROM THE REINDEER ON THE WALLS OF CAVES TO THE CLIFFS OF MONET — FROM THE HUNTERS, THE FISHERMEN WHO INHABIT THE TOMBS OF EGYPT, THE COMICAL SCENES OF POMPEII, THE FRESCOES OF PISA AND SIENA, THE MYTHOLOGICAL COMPOSITIONS OF VERONESE AND RUBENS, FROM ALL THESE THE SAME SPIRIT COMES DOWN TO US . . .

Paul Cézanne

WHEN YOU PAINT

A complete guide for practicing artists

by WARD BRACKETT

a North Light Book

McGRAW-HILL BOOK COMPANY

NEW YORK, ST. LOUIS, SAN FRANCISCO, DUSSELDORF, LONDON, MEXICO, SYDNEY, TORONTO

NORTH LIGHT PUBLISHERS,
a division of FLETCHER ART SERVICES, INC.,
37 Franklin Street, Westport, Conn 06880.

McGRAW-HILL BOOK COMPANY
1221 Avenue of the Americas, New York, N.Y. 10020

Library of Congress Cataloging in Publication Data

Brackett, Ward.
When you paint; a complete guide for practicing artists.

1. Painting — Technique. I. Title.
ND1500.B66 751.4 74-77082
ISBN 0-07-007029-6

Edited by Walt Reed
Designed by Ward Brackett

Composed in Optima by John W. Shields, Inc.
Printed by Connecticut Printers, Inc.
Bound by Economy Book Binding Corp.

Manufactured in U.S.A.

First Printing 1974.

This book is for Dolli and Gordon

ACKNOWLEDGEMENTS

I would like to start by thanking Walt Reed, our editor, for his much needed guidance and encouragement in seeing this book through. I am grateful to my wife for her help in curbing my rhetoric when it rambled and my syntax when it floundered; and to publisher Bill Fletcher for his unfailing patience with my lateness. Finally I want to thank Howard Munce who suggested I do the book in the first place.

CONTENTS

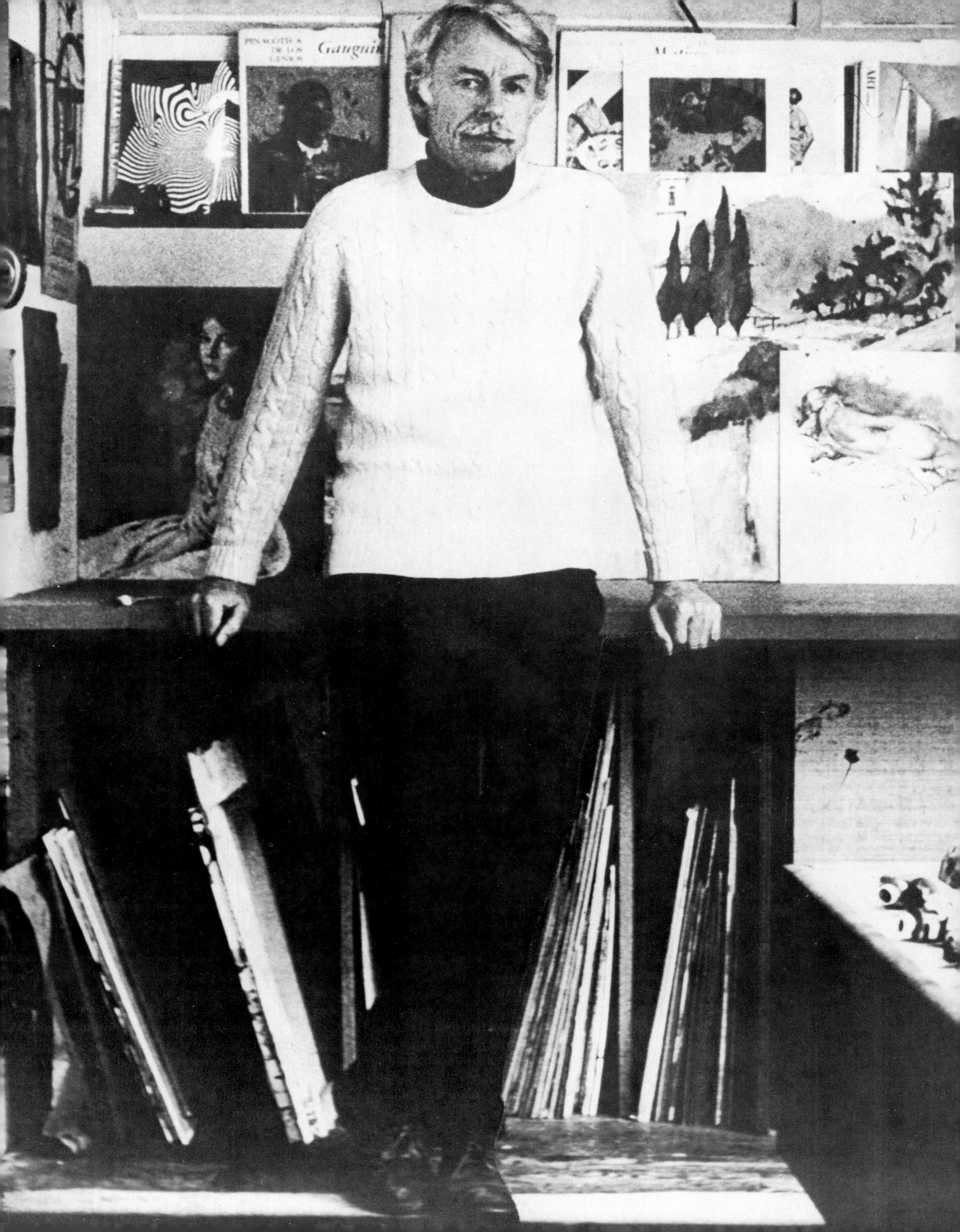
PINACOTECA DE LOS GENIOS
Gauguin

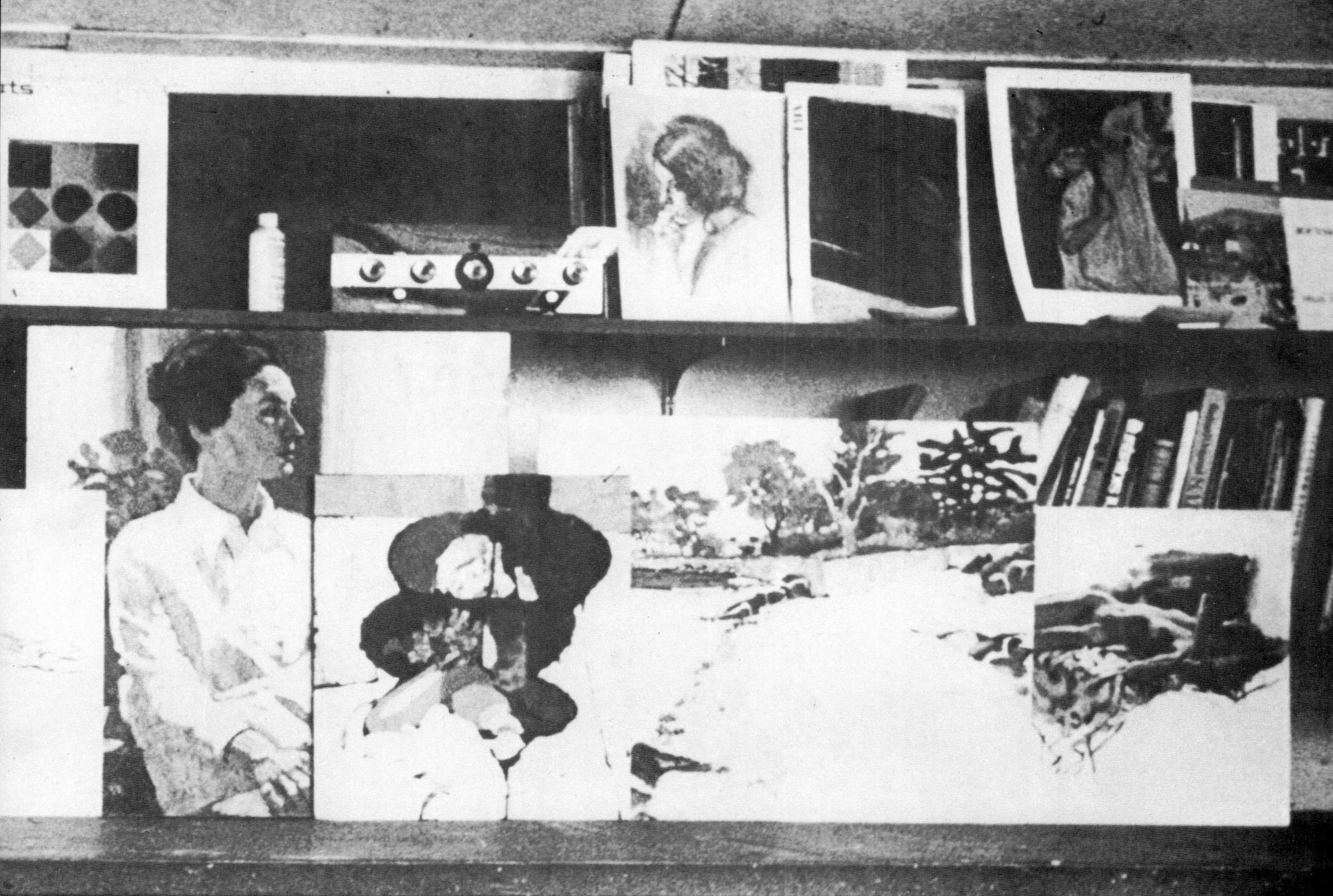

My aim in writing this book is to bring to the reader fundamentals of drawing, painting and design. Practical matters such as materials and methods, techniques and procedures will be discussed at length and in detail. We will discuss more advanced subjects like color, concept and the psychology of shapes.

Since this is basically a book about my personal discoveries and experiences as a professional artist, you will be exposed to some of my minor victories and misadventures at the drawing board. When I say discoveries I mean just that, because I believe every artist has to make his own, just as though they had never been made before by anyone.

In the pages that follow you will find the gleanings of much researching and talking to myself. A lot of this material was culled from notes taken during a break away from work or a pause in the midst of painting a picture.

Considerable thought has gone into the selection of subject matter. What I particularly wanted were those subjects that would be as relevant as possible to the students' special needs and problems.

Today, more than ever, the approach to painting must appear, to the student, baffling and contradictory. The last two decades have seen the introduction of new materials, new methods, and new concepts.

This book intends to show that any method or technique, whether it be old and traditional, or new and experimental, should remain the tool of the artist — the transmitter of concept and no more. It must not be allowed to outshine the original purpose, the idea. A picture that screams its technique at you at the expense of everything else is little more than a demonstration of craft.

One of my hopes is to save the student some initial groping and confusion in his approach to picture making. Much waste motion can be averted if he will take the time to familiarize himself with the ways and methods of artists who have gone before him. The more he acquires of this knowledge, the sooner he will be ready to decide for himself which way he wants to go and which technique is best for him.

You may notice that I have not been bothered by any feelings of modesty in the way I intermix examples of my work with those of people like Vermeer, Matisse and Picasso. The fact is, wherever I found them helpful in demonstrating a point or serving as an example, I have not hesitated to put them to work. I have tried to avoid tricks and gimmickry as unnecessary diversions.

You will find that I make no particular distinction between "fine" art and commercial art, but treat both as one.

Finally, I would like to say that the experience of writing this book has been full of rediscoveries for me, not the least of which is that the creative artist never stops learning.

W. B.

SEEING WHAT'S THERE

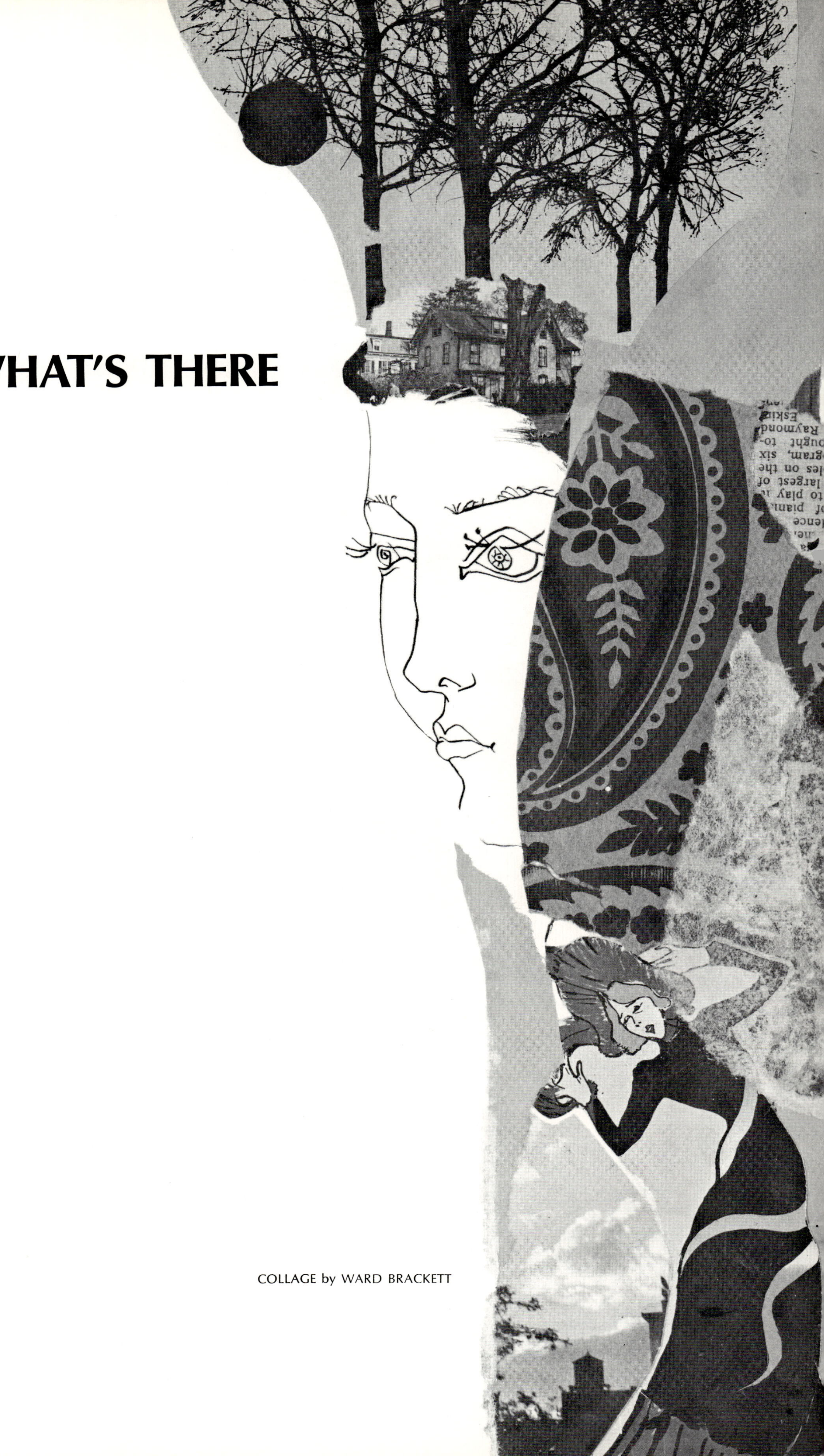

COLLAGE by WARD BRACKETT

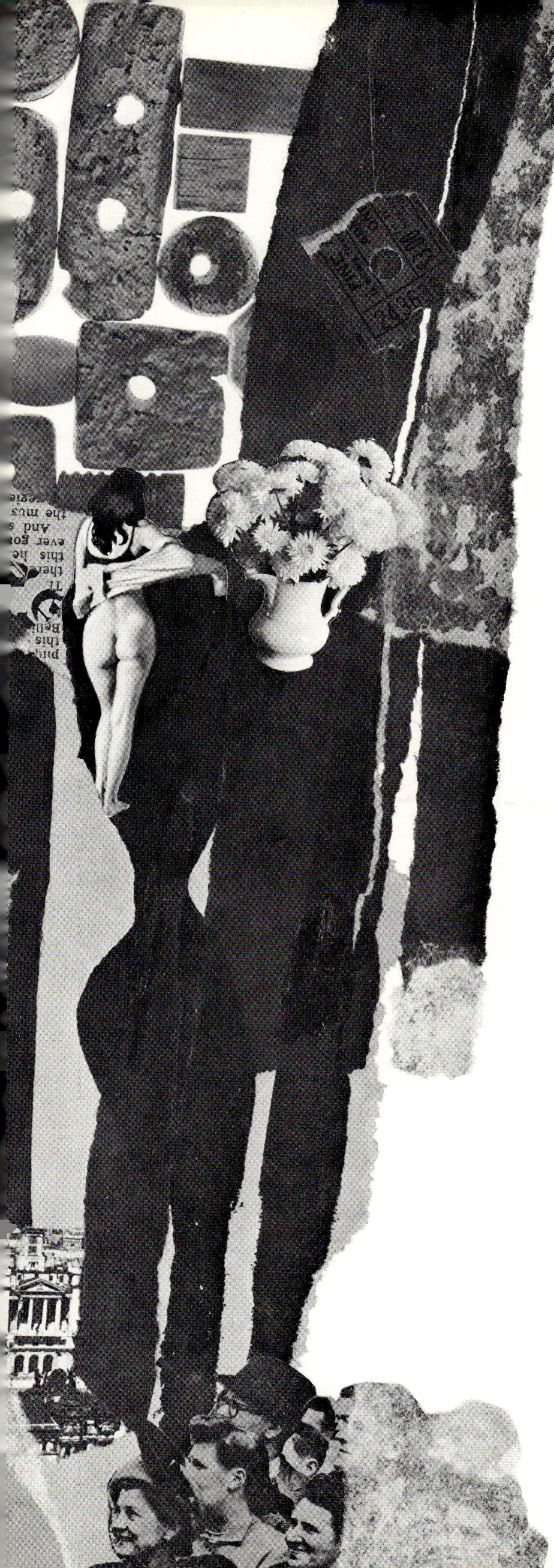

THINKING IS MORE INTERESTING THAN KNOWING, BUT NOT SO INTERESTING AS LOOKING.

Goethe

When I was about five years old I came home from school one day with a wash drawing of a peach. My mother took one look at it and decided then and there I must be a *wunderkind,* and should be introduced to art without further delay. As a result, I was taken to the Milwaukee Art Institute and let loose in a couple of acres of paintings, mostly German, English and American in origin, and all very traditional.

I remember the paintings seemed enormous to me at the time and awesomely "natural" looking. Also, I remember coming away with another reaction: the feeling that artists must be different from ordinary people. How else was it possible for them to see so much if they didn't have a special kind of vision. It wasn't until years later that I learned that the artist is not gifted with any super vision. But there is a difference. And that is in the way he **uses** his eyes.

Sooner or later every artist learns that the eyes can be trained and must be trained to go far beyond the requirements and demands of everyday living. It is this training that makes the artist unique.

An example of the sort of observation I'm talking about would be to walk along a route that you have driven along many times before. When you are in a car your eyes may do a perfectly good job of alerting you to traffic and to getting you where you want to go. But on foot and suddenly free to use your eyes in all directions, you will be amazed at how much you have missed.

When we consider the world around us with an eye to drawing and recording it with accuracy and understanding, we are required to use our eyes in a very particular way, if we are going to understand it. We cannot understand it if we have not first observed it with complete objectivity.

Some schools follow a completely uninhibited approach to drawing and give the student his head if he wants to bypass the academics of formal and conventional drawing. The student is encouraged to draw as he imagines his subject rather than as he sees it. This may be fine, but I think this sort of conceptual expression should come only as a natural consequence of learning and developing, of evaluating and experiencing. In short, I believe that to draw as one imagines, one must first learn to draw as one sees.

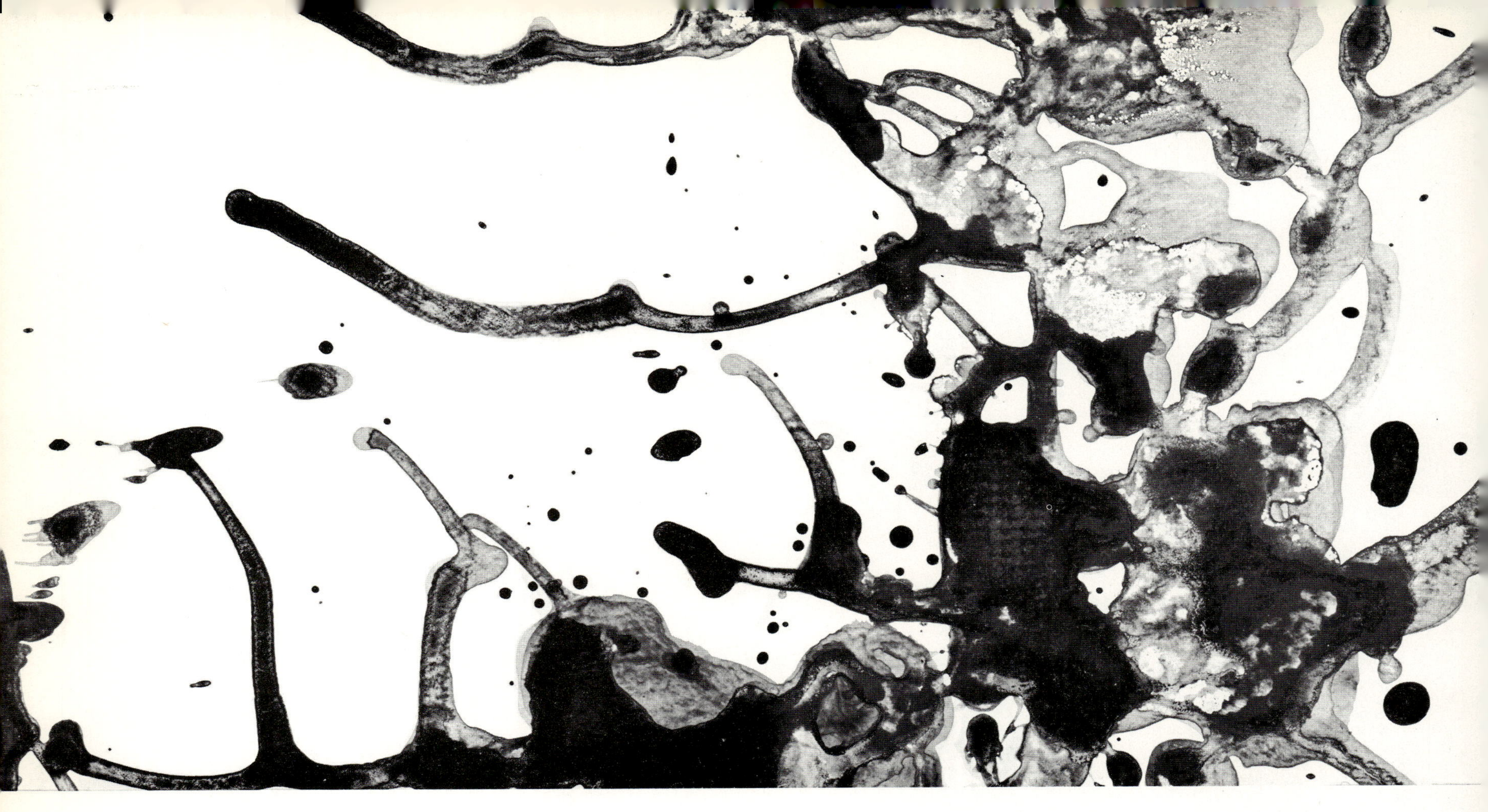

PART 1· SHAPES and COMPOSITION

The first things a baby sees are shapes. To its wondering, unfocussing eyes, the world is a scene of vague, shadowy forms. By the time it learns to see things sharply, its reaction to form is instinctive. And even though it soon loses all conscious interest in these first impressions, they are never altogether forgotten. They are stored away in the subconscious, waiting for just the right kind of stimuli to awaken them. Here's what Paul Klee has to say about memory:

"All art is a memory of age-old things, dark things, whose fragments live on in the artist."

Anyone who has ever seen the primitive, purely impulsive paintings of kindergarten children must be struck by their direct, unaffected and unmannered concept. To me, the most remarkable thing about these paintings is the shapes that are used, and even the soundness of the composition. But mostly it is the shapes that come through; boldly, powerfully and with the greatest directness. As they get into the higher grades the approach becomes more intellectual. Their paintings tend to lose much original impact. Colors become less primary, shapes more vague and composition

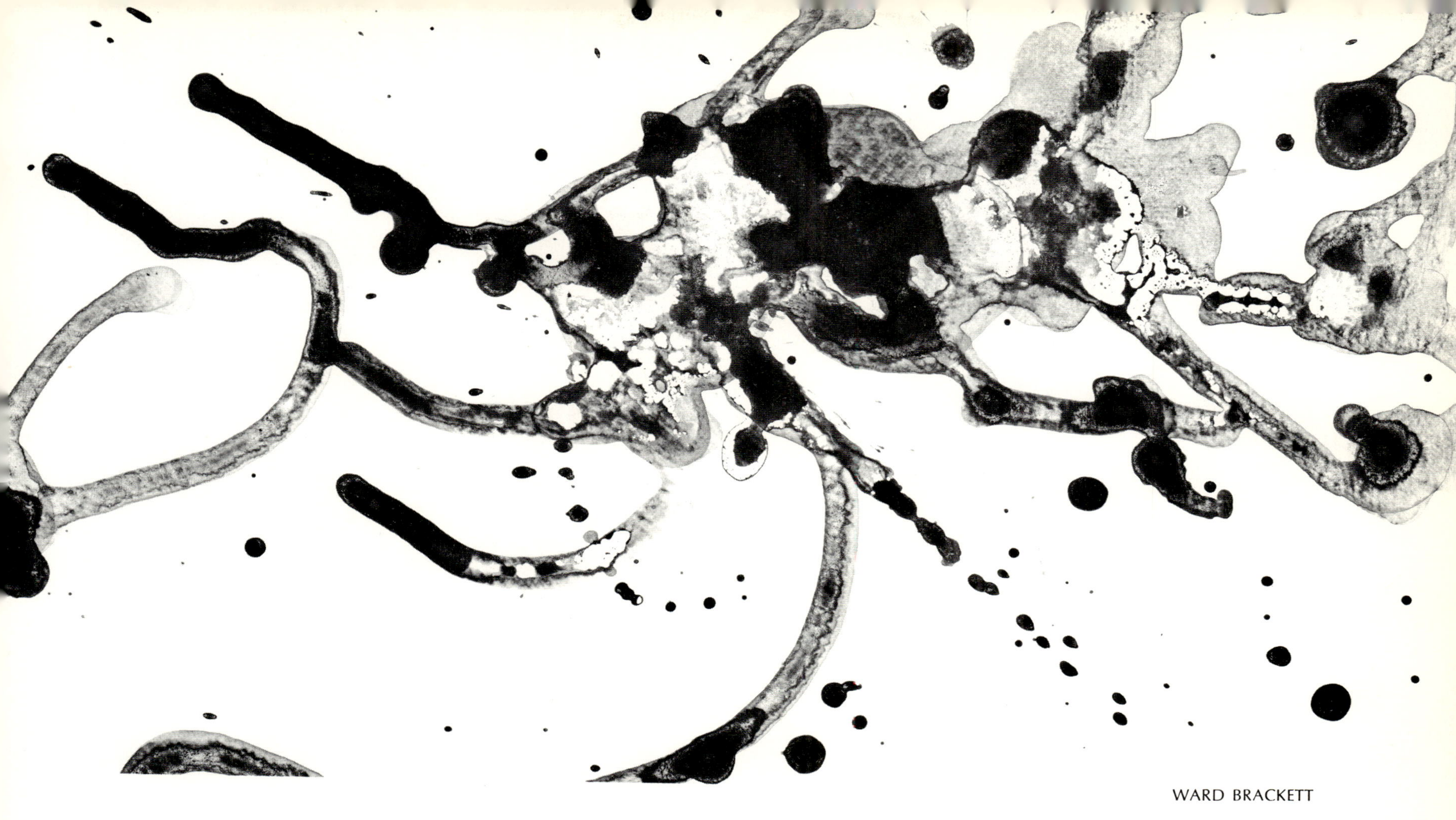

WARD BRACKETT

is often confused or unresolved. The greatest loss, I think, is in the shapes. Concept of form is overshadowed or replaced by detail as reasoning takes over. Matisse was aware of this. He instructed his pupils to strive to "—see like a child and paint like an adult."

The lesson to be learned here is simply— shapes. In the next few pages I would like to go into this subject and discuss every aspect of it — where they originate and how they affect and influence the artist. A little further on we'll see how shapes can be used to stimulate the power of suggestion and how they work on the subconscious mind of the viewer. Painters like Dali, Chagall, Miró and Gorky, to name only four, are famous for their ability to take shapes and make them generate moods and sensations of excitement or serenity; joy or horror; mystery or nostalgia.

A world of shapes awaits us, in an infinite variety of forms. Architectural forms, natural forms, animal and vegetal forms, sky, sea and earth forms. There is literally no limit to this vast reservoir of raw material. The artist who chooses city shapes for his motif will naturally be working more with architectural forms, just as the landscape and seascape painter will find himself involved primarily with shapes that are created and conditioned by nature rather than by the hand of man.

In the following six pages we're going to take a hard look at some of these shapes, the idea being to become as familiar as possible with their wide variety. We will see how the visual material found in nature (as well as that from man's created world) can become the motif for design. The illustrations are designed to show that it is not enough to take what we see for granted. Being selective in choosing our subject means being aware of what's there and knowing how to use it. Taking things for granted, in fact, usually leads to dangerous generalizing, with the result that we do not become sufficiently involved with our subject.

The first half of this chapter on shapes and composition deals with the subject of forms. Virtually all forms fall into two categories — **organic** and **geometric.** For the sake of easier identification and description, we will be referring to them by these names throughout this book.

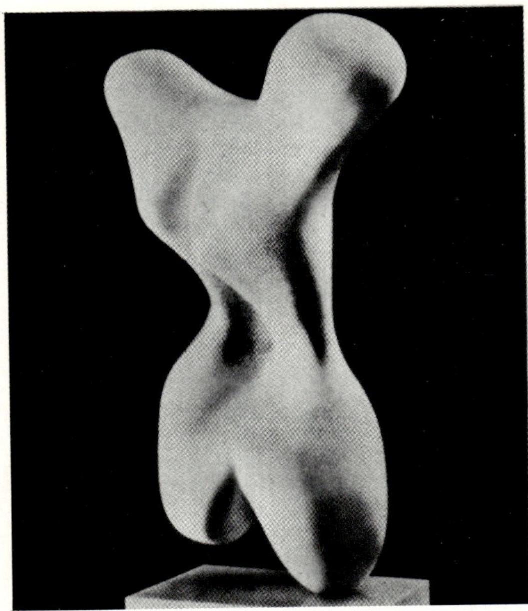

TORSO by HANS ARP
Muller-Widman Collection, Basel

FORMS: ORGANIC

Organic shapes are perhaps the most fundamental, both to our consciousness and to the meaning of art itself. Actively or subconsciously we think of curving, rounded shapes as being analogous to growing, living things. In much the same way we have been conditioned by environment and habit to accept rectilinear, triangular and cylindrical shapes as a product of man. But let's start with the free forms of organic shapes. On the opposite page I've assembled eight examples.

1. This is a close-up shot of a clump of seaweed taken at low tide. Here are some basic vegetal shapes you'll probably recognize from wall paper and textile designs. It also suggests the action painting of Jackson Pollock (see page 25) or simply random brush strokes.

2. These beach stones and pieces of wood have been well worked over by the forces of nature. They probably started out as angular, geometric shapes, but the processes of erosion and abrasion have left them quite organic in form.

3. Here's one you may not recognize. I'll admit it's a bit tricky but I couldn't resist it. I discovered it in the tray in my darkroom one morning and took a picture of it. It's nothing but crystallized hypo, but if you take another look it seems to be jumping with all sorts of symbols and prehistoric images. To me it suggests ancient cave painting or rock engraving. I also think of Paul Klee or Dubuffet.

4. Onions, limes, mushrooms and a green pepper contributed to this arrangement. Vegetal forms like these are the most common of all motifs. Look for them in modern art.

5. Turn your imagination loose and you will find all kinds of shapes in a sky full of clouds. Human, animal, vegetable, symbolic — they're all there. Notice how often the cloud motif pops up in modern abstract painting.

6. The cracked clay of this dried river bed makes an interesting mosaic something like that of a jigsaw puzzle. Here is abstract pattern straight from nature.

7. Bones, sea shell and coral. These forms have furnished a basic concept for quite a few modern artists. Henry Moore, the English painter-sculptor, for example, has taken animal bone and made it a motif for much of his art.

8. This growth of barnacles has good possibilities for an abstract design. It presents an overall pattern very similar to that of a field of flowers or a crowd of people viewed from overhead.

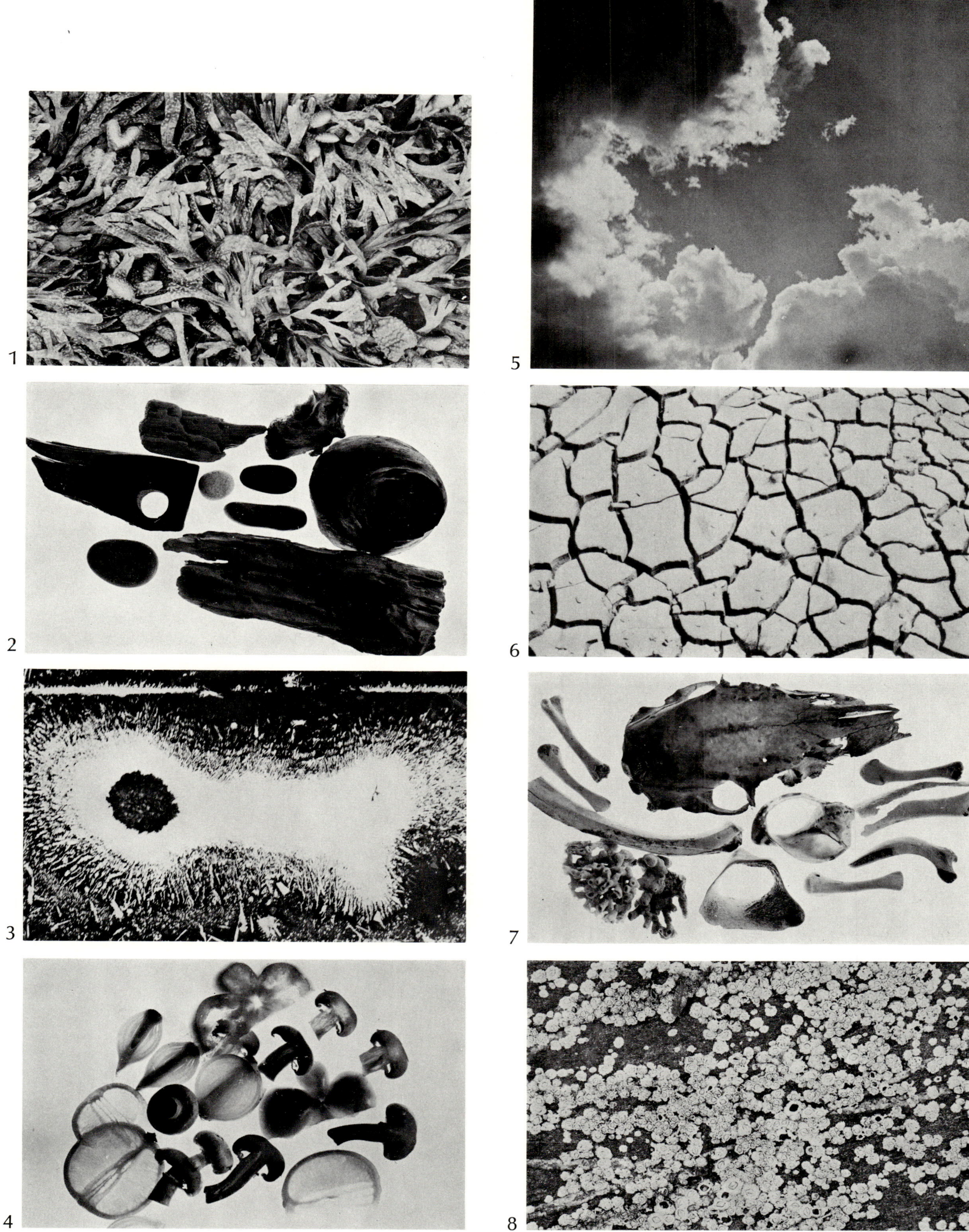
1
2
3
4
5
6
7
8

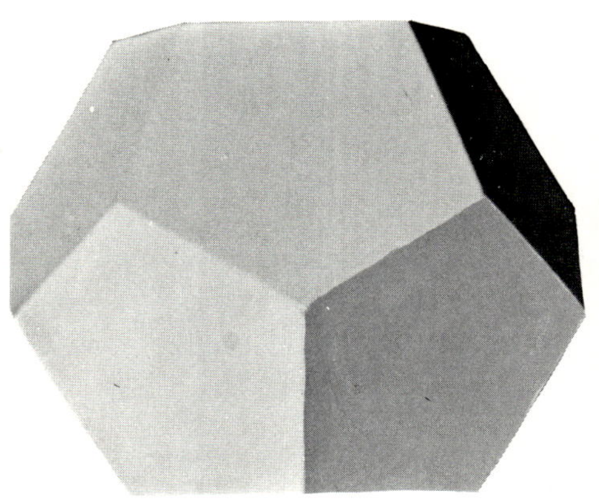

FORMS: GEOMETRIC

Although we're in the habit of thinking of **geometric** shapes — squares, spheres, rectangles, cones — as being man-made and we associate these forms with man's created world, the world of cities, science and architecture, not all geometric shapes are man-made. Let's take a look at a few of the products of both man's and nature's handiwork.

1. The shapes in this picture of the Eiffel Tower looked to me like mirrored designs in a kaleidoscope. I took this photo, shooting up from the base center, at ground level.

2. Here are some natural formations of triangles, rectangles and hexagons that are geometric in shape, yet they appear here in their natural form, just as nature shaped them.

3. Le Corbusier's CANDIGARH IN INDIA is a graphic example of a systematic use of geometrics in modern architecture.

4. A bee's honeycomb, a natural cellular construction that is geometric by necessity. It is the most efficient way of packing cells into a given space. Animal and vegetal cells use a very similar pattern of structure.

5. Look at the triangles, rectangles and trapezoids in this wall of exposed granite. The process of erosion and decay already is beginning to reshape them. In time they will be returned to rounded, organic shapes.

6. It would be hard to find an abstract painter who could not use the squares and rectangles in these rice paddies as a point of departure. Man-made though they are, the natural contour of the land has had a hand in shaping the overall pattern.

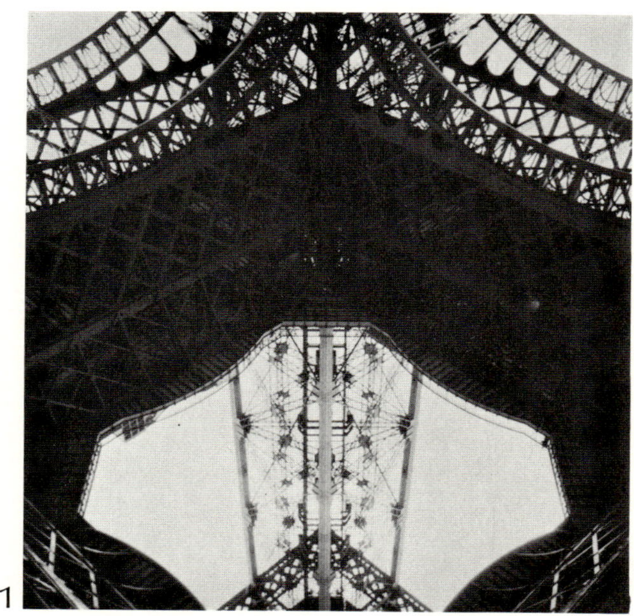
1

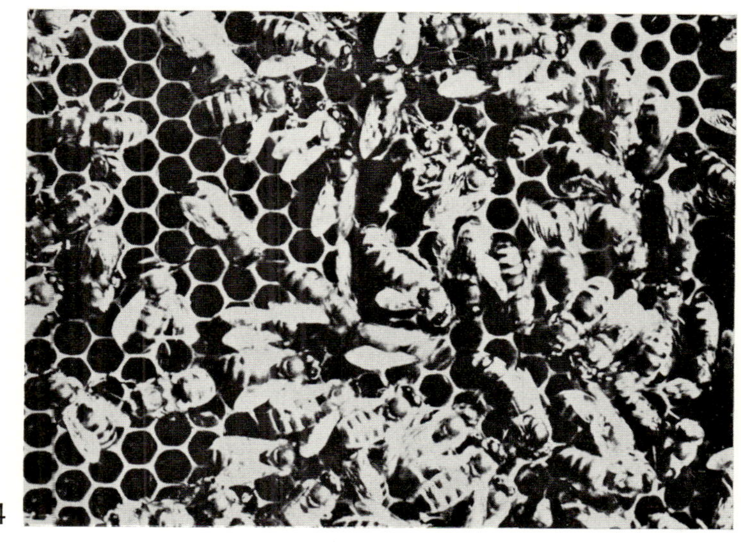
4

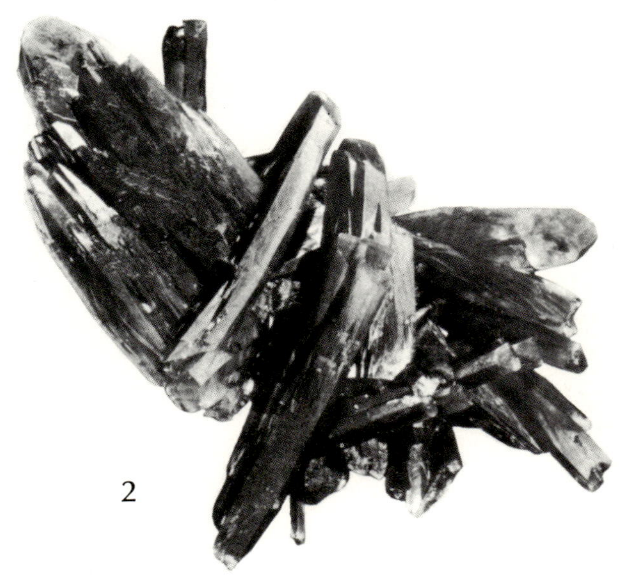
2

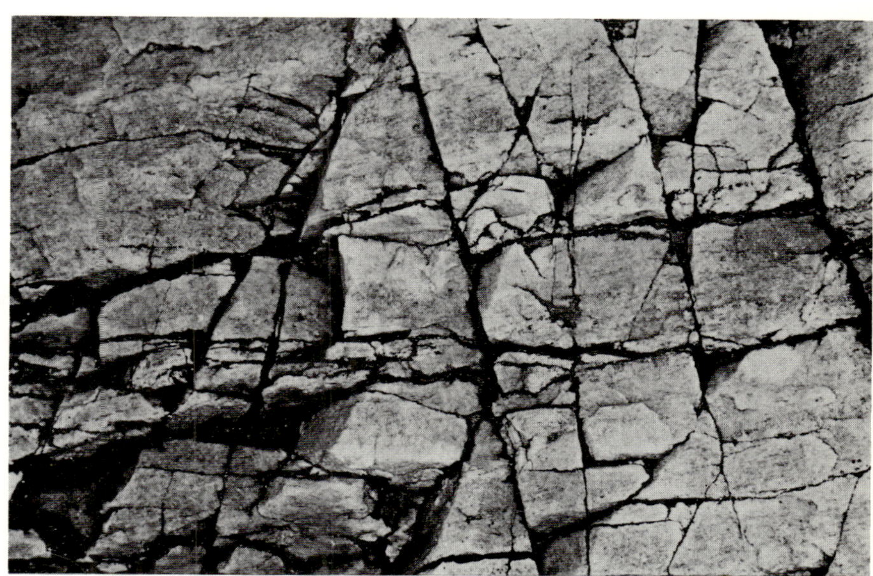
5

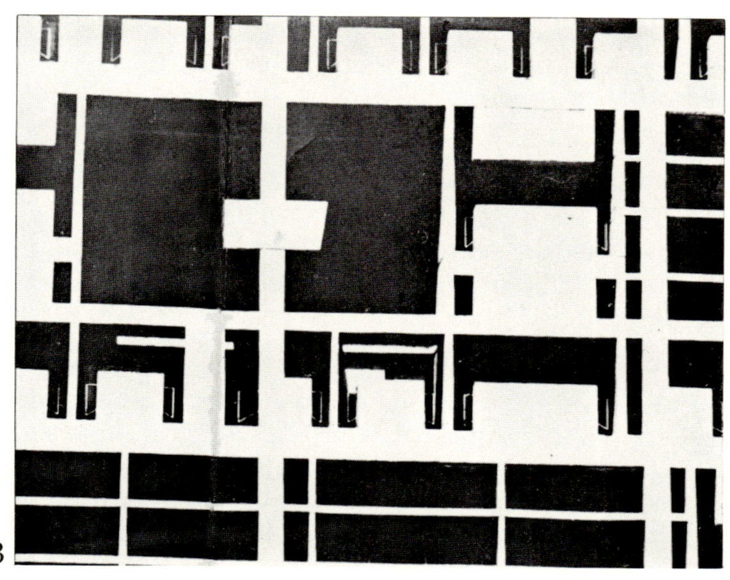
3

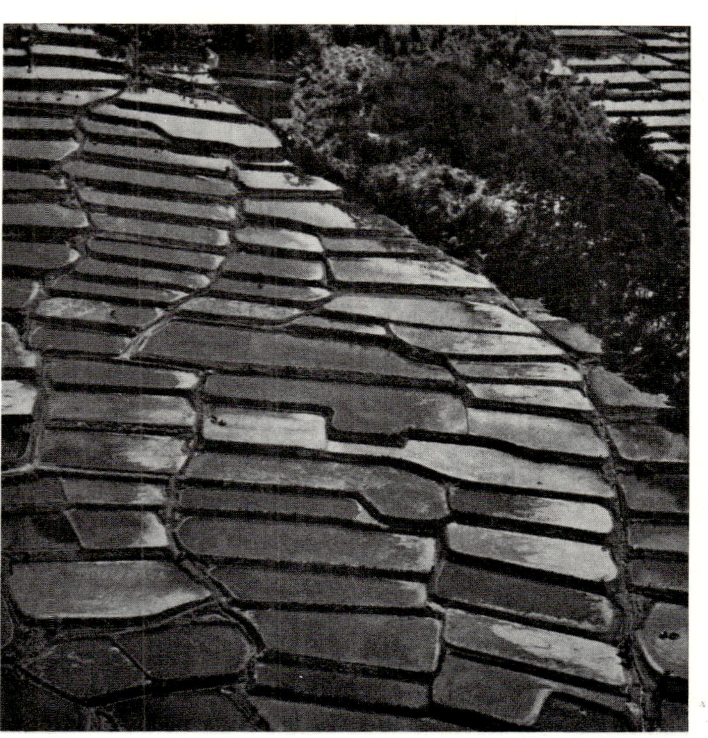
6

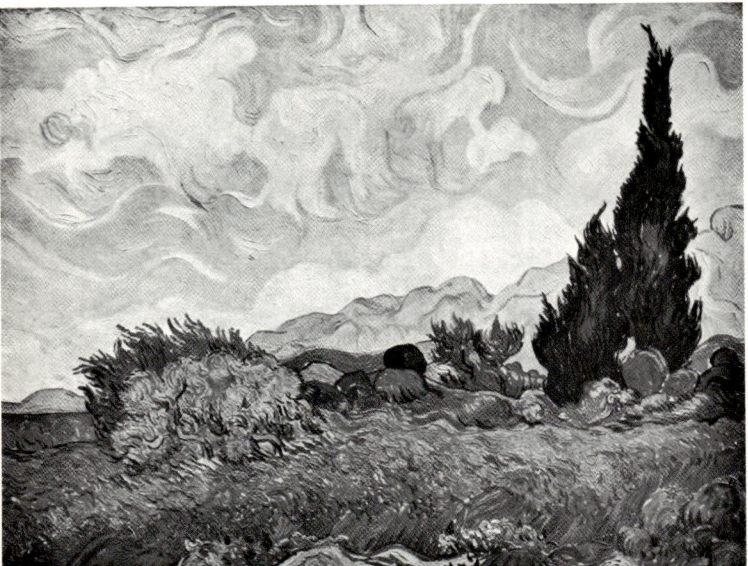

WHEAT FIELD WITH CYPRESSES by VINCENT VAN GOGH a.
Tate Gallery, London

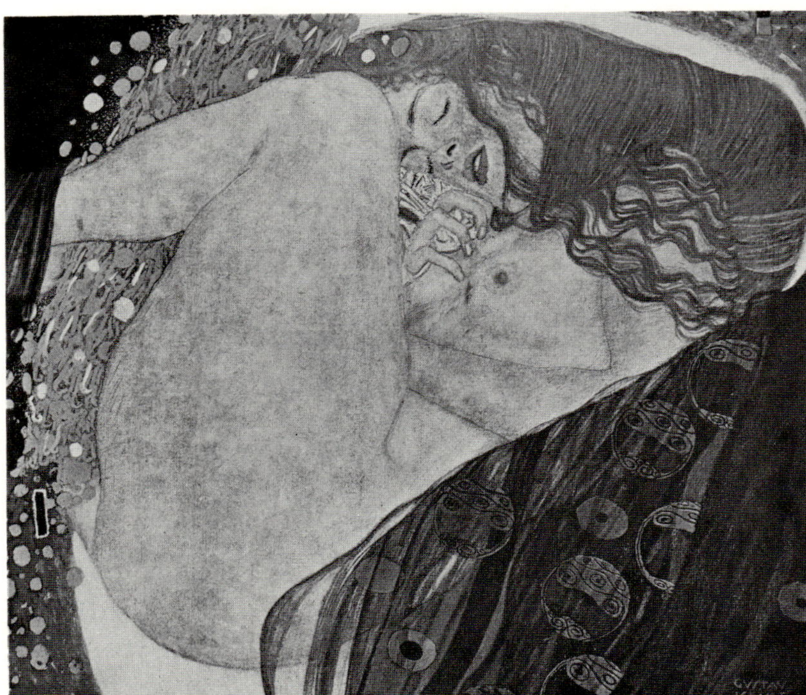

DANAE by GUSTAV KLIMT d.
New York Graphic Society

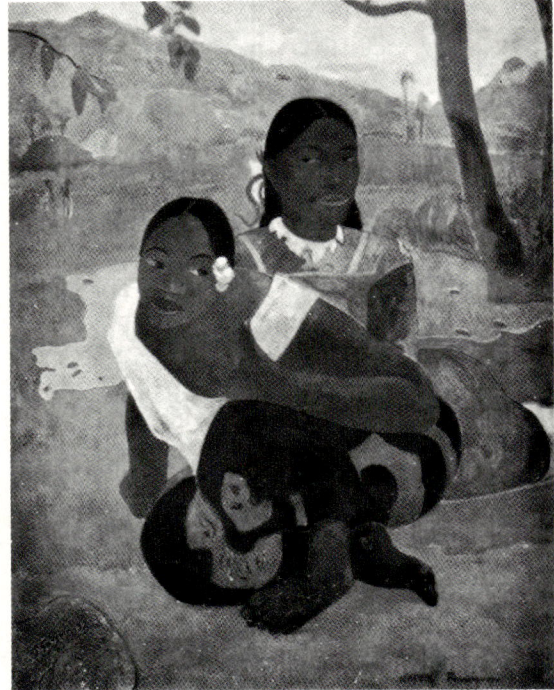

NAFEA FOA IPOIPO by PAUL GAUGUIN b.
Rudolf Staechelin Collection, Basel

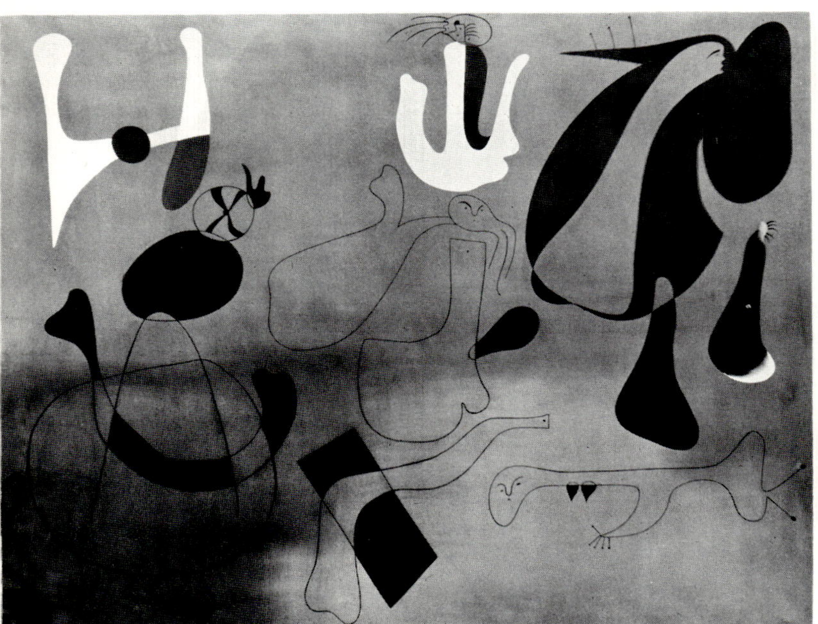

PAINTING 1933 by JOAN MIRÓ c.
Wadsworth Atheneum,
Ella Gallup Sumner and Mary Catlin Sumner Collection

USE of ORGANIC

The pictures on this page have been selected for their different interpretations of organic shapes. Let's start with the most obvious — Van Gogh's WHEAT FIELD.

a.
This painting is the absolute essence of an organic shape concept. There are no geometric shapes in it anywhere. Animal forms can be found in the clouds, and cloud forms in the underbrush and mountains. In fact, just about every organic form is represented here.

b.
Gauguin interpreted shapes in a more primitive and abstract way. His use of natural form depended on rhythmic planes of color. He never seemed to worry about the third dimension, but was concerned primarily with the lyricism of color and form.

c.
Miró's COMPOSITION draws on animal forms, abstracted and very precisely arranged. He used shapes that were fluid and curvilinear, never geometric. Compare this painting with Figure g , page 19.

d.
Fluid line and curving forms combine to make this sensuous design by Gustav Klimt a study in organic shapes.

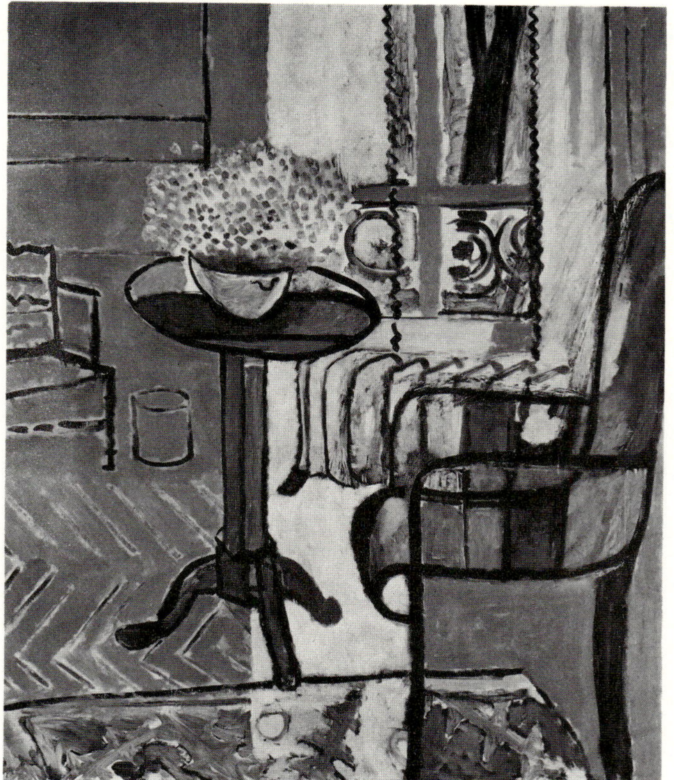

THE WINDOW by HENRI MATISSE e.
Detroit Institute of Arts

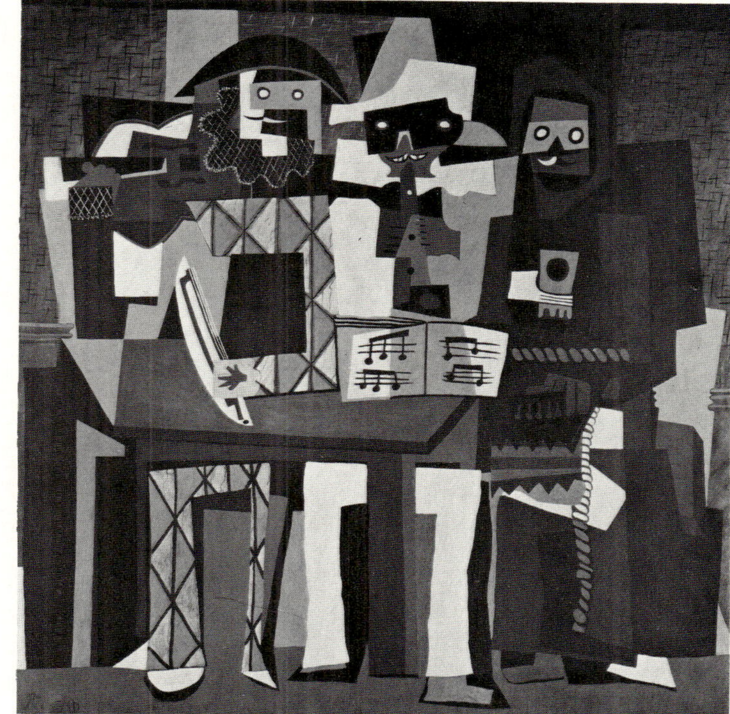

THREE MUSICIANS by PABLO PICASSO f.
Philadelphia Museum of Art

and GEOMETRIC FORMS

e.
In this picture, Matisse has taken an interior and extracted from it a rectilinear theme. Notice how the sunlight and shadow areas have been abstracted to force this effect. Bold curves in the chair, table and balistrade serve as counterpoints in this composition.

f.
Picasso's masterpiece of cubism, THREE MUSICIANS was designed like a collage, the separate pieces fitted together as deliberately as architectural blocks. Braque used shapes in much the same way. (See **overlaps and silhouettes,** page 22.)

g.
Many of Utrillo's street scenes are architectural in detail and, hence, geometrical in concept. Here is a composition that is totally committed to triangles, trapezoids and rectangles, but especially to triangles. I counted ten of them.

h.
Geometric forms have been powerfully wielded in this abstract by Nicolas de Stael. Although his most important work was done with palette knife, he was also a great collagist and collage forms very definitely show up in his paintings done with brush and palette knife.

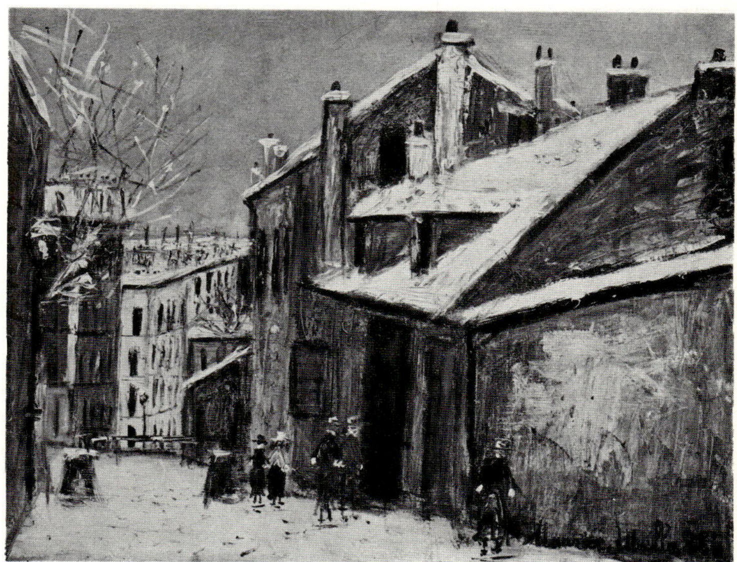

MAISON MIMI by MAURICE UTRILLO g.
Private Collection

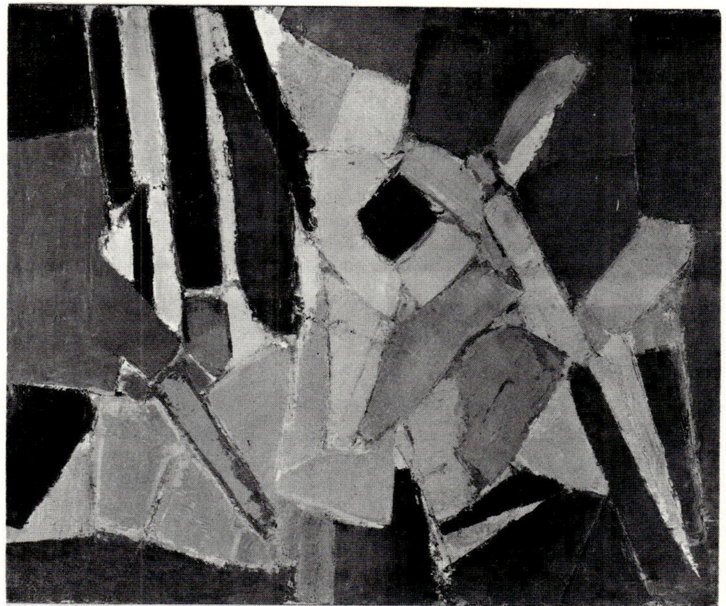

RUE GAUGET by NICOLAS DE STAEL h.
Museum of Fine Arts, Boston

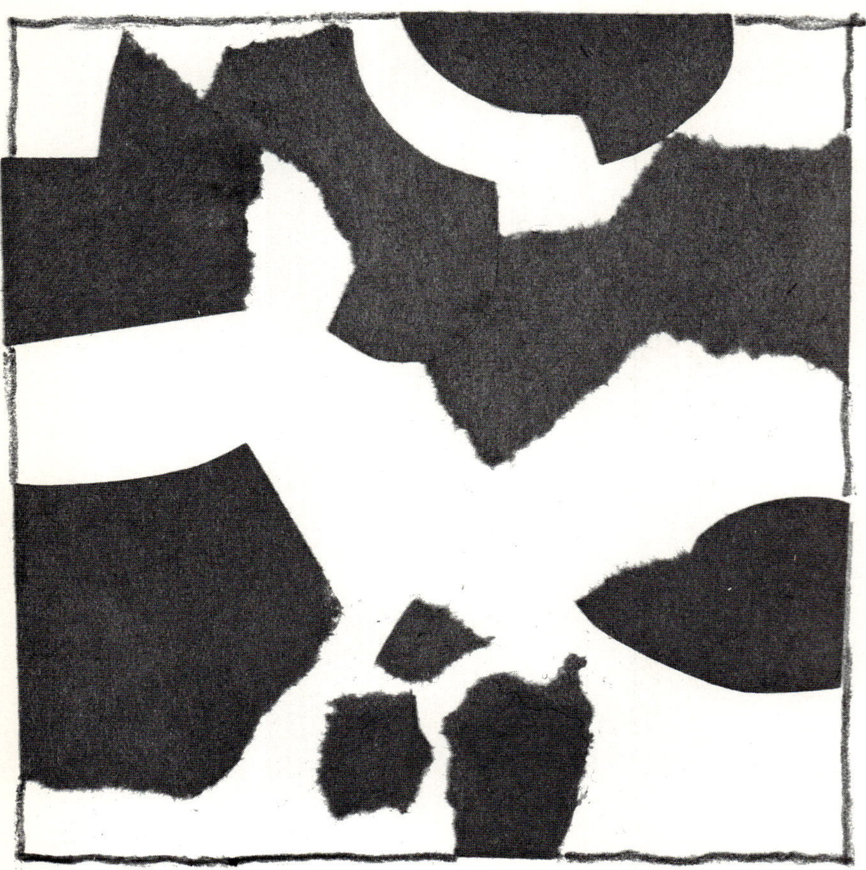

1

NEGATIVE SHAPES

GREAT PAINTING IS PAINTING IN WHICH THE SPACES BETWEEN THE FIGURES ARE CHARGED WITH AS MUCH ENERGY AS THE FIGURES THAT DETERMINE THEM.

André Masson

So far, in our exploration of the world of shapes, we've been discussing positive shapes. We have seen how rock forms, buildings, trees, animals, fields, sky, and water — in fact virtually anything that exists in visual form — is raw material for the artist. Still life, landscape, interiors, even portraits and figure painting all have to start with an arrangement of shapes put together with some kind of order.

When this assembling of shapes takes place a strange thing happens. A secondary pattern of **negative** shapes is created . . . automatically, though quite by accident (until you learn to control it). These negative shapes can be found in the "background" area of a picture, filling in between and around the deliberately planned shapes. Though they may seem a sort of by-product of the original forms, don't ever ignore them or underestimate their importance. They should be regarded as being strictly abstract in form. Get into the habit of looking for them even before you begin to think about drawing. Remember, almost all painters work with negative shapes in developing their compositions. Look for them in reproductions of paintings.

I was only vaguely aware of them until I began studying under Reuben Tam at the Brooklyn Museum School. Here I learned to look for them — in any subject — then to utilize them in designing a picture. To me, negative shapes have become almost sacred. I see them, not only in the two-dimensional plan of a picture but in the actual viewing of the scene itself . . . in the view through the window, the street scene, or in the silhouettes formed by figures against a background. They are one of the most pervasive forces in the concept of design — figurative or abstract.

The abstract arrangement of shapes in Figure 1 is made up of pieces of construction paper that were torn and cut at random, with no design plan in mind. They were then quickly assembled, but with attention concentrated on the white, "negative" spaces, disregarding as much as possible, the dark positive shapes. Squint your eyes and you will see these negative shapes clearly. Their influence on the overall design is obvious. Notice, too, how the edges and corners of the frame have had a hand in shaping the design. Negative shapes, though seemingly accidental, should never be ignored. Develop your awareness of them until you intuitively feel their presence.

Figure 2 at first glance appears to be an abstraction of swirling, nebulous shapes: something like spilled ink. Actually

2

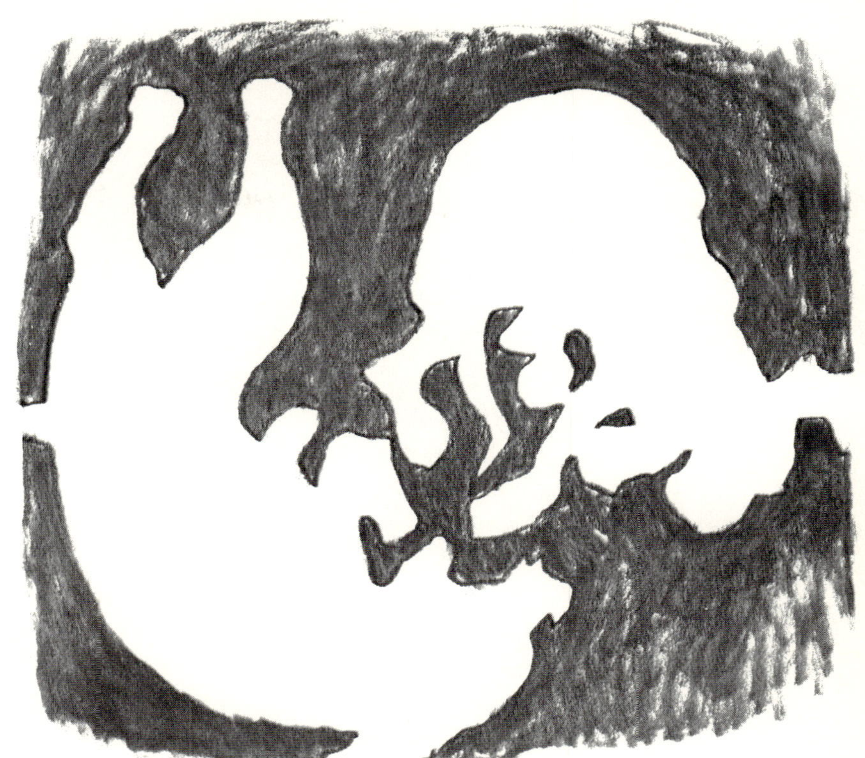

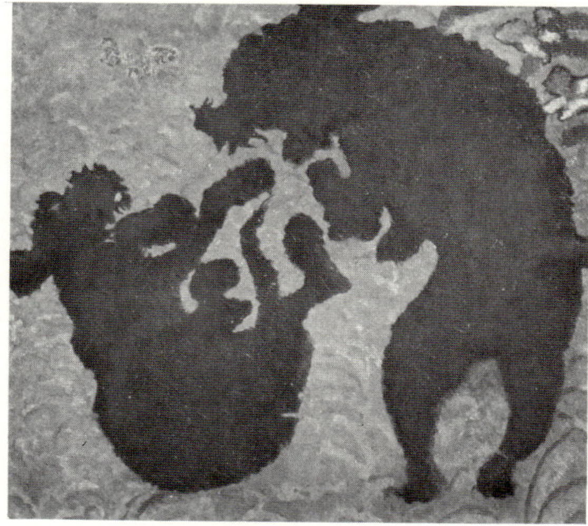

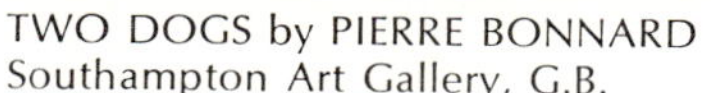

TWO DOGS by PIERRE BONNARD 3
Southampton Art Gallery, G.B.

it is a carefully traced drawing in negative of a painting by Bonnard. I have turned it upside-down to de-emphasize its figurative quality — to make it less recognizable. Now, if you will turn it right-side-up you will see it for what it is — two dogs at play (3). Note the effect of the negative shapes on the design. Stare at it a while and the shapes begin to take on all sorts of abstract meanings. Bonnard painted this when he was 24 years old. It shows a great regard for negative shapes, at an early stage in his career. His concern for these shapes is apparent in all his later works, right up to his last, a simple painting of a basket of fruit painted in 1946 when he was 79 years old.

Another example of negative shapes at work is in Matisse's VENUS, a collage done in blue on white (4). I've made a drawing of it in negative (5) to show how the negative form balances and compliments the design. I think you'll agree, it's hard to say which forms dominate, the positive or negative. Matisse delighted in the alternation between positive and negative, particularly in his latest works, which were mostly collages.

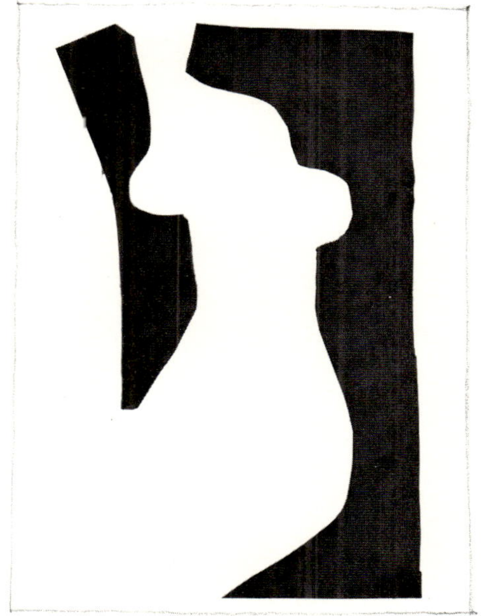

4

VENUS: after collage by HENRI MATISSE

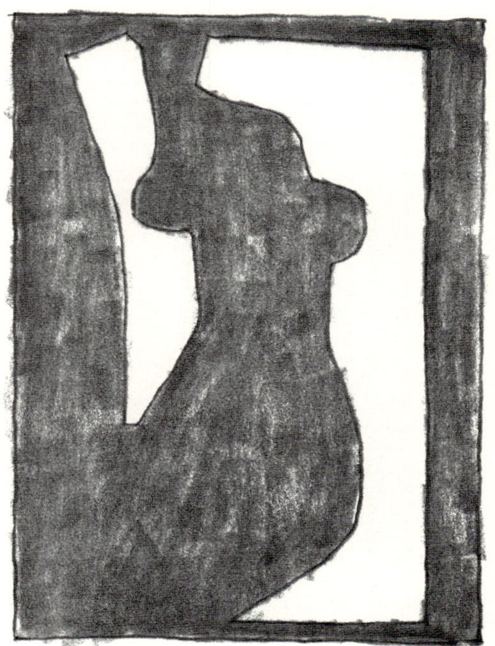

5

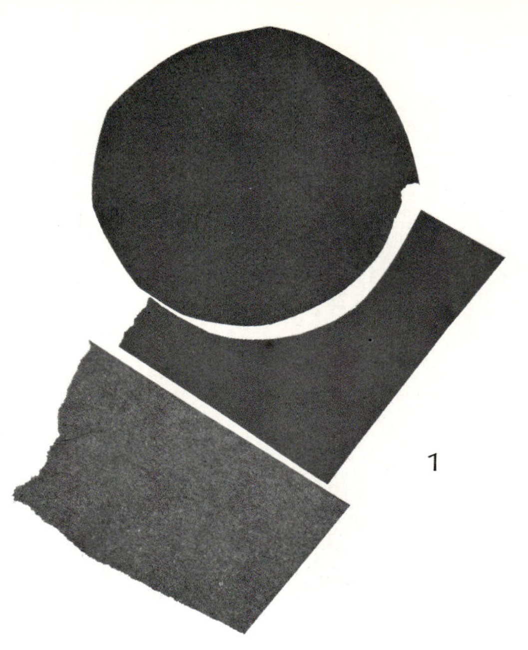

1

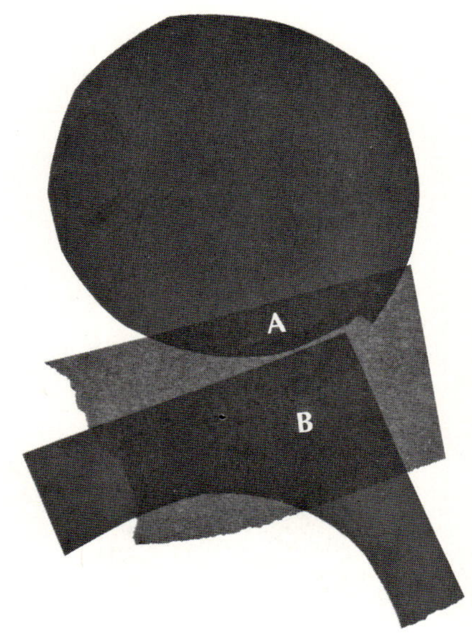

2

OVERLAPS and SILHOUETTES

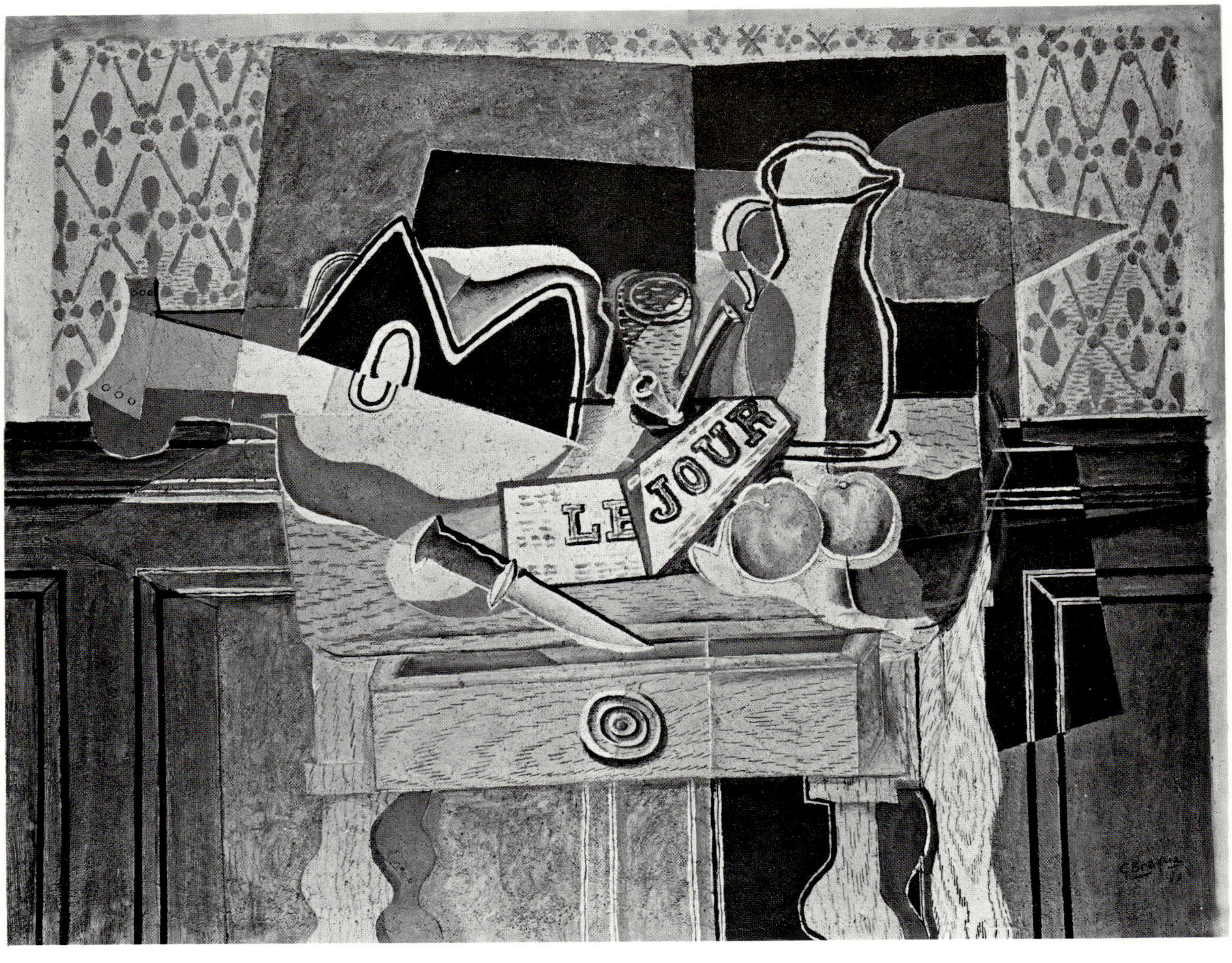

STILL LIFE: LE JOUR by GEORGES BRAQUE
National Gallery of Art, Washington, D.C., Chester Dale Collection

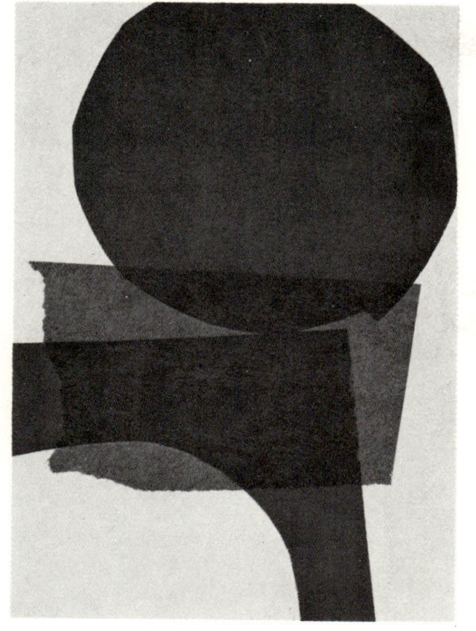

3

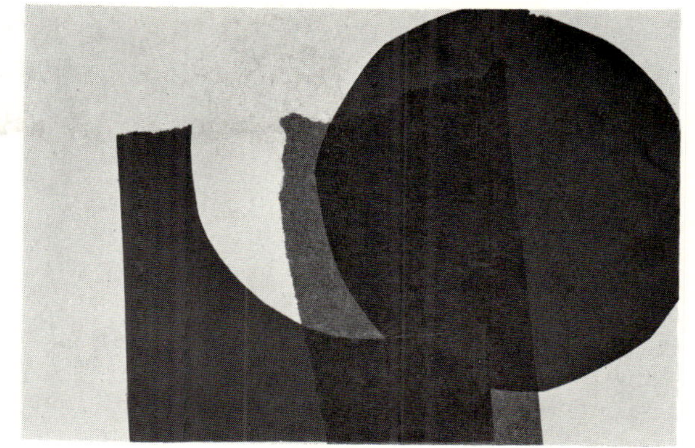

4

INTERACTION of SHAPES

5

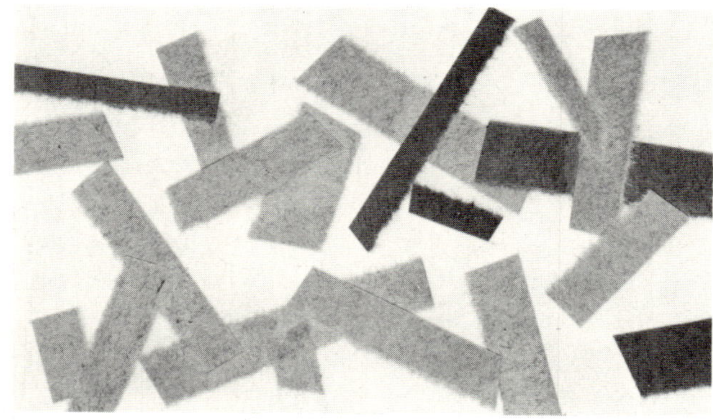

6

Let's leave negative shapes for a while and move on to a subject that is closely related but perhaps a little less obvious. I'm referring to **overlaps.** Overlaps are a sort of by-product, formed when one shape is allowed to overlap another, creating a third. A good way to demonstrate this is to take a simple exercise, something like the one on page 20, and carry it a bit farther. Just to force the effect I'm going to use transparent tissue paper for this one. I've cut three pieces, roughly geometric in shape (Fig.1). They should be light enough in color (I used Christmas wrapping paper) to get maximum contrast when overlapped. In Figure 2, I've brought them together. Now there are two new overlap shapes (A and B). Note how the process of overlapping has created new negative shapes as well, especially in the circle and rectangle.

Now let's go another step and see what happens when we take these three simple shapes and enclose them in a rectangle (Fig. 3). By framing (cropping) I have arrived at a picture of sorts — an abstract composition. Again, notice the negative shapes that have suddenly materialized out of what was empty background space. The four corners of the picture have become very important. In Figure 4, I have used a different arrangement of the same three shapes to create different overlaps and . . . there we go again . . . more negative shapes.

Look at the paintings of Braque and Picasso. They are full of overlaps, especially Braque's still lifes. Some of their cubistic effects are achieved with overlaps. (See Braque's LE JOUR, opposite page.)

Interaction of forms is what gives a picture energy and excitement. A simple form can express little action all by itself. It remains more or less inert until it is placed in opposition to other forms. Then, when interaction takes place within the four sides of a picture, a sort of visual energy is produced. If we take these forms and place them quietly, side by side, the combined effect is still one of inertia. Let's illustrate with a simple experiment.

In Fig. 5, I have made a composition of sorts out of some bits of construction paper by laying them in an orderly, parallel fashion. The result is a calm, quiescent design.

Now let's take the pieces and scatter them about until they oppose each other in all possible attitudes (Fig. 6). They now react vigorously with one another. Immediately the composition comes to life when these same forms are placed in opposition and in collision with each other. Energy is actually generated by this scattering of forms over the picture surface. Study page 19 for examples of opposition and interaction of forms in four distinctly individual styles.

KINDS of COMPOSITIONS

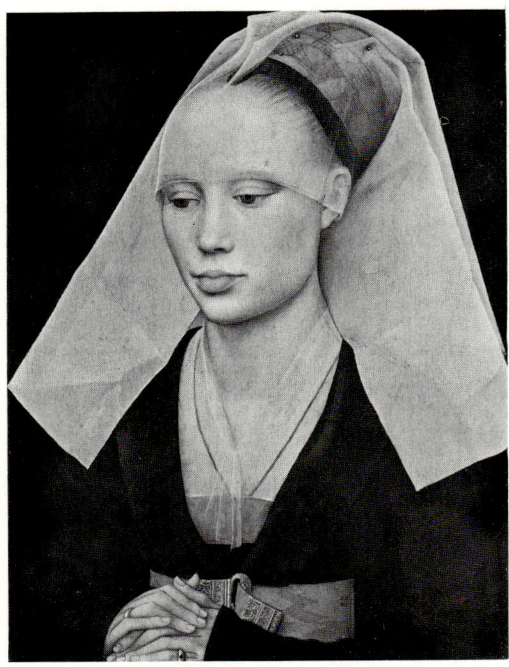

PORTRAIT OF A LADY
by ROGIER VAN DER WEYDEN
National Gallery of Art, Washington, D.C.,
Chester Dale Collection

When we draw anything — any object — any form in its immediate environment or setting, we are composing. As soon as a figure or a still life is combined with a background a composition is born.

Think of composition as the sum total of forms and empty spaces. It should be thought of as a by-product of design and not as an end in itself. Good composition is a result of good organization in planning a picture.

For the sake of discussion let's say there are three basic types of compositions, **symmetrical, asymmetrical** and **mosaic.** Van der Weyden' elegant PORTRAIT OF A LADY is a classic example of symmetrical design. Many portrait painters use this kind of formal construction for their compositions. Draw a line down the middle of the picture and you'll find that both halves are about equal in "weight." Hobbema uses this same symmetrical plan.

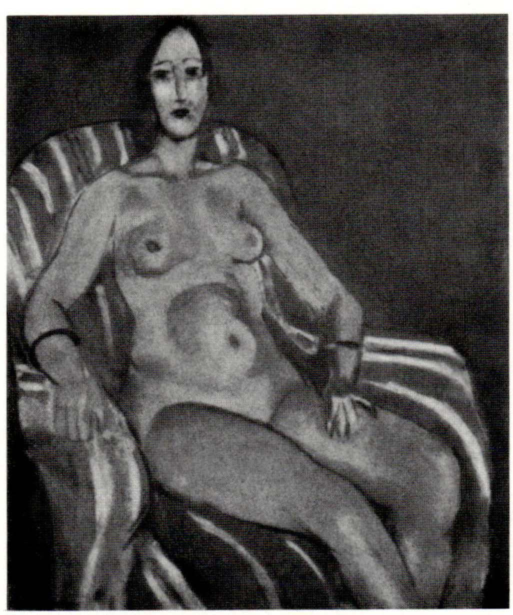

NU SUR FOND ROUGE by HENRI MATISSE
Musée National d'Art Moderne, Paris

But a great majority of compositions are asymmetrical. They will not balance if divided into two equal parts, but rely on more subtle devices to make them work. Let's look at a simple figure painting of Matisse's. The figure, at first glance, appears to be rather arbitrarily placed. It is way off center, but the composition balances very nicely. Why is this? It's because the design flows to the right, in contrast to the above compositions which are static. This left-to-right movement keeps the composition from becoming lop-sided and is supported further by the fact that the figure's eyes are directed to the right hand side of the picture.

In Degas' AT THE RACES, again, all the action is moving to the right. In this case, the composition is kept in balance by two things. One — the wheels which serve to radiate action back into the picture, and two — the rider on the left side of the picture, who, though smaller, is silhouetted and therefore commands much more attention than any of the other figures.

The third category is in marked contrast to the above compositions in that open space is not utilized. Instead, small units are used to arrive at an over-all pattern something like a mosaic or patch-work design. This kind of composition is demonstrated in the chapter **Interaction of Shapes**, page 23. Besides Klee and Pollock, illustrated here, abstractionists like Mark Tobey, Piet Mondrian and Wassily Kandinsky created designs of great energy and power using this kind of pattern. Their paintings have a built-in force that comes from an active use of form and tension.

Much of today's abstract painting uses a mosaic design plan and even though the results may be totally non-representational and seemingly miles away from nature, still the forms used quite often lead directly back to nature.

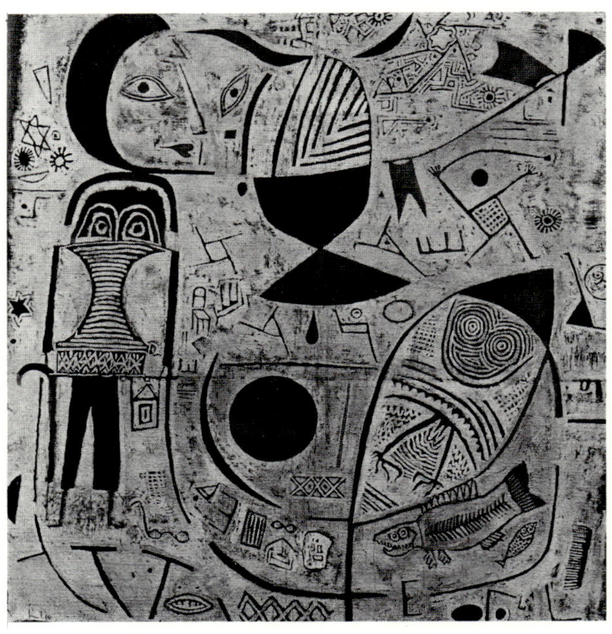

PICTURE ALBUM, 1937 by PAUL KLEE
Phillips Collection, Washington, D.C.

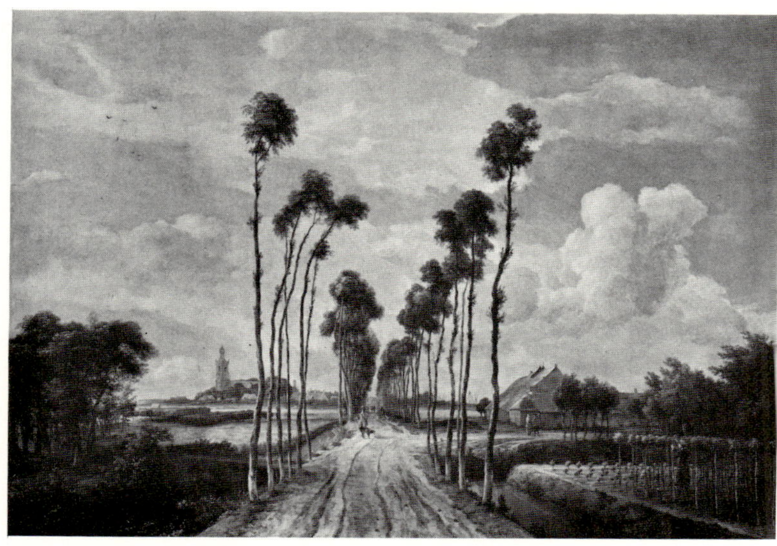
THE AVENUE by MEINDERT HOBBEMA
National Gallery, London

SYMMETRICAL – FORMAL

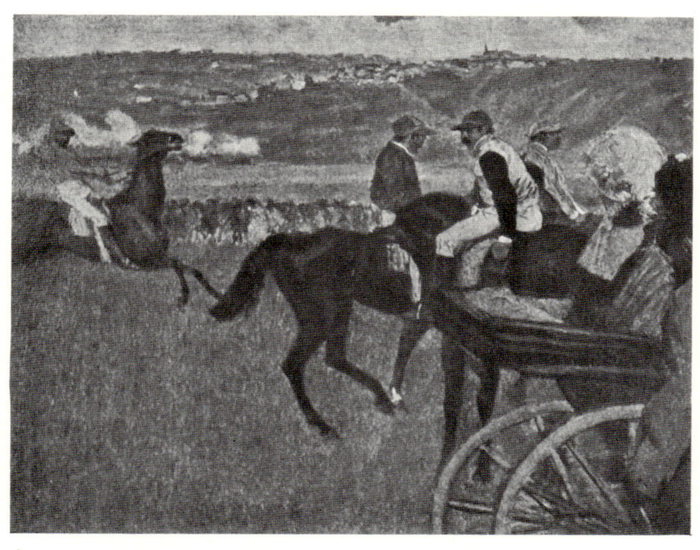
AT THE RACES by EDGAR DEGAS
Louvre

ASYMMETRICAL – INFORMAL

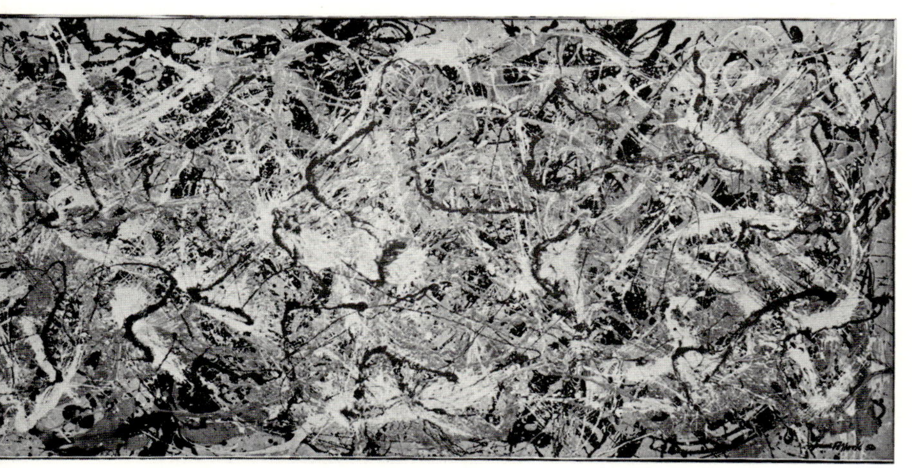
NUMBER 27 by JACKSON POLLOCK
Whitney Museum of American Art, N.Y.

"MOSAIC" – OVERALL DESIGN

INVENTED COMPOSITIONS

A PAINTING THAT IS WELL COMPOSED IS HALF FINISHED.
Pierre Bonnard

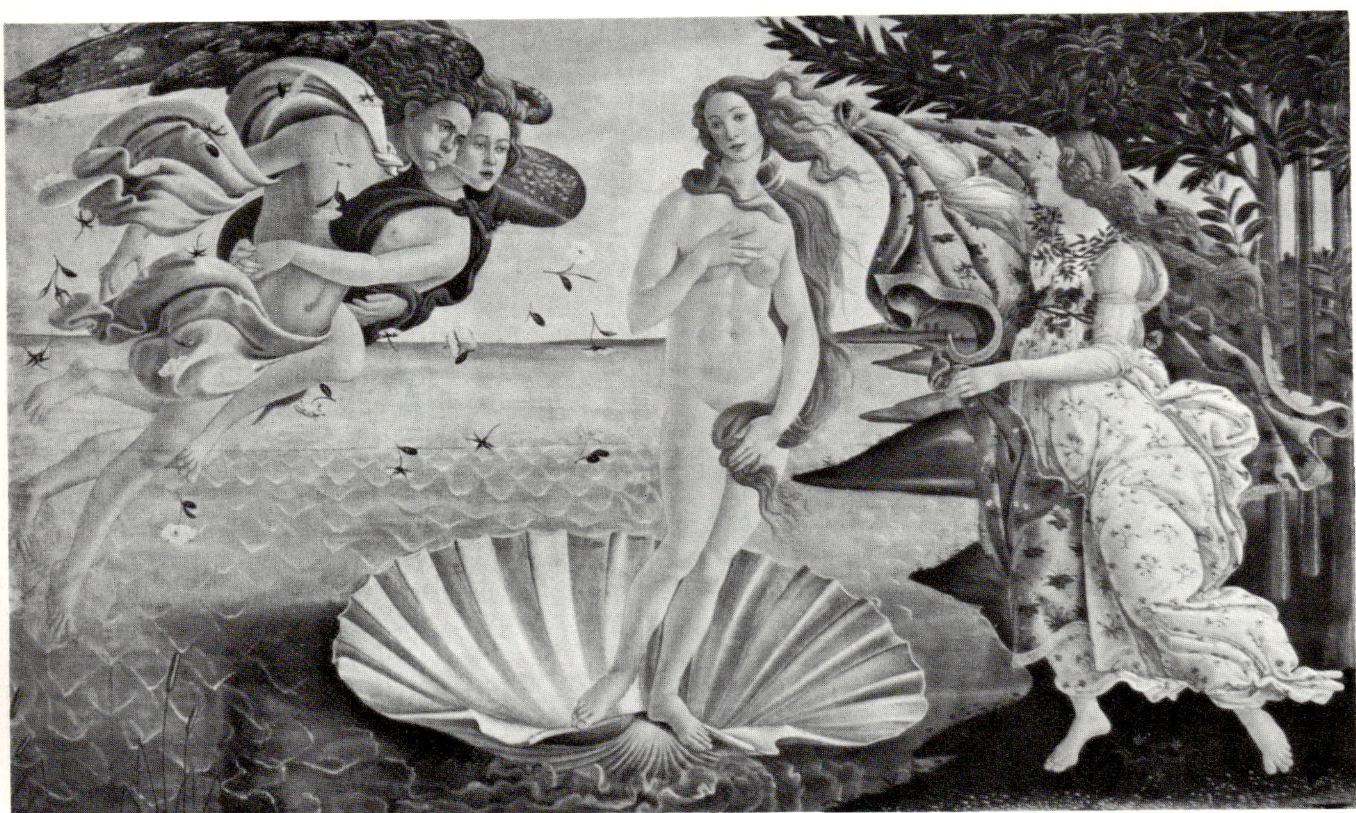

1

THE BIRTH OF VENUS by SANDRO BOTTICELLI
Uffizi Gallery, Florence

Any composition is an invention of sorts. The term **invented compositions** is used here in a strictly figurative sense. I want to point out that there is a difference between a composition that comes mainly unaltered from nature, and one that is an invented arrangement of the scene.

Figure 1. A classic example of this kind of concept and a piece of pure confection is Botticelli's THE BIRTH OF VENUS, sometimes irreverently referred to as, VENUS ON THE HALF SHELL. Like so many of the paintings of the Renaissance, especially the ones depicting the supernatural, this painting, though quite realistic, is all invention, compositionally.

The paintings of the Impressionists, by contrast, were much more dependent on that which was seen. These painters,

2

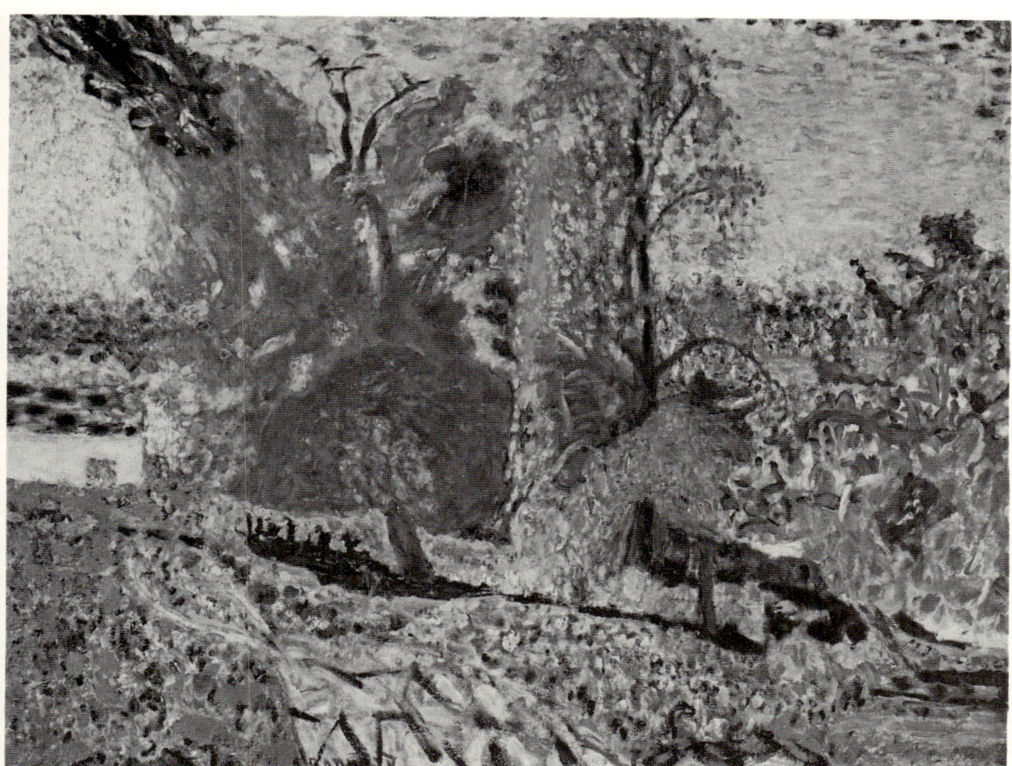

LANDSCAPE OF THE MIDI by PIERRE BONNARD
Smith College Museum of Art

3

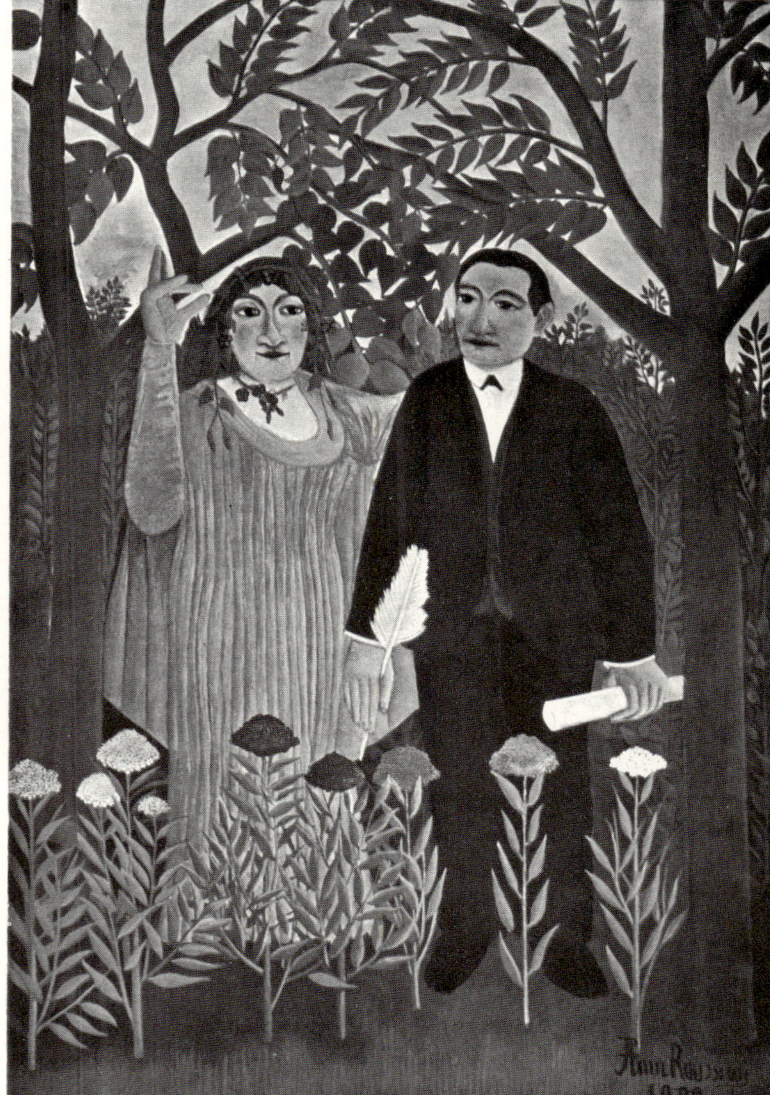

THE POET AND HIS MUSE by HENRI ROUSSEAU
Kunstmuseum, Basel

putting classicism and romanticism behind them, began to paint what they saw. Traditional subject matter and academicism was being replaced by a "candid" view of life. Street scenes and cafes, prostitutes and middle class people were recorded quickly, quite often at the moment of observation. Some of these artists painted the same scene over and over again. And the same scene, painted by different artists, showed that they did not alter, substantially, the composition; only the point of view.

Figure 2. One of the most inventive and venturesome of naturalist painters was Pierre Bonnard. He did not paint directly from nature, but from memory, quick sketches and notes. His compositions, landscapes in particular, are worth noting for their inventive quality. He never wandered far from nature in his painting. At the same time he displayed a curious independence of nature. Bonnard's painting, at times capricious, arbitrary, naive, abstract — was always inventive.

Figure 3. Rousseau's painting is almost impossible to classify. I guess it comes as close to fitting the description of primitive art as anything else. Everything he painted he invested with dignity and a touch of grandeur. Though he was never much of a traveler, he created some of the most exciting and exotic landscapes almost entirely from imagination. Most of his information must have come from illustrated catalogues and botanical handbooks. Even his perspective (his backgrounds look like painted backdrops) is an invention of his own.

RHYTHMS and ORCHESTRATIONS

1

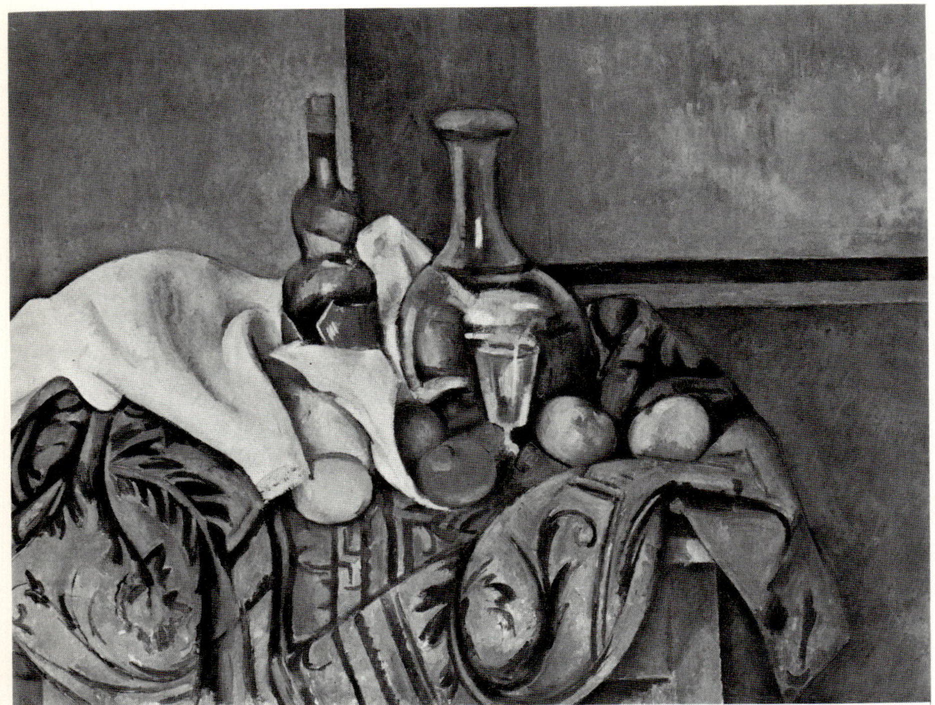

STILL LIFE by PAUL CÉZANNE
National Gallery of Art, Washington, D.C., Chester Dale Collection

All good compositions employ a process of linking-together of forms. Consciously or unconsciously this happens in the planning of a design, no matter what the subject. These exaggerated diagrams have a mail order, "drawing made easy" look, I'll admit. Their purpose simply is to trace the rhythms, some obvious, some not so obvious, that flow through a picture, connecting and binding one form with another. Finding these rhythms and "echos" in a well-composed picture is fairly easy. Let's examine some good compositions and see what it is that makes them good.

Cézanne is an example of classic perfection in composition. Analyze any one of his compositions and you will find that it has an architectural structure quite independent of mechanical perspective. Look at the rhythms in his still life (Figure 1). What sets them in motion? One interpretation is shown in Figure 1A. Try it yourself — you may have another version. Notice how forms echo each other and how lines are made to contribute to the unity of the design as a whole.

1A

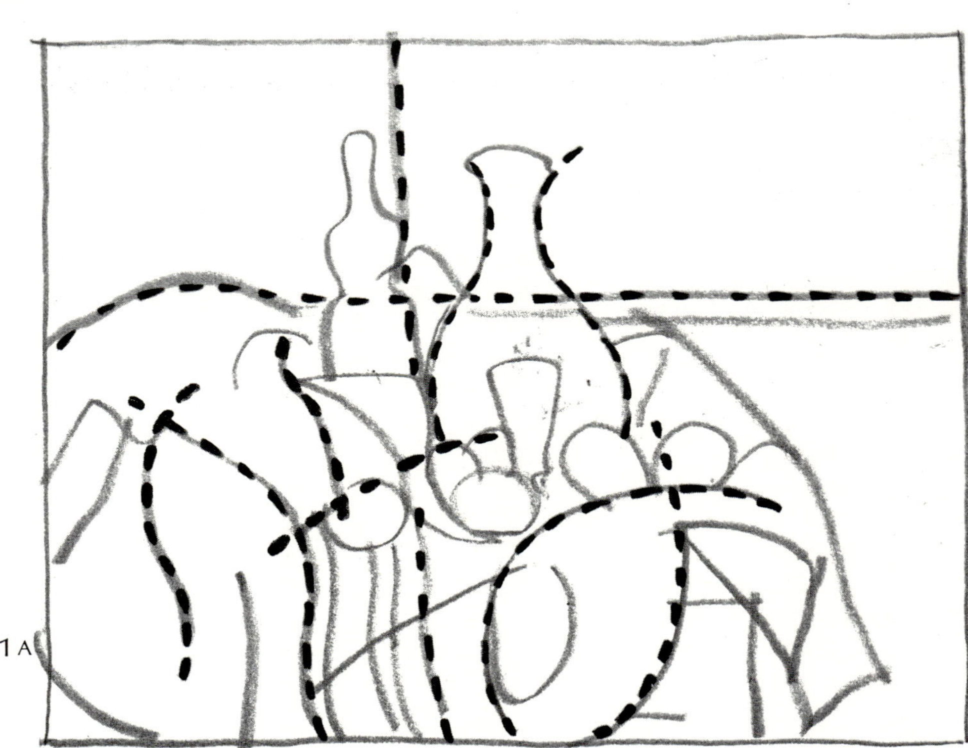

2

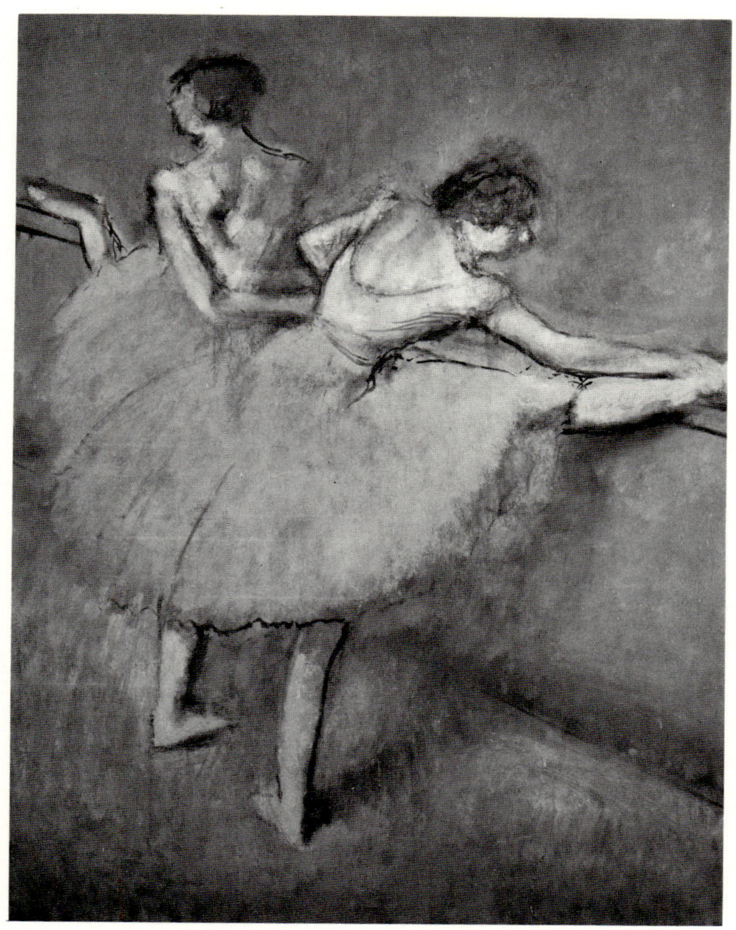

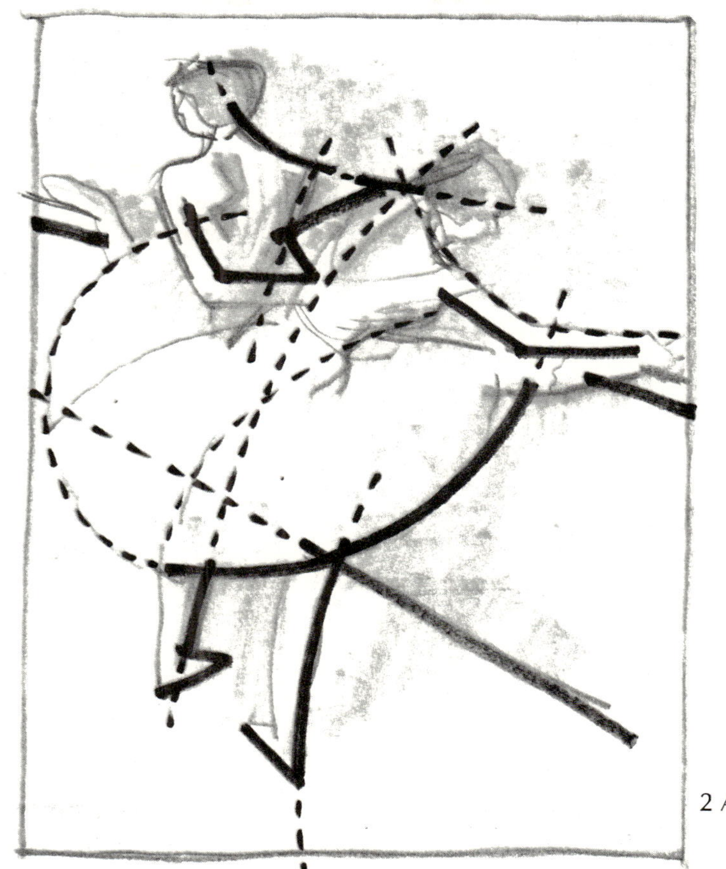

2 A

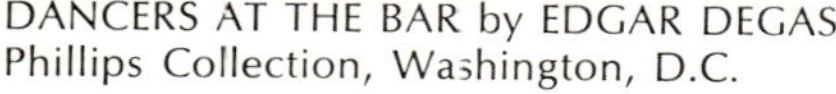

DANCERS AT THE BAR by EDGAR DEGAS
Phillips Collection, Washington, D.C.

I vowed this was going to be one book that did not include any Degas dancing girls, but this is such a good example of rhythmic connections I had to use it. It is also a good demonstration of interaction of forms and angles. Notice how skillfully he has put angles and connecting lines to work, opposing and echoing each other. The result is a composition that's charged with energy and movement (Fig.2).

Gauguin's critics have said that he leaned a little heavily toward the exotic novelty. That may be, but what they can't deny him is his genius for the decorative and for his mastery of color.

He had a special gift for taking nature and synthetizing it to suit his own purposes. His DECORATIVE LANDSCAPE, 1888, is a good example of this. Even in black and white, there is a beautiful harmonic balance between curving baroque and angular geometric. Here is a classic demonstration of rhythmic line and well-orchestrated value pattern. It is also, I think, a remarkable abstraction when you consider that it was painted before the turn of the century.

3

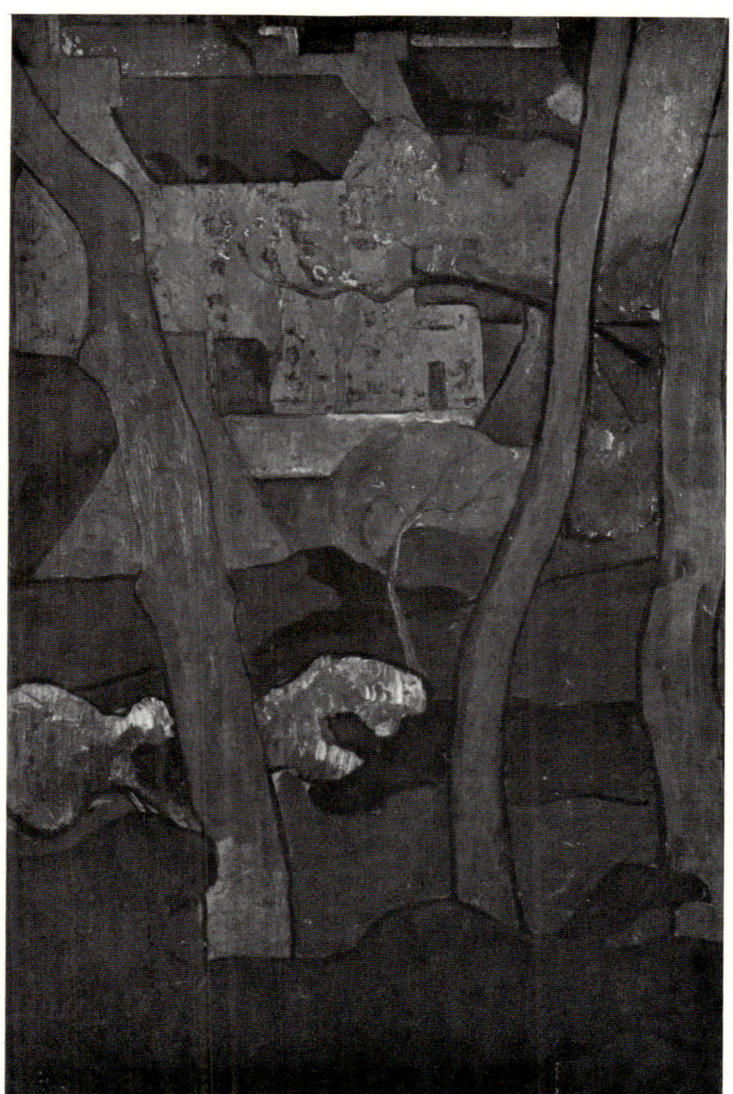

DECORATIVE LANDSCAPE by PAUL GAUGUIN
National Museum, Stockholm

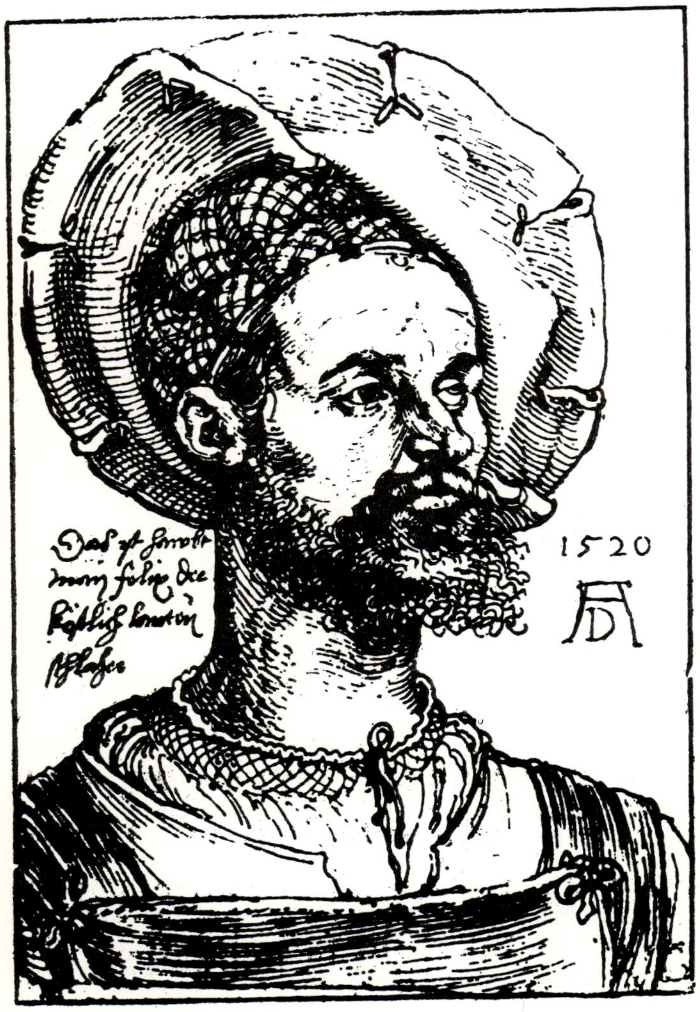

ALBRECHT DURER

PART 2· DRAWING

To the layman, drawing must seem a somewhat frivolous pursuit, something like a juggler's act or a sleight-of-hand demonstration. Remarks like, "I can't draw a straight line with a ruler"... or that real classic, "I don't know anything about art but I know what I like," have been heard round the world since the time of cave painting. Possibly the greatest misconception of all is that the artist was born lucky. All my life I've had people tell me how lucky I am that I can draw. In looking back I'm sure some of them were trying to tell me how lucky I am that I don't have to use my head.

With the exception of that rare phenomenon, the genius, there's about as much luck involved with drawing as there is in playing the violin. Contrary to popular belief, the ability to draw comes from practice, and once learned, requires continued practice and application to remain operable. Drawing must be learned, and it can be learned. But, like any other acquired skill, it comes easier for some than for others.

Drawing is communicating. Communicating or converting an idea or concept into a visual statement is the whole purpose in drawing. It follows that the greater an artist's mastery of drawing, the more articulate he will be in expressing what he wants to say. And drawing really starts with seeing. It begins with the process of form conception. **How** we translate and interpret what we see is what determines the way we draw.

For practical purposes of discussion there are two kinds of drawing. The first is the kind of drawing that is referred to in a painting. Good or bad, it is the framework upon which a painting is built. Like a badly constructed house, if the drawing is bad, the painting will fall apart or sag. This sort of drawing is so much a part of painting that the two are inseparable. Drawing becomes painting, and painting in a similar way can be regarded as drawing with a brush. Either way, drawing should be the artist's first consideration when he starts his adventure in picture-making. The second category is drawing as an end in itself. Artists like Ingres,

IT IS A FALSE IDEA THAT DRAWING IN ITSELF CAN BE BEAUTIFUL. IT IS ONLY BEAUTIFUL THROUGH THE TRUTHS AND THE FEELINGS THAT IT TRANSLATES.

Auguste Rodin

Delacroix, Durer and Degas are good examples of great painters who used drawings as a complete art form. Colorists like Bonnard, Vuillard and Monet, as well as many of the painters of today, think of drawing as a means to an end. In fact, some of Bonnard's drawings are little more than naive-looking scribblings . . . short-hand notes used to identify and record his impressions of a scene.

In a very broad sense drawing is a matter of getting things the right size, the right shape, and in the right relationship to other shapes.

There are books on the market that purport to teach people the "proper" way to draw. Things like trees and flowers, clouds and rocks are used in demonstrations of the right way and the wrong way. All precepts such as these are based on one artist's preconception of what these objects should look like. The big danger in this fuzzy kind of thinking is that the student is led into using conventions in drawing instead of using his own eyes and judgment in observing and translating from nature.

If we examine the drawings of some great draftsmen like Michelangelo, Durer, Ingres and Picasso, we will find little evidence that there is any "proper" way to draw. It stands to reason that if there were, there would be some sort of method, some plan or system easily detectable in the work of all these masters of drawing. In fact, every drawing might look exactly alike. What is evident in the draftsmanship of any good artist is drawing that is creative and highly individual. It is this creative form of drawing, not mechanical rendering, that we are going to concern ourselves with in this book.

Putting pencil to paper is a moment of truth; something like an actor about to walk on stage. I have always felt intimidated to some extent when I find myself face to face with the subject and that blank, unviolated pad. I am about to be put to the test. What I manage to achieve in my drawing depends a lot on how well I understand my subject. If what happens on paper is tentative or incomplete, then I must go back and look at the subject some more.

We have said that drawing is a matter of getting things the right size, the right shape, and in the right relationship. Although this may sound pretty academic, I don't think anyone will argue that these things must be mastered before we can begin to draw freely and naturally. But for now let's concentrate on one thing — being precise with the forms, angles and relationships we find in nature. Many students let themselves be tempted into taking shortcuts around the basics of drawing, skipping the groundwork. Like the music student who doesn't practice his scales, they are handicapping themselves. Sooner or later they must realize that all good painting, including abstract, is derived directly or indirectly from natural form. Take Picasso as an example. Many of his abstracted pictures are arrived at through a series of drawings that start with a realistic, literally drawn sketch.

The trouble with most beginners is that they tend to generalize in what they see. Out of timidity or perhaps faulty observation they are apt to soften the angularity of some objects or fudge a bit on the details of others. Generalizing almost invariably leads to sloppy drawing and clichés in interpretation.

A tool like charcoal or soft pencil is probably best for your first exercises since alterations and erasures are easier. But don't worry about neatness at this stage. I've seen lots of perfectly beautiful pencil and charcoal drawings that were smudged and somewhat messy looking.

Unless you have a camera eye and a memory like a computer, you will find that drawing from memory is one of the most difficult things to do convincingly. All your preconceptions and predilections take over and you find yourself guessing and faking what you think is right. This is **conceptual** interpretation. It goes hand in hand with expressionism, abstraction and symbolic art and relies heavily on intuitive gesture. Good conceptual painting is based on observation of nature and plenty of experience in dealing with nature's forms and motifs. Starting out you will be on much safer ground in confining yourself to a **perceptual** interpretation of what you see.

MATERIALS

Artists vary widely in their working habits. There are painters and illustrators who seem to be able to work successfully and efficiently in a studio with no apparent system of order. Every square inch of counter space and window ledge, tabouret and file cabinet top will be buried in an effluvium of pencil stubs, ruptured tubes of paint, discarded boxes, paint - encrusted brushes and palette knives, paint rags, charcoal, marking pencils, ink bottles, etc. I once asked a friend of mine where he kept his phone book. He thought a moment, then said — "I think it's under that pile of file holders with the sketch box and coke bottle on top."

I know another artist whose studio is as neat and orderly as a hospital operating room. Everything is labeled and arranged in showcase order. When he embarks on a job, it becomes a carefully choreographed event.

For me the answer lies somewhere in between these two extremes. The messier my studio becomes, the longer it takes me to find things and make decisions.

I guess the point I'm trying to make is that the artist should make it his business to know his materials and keep them ready and in good working order. Making a fetish of it can obscure the real object, the business of converting ideas into visual form and, moreover, to do it with a minimum of ceremony and mechanical gimmicks.

No two artists are going to require exactly the same assortment of drawing materials. A tool that may be an ideal means of expression in the hands of one artist can be awkward and unsympathetic in the hands of another. Nothing but experience can tell you which tool is right for you.

Most of the materials I have listed here are those which are used in the drawings in this chapter. They are typical of what you will find on the tabouret of almost any professional artist.

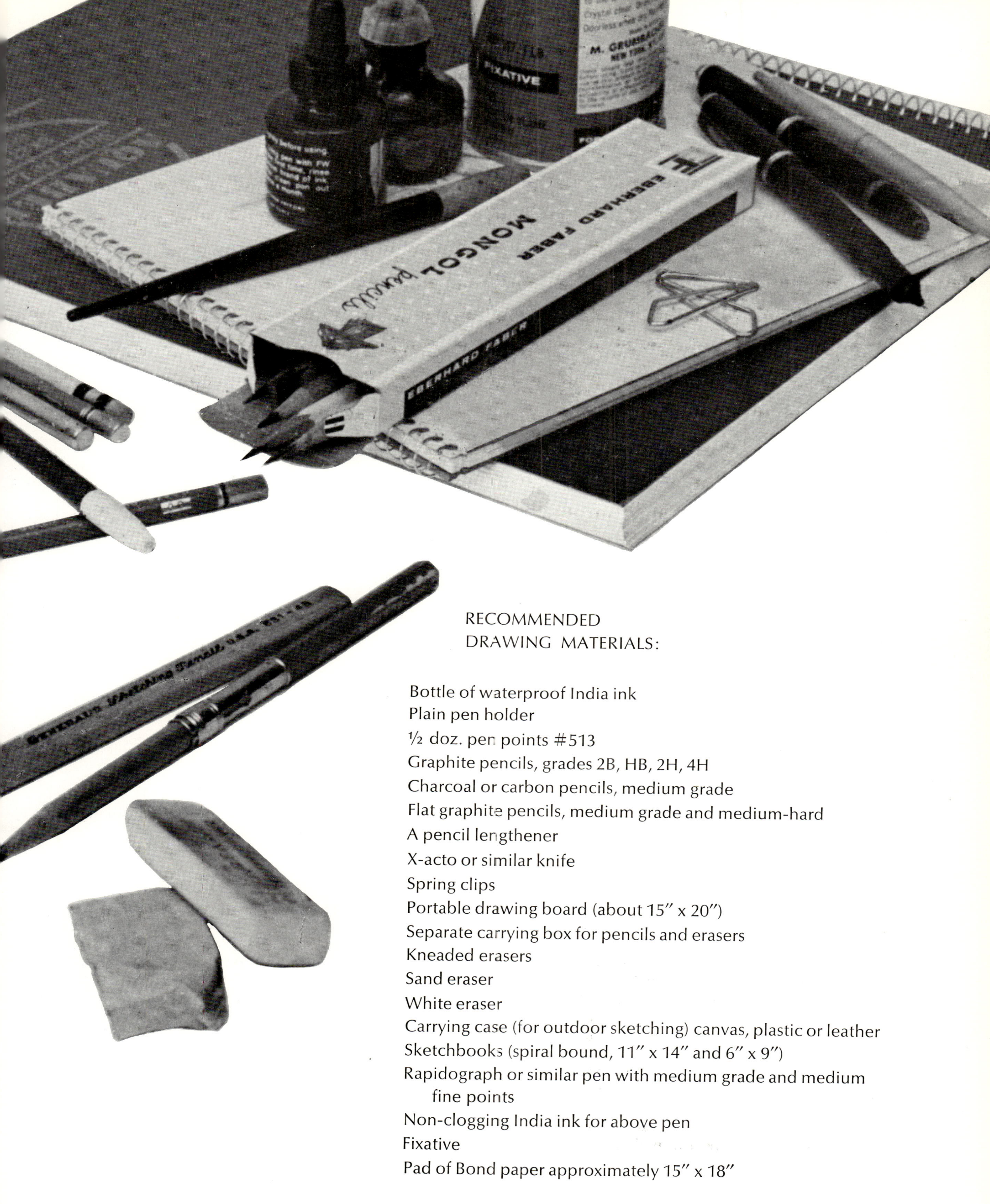

RECOMMENDED
DRAWING MATERIALS:

Bottle of waterproof India ink
Plain pen holder
½ doz. pen points #513
Graphite pencils, grades 2B, HB, 2H, 4H
Charcoal or carbon pencils, medium grade
Flat graphite pencils, medium grade and medium-hard
A pencil lengthener
X-acto or similar knife
Spring clips
Portable drawing board (about 15″ x 20″)
Separate carrying box for pencils and erasers
Kneaded erasers
Sand eraser
White eraser
Carrying case (for outdoor sketching) canvas, plastic or leather
Sketchbooks (spiral bound, 11″ x 14″ and 6″ x 9″)
Rapidograph or similar pen with medium grade and medium
fine points
Non-clogging India ink for above pen
Fixative
Pad of Bond paper approximately 15″ x 18″

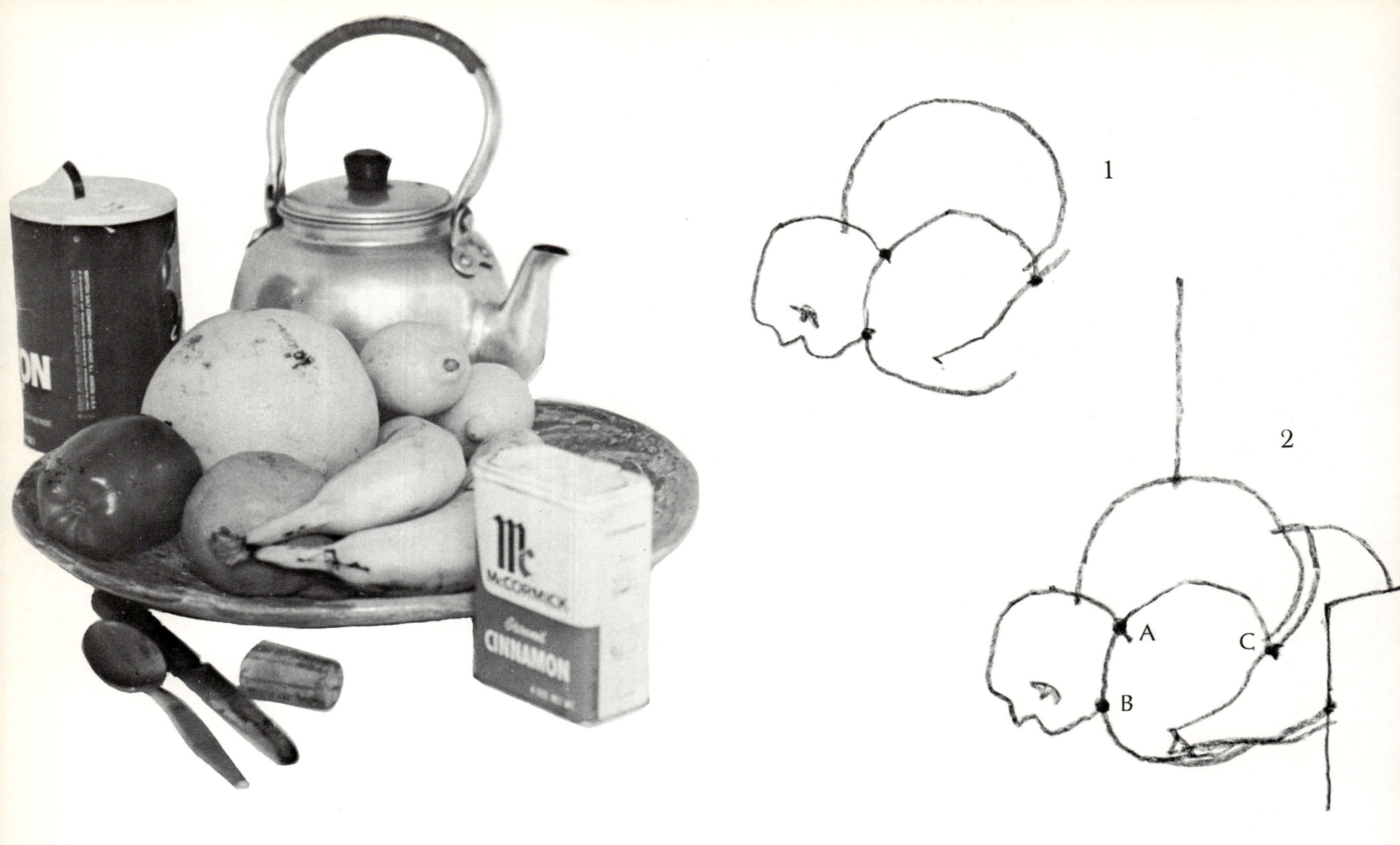

CONTOUR DRAWING

Begin your drawing at the place where your eye wants to go first. This focal point is the natural place to start. From here you can work outwards as your eye explores the subject further. In drawing the human figure, for instance, the most natural place to begin would be the head. In the case of landscape drawing and painting, where an overall design plan is usually a preliminary consideration, this rule may not apply.

Start somewhere near the center of the still life. (1) Draw slowly at first, halting your line each time it intersects with the line of another object (2A, B and C). As you draw, be careful that the hand is not quicker than the eye. Long, graceful sweeps may look impressive but, until you gain experience, it is better to draw slowly and deliberately. Note the intersections as you come to them and get into the habit of using them as points of reference in relating one object to another. (3) Drawing from one point to the next, in a "stop-look-and-go" procedure, gives you a chance to check the relationship of one angle with another. Then, as the forms begin to take shape, they are more likely to be in proper proportion.

This stop-and-go method is suggested as a disciplined way of drawing — an exercise aimed at developing good habits of observation and precision. It is not necessarily the best way to draw by any means. Some very good artists like to start in the upper left hand corner of a picture and end up in the lower right like a house painter painting a wall. However, I don't recommend this procedure for anyone just learning to draw.

Whenever there is a vertical or horizontal in the background, put it in (or invent one). Either can be very useful as a check point in relating all the other angles (vertical, diagonal, and horizontal). Try to maintain visual contact with the borders of the rectangle in which you're working. A drawing of even the simplest object becomes a composition when it is related to, and contained within, the four sides of your pad. When you go beyond the drawing of a single object and start to put in surrounding detail — part of a window or a bit of curtain — you are beginning to create a picture.

In contour drawing, a cramped, insensitive line is often a sign of too much manual control over the pencil (or pen). Holding the pencil further from the point (see photo) can remedy this. A wobbly, less controlled line is usually more interesting than a mechanically accurate one. It has more "character."

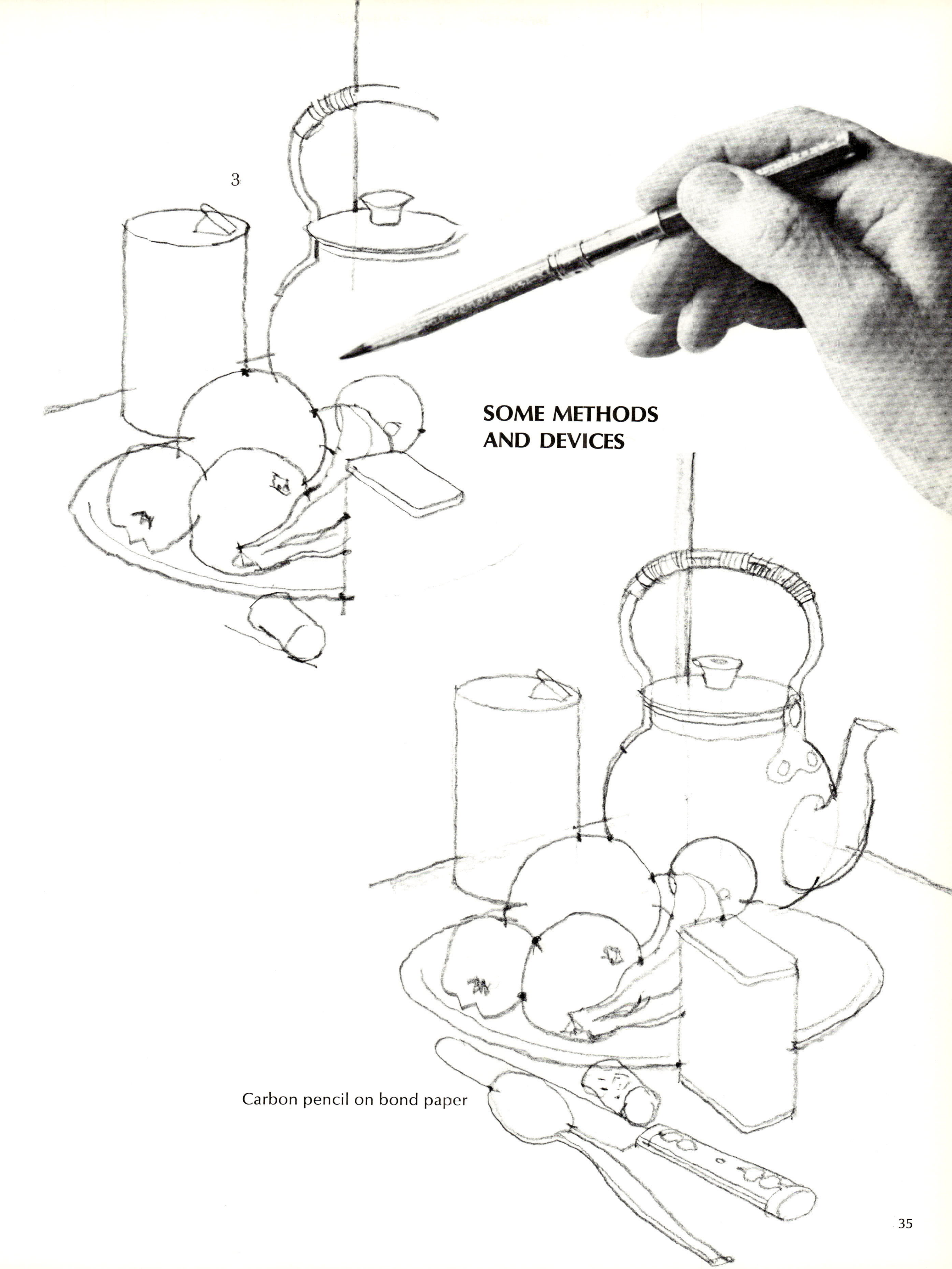

SOME METHODS AND DEVICES

Carbon pencil on bond paper

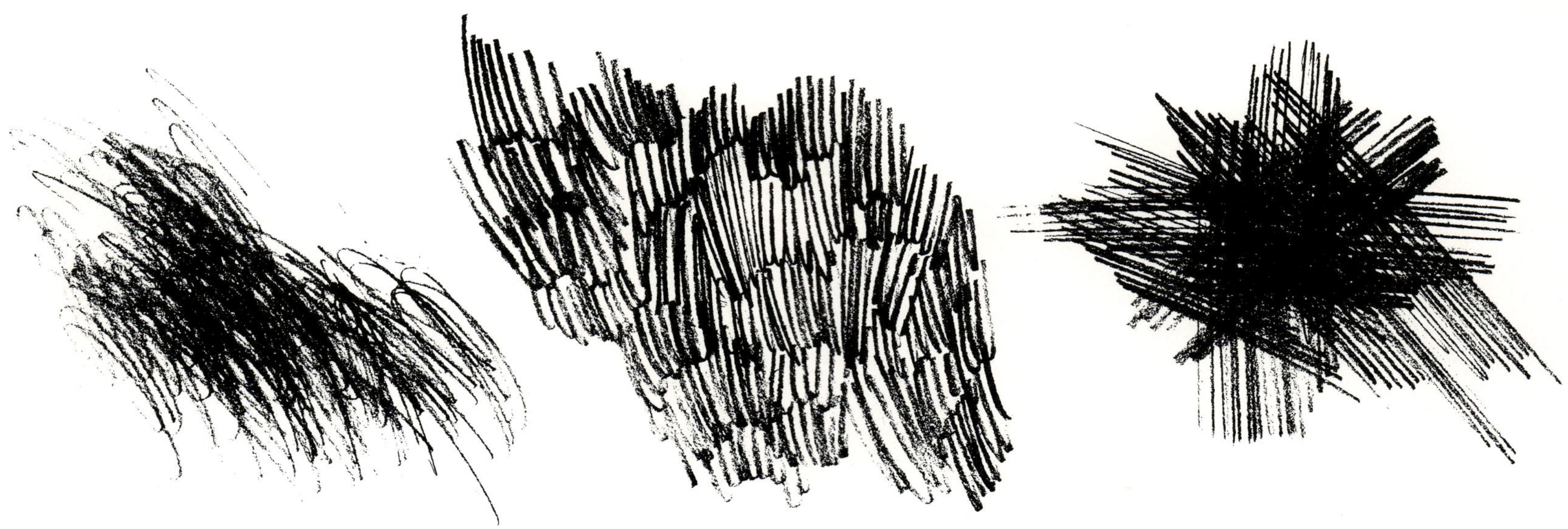

MODELING with LIGHT

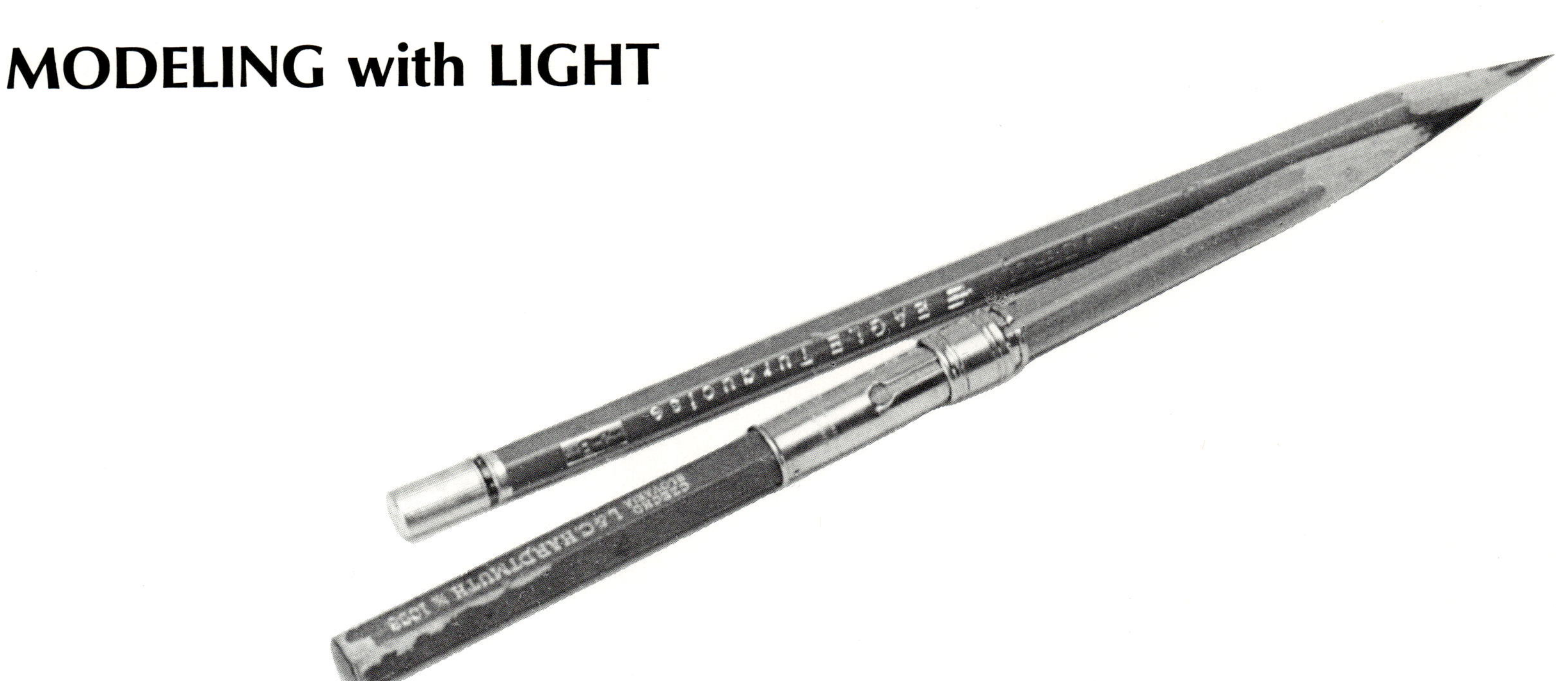

I mention the word "shading" only because it's a very familiar one. It is also an inappropriate and misleading one. The word "modeling" comes much closer to expressing what we want to say when we are talking about suggesting solid form. When drawing, modeling is using light and shade to suggest an object's roundness, its depressions, folds, bumps, etc., in other words, its three dimensions.

Let's pick up a graphite pencil and try modeling with light.

Start with some very simple objects — a vase, some fruit, a cup and saucer, a piece of crumpled up paper.

Place your subjects where they will be strongly lit from one side. Avoid top lighting or flat lighting (source of light, directly behind you). Flat light is shadowless and virtually eliminates modeling. Use side light, preferably one coming from a single window or lamp. Bear in mind that any confusion of shadows or reflections will make it harder to see the solid form. As you draw, concentrate on the light and shade, not on the outer contours of the forms. And again, aim for precision and accuracy in these first experiments. Try to "feel" the form and irregularities as you draw them just as a sculptor working in clay would do.

In drawing the light that falls on an object we automatically draw the form of that object. It is the most direct way of arriving at three-dimensional drawing. Moreover, it is one of the best exercises in developing good comprehension of form. It should not be thought of as a technique or style but rather as method — a means to an end. This modeling with light is a form of "painting with a pencil." In the chapter on **Figure Drawing** we will see how important it is when it comes to drawing the human figure.

When you begin to feel at home with an ordinary graphite pencil try switching to a carbon pencil, then to pen and ink, felt tip pen and bamboo pen.

A piece of crumpled paper is ideal for practicing modeling with light. For my subject I took a piece of brown wrapping paper about eight inches square and crumpled it, not too tightly. In drawing, I kept the pen moving constantly, in a sort of "handwriting" action, using more arm than wrist. Try it in pencil first.

The still life was done with a 2B graphite pencil.

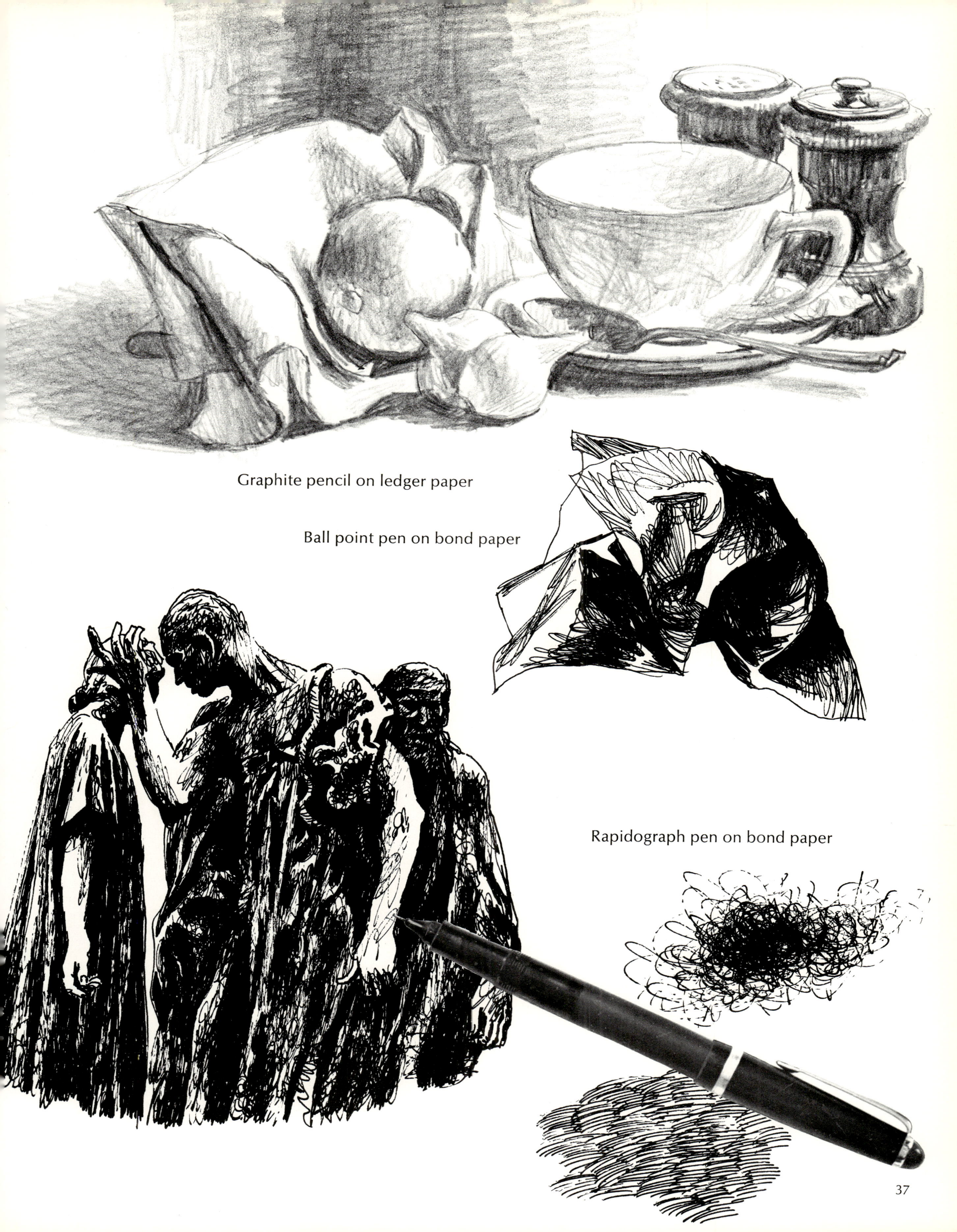

Graphite pencil on ledger paper

Ball point pen on bond paper

Rapidograph pen on bond paper

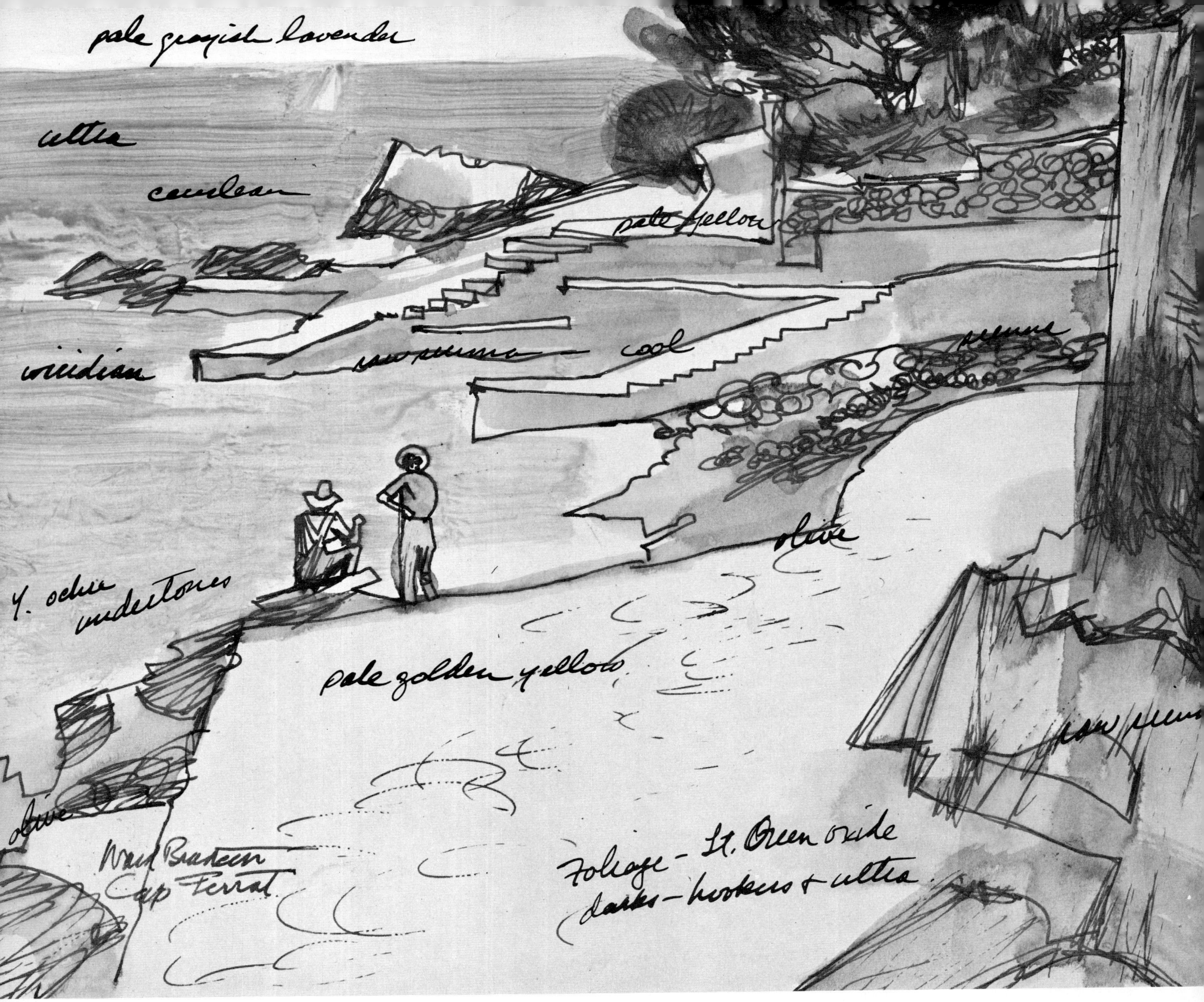

OUTDOOR DRAWING

If you are by nature curious (and what artist isn't?) and in addition if you are imbued with a spirit of adventure, then you already are halfway there when it comes to outdoor drawing.

Almost every picture I make, whether it's an on-the-spot sketch, a portrait, an illustration or an abstract, begins with a pencil drawing of some kind. In fact, I would be lost at this formative stage, without a pencil in my hand. I don't think there is anything quite like it for catching an idea on the wing and recording it quickly. It's the most familiar, easiest-to-use drawing tool there is. It's erasable, it will not clog or blot like a pen, and it is compatible with other mediums — a considerable virtue in today's anything-goes-world of art. I'd suggest you use it for your first excursions into outdoor drawing — and let yourself be guided by subject matter that interests you. Don't let anything hurry you at this stage or you are liable to miss things, and it will show up in the drawing — it always does.

The best way to get to know your subject is to draw it. Drawing from nature forces us to observe and analyze. Learn to simplify, exaggerate and rearrange what you see. Don't be afraid to disregard perspective and dimension in favor of pure flat pattern if this sort of concept will enhance the ultimate design of the picture.

The above drawing, done with a Rapidograph #2 pen, is a typical on-the-spot sketch. I made it without any particular regard for the end result. I was trying to catch a feeling of the excitement of moving trees and water, and especially the sparkling sunlight. About all I came away with was a record of the crazy shapes in it. I'm afraid that trying to portray the French Riviera without benefit of color is something like playing Debussy's "La Mer" with a three piece combo. But anyway, I now had a pretty descriptive record of the scene that could be referred to later if I wanted to make a painting of it.

I used a thin ink wash to indicate shadow and sunlight. The color of the trees and water was put in with transparent green and blue acrylic. When making color notes on location, be as specific and descriptive as possible. Blue for water and gray for rock will not do. Nail down the actual color as accurately as you can. The wash of green and blue, incidentally, was very little help as a record. It served only to establish a pattern of values.

Take along a box full of sharpened pencils — you won't want to stop in the middle of a flush of inspiration to sharpen one. They should be fairly soft, 2B or softer. You can vary your drawings with charcoal pencil when you feel you're ready. Use a medium grade.

Take the time to decide what to draw and how to draw it. But don't spend all day looking for a ready-made subject. You may never find it. Be prepared to improvise and regroup your subject matter from scattered elements. Don't hesitate to borrow from one scene anything that will help the composition of another. It's possible for a scene to be full of interesting detail and subject matter, yet be monotonous and uninspiring. Sometimes it needs only the addition of some foreground shape to liven it up. Look around you for something that can be adapted — rocks, grass, a tree stump, anything compatible that will pep up your composition and make it more dramatic, more pictorial.

Many beginners make the mistake of trying to fill all the space on the paper. Fine detail, no matter how exquisitely rendered, needs relief and contrast to compliment it. Give the white space around your drawing a chance to work for you.

Learn to extract what you want from your subject instead of just methodically copying it.

More good drawings have been ruined because the artist didn't know when to stop.

NORMAN MAC DONALD

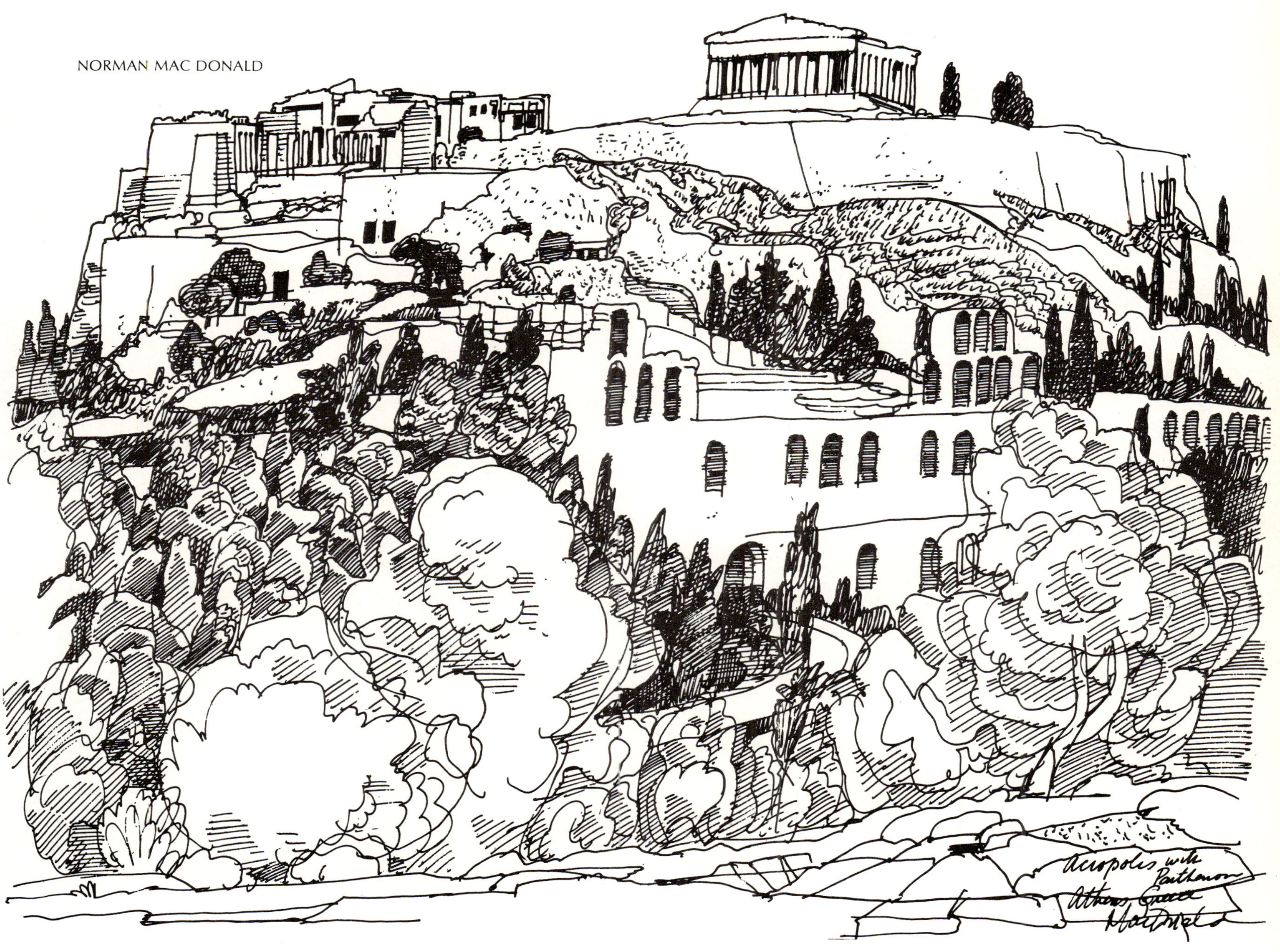

A dictionary definition of perspective tells us that perspective is "the art of depicting landscape, etc. on a flat surface in such a way as to express dimensions and spatial relations." As painters we all inherit the same problem: to suggest a completely dimensional experience on a flat, two- dimensional surface.

Up until the time of the French Impressionists, about 1870, the only perspective known to art was the classical, rigidly formulated perspective of the Renaissance. Ever since Durer, da Vinci and Uccello, its laws had gone unchallenged and unchanged. Cézanne was the first to take liberties with these laws. He developed a whole new system of space representation that was virtually independent of the old rules of converging lines, vanishing points, and immutable eye levels. The result was a synthesis of visual form and imagined reality. Like most revolts in art, it was greeted by the public and the critics with outraged disapproval. Only Cézanne's fellow artists were wise enough to know that he was indeed onto something. His remarkable insight into form, volume and relationships revolutionized painting and paved the way for the Impressionists and Twentieth Century Art.

As an art student you would probably be handicapped without a basic knowledge of classical perspective. But, like studying anatomy, it's a good thing until it becomes an obsession. The mathematics of perspective should never be allowed to stifle creativity.

As you develop in your ability to draw, you will find that your sense of perspective becomes less mechanical and more intuitive. You should then be more concerned with the relationships of forms and how they can be made to function in **suggesting** distance and foreshortening, which is, after all, the essence of perspective and spatial conception. Cézanne discovered and put into practice the methods of

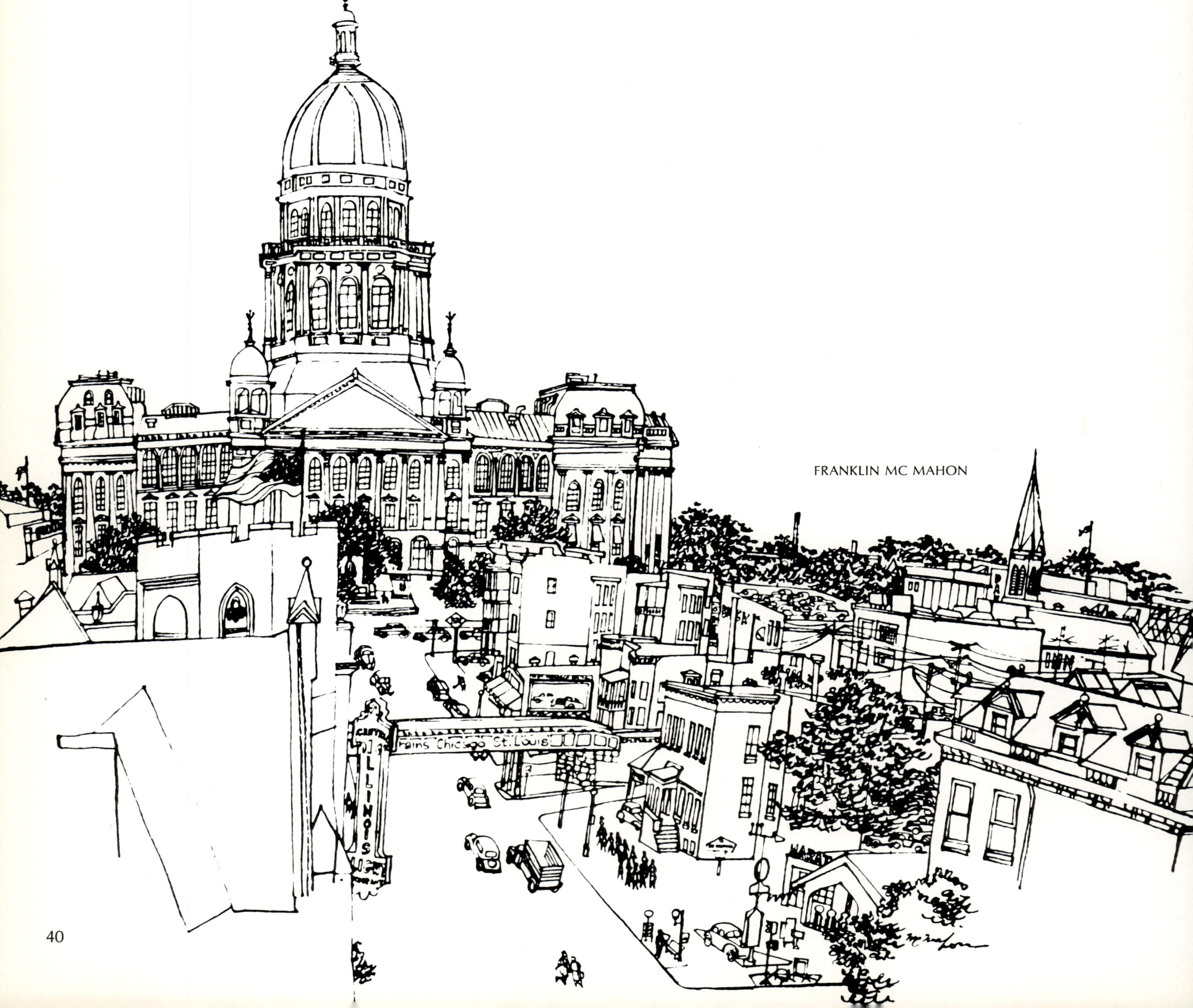

FRANKLIN MC MAHON

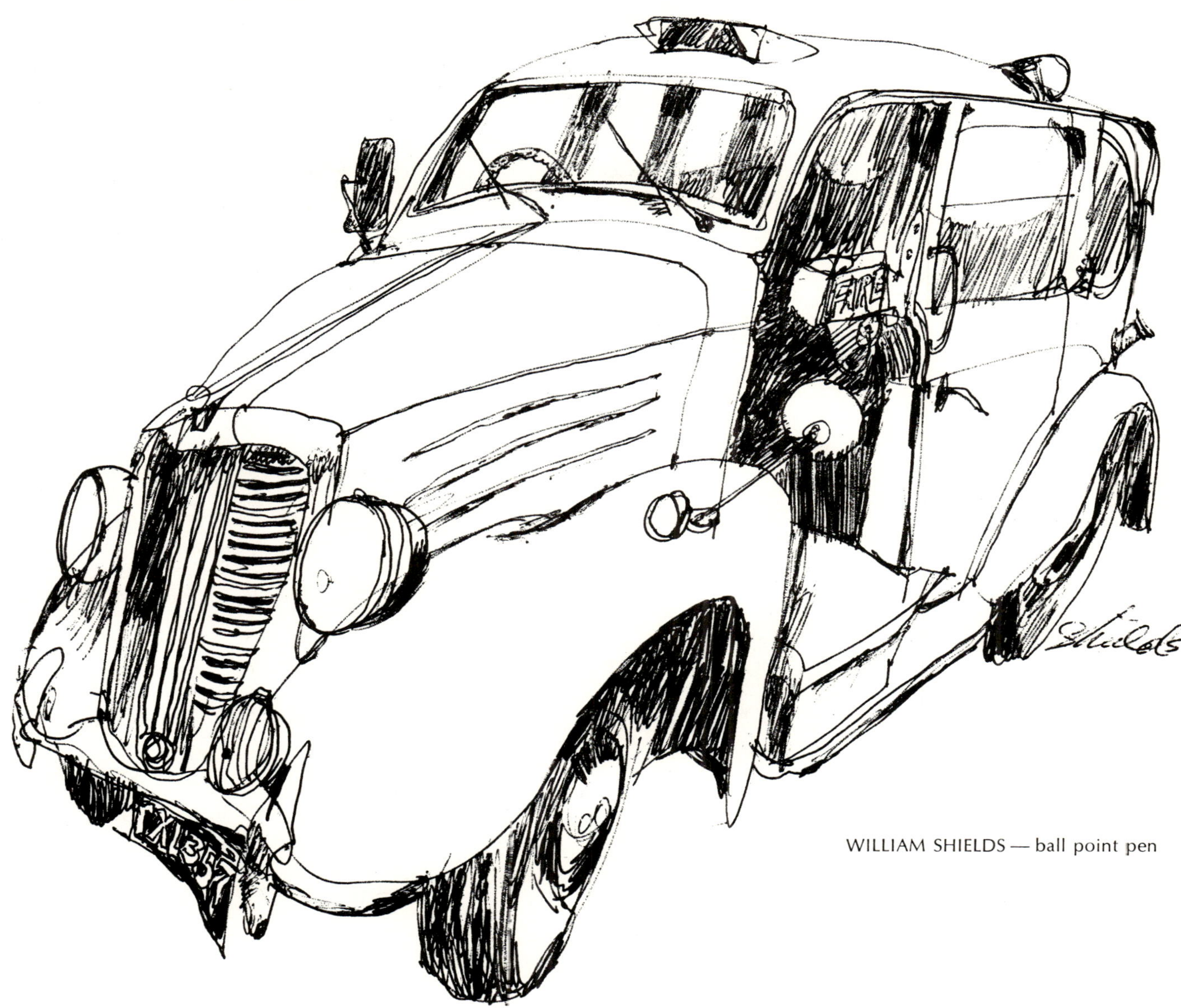

WILLIAM SHIELDS — ball point pen

suggesting the near and the far by the use of color alone.

Many of the paintings of Bonnard and Matisse are almost totally free of any formal perspective. Horizon lines are tilted or unconnected, planes are two-dimensional. Interiors and still-lifes are sometimes completely lacking in vanishing points. By deliberately flattening out perspective, shapes and abstract design are given greater freedom to work. Strangely enough the feeling of space and volume is there without the static correctness of academic perspective. A more natural kind of painting can result when visual interpretation does not have to compete with mathematics.

Much of what we see comes to us through our peripheral vision. This wide area, which lies outside the point of focus, is an essential part of seeing. To demonstrate — fix your eye on some conspicuous object across the room or out the window; really nail your vision to it. Now, without moving your eye even for an instant, try to define accurately some object outside this point of focus. You will find you cannot do it. Unless you shift your eyes you will see everything in this marginal area pretty much in terms of vague, soft-edged shapes. Even prominent forms seem to distort and undulate, though we may not be consciously aware of it. Windows and houses lose their rectilinearity and appear more "free form" in shape. Some artists put this distortion to work. By softening some forms and exaggerating others, they actually re-create the effect of peripheral distortion in the eye of the viewer.

Edvard Munch was a painter who used these vague shapes to express sensations and emotions that were personal — without any particular bearing on realism. In his case, his predilection for gruesome subjects and his obsession with death came out in the form of ghostly tortured shapes, sometimes naive but always highly symbolic. (See page 56.) His paintings were the beginning of Expressionism.

In dramatic contrast is the way in which Bonnard used forms to express an optimistic view of life. He made vague, distorted shapes shimmer and fuse together in a sort of joyous, lyrical abstraction. (See pages 27, 58.)

Distortion really comes into its own in line drawing. Exaggeration of perspective is particularly useful in a medium where modeling and spatial form are absent. The drawing on page 43 demonstrates vividly how wide angle distortion can bring life and a feeling of space to a picture. Distortion can make even the most ordinary subjects somehow more interesting and compelling. Bill Shields' drawing of an old London taxi, above, is an example of this.

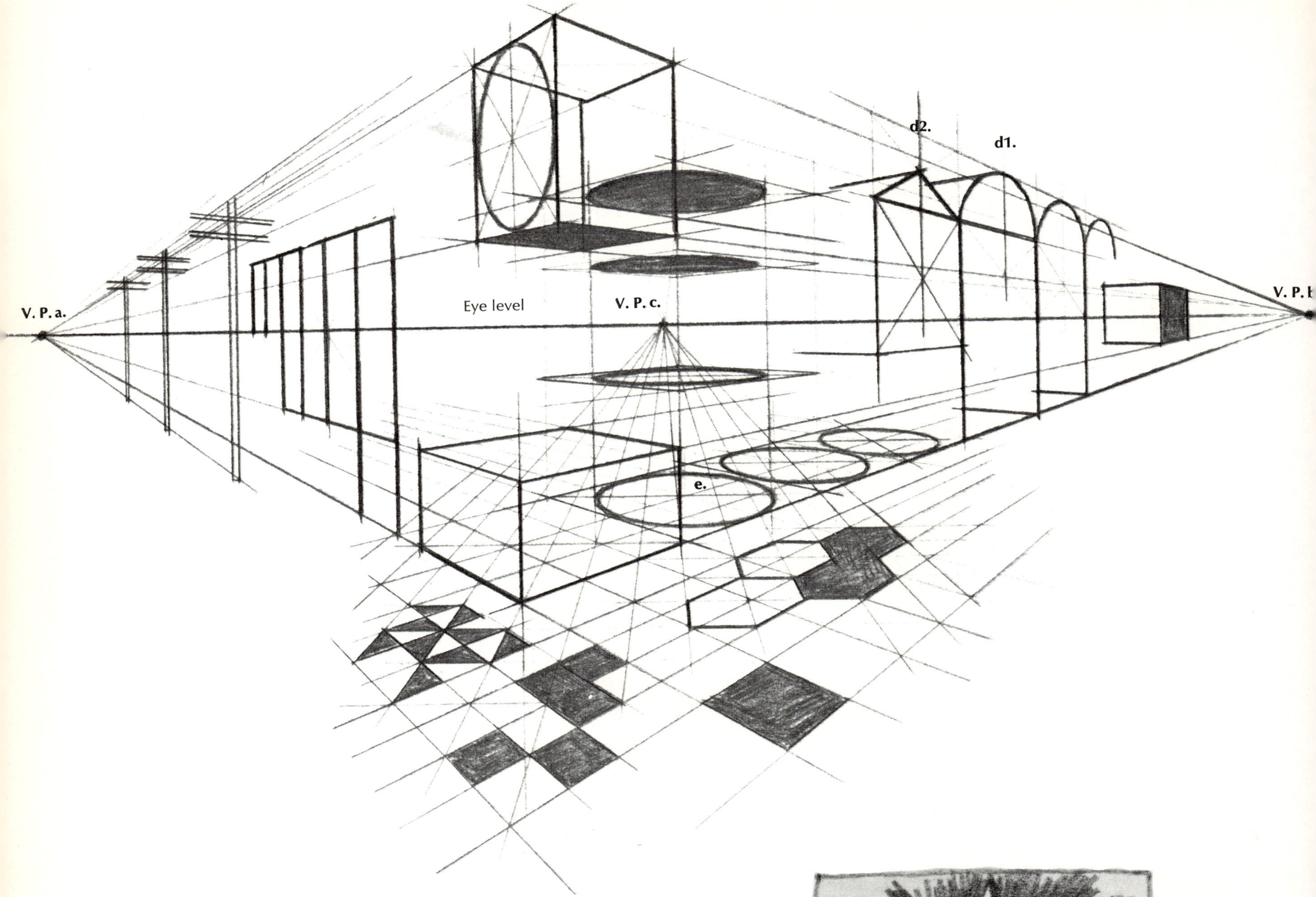

d2.
d1.
V. P. a.
Eye level
V. P. c.
V. P. b
e.

PERSPECTIVE

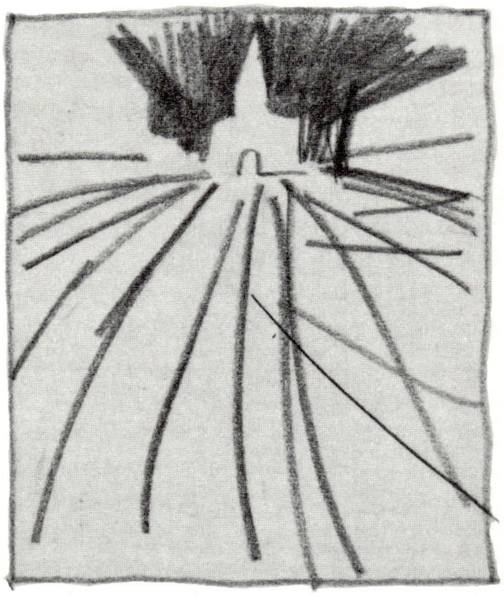

2

1
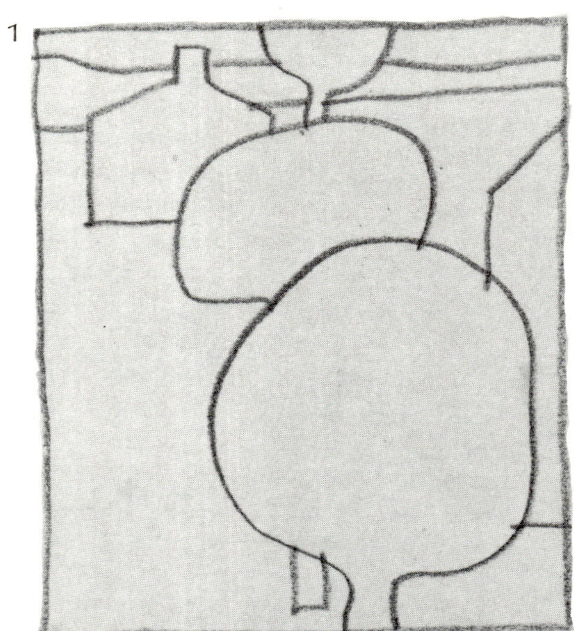

For the benefit of any readers I might have left after seeing the drawing on the opposite page — it is not a plan for some secret weapon but a composite diagram that demonstrates a few ironbound laws of perspective. *Don't* take it too seriously.

It's intended to remind you that the closer and the larger any object is to the eye, the more distorted and foreshortened it will be. Every object — cube-shaped, pyramidal, elliptical — is subject to the same laws of perspective. In the diagram every plane, every line except the verticals, shares the same vanishing points, **a.** and **b.** The exception to this is in the "diagonals" used in centering, the horizontal ellipses and squares. These lines go back to vanishing point **c.** Diagonals are also used to locate the center of an arch or the peak of a roof, as in **d1.** and **d2.** Keep in mind that ellipses, horizontal or vertical, are not perfect ovals when drawn in perspective. They distort like everything else. (See **e.**)

There is no mechanical problem in perspective that can't be figured out if you care to go into the geometrics of it and keep plodding away. The rule of the vanishing point is as unchanging and unalterable as the law of gravity.

Today the *illusion* of depth, more often, is used to convey the feeling of perspective rather than mathematics. You don't need to be literal about it. Overlaps alone, if they are kept concise and clear, will create a sensation of depth (Fig.1). Diagonals are so closely rooted to our subconscious sense of perspective that it's almost impossible to use them in a design without suggesting a certain feeling of third dimension (Fig.2).

If you are interested in pursuing the mechanics of perspective further I can recommend a book that tells it all: from the rules governing the perspective of stairways to the mathematics of cast shadows. It is E. W. Watson's book *How To Use Creative Perspective,* published by the Van Nostrand Reinhold Company.

DISTORTION-PERIPHERAL VISION

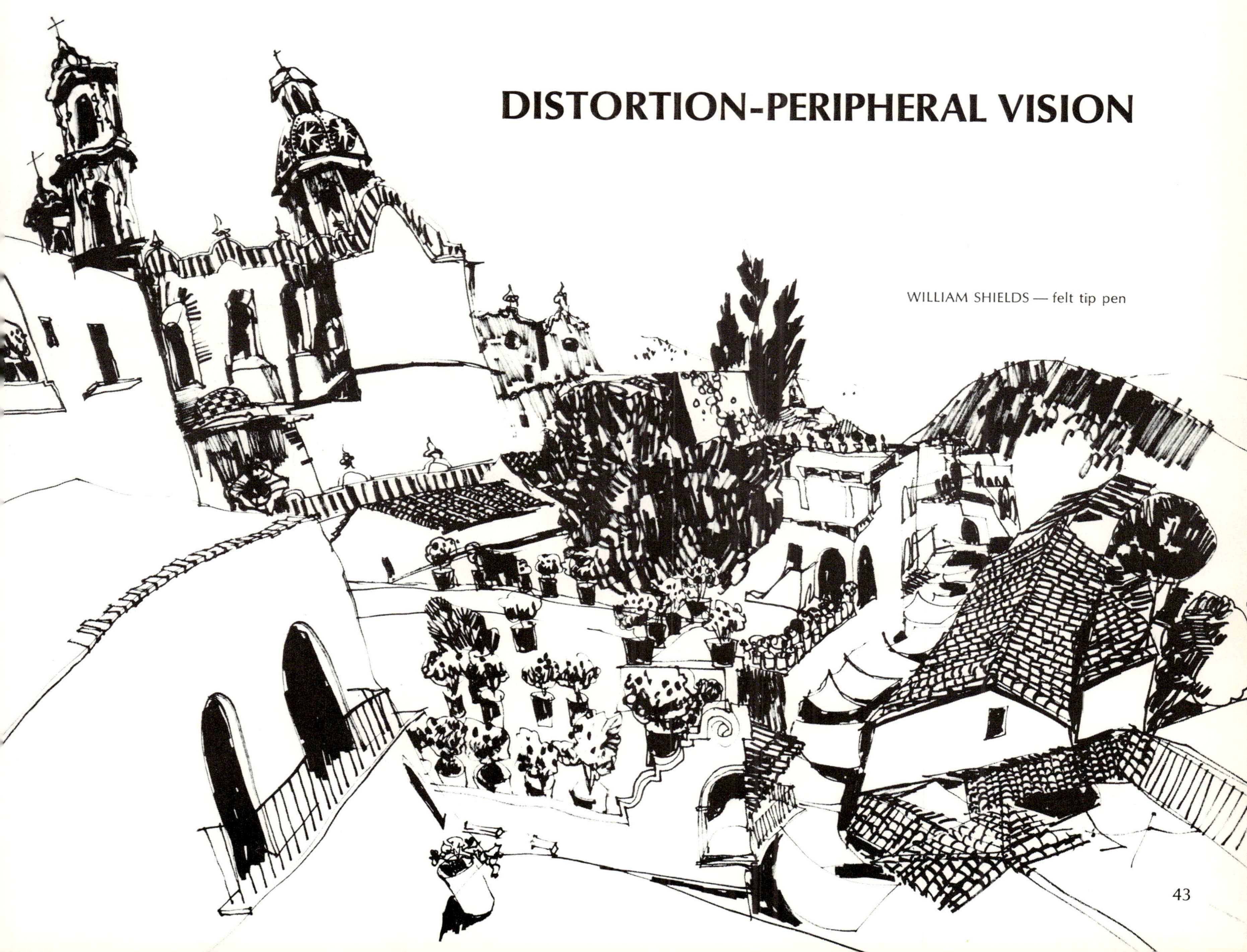

WILLIAM SHIELDS — felt tip pen

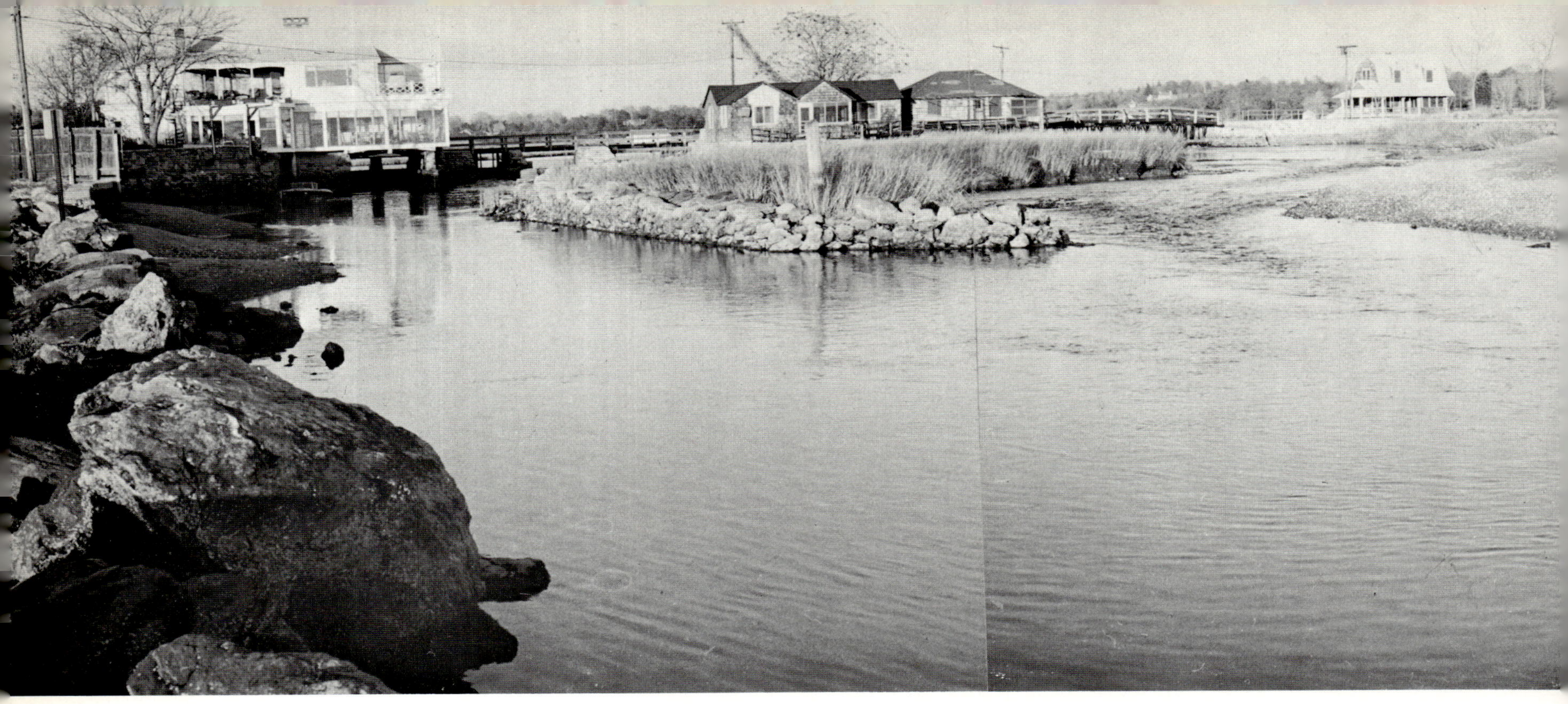

SELECTING the SUBJECT

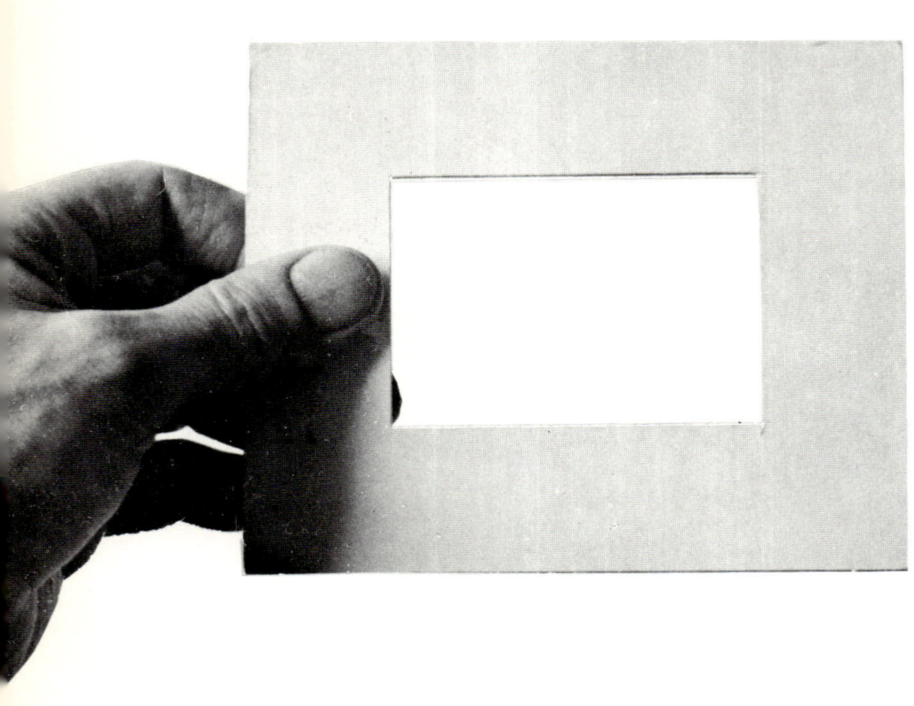

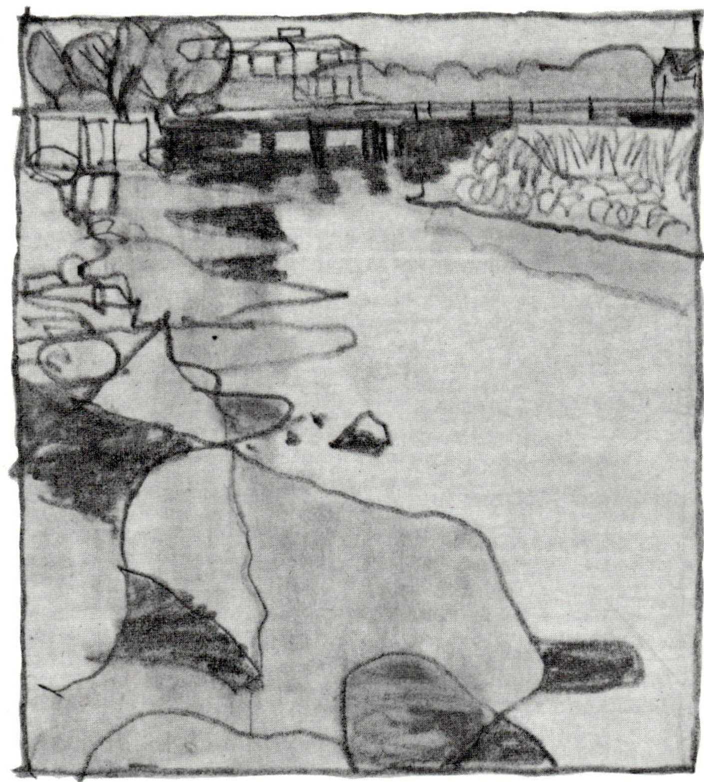

1

The first thing the artist must do is discover what he really wants to paint. He must learn to recognize his likes and dislikes and develop his preferences and natural inclinations when it comes to subject matter. Many amateurs have a tendency to go after subjects simply because they are familiar or popular. While there is nothing wrong with paintings of Paris boulevards, quaint fishing boats and weather-beaten barns, still, constant repetition has rendered them a bit sterile. Not that good pictures can no longer come out of this sort of subject matter, but it is much more difficult to take a cliché subject and come up with a painting that is anything other than a cliché. Moreover, it takes an artist with an extremely daring style and approach to deal with such conventional subjects in a way that is original and exciting.

What you paint should be determined by what you really **want** to paint. If you enjoy a single flower, enough to want

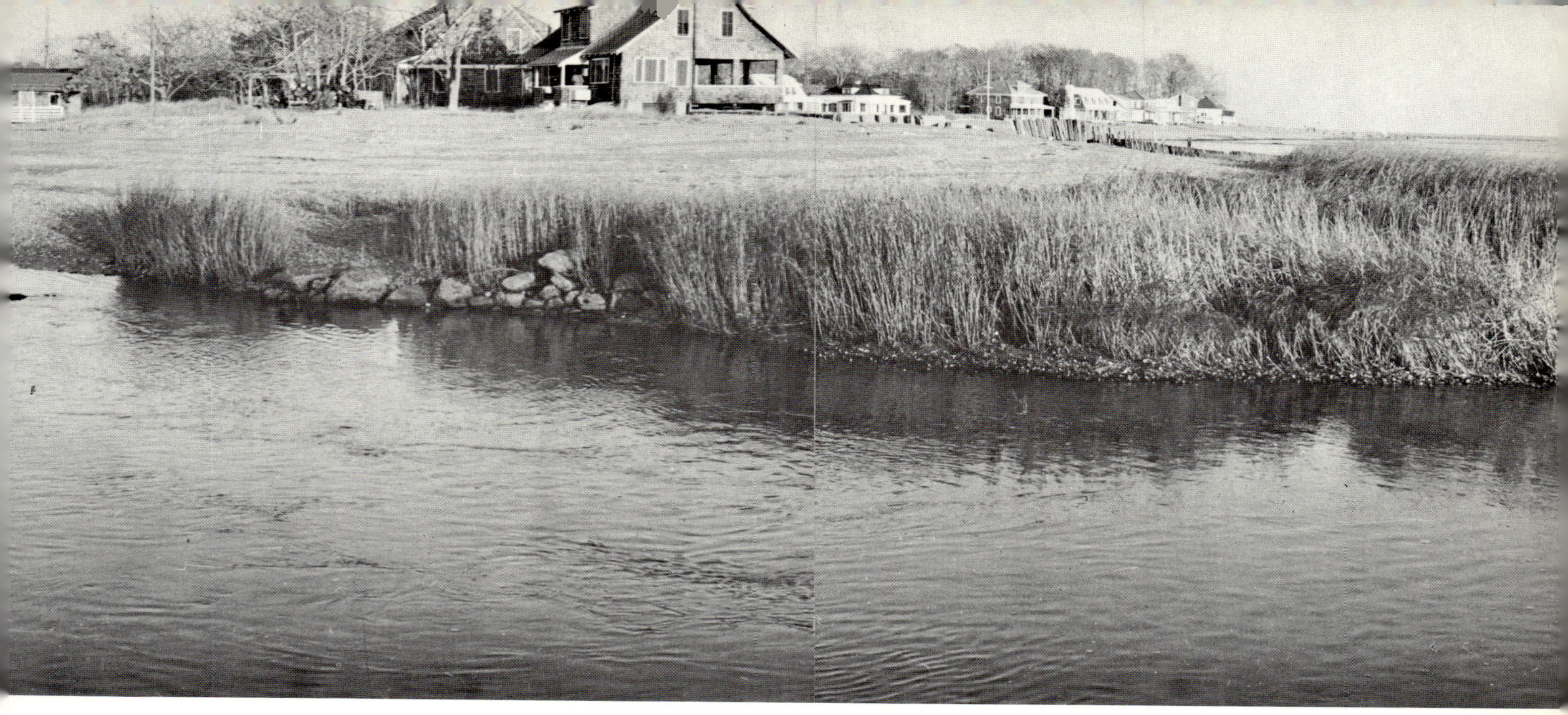

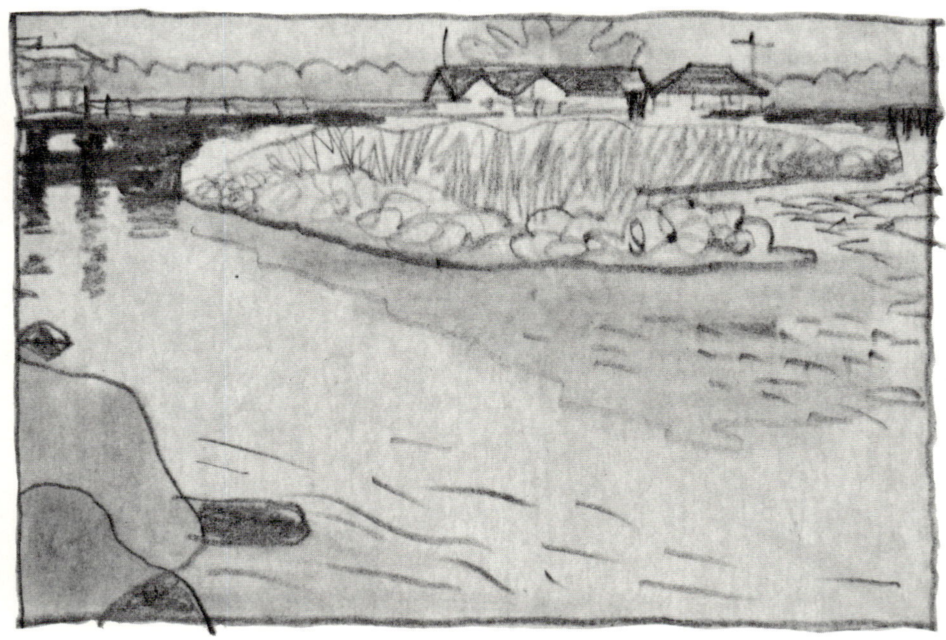

2

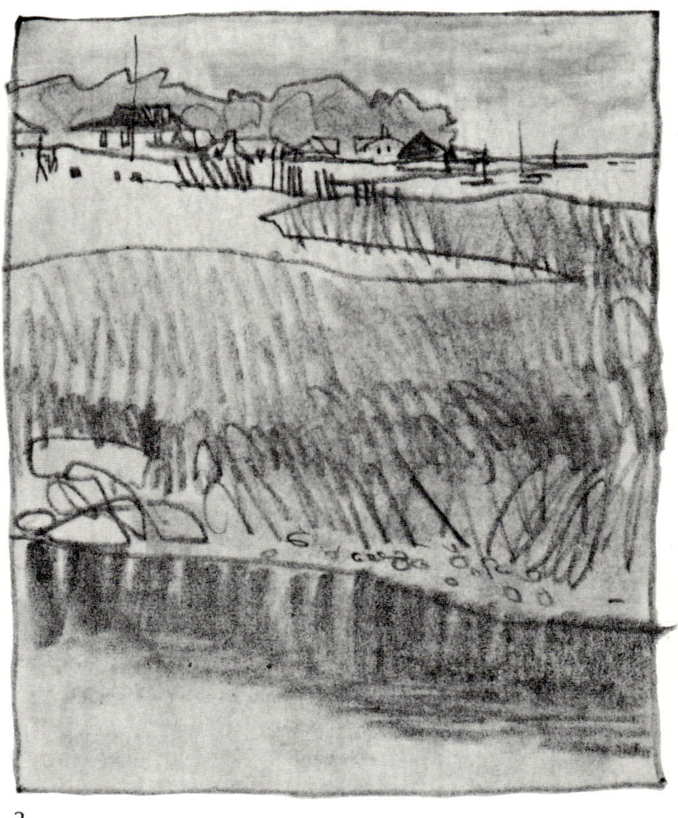

3

to paint it, for example, then you should by all means paint it. (See page 59.)

The pure pleasure and interest in your subject can generate a quality that all the intellectualizing in the world could never achieve. Nothing can ever substitute for the magic that seems to come from the enjoyment of what you are doing.

The above panorama is of a tidal inlet on Long Island Sound. I picked it because it is near my home, but more importantly, because it is so typical of this coastal area.

To anyone seeing it for the first time I would guess that it is neither very exciting nor very dull. But I have passed it many times and explored it so often, I feel as though I know it intimately. It offers enough variety, I think, for half a dozen pictures, depending on one's vantage point.

Now this scene may not be one that appeals at all to you, but for the sake of discussion let's assume that it does. Naturally you would be wasting your time trying to draw something that did not interest you.

Let's suppose you are sitting about where this picture was taken and are itching to get started. This is where many beginners make their first mistake. They don't take the time to consider all the possibilities their subject offers.

Look for the **big shapes,** and here is where a cardboard "finder" can be a big help in selecting the subject. Figures 1, 2 and 3 show three entirely different compositions taken from the same scene without moving from the spot.

You are composing in earnest now. Keep in mind the principles of balance (pages 24-25) and rhythms (pages 28-29). Here's your chance to put them to work. And once again — don't overlook those negative shapes!

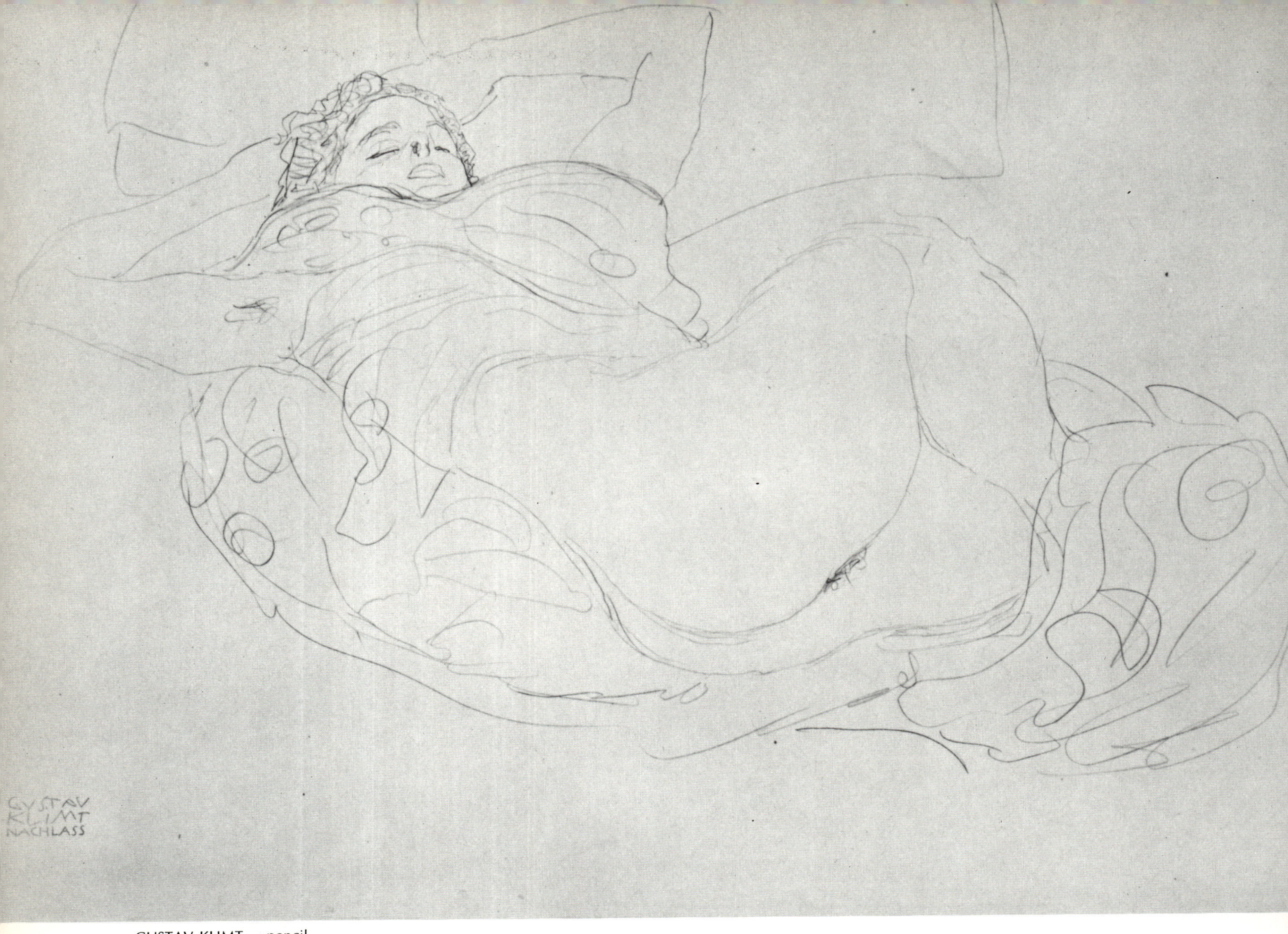

GUSTAV KLIMT — pencil

FIGURE DRAWING

There are some traditions that are hard to buck. One of the oldest and most hallowed of these is the tradition of drawing from the nude. Up to this day the human body remains the most universally accepted subject. There is a good reason for this. It's because the figure presents such an infinite variety of attitudes and so many subtleties of motion and color. No other subject offers us a wider range of interpretations or is quite so challenging to draw.

Another reason is that we identify and relate to the human body more easily. We are closer to this subject, literally and psychologically, than to any other.

The different interpretations that can be drawn from the human figure make it an ideal subject for experiment. It is a subject that should be approached with considerable respect. Nothing will demand more of your powers of observation. All the problems of light and shadow, form, composition and space relationships will challenge you. Figure drawing requires knowing your subject more thoroughly than, say, still life or landscape. It's much harder to take liberties with the anatomy of an arm or with the way a head sits on neck and shoulders than with a landscape where you are freer to exaggerate and simplify.

I find the nude far more difficult to draw than the draped figure. Clothing can be made to cover a multitude of sins (metaphor intended). Folds and wrinkles will hide as much of the underlying forms as you want. Not that this is bad by any means. But if you first acquire a working knowledge of the nude, drawing the draped figure will be easier. Your drawings will be more "solid" because you will have greater conviction of what is happening beneath the surface. By "a working knowledge" I mean a basic, fundamental command over the mechanics and workings of the human body, and not necessarily knowing the names of all the bones and muscles. It is better to learn your anatomy and then "forget" it, or rather, to file it all away in your subconscious. The hand will automatically

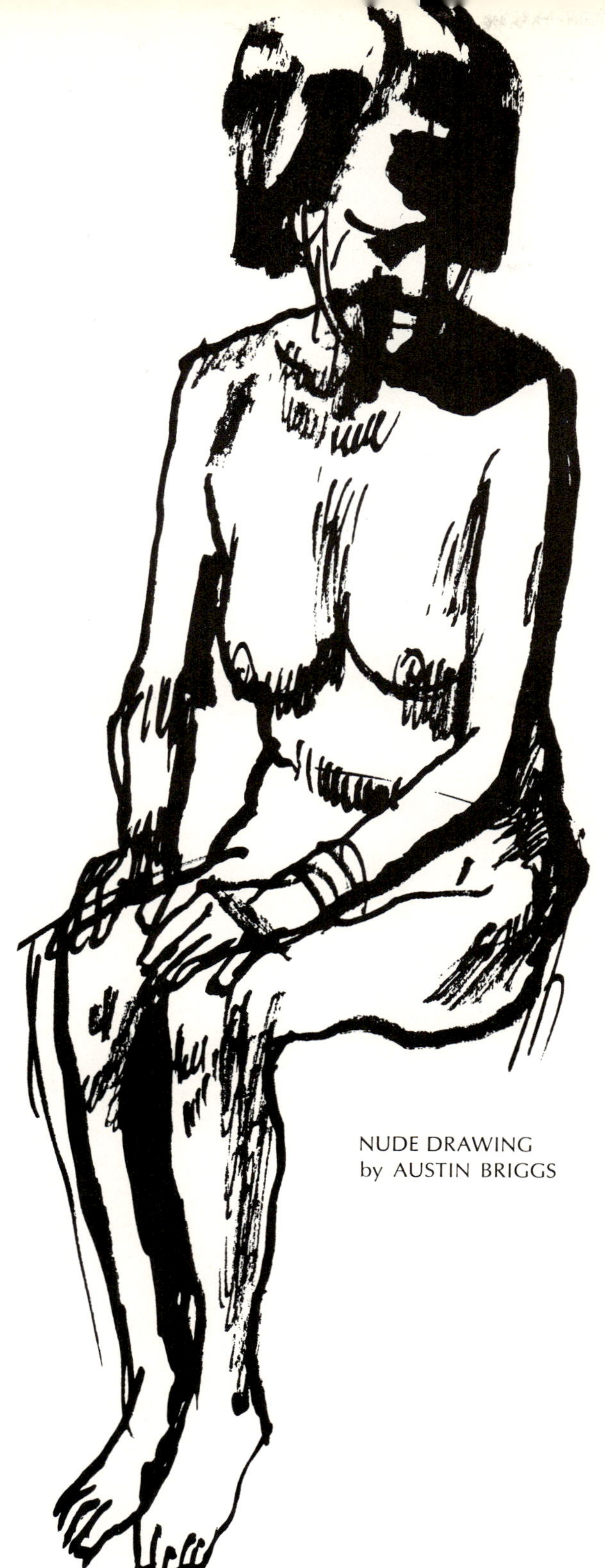

NUDE DRAWING
by AUSTIN BRIGGS

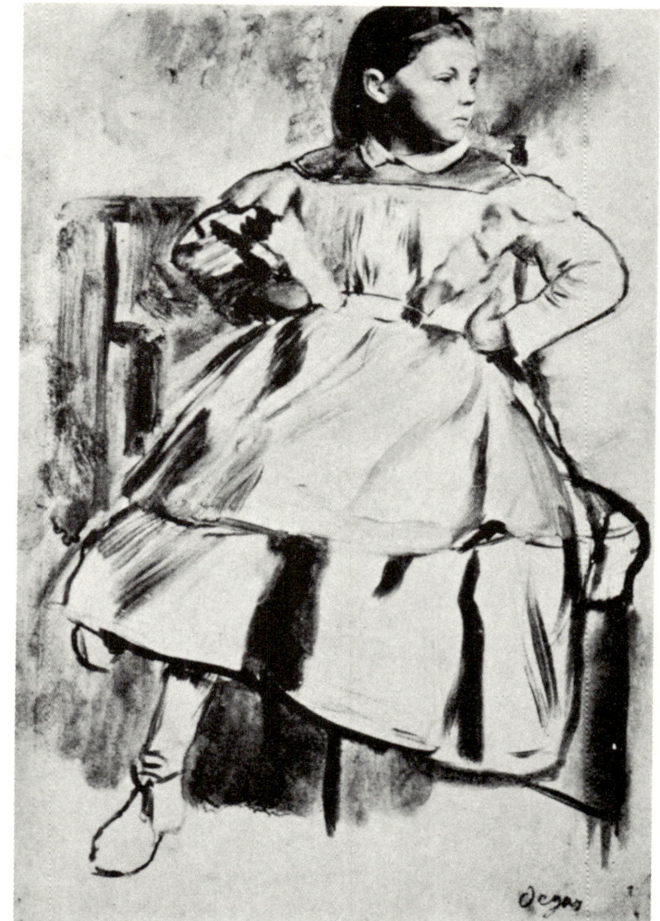

PORTRAIT OF JULIE BELLELLI by EDGAR DEGAS
brush drawing on cardboard

obey what the mind has stored away. But, when starting out, don't try to do much more than copy what you see. This is the only way I know of to learn to draw. With practice you will reach a point when painstaking copying gives way to interpretation. This is the real beginning of drawing . . . when knowledge and experience are reflected in your drawing.

Your first drawings are almost sure to have a hard edged, mechanical look. Don't worry about this. Concentrate on getting those shapes and angles and proportions right in the early stages. Sureness and flow of line should be allowed to develop naturally. That spontaneous "loose" quality owes a lot to the subconscious. It is a mysterious, elusive thing that comes only with plenty of practice. It comes with knowing what to emphasize, what to exaggerate and what to distort. Before you can hope to attain a professional look you must have an accumulated experience behind you.

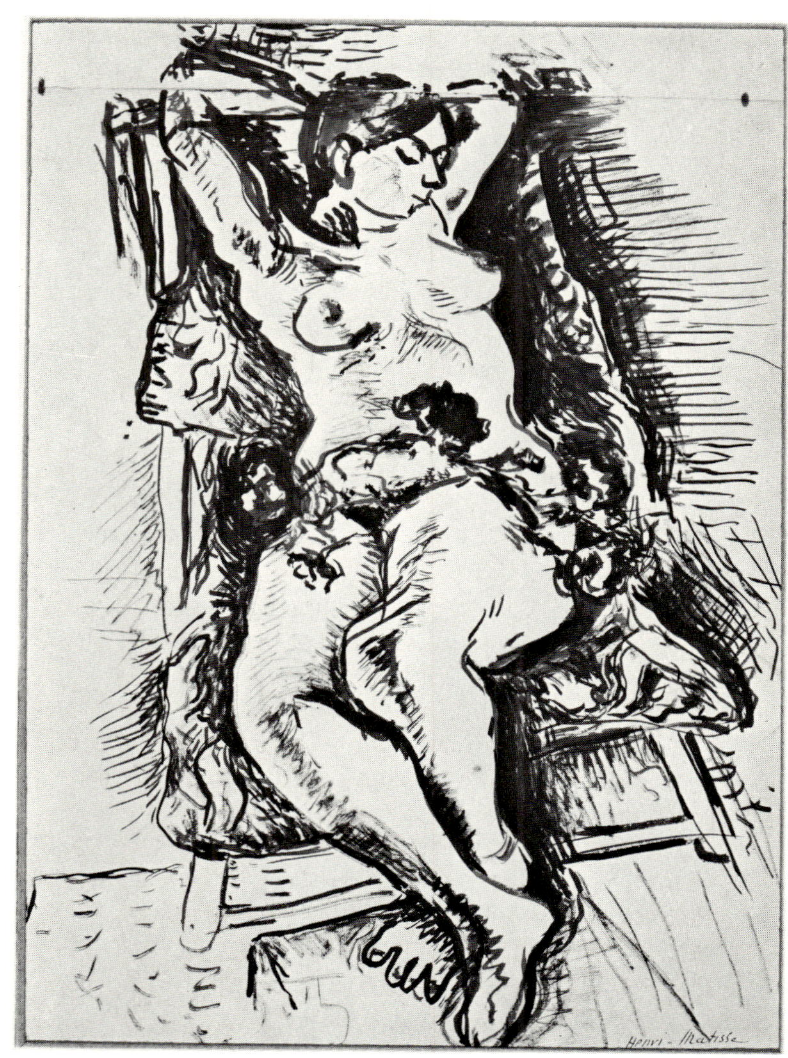

NUDE IN ARMCHAIR by HENRI MATISSE — brush drawing
Art Institute of Chicago

The atmosphere of the average life class leaves a lot to be desired. To begin with, it is almost always crowded. All except those nearest the model have to crane their necks to see around the heads and easels of the ones in front. But the fees are small; and, for the beginner, some guidance is better than none (the instructor won't have much time for you in a large class). Also, in a large class you will have little freedom to move around and almost nothing to say about the pose.

A better solution is to organize a small group of your own and limit its size to five or six people. If they are advanced students or professionals, so much the better. Seeing other people's work and other people at work is stimulating and instructional.

If you live in a small town, finding models can be a problem. But remember, they don't have to be professionals. Remember, too, that good looking people don't necessarily make the best models. Some of the plainest or most unusual looking ones turn out to be the most exciting to draw. Dancers, you'll find, know how to move more naturally. They have better muscle tone and can hold a pose longer without tiring.

So many models, particularly amateurs, fall into the most interesting poses when they are resting. The model who is too carefully posed or overdirected usually ends up in a stiff, self-conscious attitude. More than once I have found myself plodding through a tedious, uninspiring drawing because the model was in an uncomfortable, contrived pose. Often it is better to let the model pose herself. Watch out for the "pin-up girl" poses some models like to assume.

Before you begin, study your subject carefully. Aside from having two eyes, a nose and a mouth, and the same number of bones and muscles, people still vary tremendously physiologically. Find out what is different about your subject and don't be afraid to exaggerate it.

Don't hesitate to move around the model until you find a pose that is interesting, but still not too complicated. Avoid tricky lighting and excessive foreshortening, at least until you become more sure of yourself. A simple, bold, three-quarter-front lighting (as against back-lighting) will be easier to handle and will give you much more definite shadow forms. Light that falls flatly on the model will produce flat, almost shadowless modeling, and is probably the best to use for disciplined drawing. But I must confess,

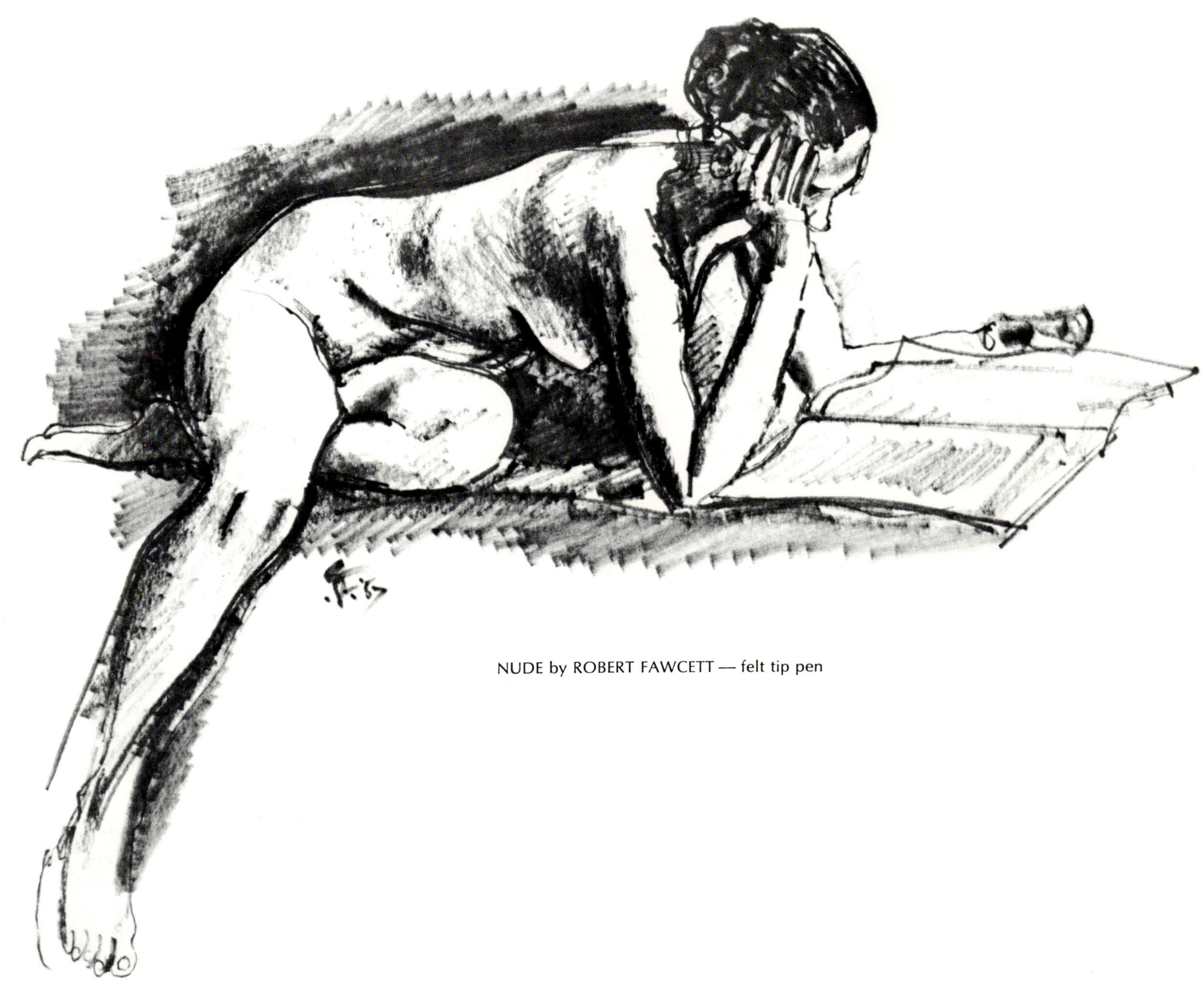

NUDE by ROBERT FAWCETT — felt tip pen

I have more fun drawing from a figure with less subtle modeling.

Study the paintings and drawings of the great artists you admire and analyze the light they used. Many of Rembrandt's figures look as though they were lighted 45 degrees overhead and 45 degrees to one side. This classic,"three-quarter" lighting had the diffused, soft-edged shadows of natural light. It's a lighting formula that is pretty hard to beat.

In beginning figure drawing, the student is often plagued by the problem of what size to draw. The only answer is, the natural size. If this sounds flip to you, let me explain.

The eye, like the camera lens, sees one size. When drawing, trouble crops up when we try to put it down at another size, out of habit or possibly through a desire to fill the page. Train yourself to draw the size that the eye sees. You will minimize inaccuracies in proportion and loss of control over the scale of the overall picture.

The size of the paper you are working on should not have anything to do with the size you draw. The size you **see** should be the only determining factor. This size is the natural size to draw and should be consistent with three things:

1. The size of the subject
2. The distance of the subject from the eye
3. The distance of the eye from the drawing

Try to keep the latter two constant while drawing. Otherwise, if you move forward or backward the sizes of both subject and drawing will change in scale.

When the subject is the same distance from the eye as the paper you are drawing on, it should be drawn actual "life" size. As the subject moves further away it becomes proportionally smaller and should be drawn at the size seen, rather than trying to transpose all of the dimensions of the subject to their actual sizes. The late Robert Fawcett called this drawing "sight size" and wrote extensively about the subject in his book *On the Art of Drawing,* published by Watson-Guptill.

Don't expect proficiency to come overnight. It will take a lot of practice before you will be drawing naturally. Get yourself some cheap newsprint pads and a large wastebasket, and don't worry about the bad ones. Keep in mind that nobody need see the results but you.

DRAWING "SIGHT SIZE"

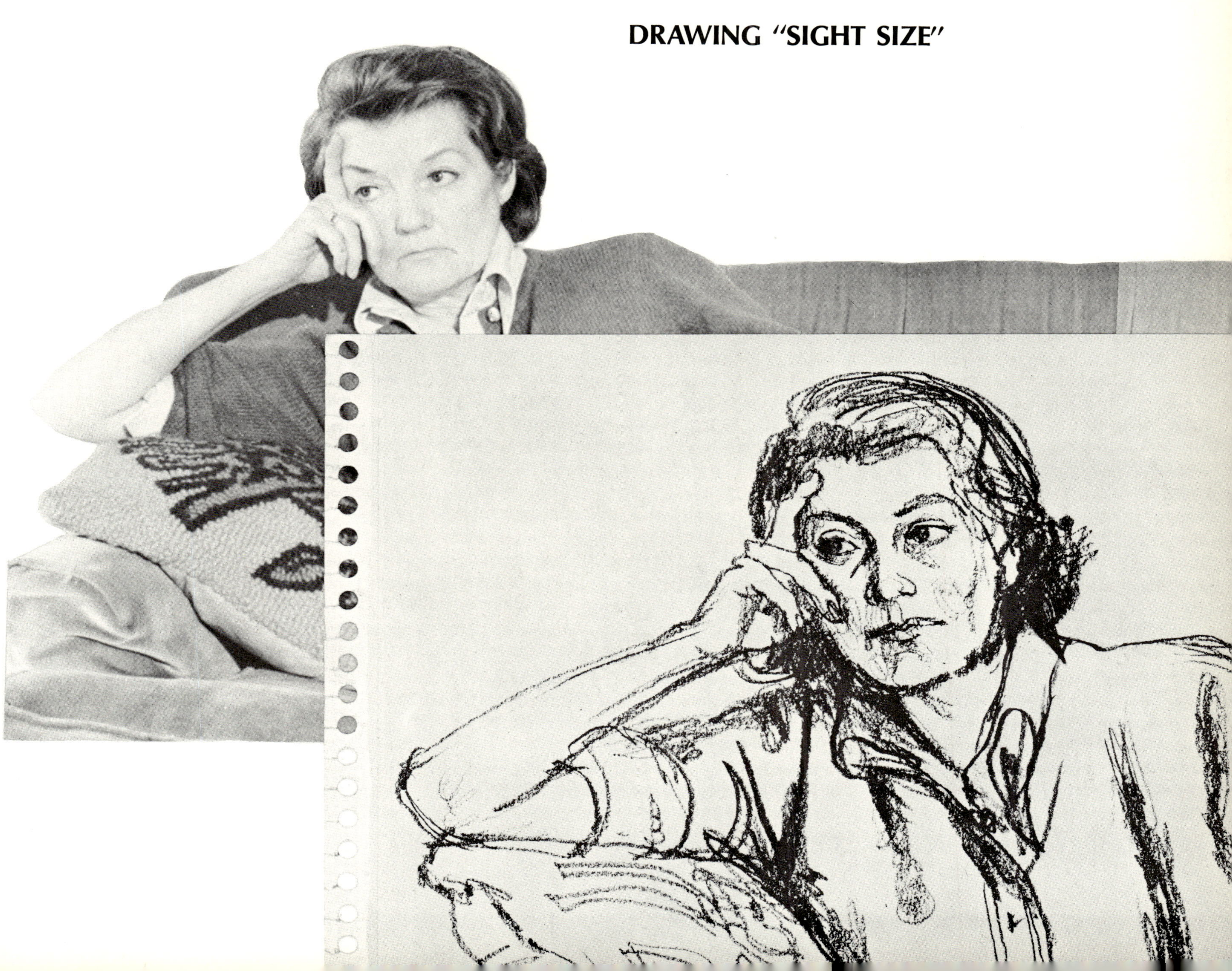

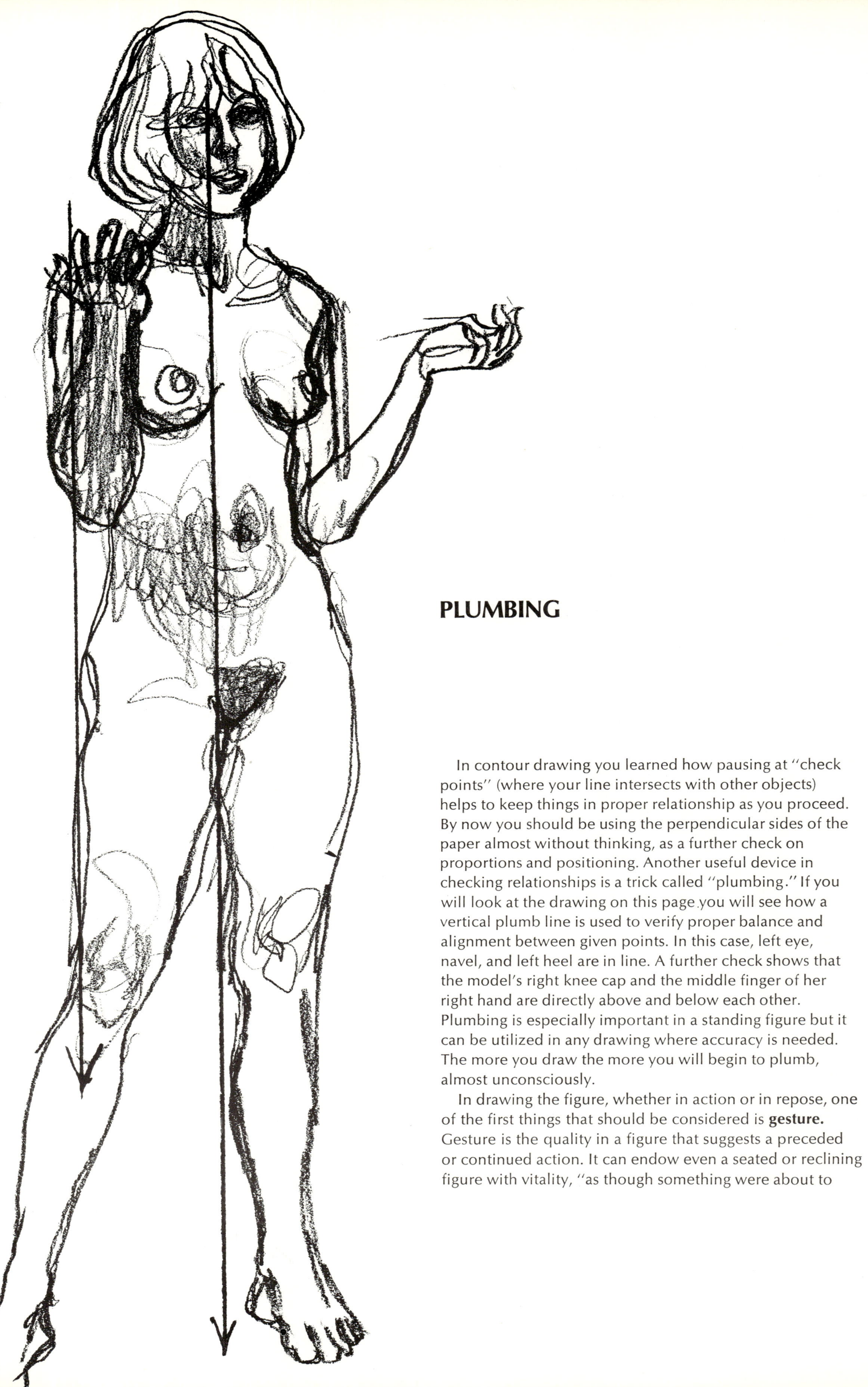

PLUMBING

In contour drawing you learned how pausing at "check points" (where your line intersects with other objects) helps to keep things in proper relationship as you proceed. By now you should be using the perpendicular sides of the paper almost without thinking, as a further check on proportions and positioning. Another useful device in checking relationships is a trick called "plumbing." If you will look at the drawing on this page you will see how a vertical plumb line is used to verify proper balance and alignment between given points. In this case, left eye, navel, and left heel are in line. A further check shows that the model's right knee cap and the middle finger of her right hand are directly above and below each other. Plumbing is especially important in a standing figure but it can be utilized in any drawing where accuracy is needed. The more you draw the more you will begin to plumb, almost unconsciously.

In drawing the figure, whether in action or in repose, one of the first things that should be considered is **gesture.** Gesture is the quality in a figure that suggests a preceded or continued action. It can endow even a seated or reclining figure with vitality, "as though something were about to

GESTURE DRAWING

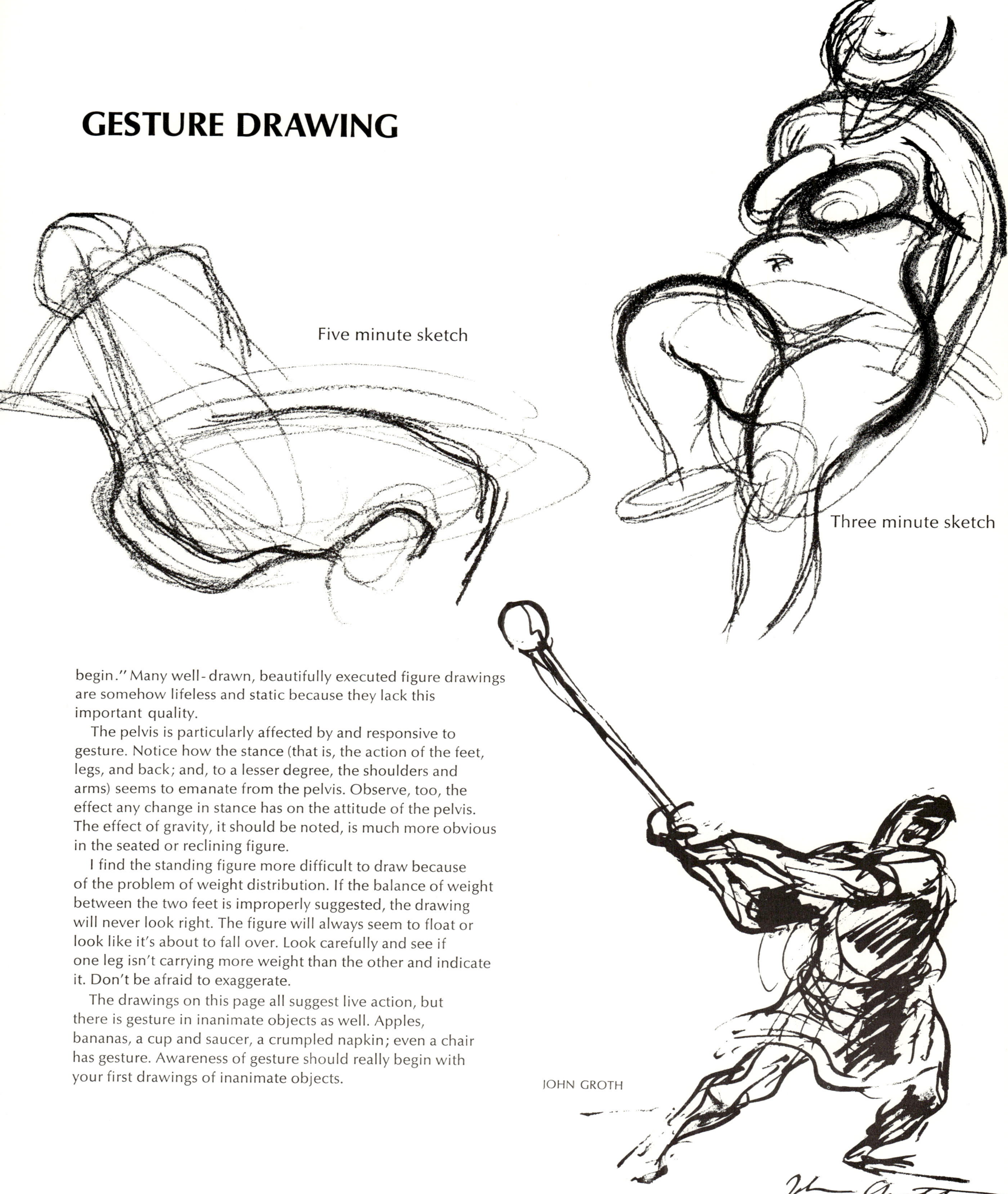

Five minute sketch

Three minute sketch

JOHN GROTH

begin." Many well-drawn, beautifully executed figure drawings are somehow lifeless and static because they lack this important quality.

The pelvis is particularly affected by and responsive to gesture. Notice how the stance (that is, the action of the feet, legs, and back; and, to a lesser degree, the shoulders and arms) seems to emanate from the pelvis. Observe, too, the effect any change in stance has on the attitude of the pelvis. The effect of gravity, it should be noted, is much more obvious in the seated or reclining figure.

I find the standing figure more difficult to draw because of the problem of weight distribution. If the balance of weight between the two feet is improperly suggested, the drawing will never look right. The figure will always seem to float or look like it's about to fall over. Look carefully and see if one leg isn't carrying more weight than the other and indicate it. Don't be afraid to exaggerate.

The drawings on this page all suggest live action, but there is gesture in inanimate objects as well. Apples, bananas, a cup and saucer, a crumpled napkin; even a chair has gesture. Awareness of gesture should really begin with your first drawings of inanimate objects.

DRAWING the DRAPED FIGURE

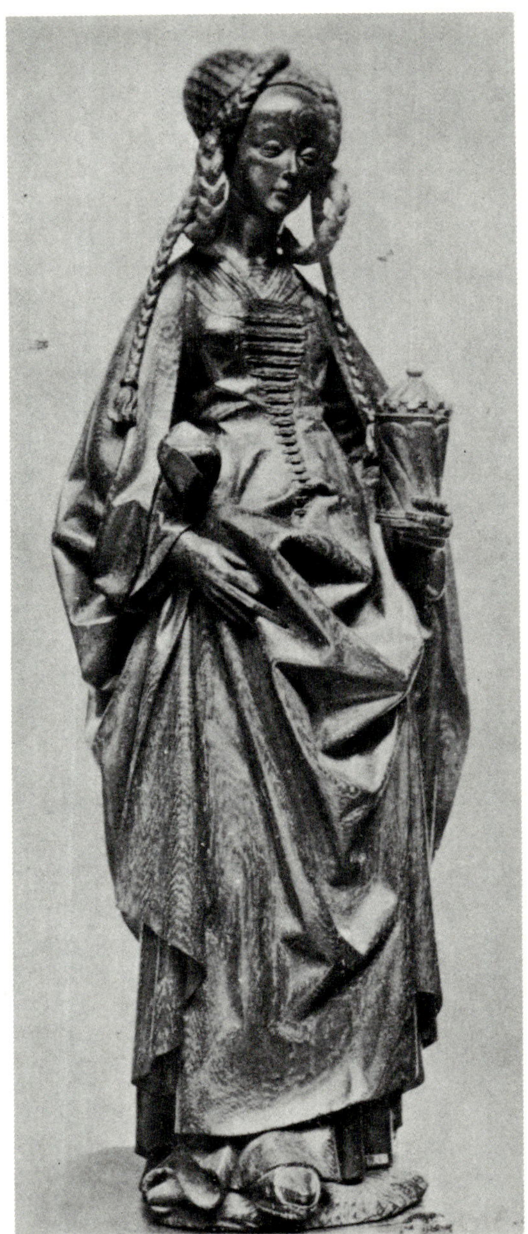

16th Century
Woodcarving
Cluny Museum, Paris

1

When you start out to draw the draped or semi-draped figure you will be confronted by an endless variety and complexity of folds. But study these folds under changing conditions and in different action and you will begin to see that almost all folds are more or less predictable. Their exact details will vary but their fundamental structure will reoccur. For instance, the folds that result each time you bend your arm are similar in character (though not necessarily in detail) and the action of bending your knee will produce a somewhat different but still a repeating pattern of folds.

A good understanding of the three basic laws that govern folds can be a big help in analyzing and drawing figures. The first is the law of **Gravity.** Gravity affects all folds to some extent. It is most obvious in full, loose-fitting drapery. **Point of tension** is the second law. It is usually but not always affected by gravity. Fig.1 demonstrates quite clearly this principle. In this case the right hand is the point of tension or support. Characteristically, the folds radiate down and away from the hand. The third law of folds is **Underlying Shape**. Whether a piece of cloth covers a table top or a human figure, its shape and folds are controlled by the form underneath as well as by the laws of gravity and tension.

The folds you draw should have a solid basis on these three laws. Be careful how you "stylize" in drawing drapery. Never lose sight of the structure underneath. When working from a draped model look first for the deep, body-hugging folds, then the secondary folds that echo and repeat each other.

All folds should be drawn decisively, directionally, and convincingly. They should not be a series of meaningless marks. Study the work of the great sculptors. The essence of the action and structure of folds is "frozen" in good sculpture. Stone, metal and wood demand an economy of expression like no other medium. See Figure 2.

Drapery can greatly enhance the interest of a composition, whether it's a figure or a still life. Just be sure it relates structurally and rhythmically with the other elements of the picture. Take advantage of how drapery helps to articulate the gesture and action of any figure, whether it be moving or in repose.

Look at Gustav Klimt's portrait study of Frau Bloch-Bauer. Here, movement and gesture have been caught and put to work with great skill. There is an amazing rhythm and vitality to this drawing that comes almost entirely from use of counterpoised, curving lines.

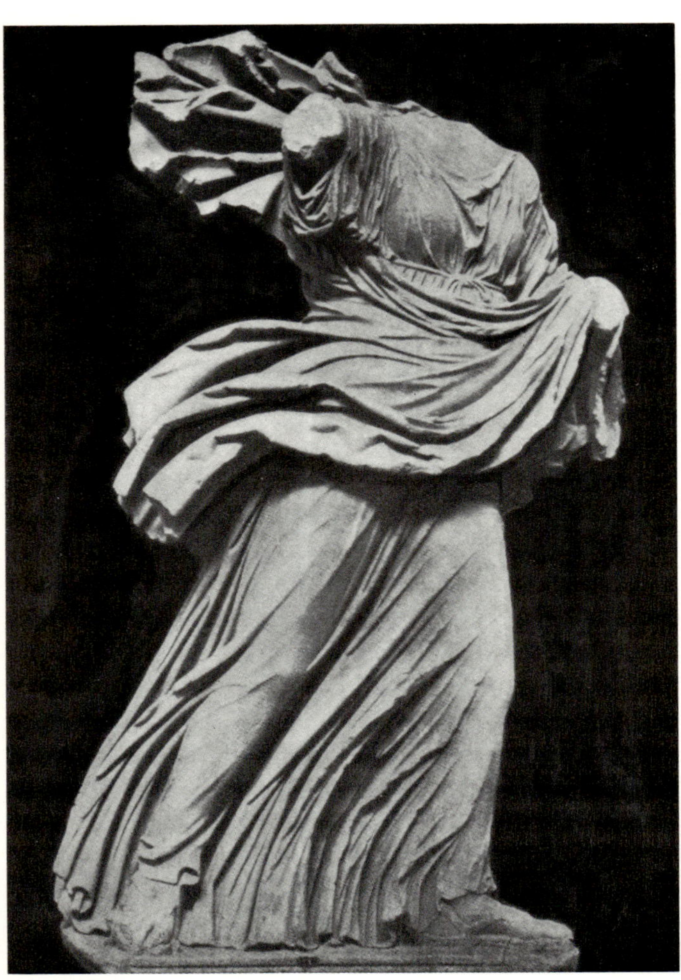

NIOBID CHIARAMONTI
Vatican, Rome

2

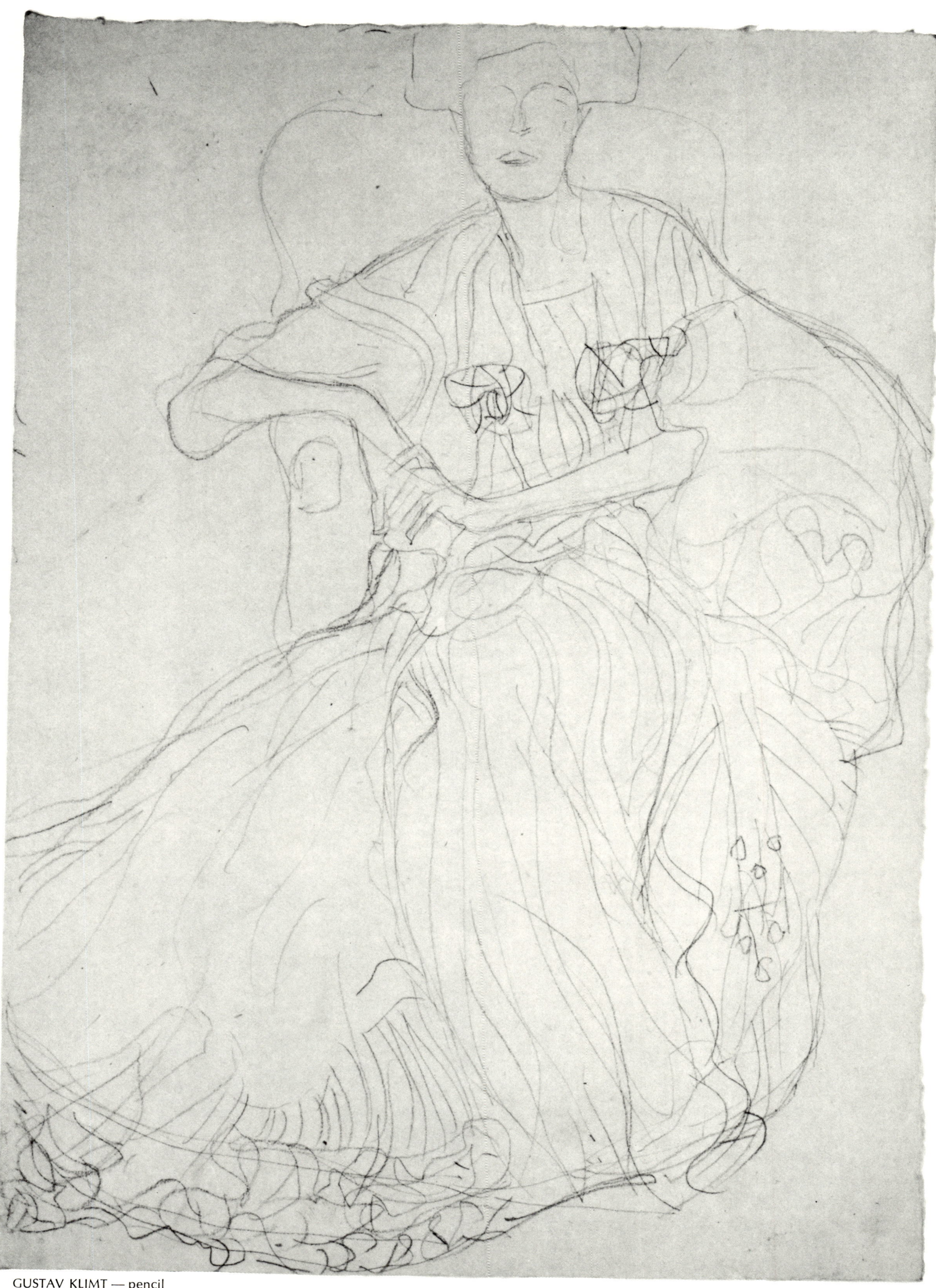

GUSTAV KLIMT — pencil

PART 3 · PAINTING

MOTIVATION

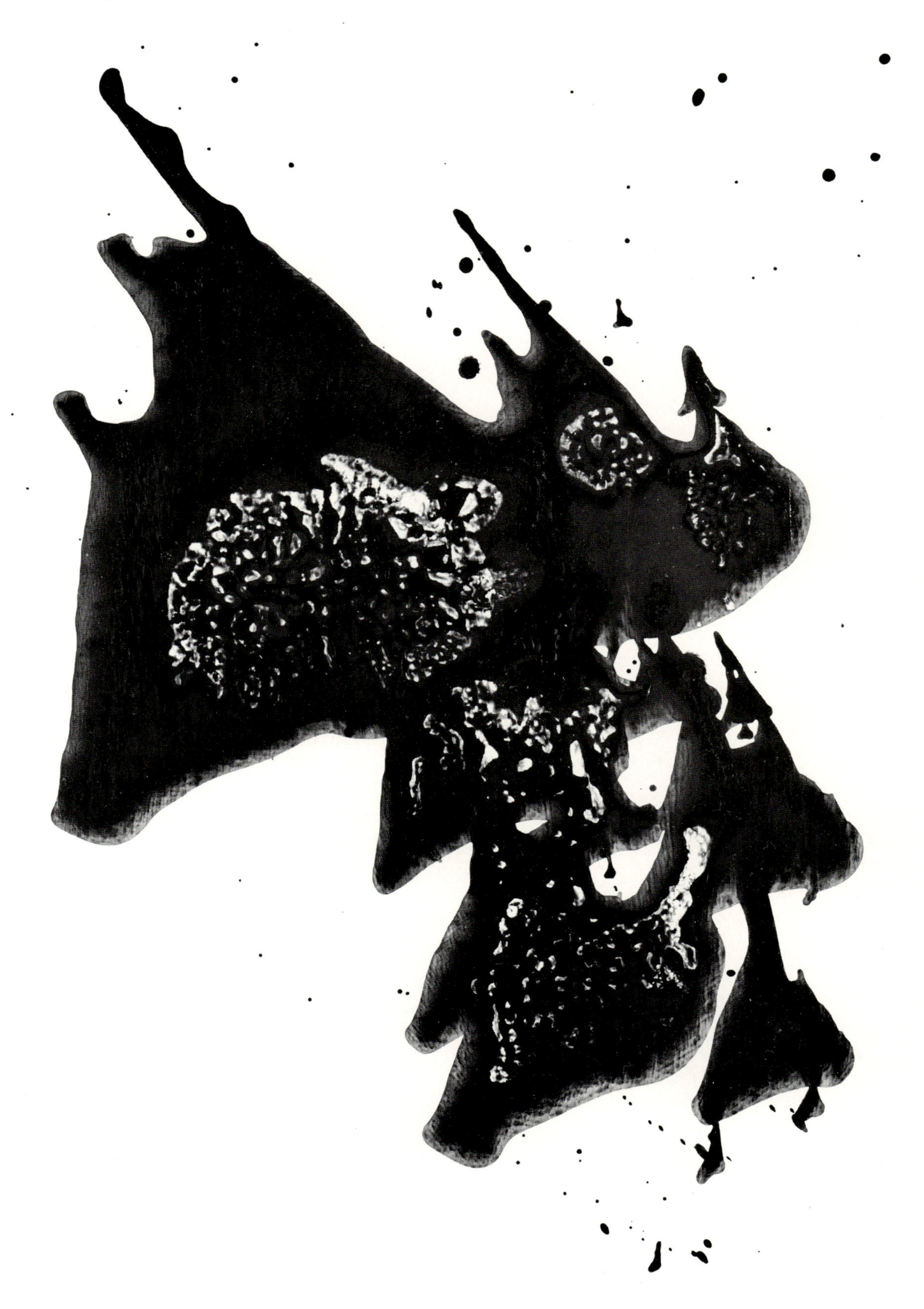

PAINTING IS SELF DISCOVERY.
EVERY GOOD ARTIST PAINTS WHAT HE IS.
Jackson Pollock

Inspiration is a word I've been hearing all my life. It seems people always talk of inspiration as though it were some sort of divine revelation. Maybe the word itself is at fault. It's too "high falutin' " for its own good. And it's been badly misused because people simply don't understand what it means.

Motivation, I think, is a much more down-to-earth word to describe the impelling force behind a creative painting. What drives a person to paint a picture? What tells him how he should paint and what he shall say? Pretty heady stuff, this. I'm not going to ponder over what poets, critics and philosophers have found imponderable. Instead, I would like to present in the following pages some motivations that were seized and acted upon with great success.

The trouble with so much art, even though it may be brilliantly executed, is that it lacks motivation. It has no reason for being, beyond that of mere decoration.

Truly creative painting calls for some preliminary self-examination. Before you begin to look for a subject to paint, stop and decide what it is that you really want to say. What you paint and how you paint it depends to a great extent on your life pattern. Meaningful painting is a matter of emotional involvement and identification with the subject.

I believe it is absolutely essential that you enjoy what you are doing when you paint. Rationalizing will not justify the results of a picture you found boring and tedious to do. No amount of stylistic bravura will cover up a lack of interest in your painting. It should be fun or there is something wrong.

Finding one's way can sometimes be very difficult for the artist. The beginner needs to look at all the art books and reproductions he can get his hands on. He needs to tramp through miles of museums and art galleries, steeping himself in every kind of art, from ancient to contemporary — from realistic to non-objective.

Discover what is most gratifying and interesting to you. Then go after it. Question your reasons for liking or disliking a picture. Be wary of sentimentalism and be just as careful never to dismiss a work because you don't understand it. All the great revolutionaries — the Impressionists, the Fauves, the Nabis, the Expressionists, the Cubists, the Abstractionists — were originally greeted with scorn and a lack of understanding.

Thinking about what you want to paint and how you want to paint it is almost as important as doing it. Almost, but not quite.

ABSTRACT
by WARD BRACKETT

HOW SHALL I PAINT?

INVENTION IS THE ESSENCE OF A PERSONALITY.
Edward Hopper

SYMBOLISM (REALISTIC)

The work of Edvard Munch has a special importance in Modern Art, not only for its individual worth but for its wide influence on art in general. Munch detested the serenity of the Impressionist painting of 1905. He associated more with writers than with painters; indeed he was concerned less with painterly problems than with psychological, religious, and ethical ones. He did not treat his painting as an objective rendering of visual things but rather as a recipient for his emotional outpourings. The cult of Expressionism was born with him. He was the source of inspiration for Ensor, Nolde, Kirchner, and Kokoschka.

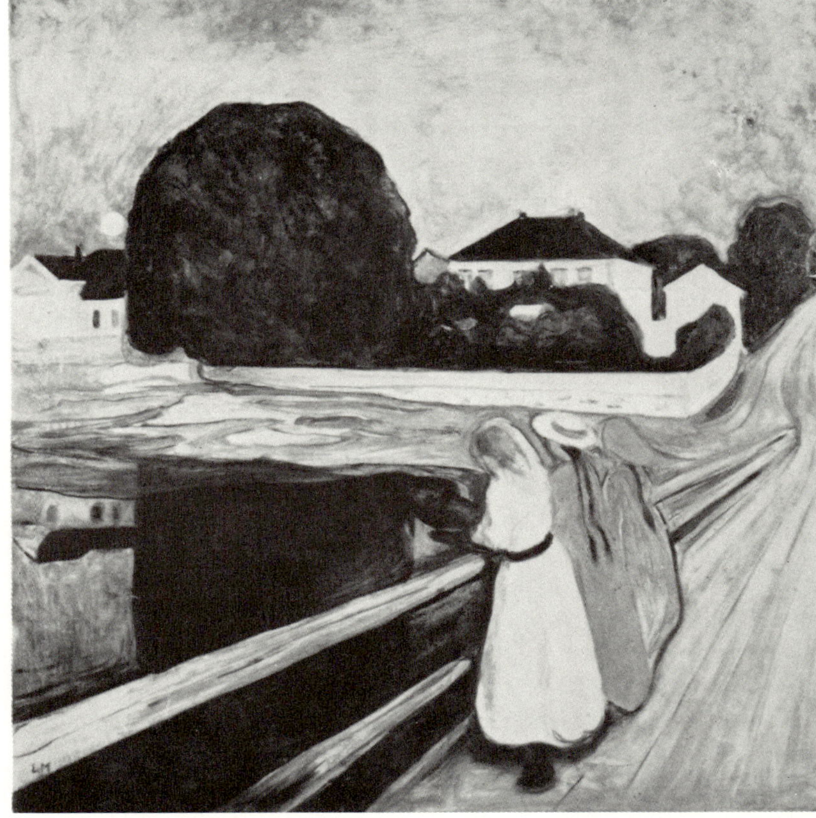

GIRLS ON THE BRIDGE by EDVARD MUNCH
National Gallery, Oslo

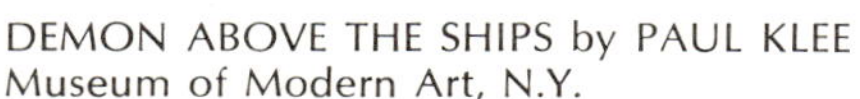

DEMON ABOVE THE SHIPS by PAUL KLEE
Museum of Modern Art, N.Y.

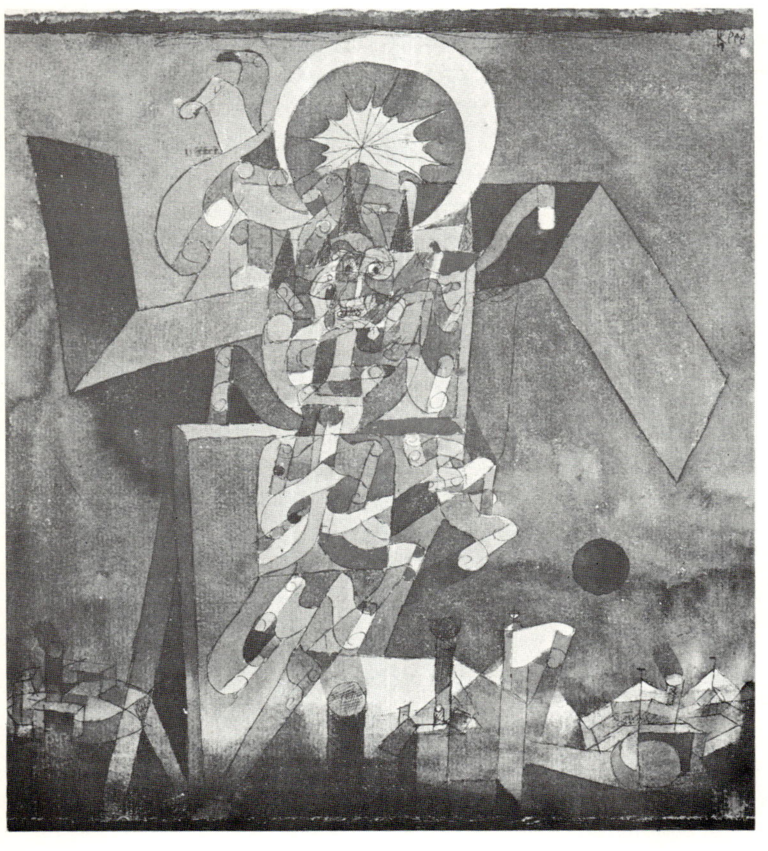

POETIC IMAGERY

Paul Klee's art is an unreal, whimsical world. Like poetry or music, it is a world full of magic transformations — where anything can happen. There is no myth, no fantasy or fairy tale his remarkable imagination could not put into visual form. In Klee's art can be seen the adult equivalent of the art of children.

He believed that art takes on a much greater significance by expressing reality rather than literally representing it.

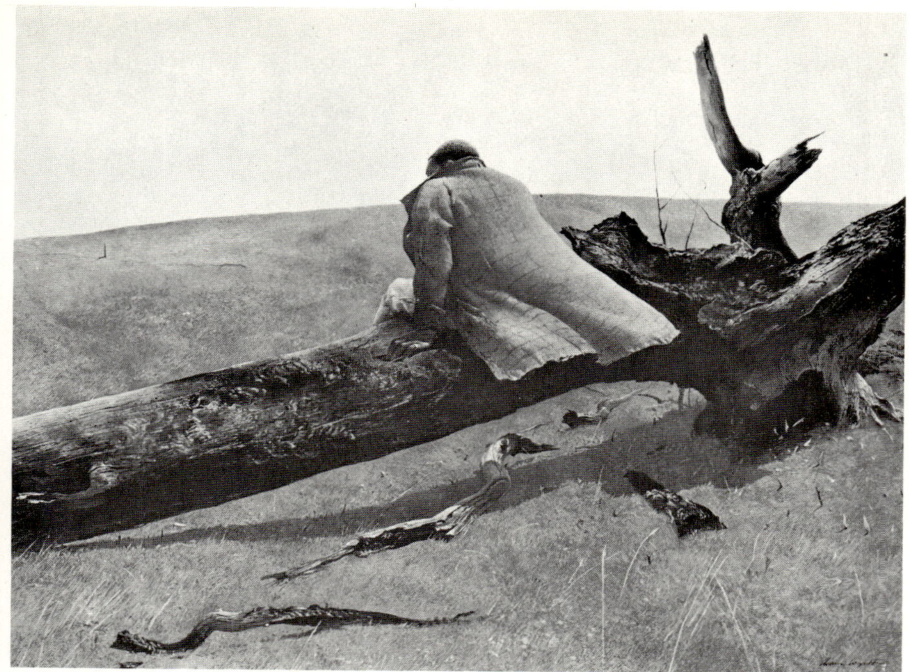

APRIL WIND by ANDREW WYETH
Courtesy Wadsworth Atheneum, Hartford

REALISM

Andrew Wyeth is no ordinary painter of realism. What makes his art unique among a vast field of realistic painters, past and present, is its appeal to a wide range of critics, from avant-garde to ultra-conservative. Everything he paints is an adventure in direct observation and truth, but it is even more than that — it is a sort of celebration of the subject. His art is, I think, a perfect example of total involvement with, and understanding of, subject matter.

SYMBOLISM (ABSTRACT)

Armenian-born Arshile Gorky had a strong influence on the Abstract Expressionists of the '40's and early '50's. His early works, semi-abstracts, were inspired by Picasso, then Miro and Leger. Later, his style and subject matter became more colorful and more personal, and he began using anatomical biological forms as his motifs. Heart, liver, breast, buttocks and genitalia became the raw materials for his most important paintings.

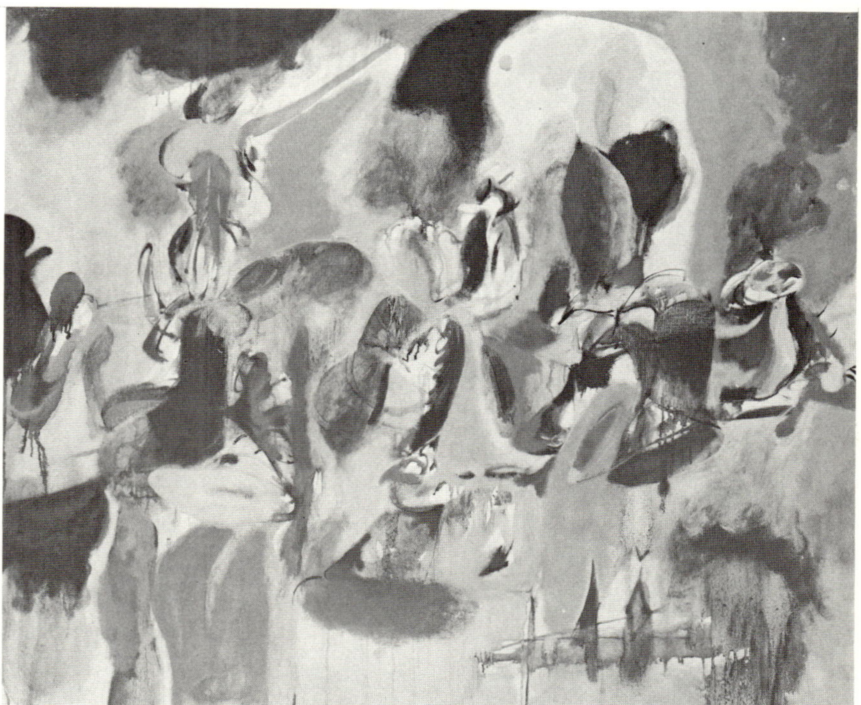

WATER OF THE FLOWERY MILL by ARSHILE GORKY
Metropolitan Museum of Art
Purchase from the J. H. Wade Fund

THE RACE TRACK by ALBERT PINKHAM RYDER
The Cleveland Museum of Art

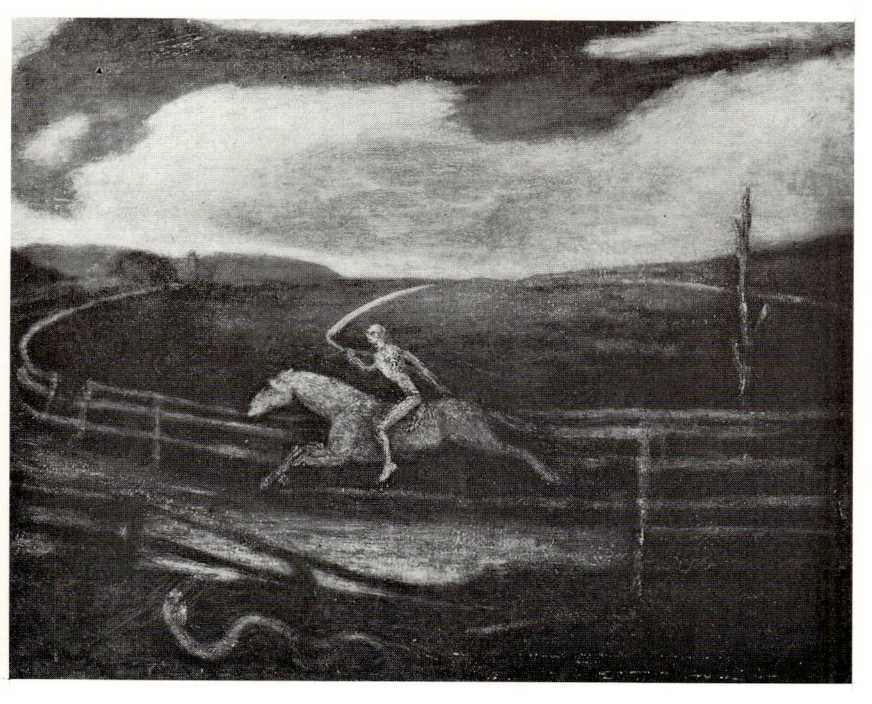

ALLEGORIC

Albert Pinkham Ryder's subject matter came mostly from the sea (he grew up on Cape Cod) and the world of his imagination. He was one of the earliest painters to play on the subconscious through the use of symbols and imagery. His RACE TRACK, or DEATH ON A PALE HORSE was inspired by the suicide of a man who lost everything on a racehorse.

WHAT DO I WANT TO SAY?

THE PASSION OF SACCO AND VANZETTI by BEN SHAHN
Whitney Museum of American Art, N.Y.

SOCIAL PROTEST

A great part of Shahn's energy went into portraying his personal reactions to the political and social upheavals of his time. Many of his paintings reflect "the tragic sense of life."

The engraver-painter William Hogarth was another artist who involved himself and his painting with the social ills of his day. He, unlike Shahn, used art to implement his social consciousness more than he served art itself.

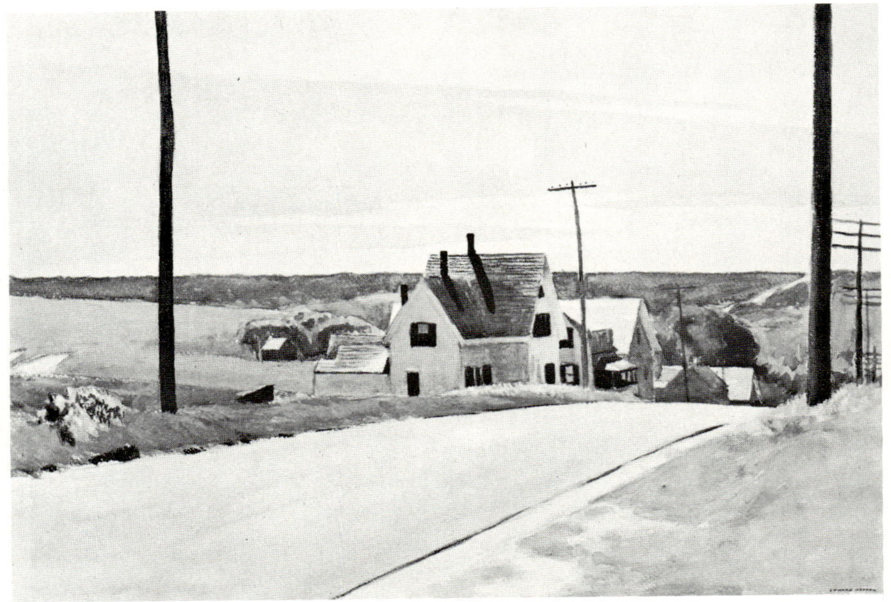

HIGH ROAD by EDWARD HOPPER
Whitney Museum of American Art, N.Y.

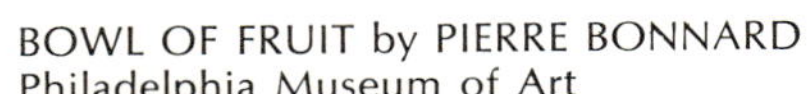

BOWL OF FRUIT by PIERRE BONNARD
Philadelphia Museum of Art

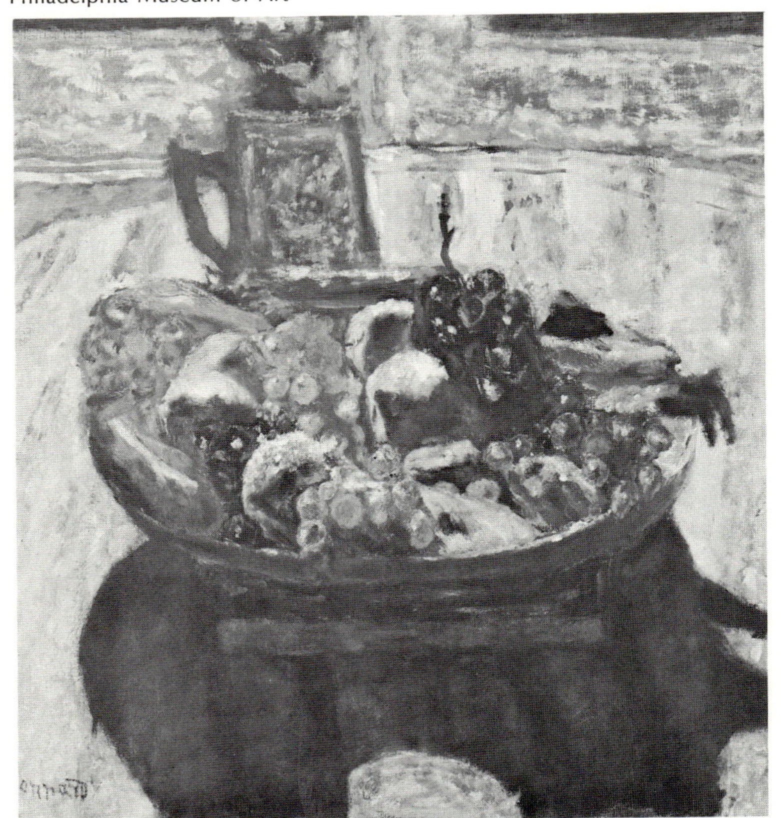

NOSTALGIA

Certain scenes take on mood and drama under a cloudy sky. Others are better expressed in terms of bright sunlight and crisp shadows. Edward Hopper drew much of his mood and statement from the stark, clean patterns of sunlight and shade. He loved particularly to paint the sparkling white light of Cape Cod. This clear, sun-washed ambience is his signature. It dominates many of his outdoor paintings.

Here is a painter who was clearly motivated by nostalgia. Its presence lingers over his paintings like a spell. Hopper saw his America and painted it with great empathy and intensity.

JOY OF LIFE

Implicit in Bonnard's painting is a belief that the artist's task is to record the beauty and pleasures of life, particularly of the natural world. The world he liked to paint was leisurely, untroubled, introspective, sometimes playfully naive. A gifted colorist and one of the least systematic of painters, he never used technique to demonstrate anything more than his passion for texture, color and earthy sensuality. His paintings are the embodiment of the impressions and sensations of what he saw.

PRIMITIVE REALISM

Mention primitive art and the names Rousseau and Grandma Moses immediately come to mind. Another in this field, perhaps not so well known, is the American, Joseph Pickett. His painting MANCHESTER VALLEY typifies a popular style that once flourished in America. It might be more accurately classified as folk art. In this kind of painting, elements like perspective and scale are taken very casually or ignored altogether. Naive though it is, there is a bold honesty and directness to it that seems to survive the refinements of academic art.

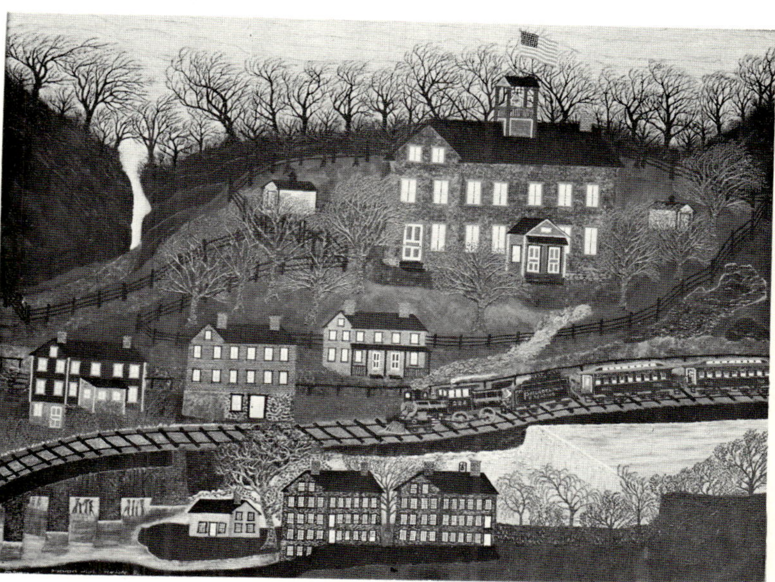

MANCHESTER VALLEY by JOSEPH PICKETT
Museum of Modern Art, N.Y.

ECLIPSE OF THE MOON by REUBEN TAM

MYSTERY

I am fortunate in having the artist himself describe the motivations that drove him to paint this compelling, poetic picture.

"One of my most haunting experiences in many years of living by the sea was that of witnessing a lunar eclipse from a cliff on Monhegan Island, Maine, where I have a summer studio. That night, as the full moon blackened, light and dark seemed to be reversed. The ocean and the sky, alternately cold whites and warm darks, pressed against a tentative horizon that was the quivering edge of earth itself.

" The sea seemed to rise and fall to unusual levels, exposing shoals and misting the night air. I wanted in my painting not so much a depiction of the phenomenon, as an evocation of the very special experience in all its cosmic mystery.

"In the painting, horizontals and verticals and diagonals are played against one another, as are the extreme darks, the luminous pale areas, and the in-between neutrality of night space."

ELEGANCE

Although this is not typical of Georgia O'Keeffe's work, it is a good example of how a theme can be developed from a single object. Here is a very ordinary subject that has been enlarged and exploited into an elegant design without departing very much from nature. Her most typical paintings, skulls, animal bones and botanical studies, come closer to the abstract. They are powerfully painted and starkly simple. All her work is directed by a passionate regard for purity and elegance.

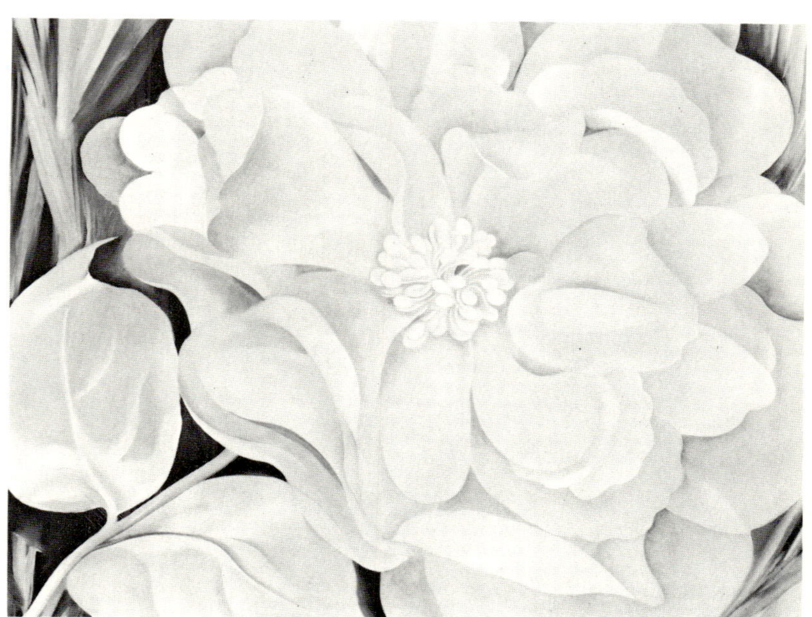

THE WHITE FLOWER by GEORGIA O'KEEFFE
Whitney Museum of American Art, N.Y.

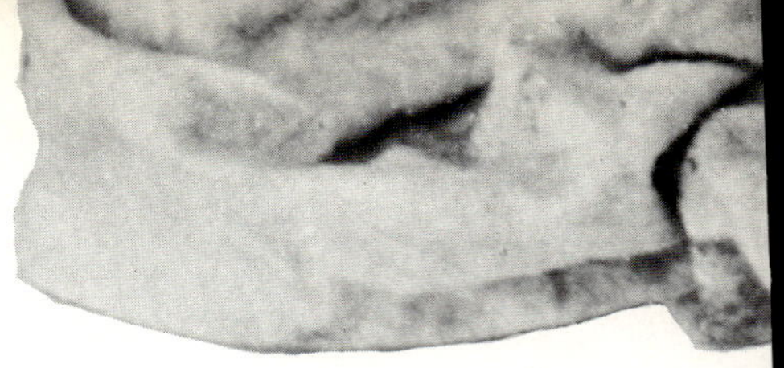

RECOMMENDED PAINTING MATERIALS

WATER COLORS, GOUACHE, CASEIN	Sable brushes: #3, 5, 8: "Single stroke" — ½ and 1 inch. Colors: Lemon yellow, cadmium yellow medium, cadmium red light, alizarin crimson, cobalt blue, ultramarine, manganese blue, viridian, permanent green light, Hooker's green, terra verte, yellow ochre, raw sienna, burnt sienna, raw umber, burnt umber, ivory black, casein white.* Palettes: For studio use — porcelain tray. For field use — disposable paper pad (see page 62). Porcelain mixing tray. Painting surfaces: Illustration board, water color drawing pad — medium or heavy weight paper, approximately 15" x 18". Water bowl of glass or plastic. For outdoor painting — plastic bucket. Small folding seat for field use. *These are basic colors. You may want to experiment later with superbrilliant colors like: rose carthame, rose malmaison, cyprus green, marigold yellow. Most manufacturers mark each tube for permanency.
ACRYLIC	Bristle brushes: #2, 4, 6. Rounds — #2, 4, 6. Filberts — #5, 8. House painting brush: 1½ or 2 inch nylon. Colors: Yellow light Hanza, cadmium yellow medium, indo orange red, cadmium red light, cadmium red medium, napthol red light, napthol crimson, acra violet, cobalt blue, ultramarine, thalo blue, thalo green, permanent green light, light green oxide, chromium oxide green, Hooker's green deep, yellow oxide, raw sienna, burnt sienna, raw umber, burnt umber, titanium white, mars black, tube of gel. Palettes: For studio use — porcelain tray. For field use — disposable paper pad (see page 62). Painting surfaces: Canvas, canvas panels, gesso panels (see page 63). Painting knives: see photo. Natural vine charcoal sticks. Easels: (see page 63). Water bowl of glass or plastic. Small sponge. Outdoor equipment (see pages 75 and 78).
OILS	Bristle brushes: Flats — #2, 4, 6. Rounds — #2,4 ,6. Filberts — #5, 8. House painting brush: 1½ or 2 inch nylon. Colors: Lemon yellow, cadmium yellow medium, cadmium red light, cadmium red medium, scarlet, alizarin crimson, cobalt violet, cobalt blue, ultramarine, viridian, manganese blue, terra verte, permanent green light, yellow ochre, raw sienna, burnt sienna, raw umber, burnt umber, titanium white, ivory black. Cobalt drier (see page 62). Cup for turpentine (see photo).* Palettes: For studio use — wooden palette. For field use — disposable paper pad (see page 63). Painting surfaces: Canvas, canvas panels, gesso panels (see page 63). Painting knives: See photo. Natural vine charcoal sticks. Easels (see page 63). Outdoor equipment (see pages 75 and 78). *Mineral spirits for those who are allergic to turpentine.

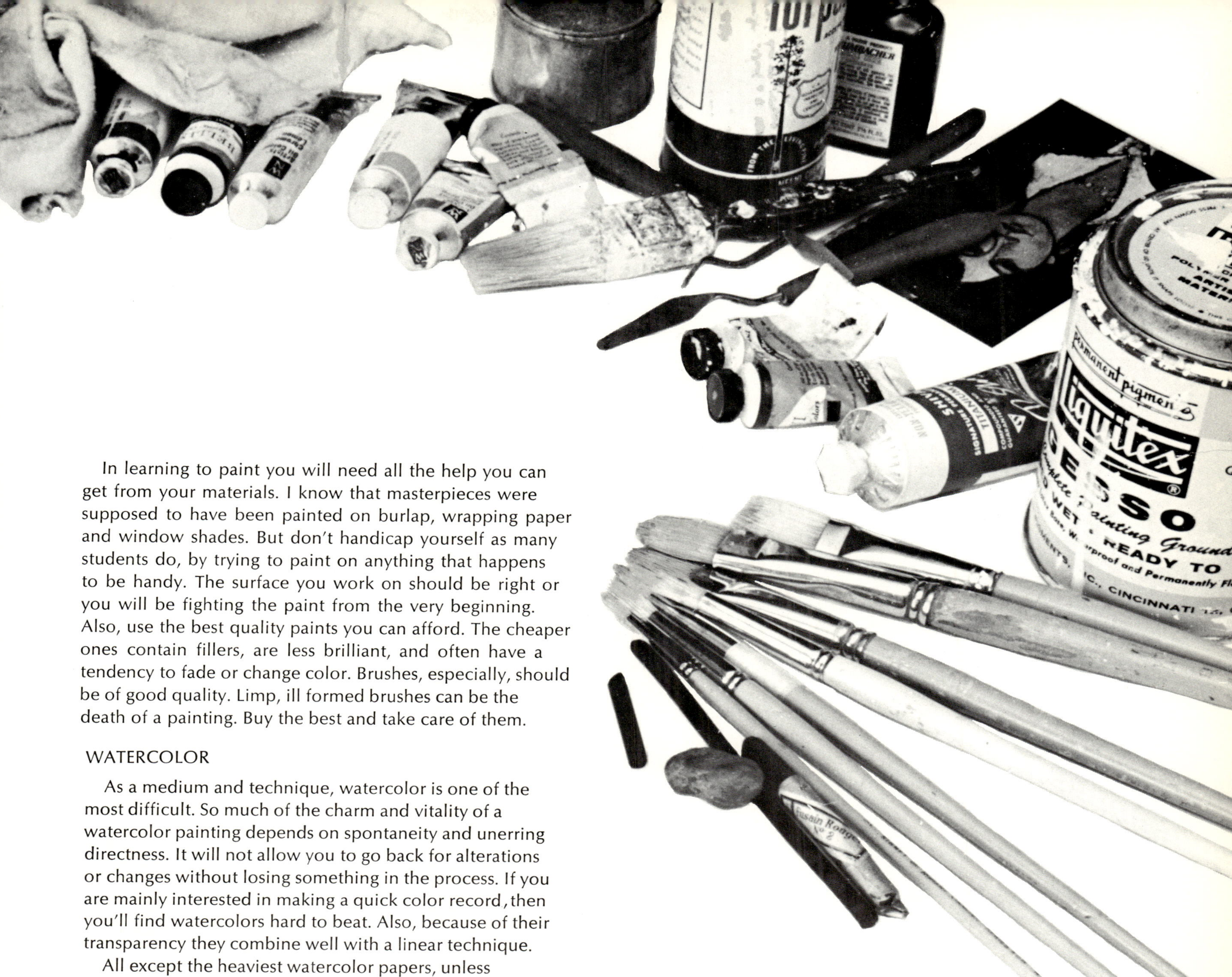

In learning to paint you will need all the help you can get from your materials. I know that masterpieces were supposed to have been painted on burlap, wrapping paper and window shades. But don't handicap yourself as many students do, by trying to paint on anything that happens to be handy. The surface you work on should be right or you will be fighting the paint from the very beginning. Also, use the best quality paints you can afford. The cheaper ones contain fillers, are less brilliant, and often have a tendency to fade or change color. Brushes, especially, should be of good quality. Limp, ill formed brushes can be the death of a painting. Buy the best and take care of them.

WATERCOLOR

As a medium and technique, watercolor is one of the most difficult. So much of the charm and vitality of a watercolor painting depends on spontaneity and unerring directness. It will not allow you to go back for alterations or changes without losing something in the process. If you are mainly interested in making a quick color record, then you'll find watercolors hard to beat. Also, because of their transparency they combine well with a linear technique.

All except the heaviest watercolor papers, unless mounted to fairly heavy cardboard, will buckle and ripple under wet washes of color. Many watercolor painters overcome this by first soaking the paper thoroughly in clear water, then taping it securely on all four edges (with water soluble tape) to a stiff piece of board that can be taken into the field. The paper will dry drum-tight and will not buckle when remoistened. Since I do not do watercolors that are any more ambitious than quick, reportage sketches, I content myself with sketch pads bound with a fairly heavy multi-purpose paper of 100% rag content.

Some of the juiciest, zingiest watercolors I have ever seen were those done with inks (dyes). Most colored inks are waterproof and as such can be applied layer upon layer with an increasing brilliance, a technique that is not possible with watercolor.

Inks can be coaxed into drying with some crazy effects and if you are an exploiter of these "accidentals" then this may be your medium. A word of warning — most inks are not color fast so if you are looking for permanence you had better think twice before using them.

Materials and a kit for outdoor sketching are described on page 75.

RECOMMENDED PAINTING MATERIALS

ACRYLICS

Since their introduction to the market a few years ago, water-based acrylic paints have been used by illustrators, designers, water-colorists and hard-edged abstract painters with great success. These paints can even be made to simulate oil, but the results often have a harsh, spurious look. Fast drying, they become water insoluble in minutes and can be painted over almost immediately. This makes them very adaptable to underpainting techniques.

However, there's a big disadvantage to them. If you are used to keeping paint on your palette longer than five or ten minutes you are not going to be very charmed with their fast drying characteristics. There is a retarder available but I have never had much success with it.

A variety of brushy, stylistic effects are possible with acrylics — especially if they are used with medium. Brushes must be kept washed out. Acrylics will dry in them like portland cement. Then, the only thing that will save them is soaking and resoaking in lacquer thinner. Another thing that's hard to get used to — they dry slightly darker, especially colors in the middle value range. But they dry with an extremely tough surface and a permanency that I'm sure will outlive us all.

GOUACHE

Gouache is a fancy name for opaque watercolor and poster color. Water-soluble and quick drying, it contains a gum binding medium but will not dry waterproof. It is used like oils — that is, opaquely. The paint is favored by professional designers and illustrators, but the colors, though brilliant, are untrustworthy. Some will bleed through subsequent layers of paint, other colors are not fade proof. Gouache can be used on just about any ground. It dries lighter with a matte surface.

CASEIN

Casein, a water-based, water-soluble paint has a more creamy consistency than ordinary opaque. This is because it is made with an oil and water emulsion base that is not unlike mayonnaise in substance. It dries very slightly lighter and becomes almost waterproof in time. However, it dries with a somewhat chalky, matte surface. Like the acrylics, casein is hard on brushes, which should be kept immersed in water when not in use during a painting session. Afterwards the brushes should be washed out thoroughly with mild soap and warm water (never hot) and then shaped to dry.

OIL

Oil remains to this day the most flexible of all mediums. Diluted with turpentine it can be washed on, something like watercolor. Applied without thinning with brush or palette knife, and mixed with white, it can be built up in an "impasto" technique. As a vehicle oil seems to bring out the glowing richness of pigments more than other mediums.

Good quality oil paints have been known to keep usable in the tube for years. And their permanency on canvas is established beyond doubt.

But they do have a drawback. They are slow drying. The use of cobalt drier (Linoleate) will accelerate drying time but mix it in sparingly. Too much can cause color changes, especially with white — it can also cause cracking and flaking. You might be safer with a product called Gel, obtainable at your local art supply store, which has a built-in drying agent.

With oil, brushes should first be cleaned with turps, then washed out with soap and warm water.

PASTELS, CRAYONS, COLORED PENCILS

Sidewalk artists and mail-order portraiture have given pastels a grim reputation. But you have only to look at the vibrant, glowing pastels of Degas, Vuillard and Toulouse-Lautrec to see the potential of this medium. Some very interesting and unusual effects are possible when crayons are combined with wash or gouache. Any water-based paint will bead, with some original and unpredictable results, when applied over a waxy surface.

COLLAGE

Collage, a French word that means gluing or pasting, is an art form unique and important enough to rate a whole chapter on the subject. Terminology, techniques, materials and methods are taken up and discussed in the chapter starting on page 94.

PALETTES

I have never found anything that beats an enameled, metal butcher's tray. When working in acrylics I keep two of them going so that one can be soaking in the sink while the other is in use. They can even be used for oil if you tape a sheet of thin acetate to the four corners of the tray. This gives a white, discardable surface that can be peeled off in a second and saves a lot of scraping and cleaning. A rubber squeegee does a beautiful job of removing acrylics from a tray that has been presoaked. I would not be without one. For outdoor sketching a disposable paper palette pad is satisfactory.

BRUSHES

The best brushes you can buy will pay off in the long run, both economically (they last longer) and in the sheer pleasure of using them. I use white hog bristle brushes for everything but transparent washes and for glazing over painted areas. Then a soft sable is better, the size depending on the area you want to cover. Make a fetish of washing out your brushes if you expect them to last.

You'll have to experiment to find which painting knives are right for you. The ones I use appear in the photo on page 61.

EASELS

The kind of support you will need depends on the kind of work you'll be doing. Some painters like to spread their canvas out on the floor or tack it to the wall. But most of us require an easel both for studio work and for outdoor use. If you work large, a studio easel is best. It is sturdy and can be raised and lowered easily. An architect's table with saw-buck legs is even sturdier but can be cumbersome to adjust. I use a heavy, four-legged table that adjusts in a second from low to high, and from flat to vertical by virtue of a patented foot pedal. Made in France, it is the best easel I've ever found but it isn't cheap. My outdoor easel is described on page 75.

PAINTING SURFACES

It will take some experimenting to find the surface that is right for you. Most painters who use oils prefer stretched canvas because it gives slightly at the touch of a brush. Canvas panels (the canvas is mounted on cardboard) are an inexpensive substitute, ideal for students. They are made with cotton canvas instead of the more durable linen. You can save money by stretching your own canvases, and especially if you prime them yourself. The canvas must first be given two coats of sizing before it is primed. White lead is the traditional prime but acrylic gesso is also used. Ordinary gesso should not be used on canvas because it will chip.

The most convenient method and the cheapest is to prepare your own gesso panels. The best base is untempered hardboard (masonite). Tempered masonite is unsuitable because it is heavier, harder to cut and, worst of all, it has a somewhat greasy, unabsorbent surface that resists gesso and paint. Panels have an advantage over canvas in that they can be recut if necessary after the painting is finished.

Undercoating white can be used on panels without any preliminary sizing. It should be thinned with turpentine and applied freely, using a large brush. I prepare my panels with acrylic gesso since most of my work is in acrylics. It's applied the same as undercoating white except that it takes at least four coats to cover properly and should be thinned very little, if at all. The back must be given one coat to counteract warping. This is important. Drying time can be hastened by turning an electric fan on the panels between coats. Remove any grittiness with fine sandpaper.

FIXATIVE

I don't like to use fixative prior to painting for two reasons.

First, fixative seals the surface of canvas or gesso, leaving it non-absorbent. The working surface should be somewhat porous in order to "grip" the paint properly. Acrylics do not adhere properly to a fixed surface. They will, in fact, actually peel off if the working surface has been heavily sprayed. If you must spray fixative to retain the drawing on the surface, use it sparingly. And be sure to use a fixative that does not dry glossy.

Secondly, I rather like having the charcoal smear a bit as the paint goes on. The little bit of graying that results when it combines with the paint seems to help in fusing the color areas together. At least, I like the effect. If you will study Matisse's paintings you will see repeated evidence of this smearing at the edges of his color areas.

FRAMES

Some artists enjoy making their own frames, but it's an exacting, time-consuming job that demands absolute accuracy in mitering whether you use a bench saw or a miter box, plus the procedure of gluing, nailing, and finishing. If you are completely at home with these tools and have patience to spare, good luck. If not, you will save yourself a lot of time and nicked fingers by going to a framer or by buying stock frames.

However you do it, remember that a frame should never be allowed to overshadow the picture. Its purpose is to set off the picture, never to upstage it. It takes a strong and vibrant painting to compete with a heavy, ornate frame. More and more galleries and museums today are hanging pictures, abstracts in particular, with no frame at all. An easy and inexpensive solution to framing many modern paintings, especially large ones, is to use ¼″ wood stripping, 1″ to 2″ wide, and simply box in your picture by nailing it to the sides. This only works with a stretched canvas frame, however, not with panels.

COLOR

Of all the revolutions in the history of art, probably none was quite as influential in setting the course of modern art as one that took place shortly after the turn of the century. In 1905, a group of young artists, sparked by an unknown painter named Vincent Van Gogh, and led by the well-established Matisse, held its first collective exhibition at the Salon d'Automne in Paris. The exhibit included the pictures of Derain, Vlaminck, Dufy, Marquet, Matisse, Vuillard and Kandinsky, as well as the originators of the movement, Van Gogh and Paul Gaugin. Also represented was Cézanne, then 66 years old.

The show contained paintings that were to bear out Van Gogh's prophesy made 15 years earlier: "Contemporary painting promises to become more subtle, more musical and less like sculpture; in short, it promises color." What the show may have lacked in subtlety it made up for in color. The artistic establishment was not quite ready for colors that "looked like they had been squirted straight from the tube." Neither were they ready for Matisse's apple-green flesh tones and his red tree trunks. The patrons of the Salon were shocked. Shock soon turned to outrage. The **Fauves** (wild beasts), as they came to be known, were branded anarchists and bolshevists by the conservative press, a charge that had some foundation in truth. Some of them did in fact lean a bit to the left, and most of them were wild in their dress. (Vlaminck sported a painted wooden necktie and a bowler hat.)

The young revolutionaries were fair game for everything from subtle irony to open scorn and abuse. They were called madmen and their paintings described as decadent, incoherent and a bad joke.

But the wild beasts of the October Revolution had started something. Though it would be some time before the decline of academic painting, the new art with its sensations of pure color and exaggerated movement became the foundation for all contemporary painting that was to follow. Cubism, Expressionism and Abstract Expressionism all owe their beginnings to Fauvism.

The Impressionists (mainly Seurat and Signac), had already paved the way for the new order in color. They had developed a system of applying paint in separate dots of pure color that intermingled but did not overlap or fuse. The result was an "optical" mixing of color called **Pointillism.** It was the forerunner of what we call "broken color" (Fig. 1, page 66) today. This phenomenon utilized the absolute purity of spectral light. Colors, when viewed at a distance, blended with remarkable brilliance and clarity compared to traditional color mixing on the palette. Seurat's methodical system of "dot" painting had a marked influence on painting that was to follow. Van Gogh, Gauguin, Pissarro, and later Bonnard and Vuillard all took something from Pointillism. But most deserving of credit for the liberation of color was Van Gogh, probably the greatest visionary of modern painting. His influence on modern art is still in evidence in some of the most recent contemporary painting.

Color is the one thing that can be enjoyed by anyone. You don't have to know anything about drawing, form, painting or color theory. Quite possibly, an artistically gifted student could get along fine without any training in color, relying just on instinct and feeling alone. However, most of us can benefit from knowing something about the physical causes of color sensations and effects. Knowing why colors do what they do can augment our interest in them.

There are only two kinds of color that concern the artist. They are **spectral color** and **pigment color.** The first refers to the colors of the spectrum (rainbow) produced when sunlight or any other white light (which contains all colors) passes through a prism. All other colors are made from pigments. These include earth colors, chemical and synthetic colors, oxides, inks and vegetable dyes.

Think of color as having three dimensions — **hue, value** and **intensity.** Make sure you understand perfectly the meaning of these three terms before you start painting with color. Any well-organized design that uses full color relies on a pleasing relationship between these three dimensions. Let's define them.

Hue: This is the identifying term for a color. It is used to refer to a color's chromatic quality. When we say a color is red, we are designating its **hue.** There are as many hues as you can find names for. The color wheel gives us twelve precisely defined hues.

Value: Value refers to a color's lightness or darkness in

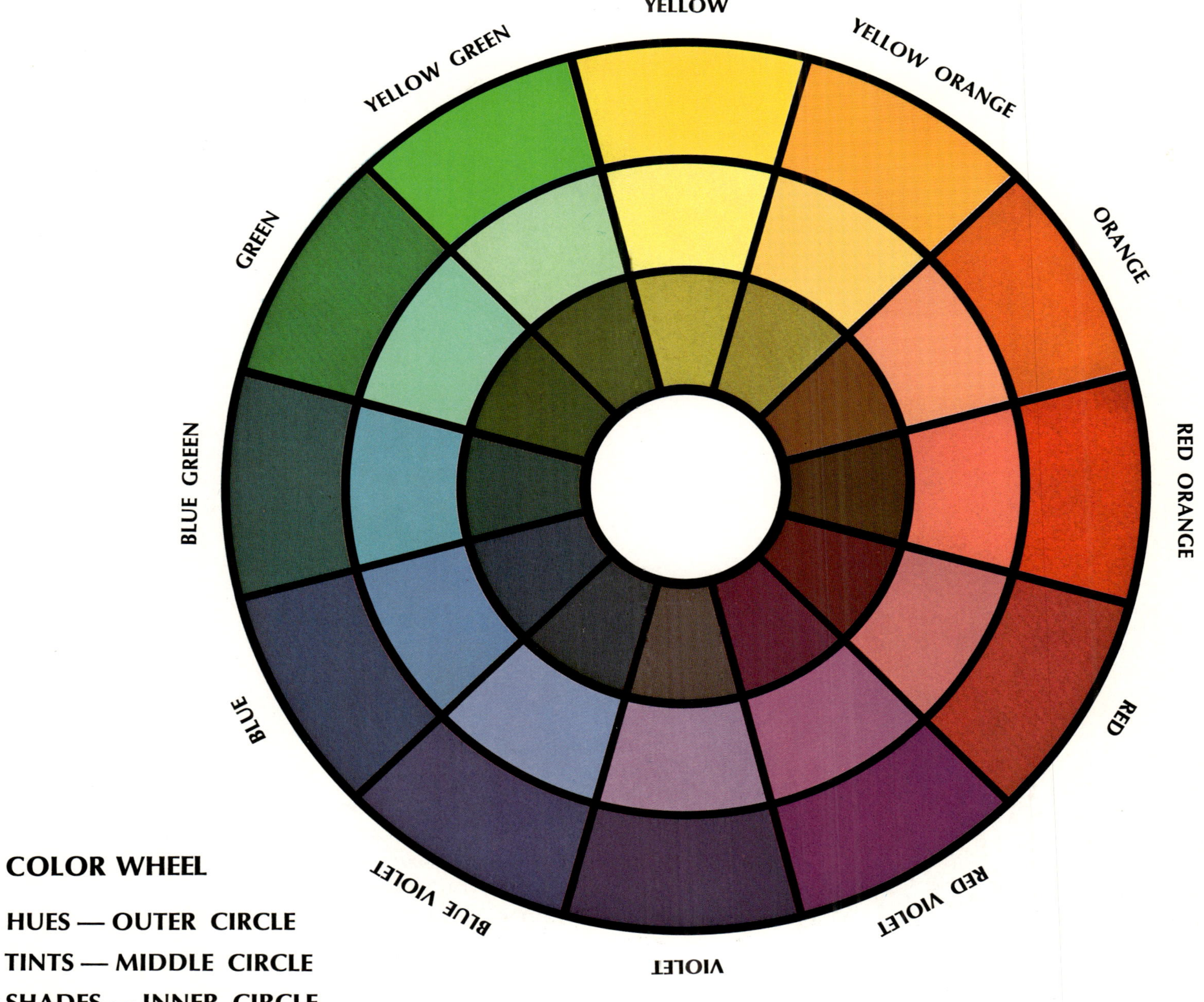

COLOR WHEEL

HUES — OUTER CIRCLE
TINTS — MIDDLE CIRCLE
SHADES — INNER CIRCLE

relation to black and to white. When one color is closer than another to white (lighter) we say it is higher in value. When it is closer to black (darker) we say it is lower, or deeper, in value. As a rule, white or black mixed with a color will change its value without changing its hue. The addition of white creates a tint, black a shade.

Intensity: Intensity refers to the color strength of a hue. It is meaningful in a relative sense only. How intense a color is depends on what it's compared to. For example, a brilliant red has more color strength than a dull red and is therefore more intense. We can diminish the intensity of a color by mixing with it a neutral gray of the same **value** — and the original value and hue will remain unchanged.

Warm and cool colors. For reasons that are physical as well as psychological, we accept red, orange and yellow as warm colors; and we think of blue, blue-green and blue-violet as cool colors. Much of the function and power of color, as far as art is concerned, is based on this association with warm and cool. Green and violet remain as borderline colors in this "color temperature" scale, according to how they are used. Their warmness or coolness is relative and is determined strictly by their placement alongside adjacent colors. For example, we can differentiate between two blues by calling one "warmer" than the other. A greenish blue (cerulean) is considered warmer than a pure blue (cobalt) because it has yellow in it. Red-violet is cooler than pure red (scarlet) because there is some blue in it. Think of color temperature in a comparative sense and you will be putting it in its proper relationship.

Nature has conditioned us to think of warm colors as coming forward, while cool colors recede. Stated very broadly, the more atmosphere we put between us and distant objects, the bluer they appear. But in painting, blue and its related colors do not always retreat into the distance. In Figure 2, page 66, blue appears closer because it has greater intensity than the warmer but paler orange. Black, because of its great intensity, will advance into the foreground of a painting that predominates in colors of lesser intensity. (See Fig. 3, page 66.)

In painting outdoors the first thing we must learn is that to reproduce the colors and tones of nature literally is an impossible job. To begin with, the tonal range we can get with pigments on a white surface is no more than a fraction of that which exists in nature. We cannot go lighter than

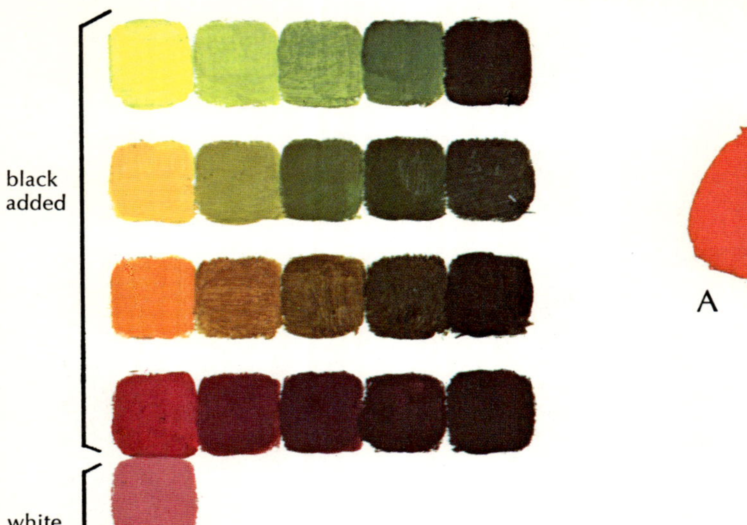

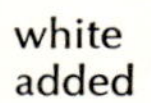

Fig. 4 Black, white and gray mixed with colors

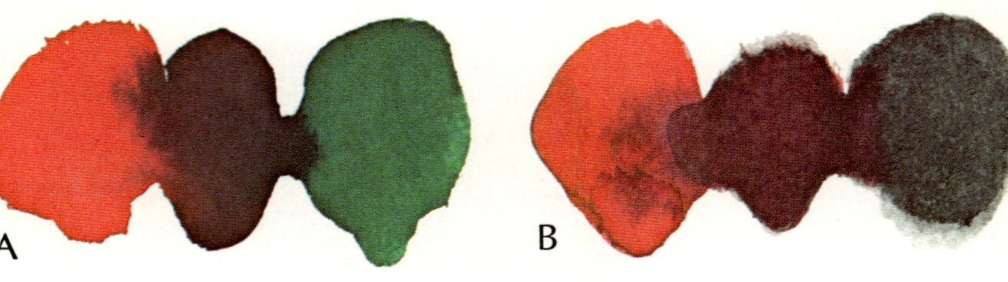

Fig. 5 Reducing the intensity of a color
A. Mixed with its complement
B. Mixed with black

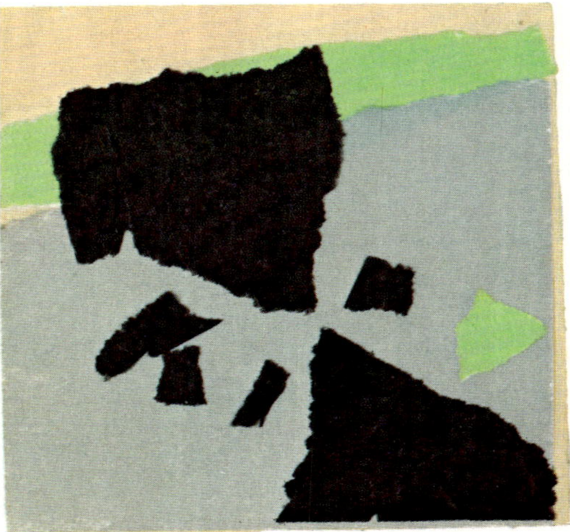

Fig. 3 Black comes forward

Fig. 2 Cool colors recede except when . . .

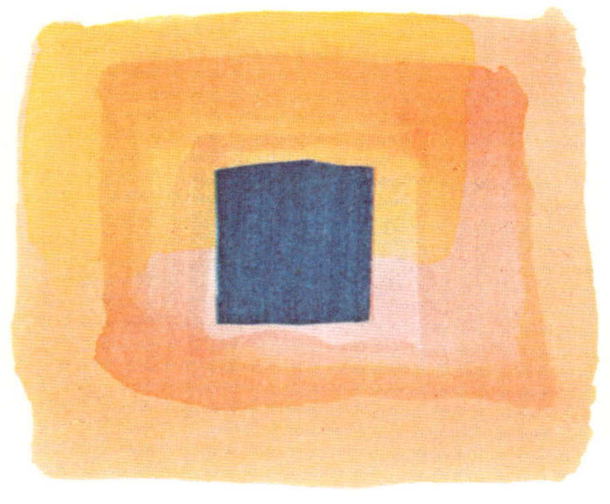

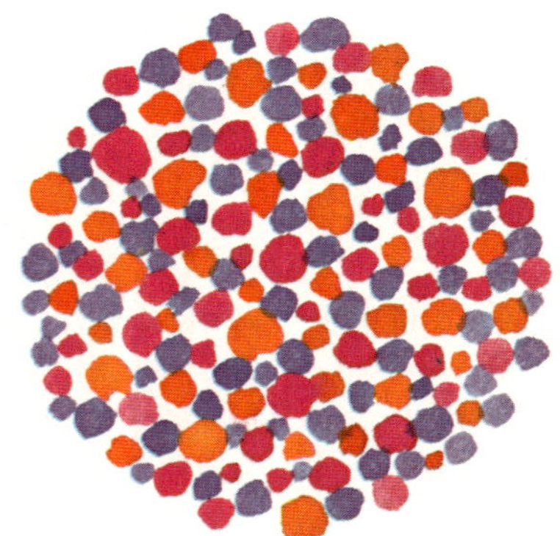

Fig. 1 Broken color

reflected white nor darker than the color of black paint. There are far more colors in an ordinary scene of field, foliage and sky than you could possibly classify, let alone put into a painting. The problem is compounded further as the light changes with the time of day and weather. Usually, you'll be better off aiming for the relative effects that colors create, rather than trying to get any certain color exactly right. It's much more important to have your colors relate to each other, interestingly and harmoniously. What happens in your picture is what counts.

It would be easy to say that color, after all, is a highly personal thing and therefore one should follow his own instincts and tastes. But it isn't that simple. Color, much like music, has a different meaning to different people. No two people are going to react the same.

It would take a whole volume just to begin to do justice to this subject. About all I can do in this book is to hit the high spots and refer you to some further reading if you wish to study particular areas of color in depth. Bear in mind that your involvement with color need not necessarily go any deeper than your interest in it. For some artists color is everything. At the same time there are many artists, including some of the best, to whom color is no more than a secondary consideration.

For further study I can recommend: *The Enjoyment and Use of Color* by Walter Sargent, a Dover Publication. It's unqualifiedly the best book on color I have ever read. I would also suggest you get the *Color Compass,* an illustrated guide for basic directions in color principles and theory, color identification, harmony, and color mixing, put out by M. Grumbacher, Inc., 460 West 34th St., N.Y.C.

It would seem nothing could be simpler than graying a hue by adding black, or lightening it by mixing white with it. But surprising things happen when we do this. Take yellow for example. Adding black to lemon yellow will produce a fairly bright green. A mixture of a warmer yellow and black makes a sort of olive tone, while orange with black goes into reddish-brown. Red with black will produce a dull violet. And red combined with white gives us distinct tints of rose (Fig. 4).

A better way to gray a color is to mix it with its complement. For this reason it is important to know with reasonable accuracy the complementary color of any given hue. Start with red, yellow and blue. The complements of these three primaries are green, violet and orange respectively. I suggest that you work out some experiments

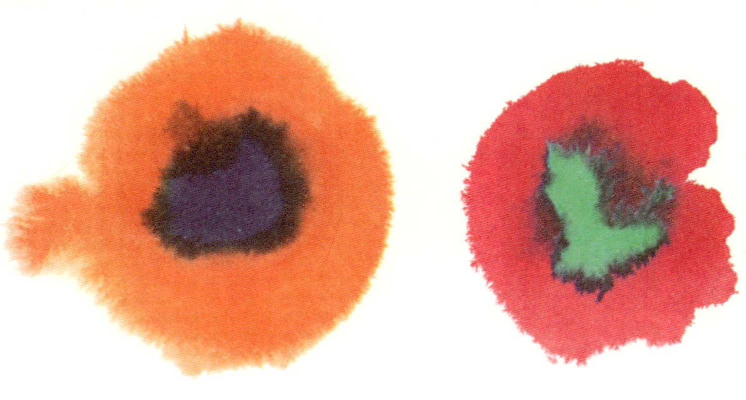

Fig. 6 Hues are intensified when contrasted with their complements

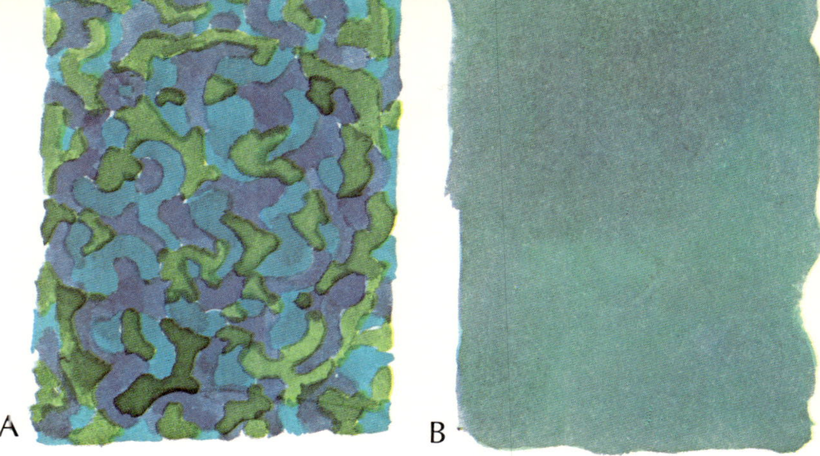

Fig. 7 A. Related hues in close proximity add vitality to each other
B. An area of the same colors, mixed

Fig. 8
Gradated color

like the ones in Figure 5 until you can pair up any given hue with its pigment complement. Make your own color wheel and use it as a guide in these experiments. (You can't always trust the accuracy of color in a reproduction of a color wheel.)

Colors intensify each other (Fig. 6). Experimenting with a few complementary pairs will soon familiarize you with the effects that are possible through combining (but not mixing) complements. Notice how much more intense the red geranium appears against its background of green leaves, and how the blue sea looks much bluer at sundown against an orange horizon.

A mass of color made up of unmixed closely related hues is usually much more vibrant and pleasing than a flat mass of thoroughly mixed color (Fig. 7). Remember that no color exists in nature under ordinary circumstances without gradation (Fig. 8). Gradation can make the difference between color tones that are harsh and monotonous and ones that are rich and glowing. This is just as true of the subtlest tints of gray (Fig. 9).

Strive for vitality in your use of color. It is the intermingling and vibration of related hues and the varying of intensities and textures that contributes to quality in color and gives beauty and power to a painting.

Grays and neutrals are often neglected by beginners. Yet the experienced painter gives just as careful consideration to the mixing and placement of his neutral colors as he does to the more intense ones. In fact, a skillful use of gray in proximity with stronger hues can greatly enhance the richness and brilliance of these colors.

We have seen that every color has one and only one exact complement, but two hues that are **near-complements.** These are the hues lying to either side of the direct complement in the color wheel. A color combination consisting of any given hue and these two near-complements is called a TRIAD. An example would be yellow, with the two hues (red violet and blue violet) that straddle its complement — violet (Fig. 10). Now if you took a piece or cardboard in the shape of this triangle and stuck a pin into the exact center you would have a triad "finder" simply by spinning the pointer anywhere within the color circle. The point to this is that in the triad you'll find the key to a wide range of color schemes that have a built-in relationship between the hues and all their intermixtures of color, from neutral hues to those of full intensity.

Fig. 9
Gray has color

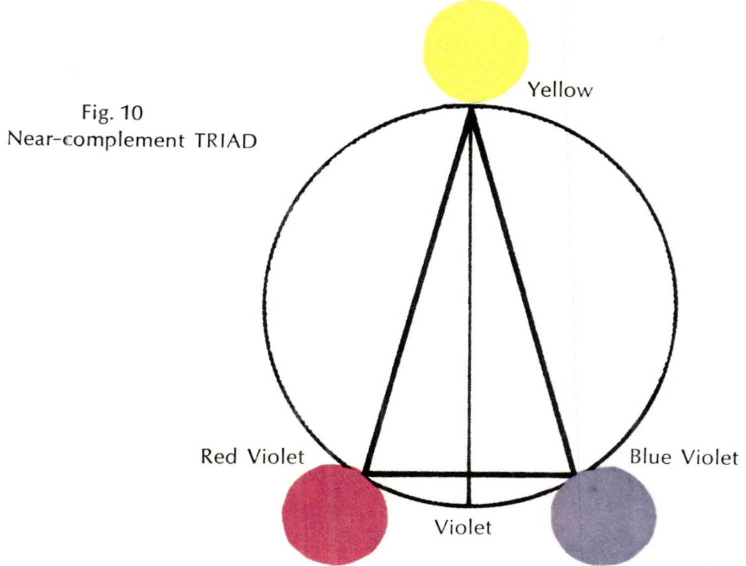

Fig. 10
Near-complement TRIAD

STILL LIFE

WHEN NATURE IS NOT THE STARTING POINT,
THE PICTURE IS INVARIABLY BAD.
Nicolas de Stael

Of all the areas of painting, no subject remains quite so consistently popular as still life. Art schools for years have used it for Lesson One, and with good reason; it is just about the ideal subject for beginners in painting.

To begin with, it's the only subject over which the artist has total control. Unlike a live model who gets tired, needs a rest, and is apt to catch a cold, it will stay put hours on end — days if need be, and no complaints. By contrast, a landscape is transient and unpredictable. Changing light is constantly altering the scene, sometimes in a matter of minutes. The immobility of a still life allows the painter a maximum span of concentration without distraction or interruption.

But over the years the still life has earned itself a bad reputation. Having been put to use so often as an exercise, it suffers greatly from overwork. Thousands upon thousands of the same stereotyped arrangements of apples and pears, pewter trays and carefully tacked-up cloths have been painted with pretty much the same dull results. The exercises may have been good practice, but the paintings that were turned out were dull because the subject matter was uninteresting. I think an exercise can just as easily be made exciting. There's no reason why the student can't become a little more involved personally with his subject.

Let's talk first about the different kinds of still lifes. Actually there are only two.

First is the arranged, set-up still life. Traditionally this has always been a more or less formal arrangement of objects, consciously selected and deliberately grouped. Some of the greatest paintings are of this formal, classic type.

Second is the existing, un-arranged still life. You might call this an accidental arrangement or assemblage of objects . . . a sort of "happening."

But setting up a still life that is interesting and exciting to paint, and yet does not look carefully and deliberately planned, is not as easy at it looks.

Start out consciously limiting yourself in the number of objects you allow in your still life. Bear in mind that some of the greatest painters used some of the humblest objects. Masterpieces have been painted of things like eggs, bread, fish, and kitchen utensils. Braque for example, could take an assortment of dishes, vegetables, books, bottles and produce a painting highly original and yet realistic. This penchant for using homely household items and portraying them abstractly, distorting and exaggerating, sets him apart from any other painter of still life.

So if in doubt, head for the kitchen and look for things that have some kind of utilitarian relationship with each other. Forget about all the still lifes you've ever seen. Exclude everything that does not seem essential or that lacks affinity with the still life. Be sure that you do not put in anything just to fill up space in the picture. Also, any elimination of objects should come before you begin to paint, not afterward. Eliminating as you paint leaves blank spaces which have to be filled with something you've invented, and almost invariably you will find that it's much harder to make the invented shape relate as convincingly as the original one.

This is an autobiographical still life comprised of the objects, animate and inanimate, in the artist's studio.

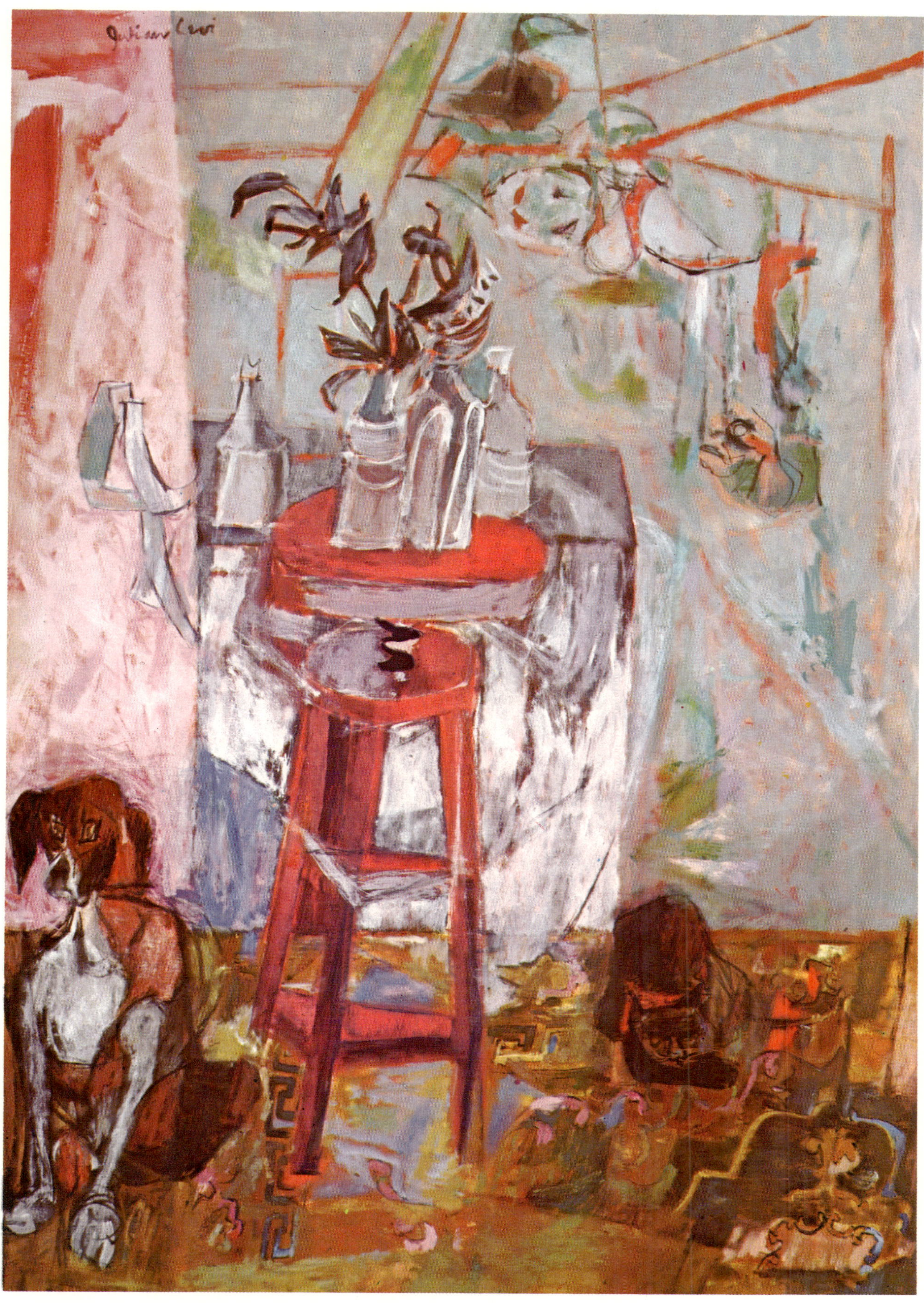

ORPHEUS IN THE STUDIO by JULIAN LEVI
Collection: Pennsylvania Academy of the Fine Arts.
Courtesy of Lee Nordness Galleries, New York

PAINTING a STILL LIFE

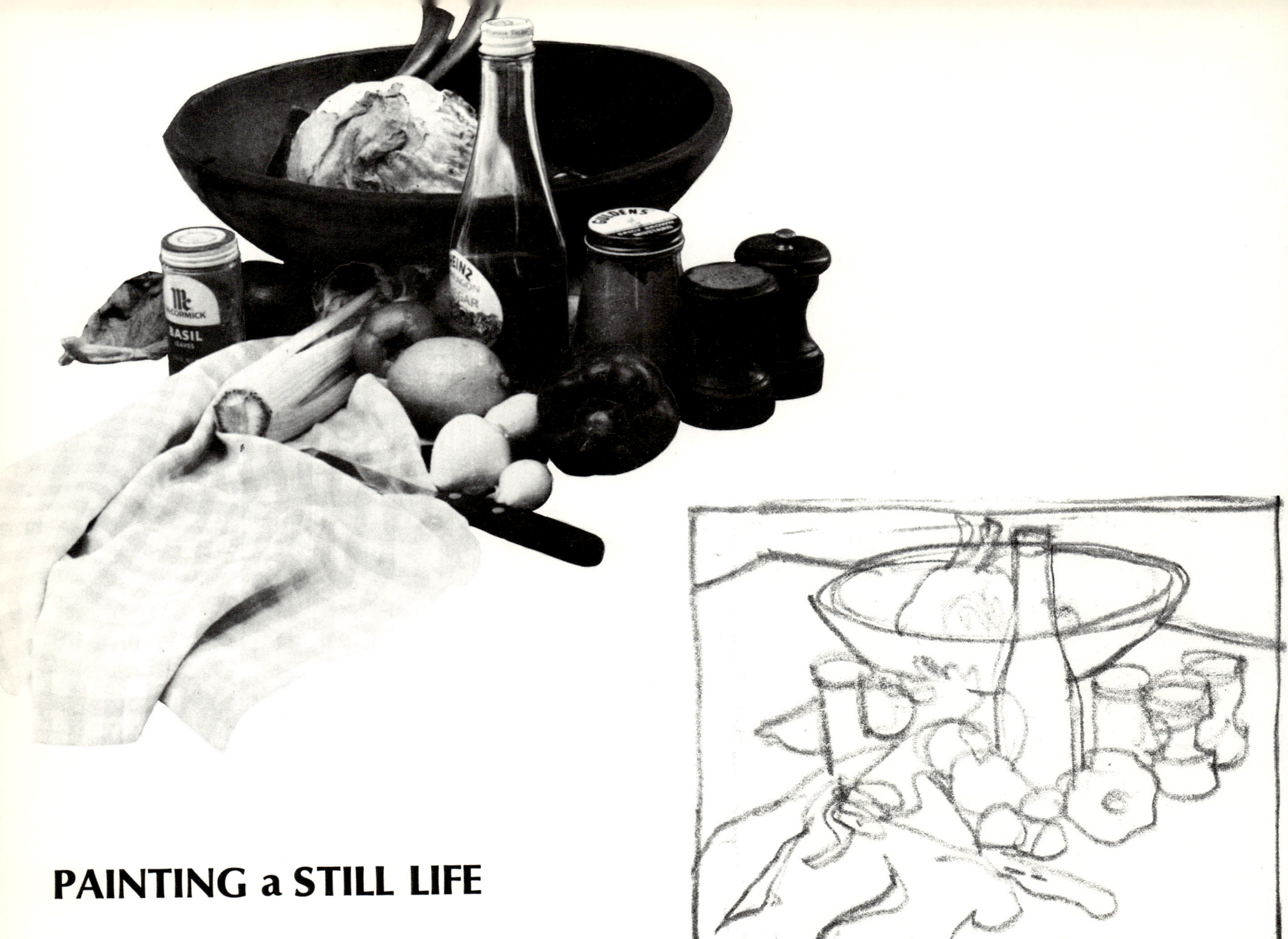

A

Many painters like to begin a painting without much preliminary planning. They may start with a few abstract shapes, then work outward, manipulating and altering elements as they go. I envy their ability to do this, but I would rather have things worked out beforehand to some degree at least, in order to find the best viewpoint and the most interesting composition. Figures A, B and C illustrate just three of the many compositional variations that are possible, simply by changing the vantage point and varying the cropping, without touching the still life set-up.

For your first still life, I suggest you use no less than three brushes. It's possible, of course, to work with one or two, but painting with too limited a range of brushes restricts variety of expression in paint application. Too often the result is a sort of production line look.

I am going to use the following brushes for this demonstration: a #10 flat, a #8 filbert, and a #5 round. A new flat will apply paint with a fairly sharp chiseled edge. A well-worn flat is very similar to a filbert, which is halfway between a flat and a round in shape. I find a filbert very useful for soft-edged effects and general use. The rounds are good for drawing with the brush and for the initial "lay-in." The brushes I have mentioned are all bristle brushes (made of hog bristle). I seldom use sables in oil or acrylics. They are too pliant to

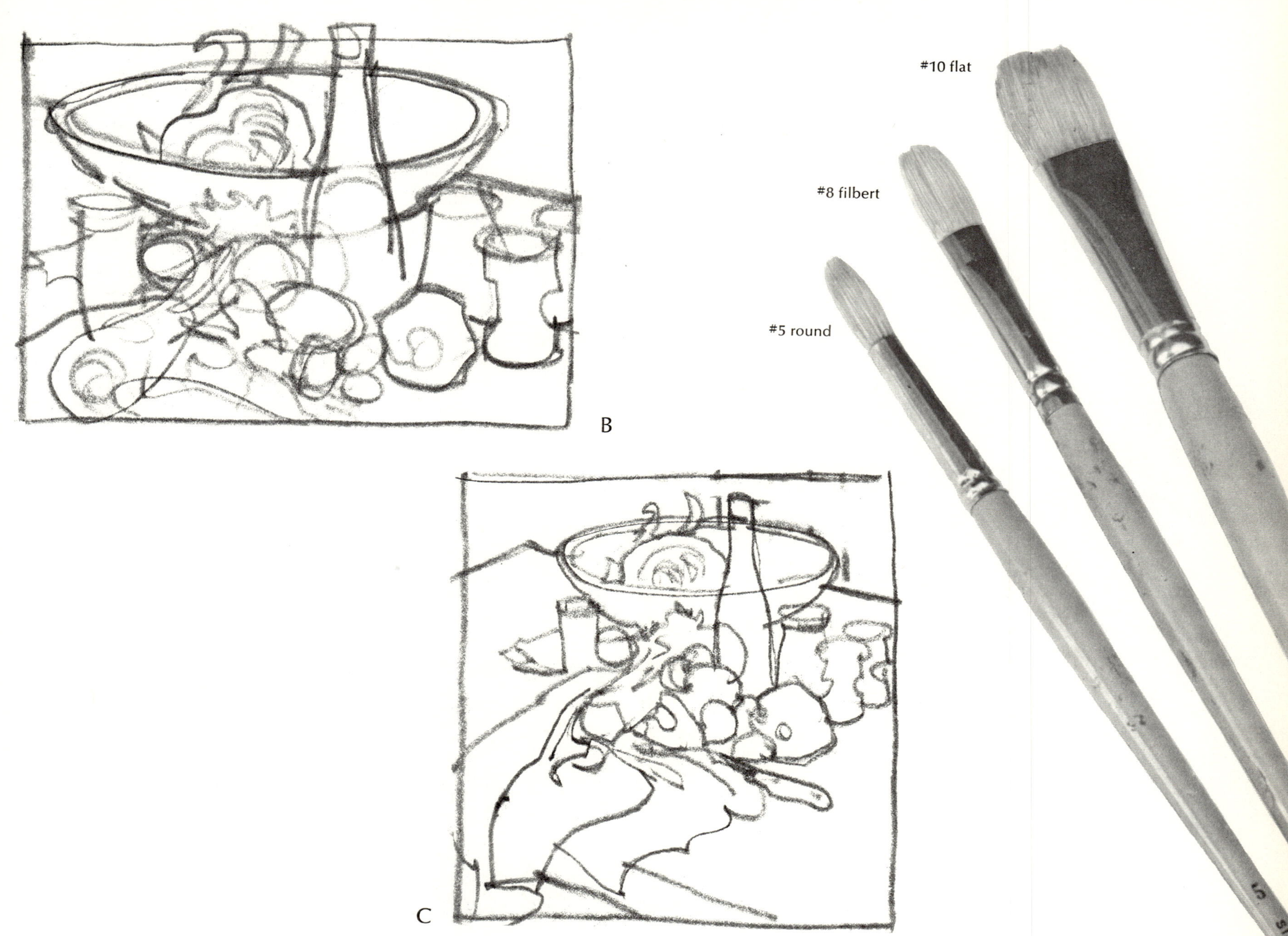

hold anything but thin washes. The palette knife can be combined with brushwork, but for this painting I will restrict myself to brushes.

There is a certain excitement to a painting in its early stages that is often hard to retain as the painting develops and the picture begins to materialize. I seem to be able to prolong my interest and excitement in a painting if I lay in the basic brushwork with as much vigor and spontaneity as I can muster, actually splashing and slopping on the paint with almost reckless abandon. Too much care and deliberation in the preliminary stages can destroy the vitality of a picture. The result then is a static, unconvincing look, and I find it almost impossible to inject new life into a feeble and indecisive beginning. If the painting is ailing at this early stage it will have little chance of gaining much excitement as you proceed. Don't be in a rush to correct the untidiness of the early stages. This "neatening up" should be saved for the final stages.

Later, with the use of smaller, more precise brush strokes and more opaque paint, you may lose a great deal of your underpainting. At this midway point you should begin to step back more and more frequently to survey what you have done. How is the pattern? Are the big shapes exerting a holding force over the composition? And do these big shapes lend abstract pattern to the picture when viewed from across the room? You may be closer to completion than you realize. There's an old saying that it takes two artists to produce a good painting. One to paint it, and another to snatch it away when it's finished. The point is that too many artists reach a stage where they become bored with a picture and don't know it. Many times this has happened to me and instead of putting it aside I have gone on mindlessly working until most of the freshness and spontaneity were gone. It's a sort of creeping paralysis that is symptomatic of painting. Be on your guard against it.

Learn to recognize this diminution of interest when it comes and do something about it. Put the painting aside and go to something else until you can return with fresh interest or you'll risk losing the very thing that moved you to paint the picture in the first place. A picture that is belabored or over-intellectualized is almost certain to betray your loss of interest.

One of the best ways I know of to head off this kind of stagnation is to keep several paintings going at the same time. Each one will (if I have been varying my subject matter, color, concept, etc., as I should be) involve a different range of problems. Then, when I tire of one painting I can go on to another, with a renewed feeling of involvement and a fresh challenge.

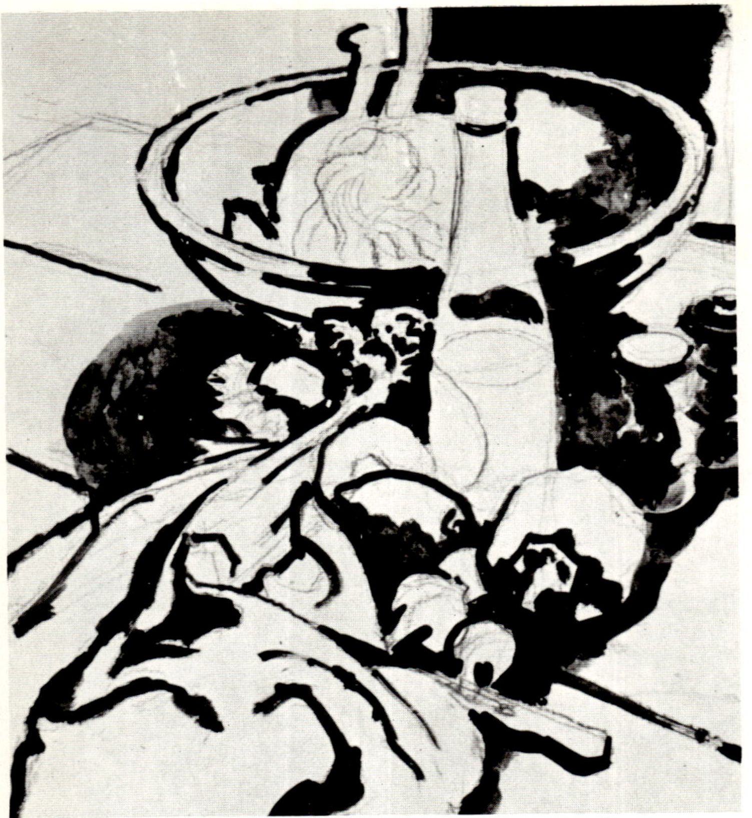

1

I painted this still life out of doors in bright shade. I especially didn't want an art school "set-up" look if I could avoid it. I was counting on the sort of natural order which seems to take place when related objects such as these are grouped together. Quite often then, all that is needed for a composition is to crop it so that the surrounding space makes interesting shapes. See figures A, B, and C, pages 70 and 71.

STAGE 1

My medium for this will be acrylics; the painting surface, a cotton canvas panel that has been extra primed with two coats of acrylic gesso. Starting with the dominant shape, the salad bowl, I put in the guidelines lightly with charcoal. Next, I do a brush drawing using a mixture of black and ultramarine blue with a #5 round bristle. This is the lay-in; it should be painted freely and boldly, simplifying shapes and lines. I'm counting on the coolness of this blue for color opposition, to set the stage for the warmer colors to follow.

Most objects have direction. The time to take advantage of this is when the still life is arranged; later, in painting the lay-in, these directions can be exaggerated.

STAGE 2

Now, with a brush fairly loaded with paint and the panel laid almost flat, I start putting in the darker objects — salad bowl, condiments, vinegar bottle, green pepper. This paint goes down wet and somewhat transparent, and in some places not completely mixed. No white yet. I want this underpainting to glow with a certain amount of transparency, and white would deaden it. Some of this primary brushwork will be left as-is, without any further working into.

2

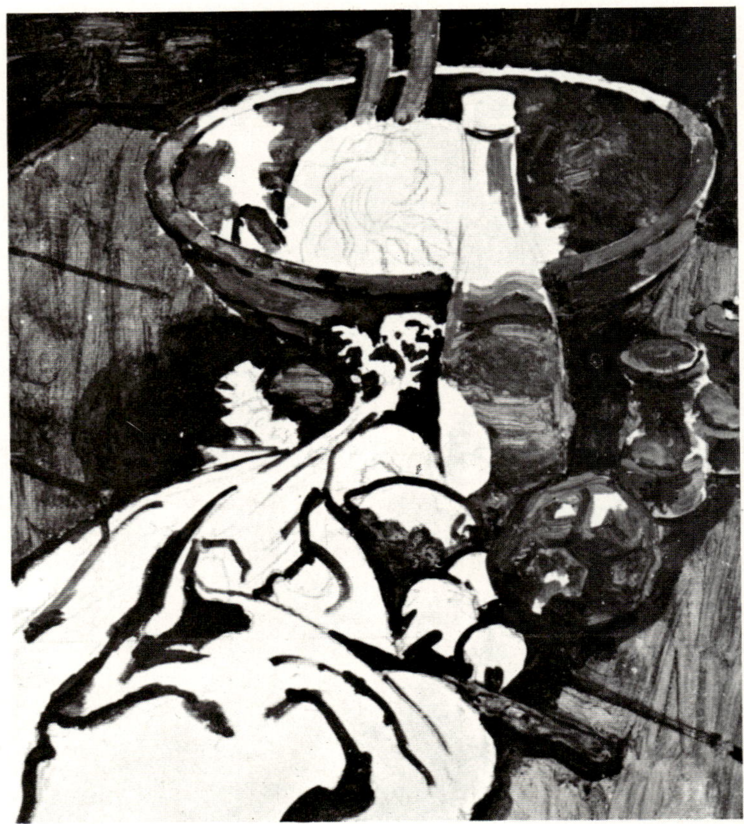

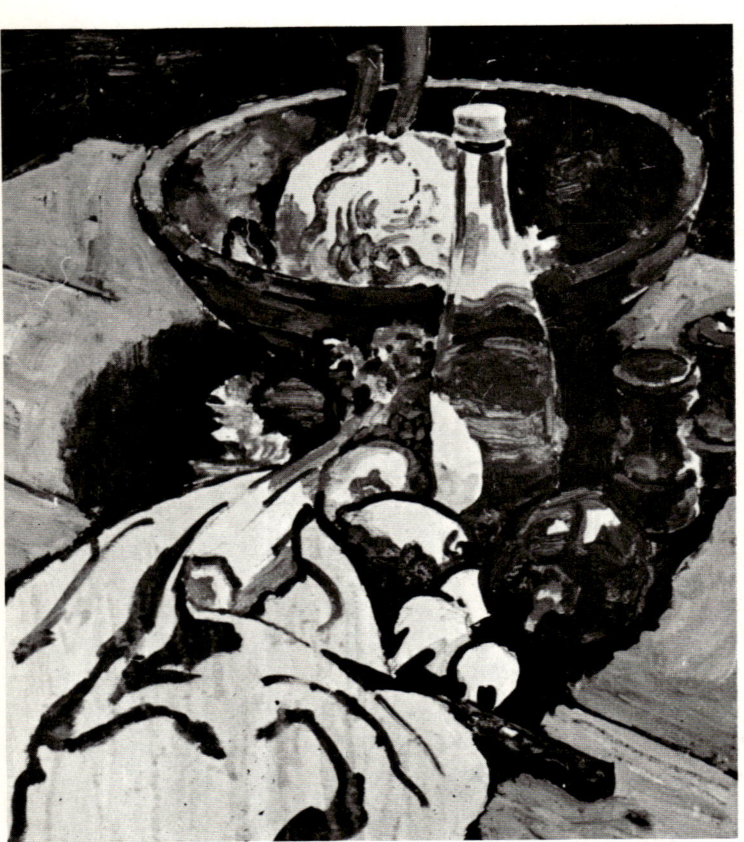

3

STAGE 3

At this point, if I don't get the blank areas filled in I'm going to be in trouble; so the next thing to go in is the table top. This gets a neutral gray made of raw sienna, cobalt blue, and white. Now the cloth is given a temporary wash of cerulean to get rid of the white space. Lighter colors follow as the paint becomes more opaque. This is the stage of completion when I have a tendency to start picking at details and overworking things, so I pause more and more frequently to check on myself and appraise the results so far. Right now the table is detracting from the still life. It needs to be simplified.

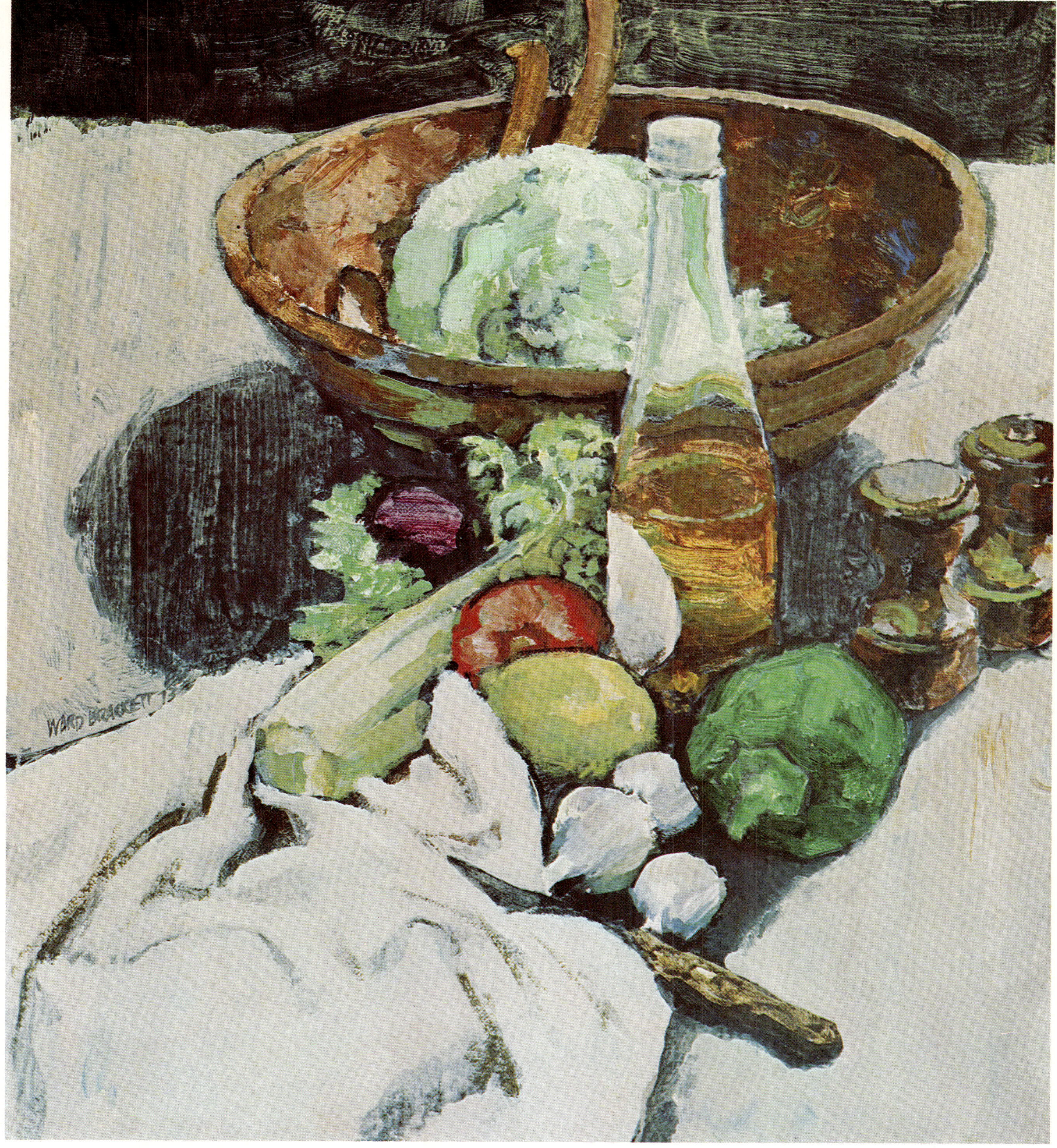

STILL LIFE by WARD BRACKETT — acrylics

STAGE 4 4

Now the last of the blank areas disappears as the lettuce and celery get a preparatory base of light green oxide. The onions are finished off with some violet, green oxide, raw sienna and white, applied unmixed. More of the same green with white in the celery and lettuce. After finishing the tomato and lemon the lettuce now looks too blue. This is remedied by "glazing," a technique of applying paint in transparent washes that alters the color but does not disturb the painting underneath. Here I use very thin cadmium yellow medium, washed on with a flat sable brush.

The cloth still looks a little flat. It lacks gradation of color. (See page 67.) The flatness is broken up with white that varies in tints of thalo blue, cadmium red light, and raw sienna. This process of applying opaque or semi-opaque pigment over dried underpainting is called "scumbling."

I said I wasn't going to use a palette knife but I couldn't resist a couple of flicks to heighten the highlights of the lettuce.

OUTDOOR PAINTING

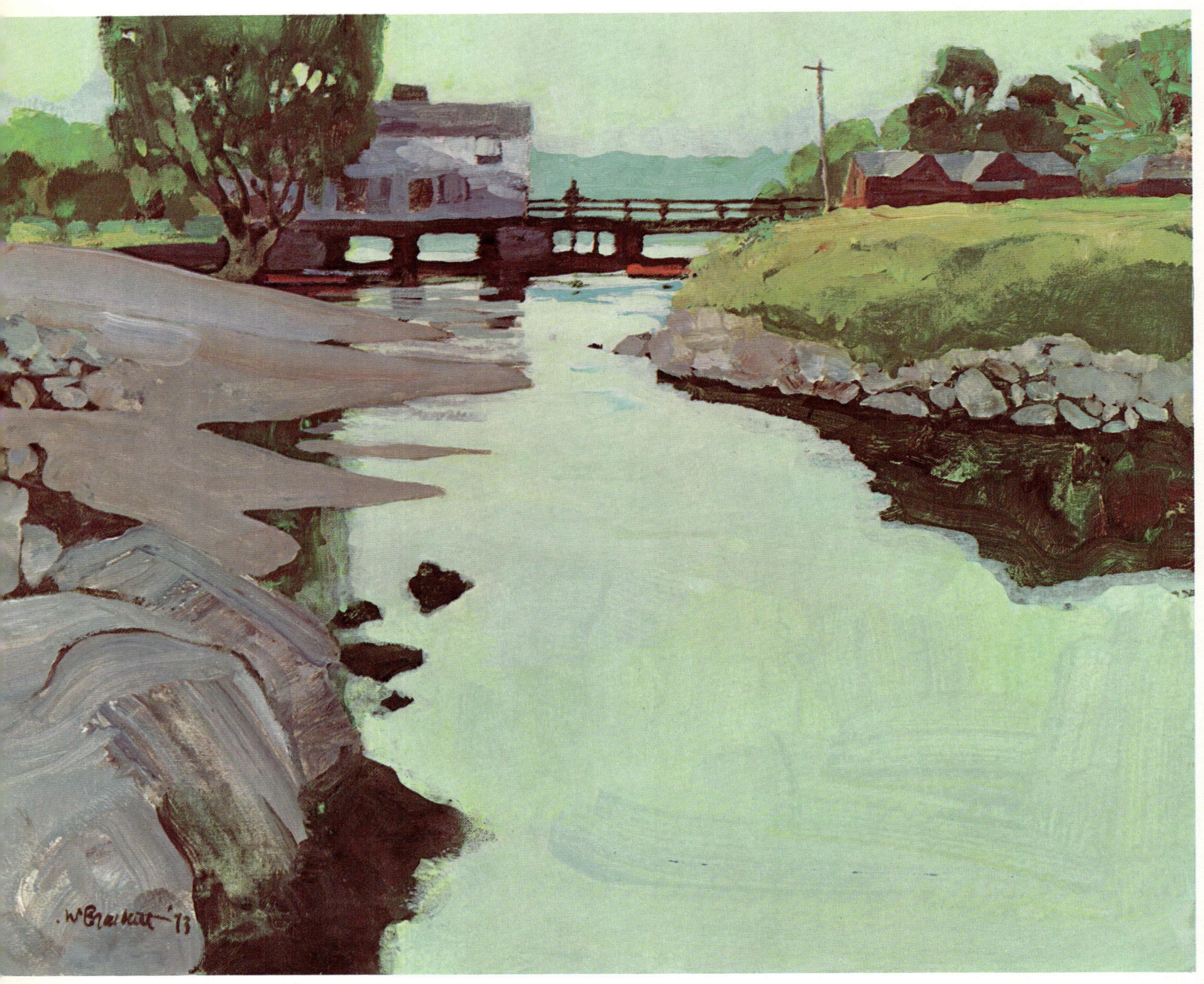

OLD MILL by WARD BRACKETT

THE ARTIST MUST BECOME ONE WITH NATURE . . .
HE MUST IDENTIFY HIMSELF WITH HER RHYTHM.
Henri Matisse

The step from still life to outdoor painting is a big one for many artists. Before you venture forth for your first encounter with landscape, consider the possibilities of your own home ground. Look around you; there may be some very paintable subjects out your window or right off the back porch.

You may as well know, the minute you appear in public with sketch box and easel, you are marked as a curiosity. Like a crew of workers or a pizza twirler you are fair game for the idly curious. They seem to materialize out of nowhere. I've even had kibitzers bring their lunch and a folding chair and break out a can of beer while they watched me all afternoon. So be prepared for an audience unless you are able to back yourself up to a wall. But maybe there's a bit of showmanship in you, in which case you are lucky. You may even enjoy an audience. Some artists do.

Preparation is the golden rule of outdoor painting. Before you start out be sure you have everything you are going to need. If there ever is a time when you must be organized, this is it. There is nothing quite as frustrating as being located and all set to start painting only to discover that you have left the sketching panels or something just as essential at home. A good way to prevent this sort of disaster is to maintain a sketching kit, complete and separate from the tools and materials you keep in the studio. In any event, use a sketch box big enough to take everything you are apt to need, except easel and painting surfaces, and a plastic bucket for water (if you are working in water color). A small, folding seat is almost an essential luxury. It's not always possible to find something reasonably comfortable to sit on. Don't scatter things around in pockets or in separate bags or you'll be sure to forget something.

The list of things that are absolutely essential for outdoor painting can be pared down to the four items pictured on page 78. They include the following (oil painters can dispense with the bucket):

1. A sketch box (mine has inside dimensions of 12″ x 15½″) with compartments to hold paints and brushes. Start out with no less than three brushes (page 71) and an assortment of colors similar to that used for the still life painting (page 73). You will need a palette as large as the box will take, a single-edged razor blade, several sticks of charcoal, a kneaded eraser and a rag. Don't forget that rag. As big a one as you can tuck into the box. Also, a palette knife and a 1½″ house brush for big areas. If you are going to be using acrylics, especially in direct sunlight, take along a tube of retarder to slow the drying of paint on your palette.

2. Painting surfaces. I prefer gesso panels or plain illustration boards to canvases for outdoor painting simply because they are not as bulky and are less vulnerable to damage. They are also cheaper. Most sketch boxes will accommodate three panels inside the cover. If you are planning to use oil then you had better include some canvas pins to keep wet surfaces separated from each other. Another thing you will need with oil is one of those little metal cups that clips securely to your palette for holding turpentine, and a bottle (or can) of turps or neutral spirits.

3. An easel. The one I use is more like a photographer's tripod in that it is made of tubular aluminum with leg tighteners that lock with a business-like twist of the wrist. I like it better than my old wooden one because it is lighter, just as sturdy and sets up with less fuss.

4. A water bucket.

The size you decide to work can vary, but don't try to cover too large an area in one sitting. You are apt to find that there just isn't enough time. On the other hand, your painting is likely to become fussy or timid if you work too small. Some beginners have a tendency to paint small out of a senseless feeling of humility and it always shows up in the results. Remember that it is no easier for most painters to do a smaller painting than it is to do a larger one. Unless it is a quick sketch done as a record and nothing more, I'd suggest that you paint no smaller than the size of a panel that will just fit into your sketch box; that is, approximately 12″ x 16″. Panels or canvases larger than this can be held together with a pair of fabric straps, fitted with adjustable buckles, to make one compact bundle.

It's best to get a fairly early start when you paint outdoors, allowing for a whole day. Give yourself plenty of time to start another painting should your first attempt go wrong.

Ideally, the best way to start is with some place in mind. It's been my experience that the most interesting places to paint are always found when I am not looking for them. Jot down the location of any good painting spot when you see it, and keep a note book of painting locations for future use.

Let's assume that you are starting out cold, with no particular place in mind. Keep your eyes open along the way. (You will see much more walking than if you are driving.) When you have found something that interests you, stop and paint it. Don't waste time trying to find the best possible view or angle. I have done this and found that the longer I looked and the more I deliberated over a scene, the more indecisive I became.

Painting a landscape is not substantially different from painting a still life. In fact, the approach and step-by-step procedure are virtually the same. What is markedly different

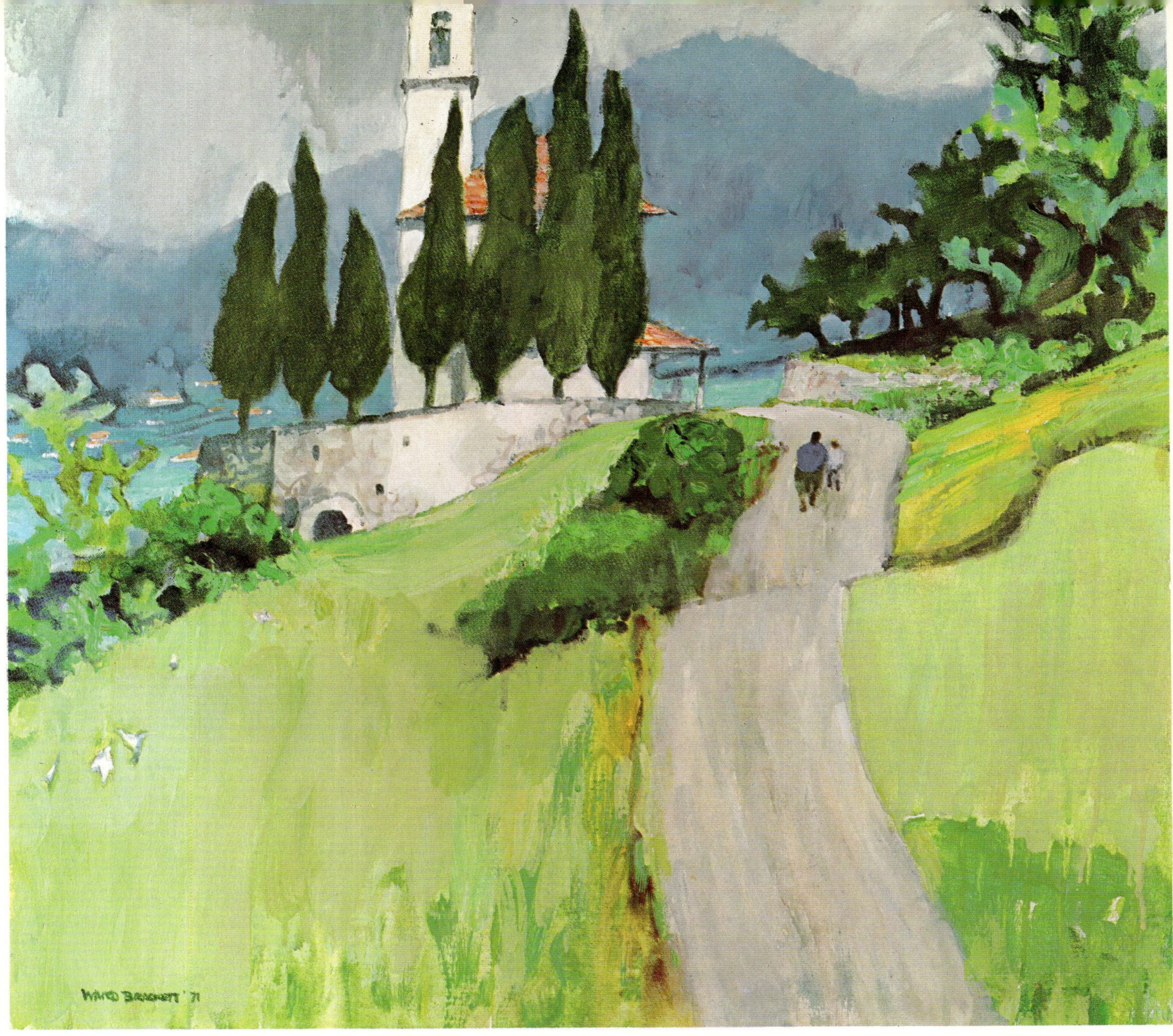

VIEW NEAR LAGO DI GARDA by WARD BRACKETT — acrylics

about it are the conditions under which you will be working. In painting out of doors you will have to contend with the vagaries of weather, changing light and shadows that have a way of disappearing and reappearing. Sometimes you will have to hurry to catch a certain lighting. And sometimes you will have to work fast to beat a threatening storm. But all in all, once you start applying paint, the problems of color, shapes and composition are the same as those involved in still life.

Your first paintings may very likely be no more than attempts to copy doggedly everything you see. There is probably something to be learned from this sort of exercise, but you can save yourself hours of painful effort if you will remember one thing . . . you can't put it all in. I am always somewhat intimidated at first sight by the abundance of raw material that confronts me in almost any outdoor scene, particularly urban areas that are complicated by the business of city life, plus architectural problems. I still have to remind myself that it is impossible to say it all in one painting.

I would suggest that you limit yourself drastically as to subject matter in your first few paintings. Narrow down your field of vision to a relatively small and uncomplicated segment of the scene you are about to tackle. See page 44.

Selecting the Subject. Bear in mind as you start to paint that there is no particular virtue in doing anything by the book. Remember that there are absolutely no rules that are inviolable. Follow your natural inclinations. It is in this direction that you will do your best work.

Do not be concerned with style, yet. Concentrate on your motivation. The things you find most gratifying to paint are what you should paint. If the vastness of waves, clouds or sky excites you, paint it. If you find a doorway or a single tree interesting enough to paint, then do it. Never feel you have to paint a big picture with everything in it simply because it's all out there in front of you. Use your finder and "close in" on the area you want. Almost any outdoor scene contains enough material for several entirely different compositions if you will take the time to look for it. It's a matter of seeing what's there, then putting it to use.

Begin early to train your eye to override the fast-changing effects of atmosphere and sunlight. Again, look for the big shapes and the negative shapes. Put some thought into their selection and placement in your picture. Oddly enough, most objects in nature seem to look right for no other reason than that they are there. Making them adapt to your design is another story.

Make your shapes decisive. If the motif is geometric take every opportunity to exaggerate and exploit triangular and rectilinear forms. If it is organic do the same with shapes that are oval and free-form. Don't be afraid to distort wherever it will add excitement and strength to the design. Try to develop a theme, a mood.

Right about now I have to contradict myself. I've been running on about formulas, and a formula is a good thing to have. I can't think of any good painters who work without one. But the painter who relies too heavily on a formula for the success of his painting, very soon begins repeating himself. He will find, if he is as self-critical as he should be, that he is turning out copies of himself. When any set formula becomes a crutch, when you are lost without it, you had better stop and see if your work is becoming mannered and predictable. Many gallery painters and illustrators have taken a formula and used it to death, although I must admit some of them have been very successful with it.

But any formula that "works" every time should be suspect. If you always know what is going to happen and how each painting is going to turn out, the way is open for clichés and generalizations. When the element of surprise is lacking, too often, so is the depth and personal quality of the painting lacking. For this reason I am careful never to let an old habit get the upper hand. This usually happens when I start working from memory. Then I find myself making the same rocks, trees, water and sky. There is such an infinite variety, in fact, to the shape of things that we need never repeat ourselves . . . if we keep our eyes open.

Don't feel you have to explain everything you do. As long as the forms you use have some basis of origin in nature, you can then become as subjective as you like. Look at Bonnard's paintings, his landscapes in particular. In them, foliage, sky, flowers, water — even human figures and animals — seem to intermingle and fuse in a way that often eludes identification. To him, the subject was secondary in importance to his images of color, form and texture. His interpretation of subject matter is so original and personal that positive identification seems unimportant.

In painting nature, strive for the **essence** of what you see. Be careful to avoid painting what you **think** you know about things. Your preconceived ideas about nature can get you in trouble if you start generalizing.

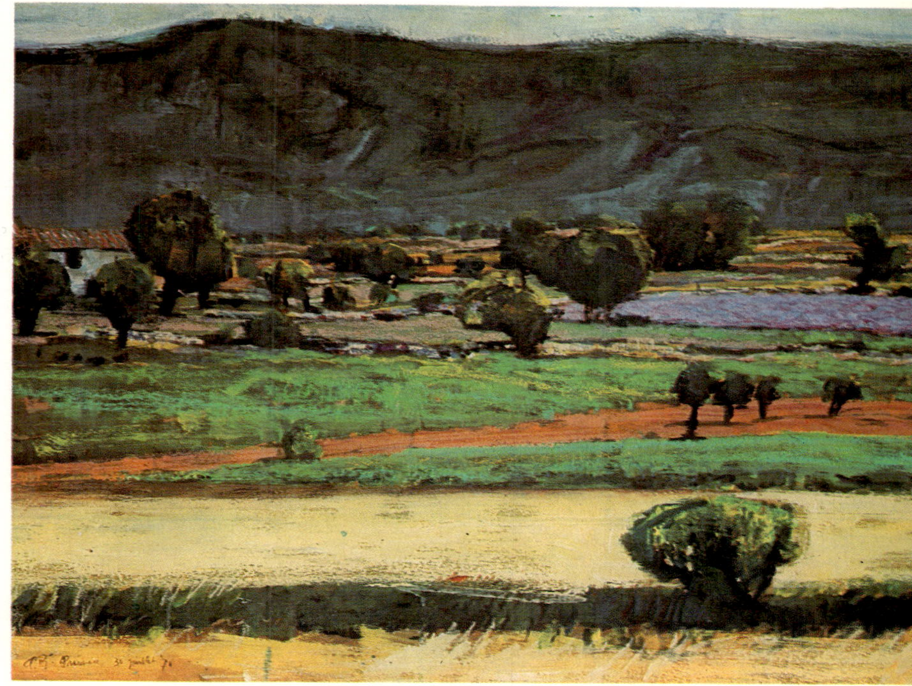

FIELD OF LAVENDER, PROVENCE by AUSTIN BRIGGS

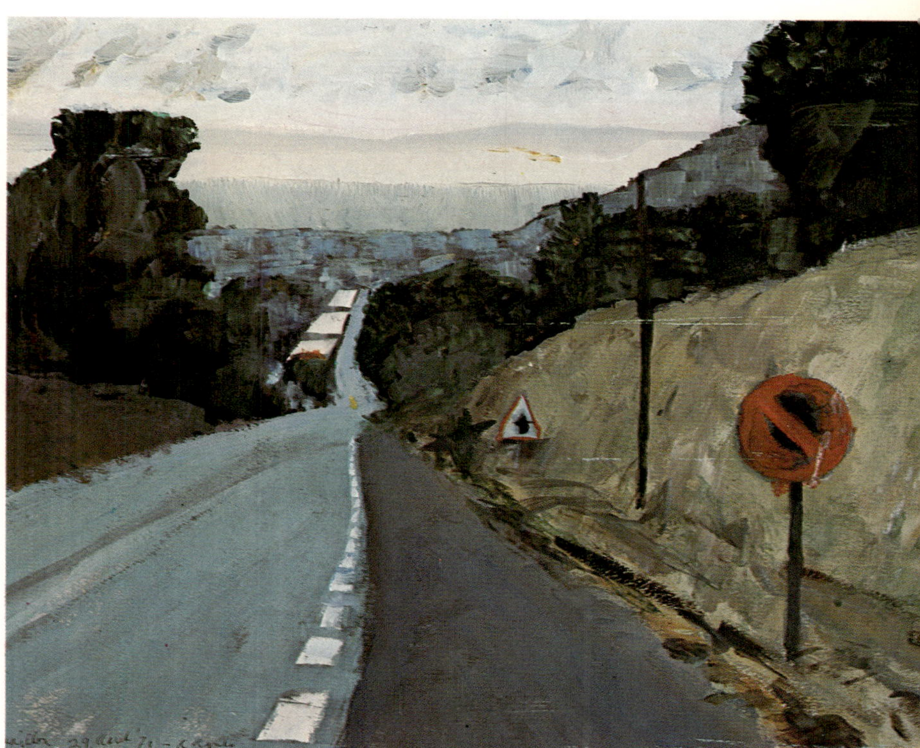

ON THE ROAD TO CAVAILLON by AUSTIN BRIGGS

One of the most successful and articulate illustrators of our day was Austin Briggs. These two paintings, done in southern France, were among the last things he did. They give us a brief glimpse of what is possible when such a talent as his is free to work without deadlines to meet or manuscripts to follow.

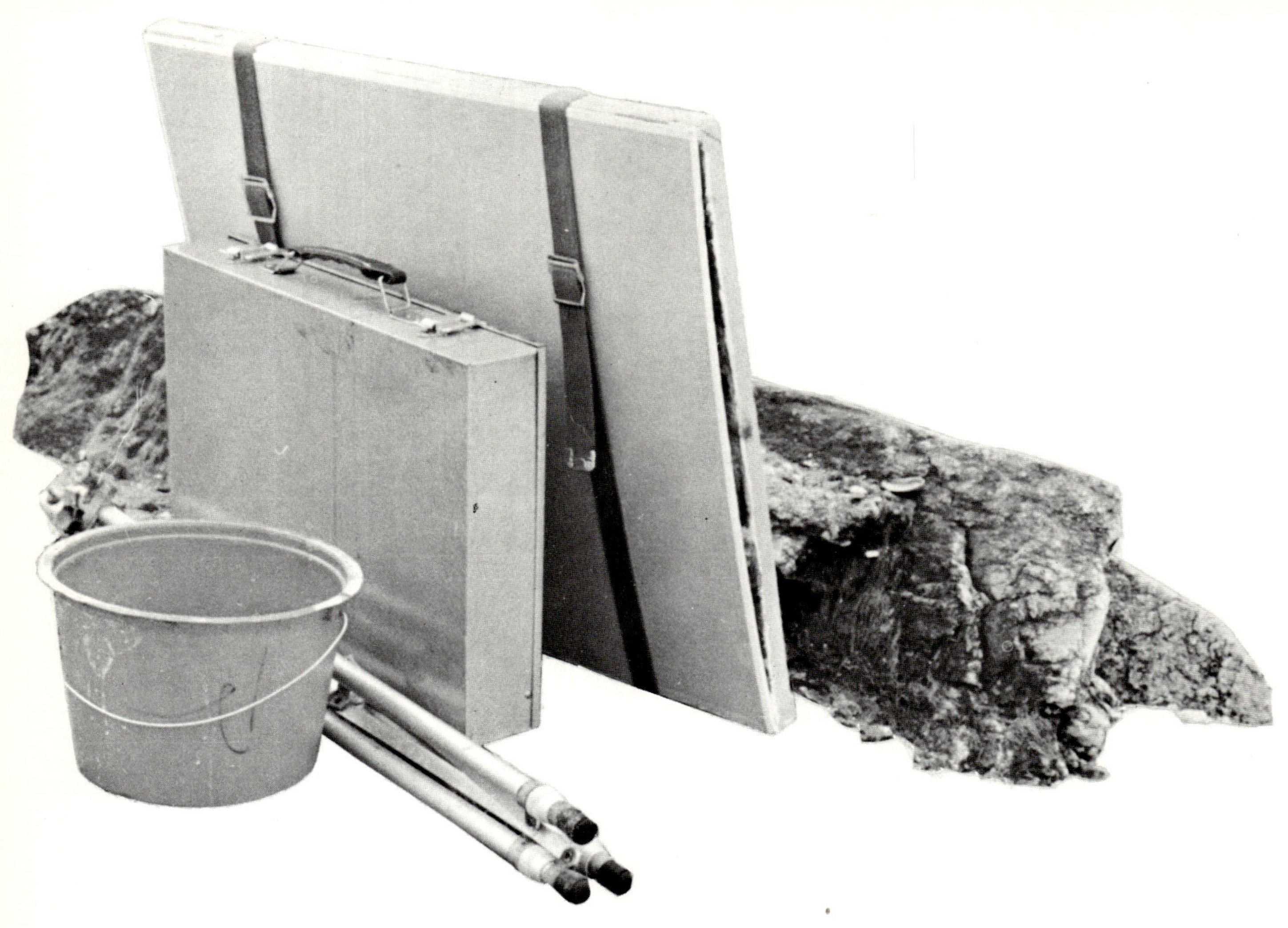

PAINTING a LANDSCAPE

When I have found the spot I want to paint, broken out the paints and set up the easel, I am ready for the next decision. Shall I take the scene pretty much as it is, painting what I see, as I see it, without rearranging nature; or is it better to try to interpret what I see into a synthetized impression of the scene?

Many artists prefer the first approach as a better way of achieving freedom and naturalness. But just as many painters, past and present, believe in taking some liberties with what they see — eliminating here, rearranging there, until they have created a design that pleases them. Turner, for instance, liked to assemble his landscapes from bits and pieces of scenes taken from his scrap book or from memory. One of his paintings is said to be a composite of details taken from nine different locations in the English countryside.

I like to work both ways. It depends entirely on the immediate conditions — the time I am allowed for painting, the prevailing weather, and whether I can sustain my interest in the scene long enough to finish it in one sitting. Often I will make a small sketch, recording color, basic details, and mood. Then I can develop the idea at my leisure, in the quiet, controlled atmosphere of the studio.

I find it harder to bring my imagination into full play when I try to complete a painting on the spot. And I still have to fight the temptation to put everything in just because it's there.

Beginners have a tendency to want to tidy up the scene. They leave things out because they find them too complicated or because they consider them unattractive. A row of garbage cans, washing on a line, telephone poles, all can provide a needed note of pattern and believability to a picture. Do not avoid man-made objects as unsightly. They are part of our environment — they belong in modern painting.

In starting out to paint, one of your objectives should be to discover what you do best. It will be easier if you let your mind remain as uncluttered as possible. Forget, for the time being, the details of any painting you've ever seen and concentrate on pure form. Details can always be put in. It's much harder to take them out.

I would advise you to approach your first few paintings without any advance planning. Your subject must have had

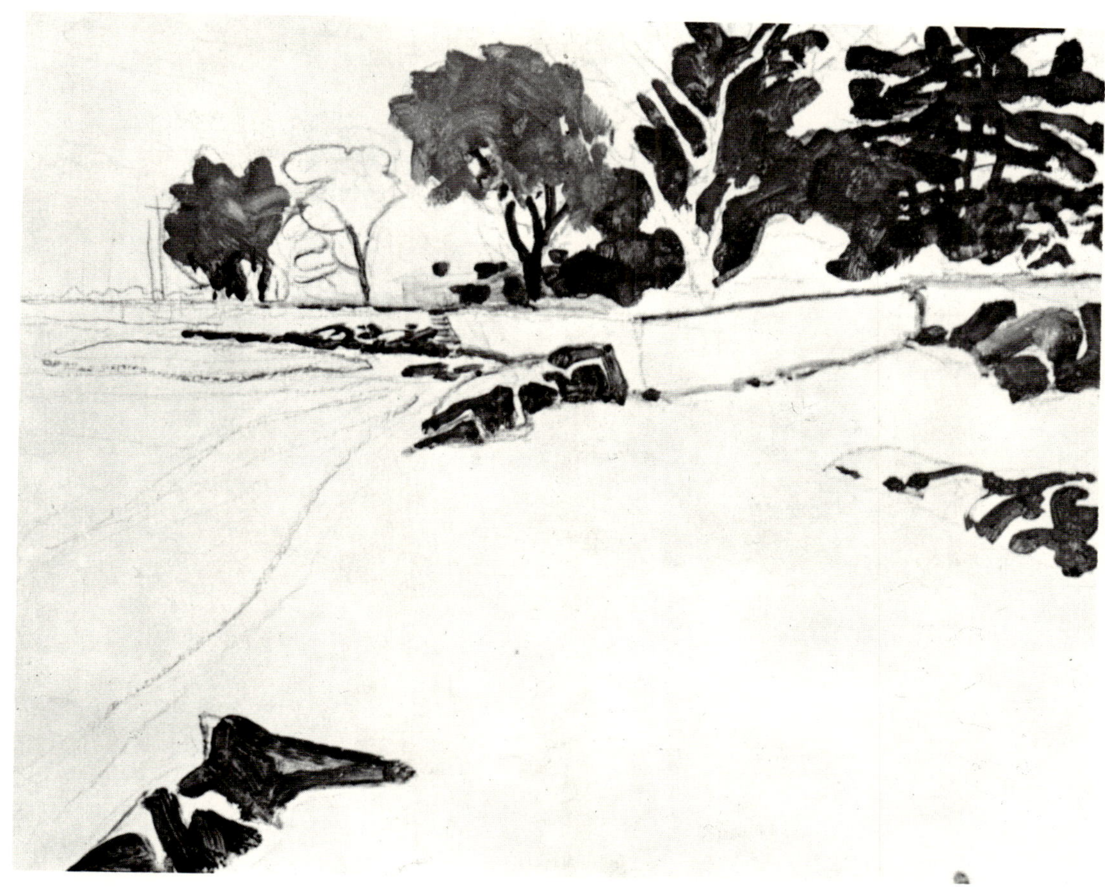

1

INSTINCT WHICH NOURISHES METHOD CAN OFTEN BE SUPERIOR TO A METHOD WHICH NOURISHES INSTINCT.
Pierre Bonnard

something interesting in it or it wouldn't have stopped you in the first place. Your aim should be to bring out what is exciting about it and elaborate on it. Never set out blindly, envisioning one goal, accepting no compromises. If you try to preconstruct every effect and plan every brush stroke in advance you will stifle intuition. Remember that it is too early to be worrying about style.

As you gain experience you'll find yourself doing things without any particular reason simply because it "feels right." Encourage this feeling when it comes; give it all the room you can. Emotion is supplanting reason, and though this might be disastrous to the scientist or the engineer, to the creative artist, this is a good thing. It is, in fact, the beginning of intuitive painting and design. Most good paintings bear evidence of this subconscious direction. Remember, as long as you continue to use your eyes and analyze what you see, your subconscious is learning too and filing away information.

Painting by intellect alone is not enough. Art begins when the artist no longer can explain positively what he is doing or why he is doing it, but knows instinctively and intuitively that what he is doing is right.

STAGE 1

This stretch of beach, near my home, is a spot I know intimately. Its outcropping of rocks, its sea wall and gravelly sand is typical of the north shore of Long Island Sound. The reason it looks so deserted is that it is supposed to be private. (I had to ignore a few "No Trespassing" signs to get to it.)

My working surface is a 20 x 24 inch canvas panel. Using acrylics, I start with the darkest darks, the background foliage. This was a mixture of Hooker's green, chromium green oxide, and ultramarine. The rocks come next in burnt sienna and ultramarine. This dark-to-light procedure works with waterproof acrylics, but with traditional watercolors the lighter colors would have to go in first.

Acrylics dry too fast on the palette, especially in sunlight, to allow much time for puttering around. I'm fortunate here to be working in the shade of an abandoned beach house.

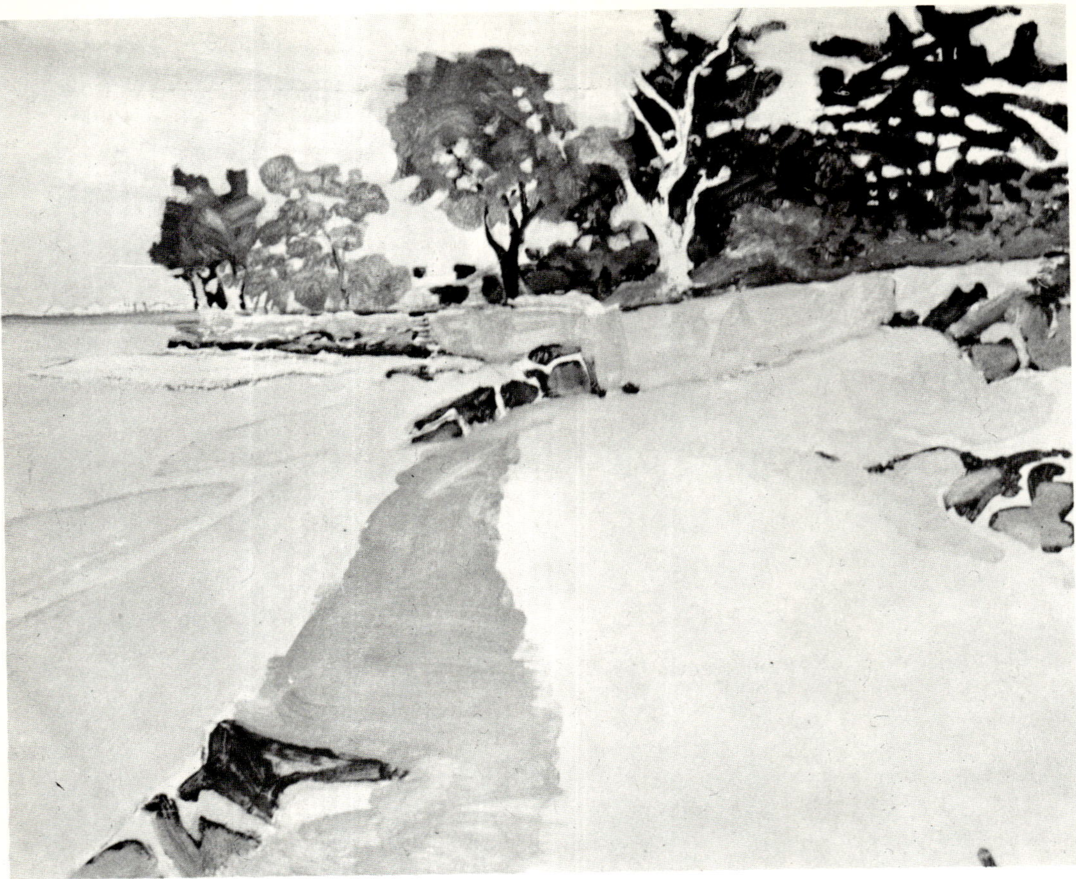

2

STAGE 2

These first shapes are somewhat tentative. Later, when all the elements are in place I will do the final shaping and altering.

There's a dramatic sweep to the sky that I want to catch and I put it in fast before it gets away. I'm feeling my way along now, letting my brush wander a bit, exploring the abstract possibilities and enjoying the effects as the paint goes on. Before the tide recedes any more I paint in the water. In an hour this area will be a mass of sea weed, mussels, and barnacles. Next, the sea wall, foreground underpainting and more foliage.

STAGE 3

Right about here is where I have to resist the temptation to start fussing over little details. The horizon gets a slate purplish color, then the sea grass, the dead elm, and some bright yellows and greens above the wall. I'm ignoring the high water line of flotsam that runs from center to lower left and give this whole area a semi-transparent wash of raw sienna, cerulean blue and white. All I want is a suggestion of this tidal debris.

Now, using opaque sky color, I go after the negative shapes in the sky, cutting back into the foliage, giving these forms their final shapes. I have eliminated most of the houses in the interest of simplifying.

3

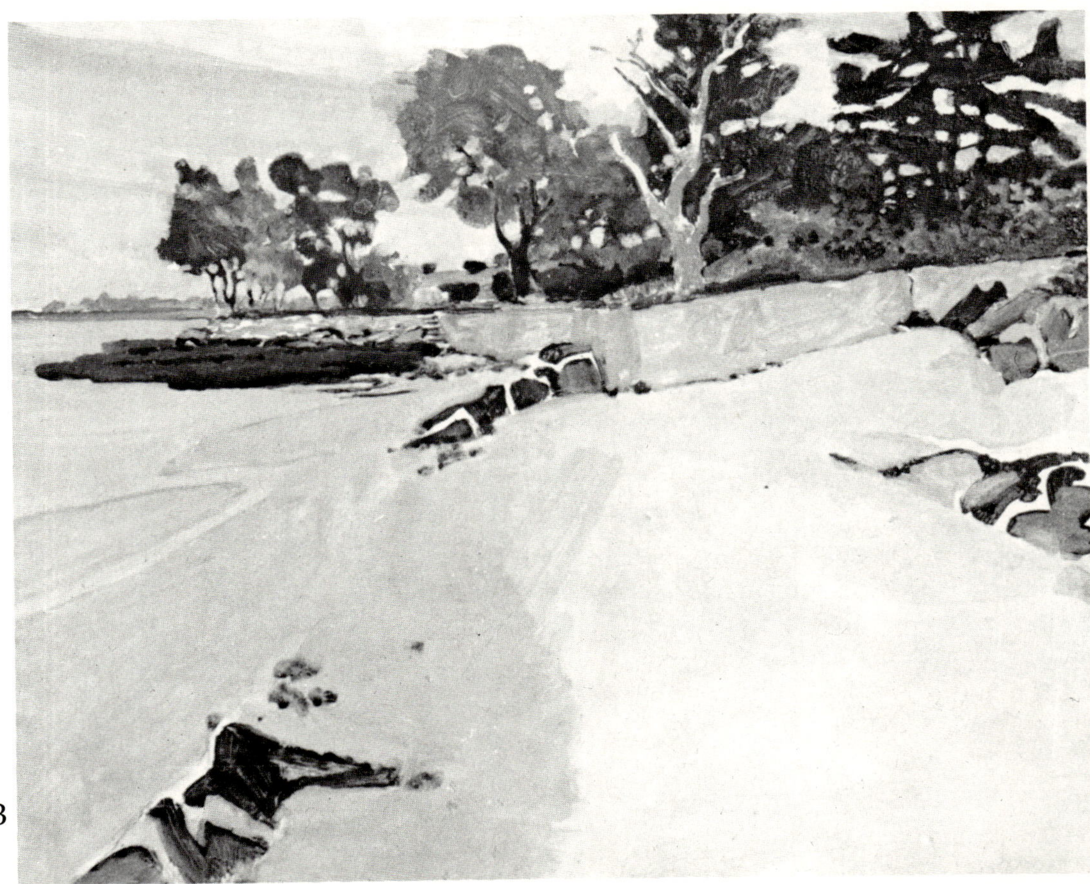

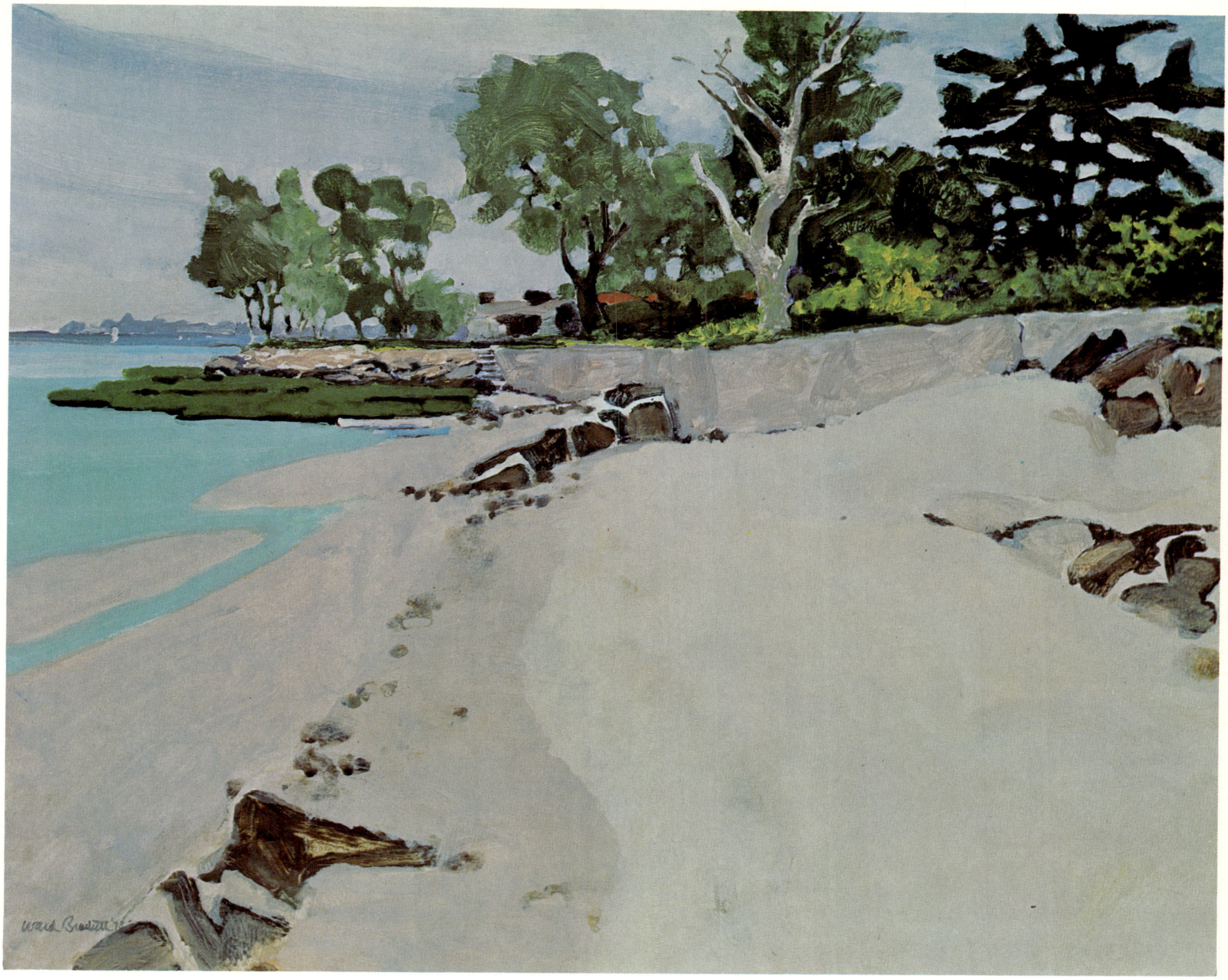

4

BLACK'S BEACH by WARD BRACKETT — acrylics

STAGE 4

In the last stage I rework the right foreground with some light, slightly translucent sand color. Notice that the wavy line running down the middle of the beach now connects with the edge of the tallest background tree. Some bits of brilliant yellow in the middle-ground foliage and finally a couple of boats to make the scene look inhabited and the painting is finished.

If you study the photograph you will see where I have taken liberties with the scene. The pine tree, for instance, was transplanted from several hundred feet away because I wanted it in my painting. The beach area, especially, had to be greatly simplified to keep it from overpowering everything.

The photograph was taken six weeks later after the diving raft had been hauled up for the winter.

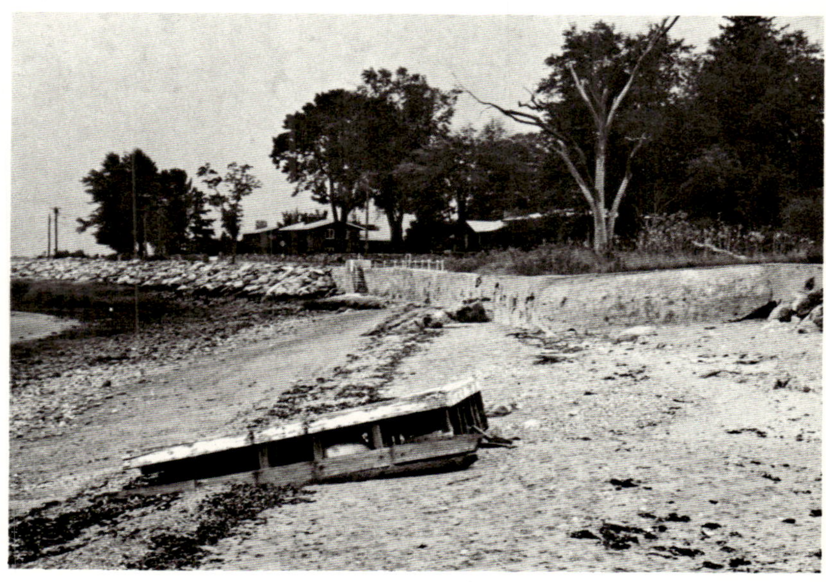

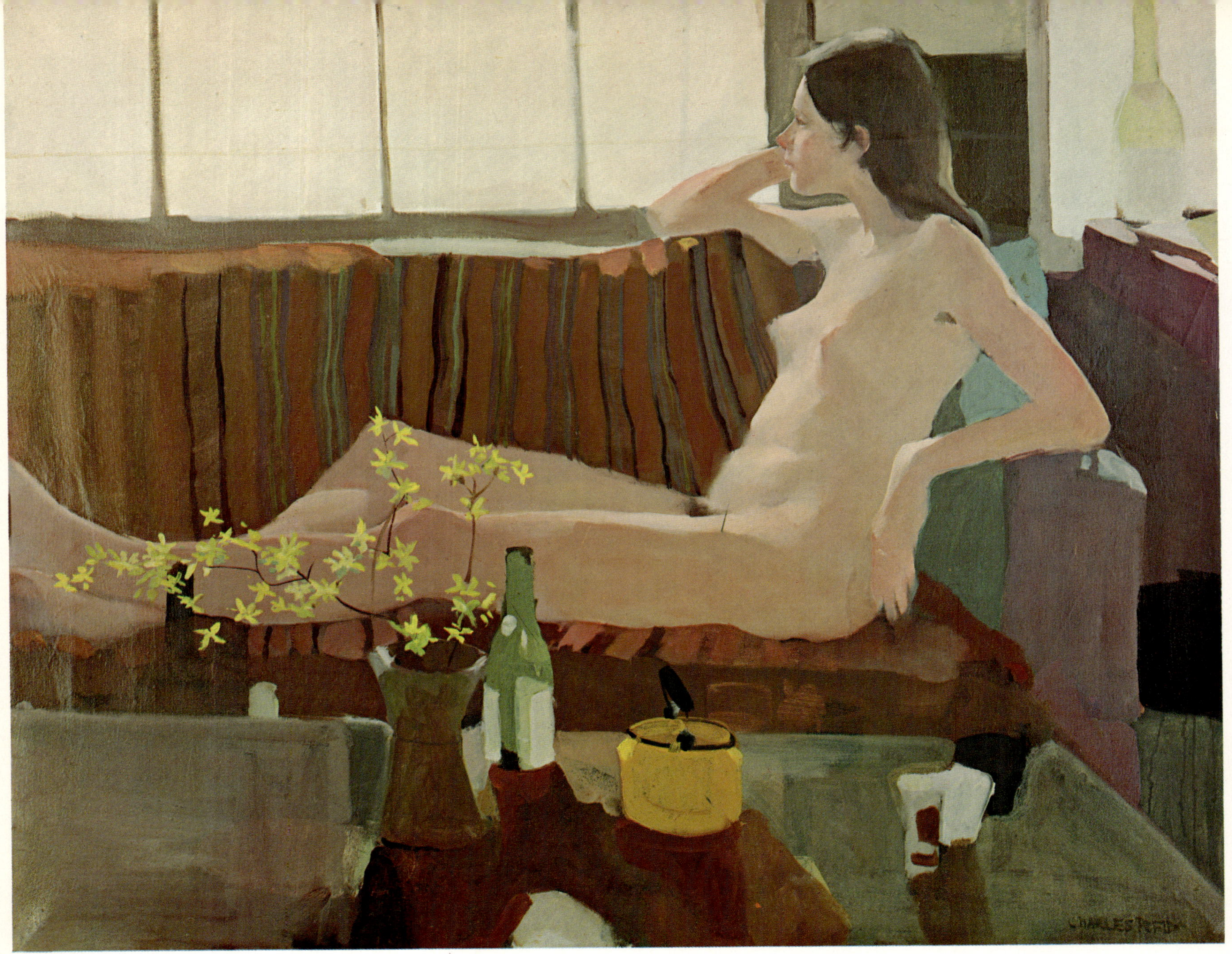

CHRIS by CHARLES REID

FIGURE PAINTING

Painting the human figure, especially the nude, is one of the hardest things to do that I can think of. There are far more problems to be dealt with than in any other kind of painting. Unless you are able to work outdoors, your first problems will be space and lighting. You will need strong, flat light on the model as well as good light on your painting.

Getting a good pose out of your model, especially an inexperienced one, can sometimes be frustratingly difficult. Anyone who has worked very much from the figure knows that frequently the best poses are "discovered" ones — when the model is taking a break or dressing or in a similarly unguarded attitude. There is something artificial and contrived looking about the "set" pose models usually get into. The model who is told to "stand with your weight on your left leg — put your hand on your hip — now look

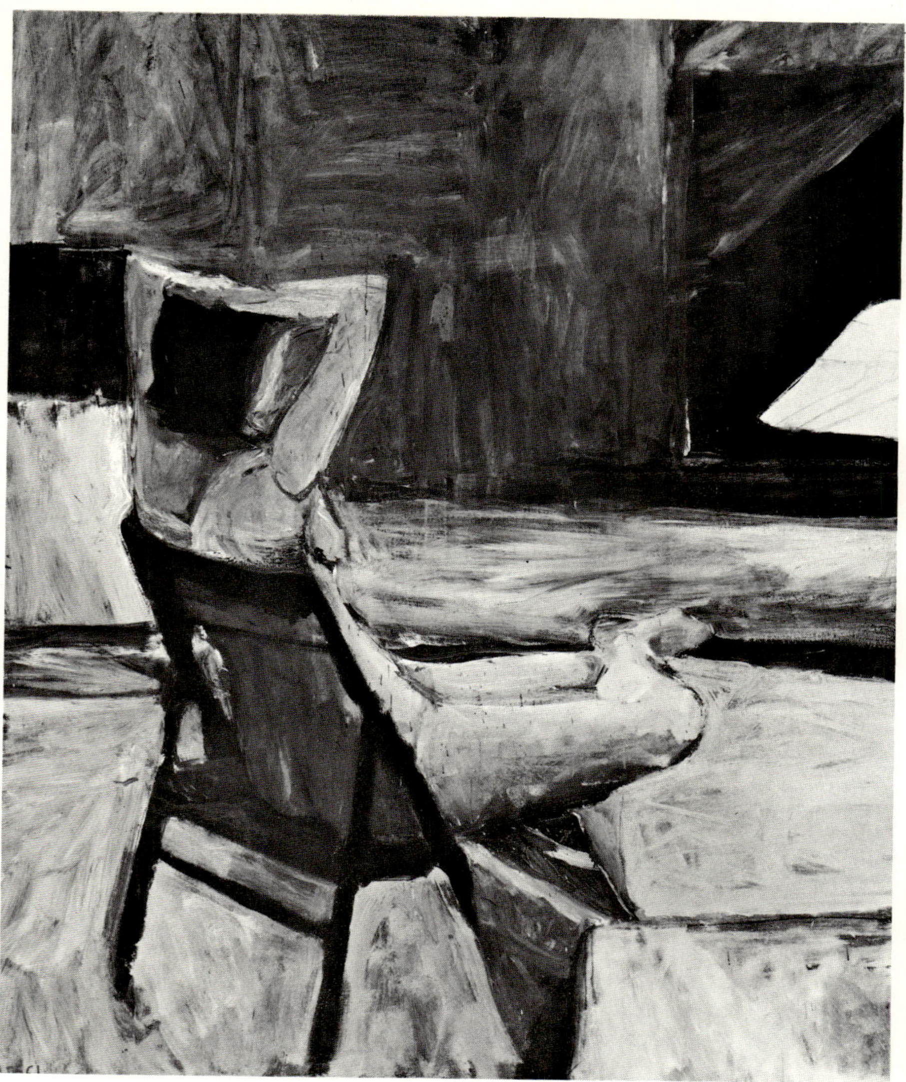

SEATED NUDE by RICHARD DIEBENKORN
Marlborough Gallery, N.Y.

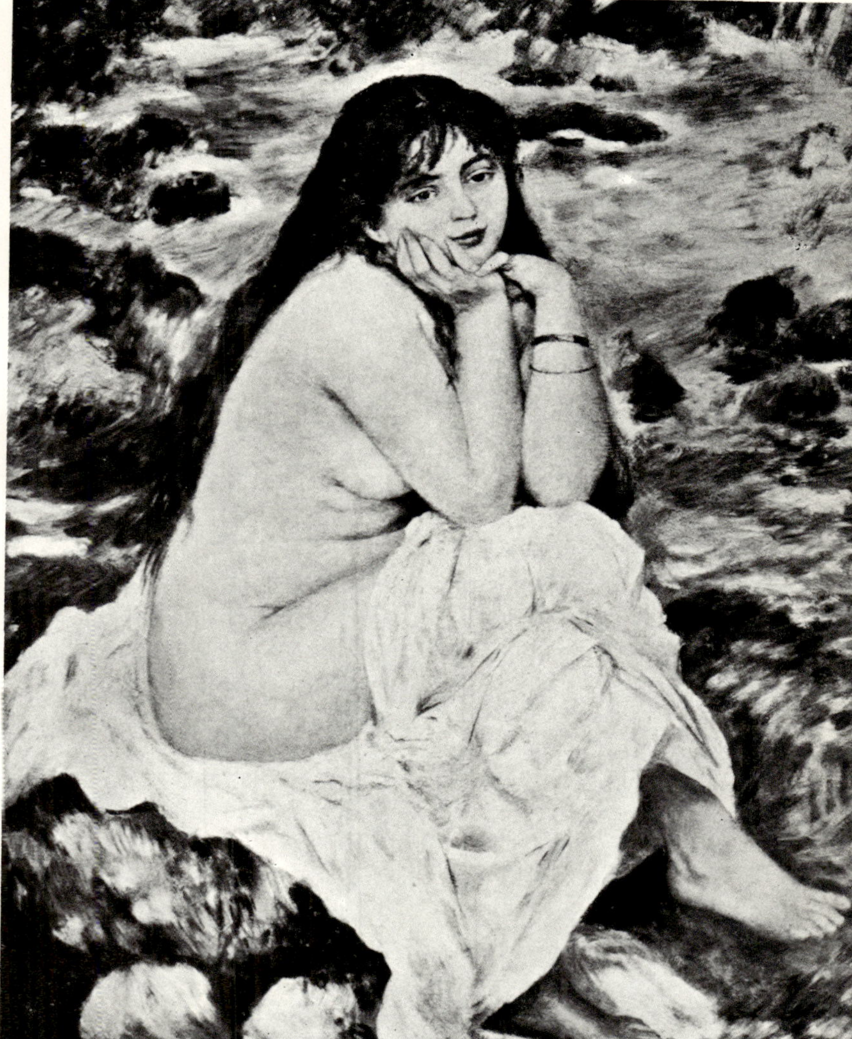

BATHING by PIERRE AUGUSTE RENOIR

over your shoulder" can scarcely be expected to come up with anything very exciting to paint. Try to avoid the art school pose. Work for "off beat," unexpected poses. Take note of the "awkward grace" of Degas' and Toulouse-Lautrec's dancing girls and prostitutes. Don't ignore the sensual aspect of the nude. Did you ever see a prissy nude by Gauguin, Rubens, or Modigliani? The best models, invariably, are the ones who are able to abandon themselves completely to naturalness.

Backgrounds should be kept simple and uncontrived if you want the figure to dominate. If the figure is to become an integral part of the picture plan you must keep a relationship going between it and all the other elements of the composition. For example — the curves (or angles) of the figure can be made and should be made to contrast interestingly and dynamically with any curves or angles in the background. There should be interaction between figure and background in the form of contrasts and repeats.

Painting in the company of half a dozen or so other people has its drawbacks. If you need total concentration to do your best work you will find them distracting. Also, you should have enough room to step back from your painting for a fresh look at it and this is not always possible in a crowded room.

But painting in a class or with a group is better than not painting at all. You are bound to learn something. Besides, not all figure paintings are done directly from the model. Many painters base their final work on preliminary drawings made from the model or even from photographs or from memory.

If there is one thing that separates the experienced painter from the amateur it's the way he mixes and applies his paint. So many beginners waste time trying to mix the exact color on the palette. It's better to approximate the color you want and try a little of it on the painting — where it can be compared with the colors next to it.

Do not add colors to your painting by mixing one color *into* another. Put down the color you want and leave it alone. You may want to change it later and, if you do, either scrape it out or cover it over. Mushing paint about on the canvas will neutralize colors and turn them to mud. It's far better to end up with an exciting combination of the "wrong" colors than with a dull, uninteresting color scheme of laboriously matched ones.

PAINTING a NUDE

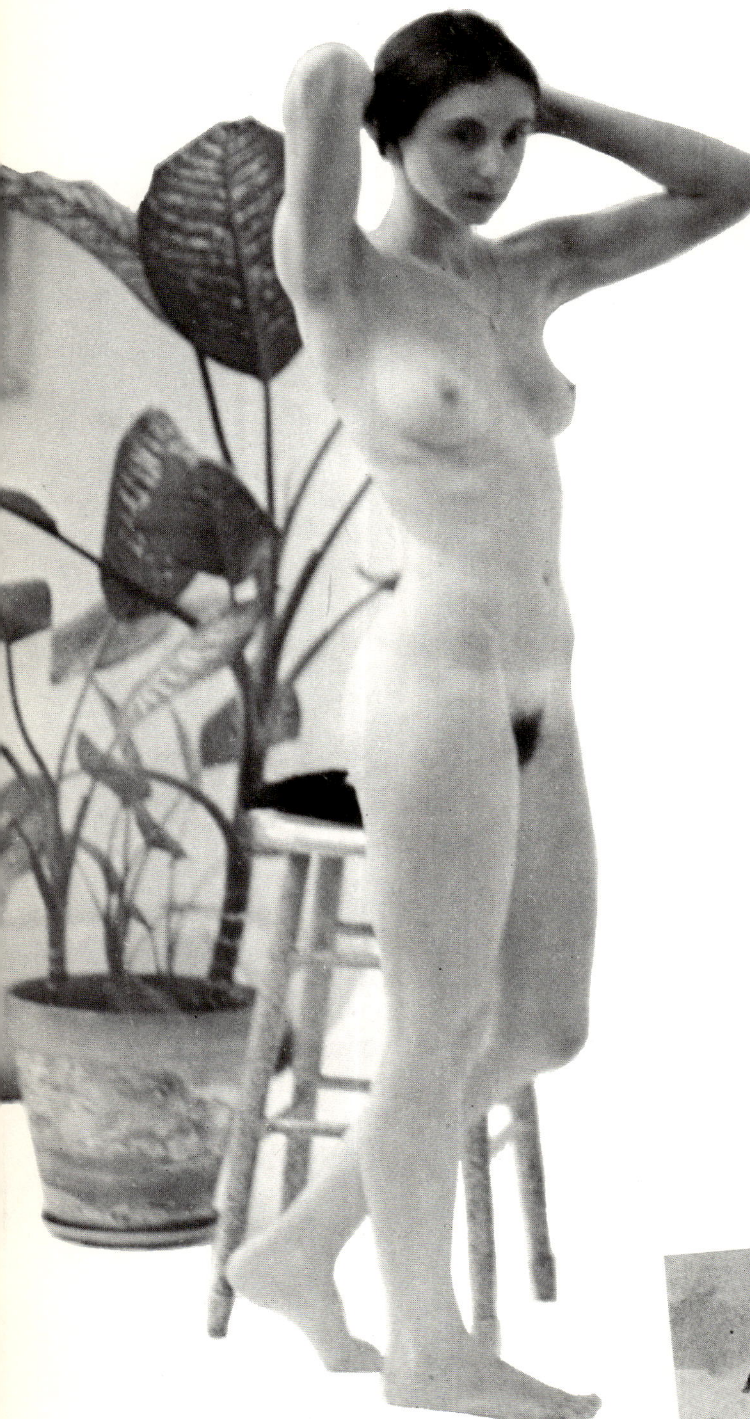

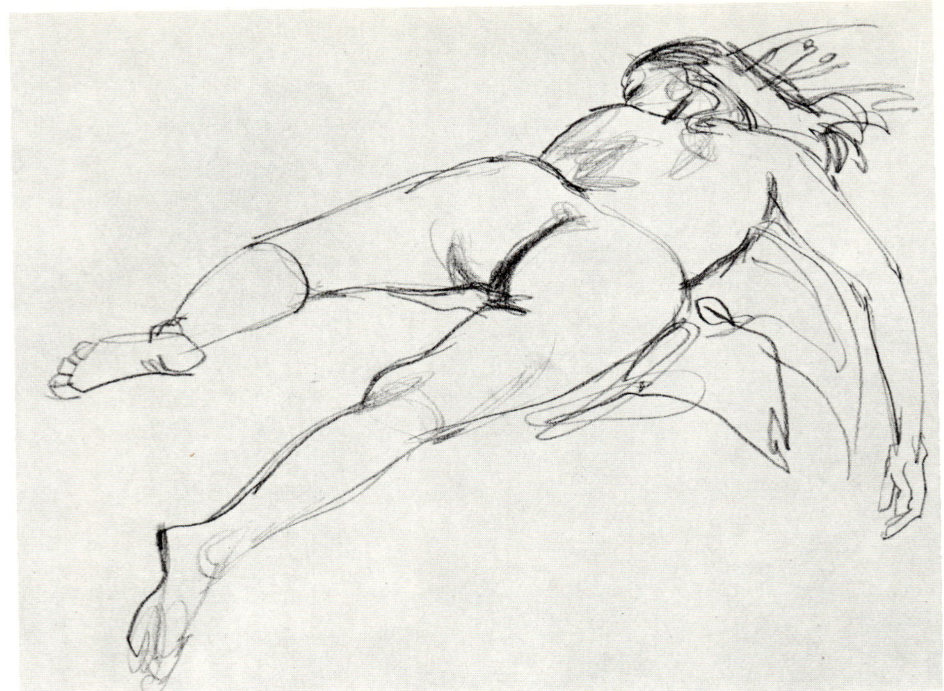

A

When you are standing six to ten feet from a human figure, especially an undraped one, structural form had better not be taken lightly if your objective is realism. In still life, for instance, all kinds of liberties can be taken with bottles, fruit, flowers, etc. However, the closer you stand to the figure, the more critical become the problems of proportion and structural form.

Working from drawings or photographs is one way to simplify the problem. Then, in a way, you are dealing with a two-dimensional subject instead of a three-dimensional one. But the next problem is naturalness and a feeling of three dimensions are often lacking. These illusions have to be injected into your painting more or less intuitively. This can be done, but it takes plenty of experience through trial and error. Whether you work from life, drawings, or photographs, you are going to need some kind of a formula. I have tried just about every method and every approach, using one system, then another, only to come back to an old way of working.

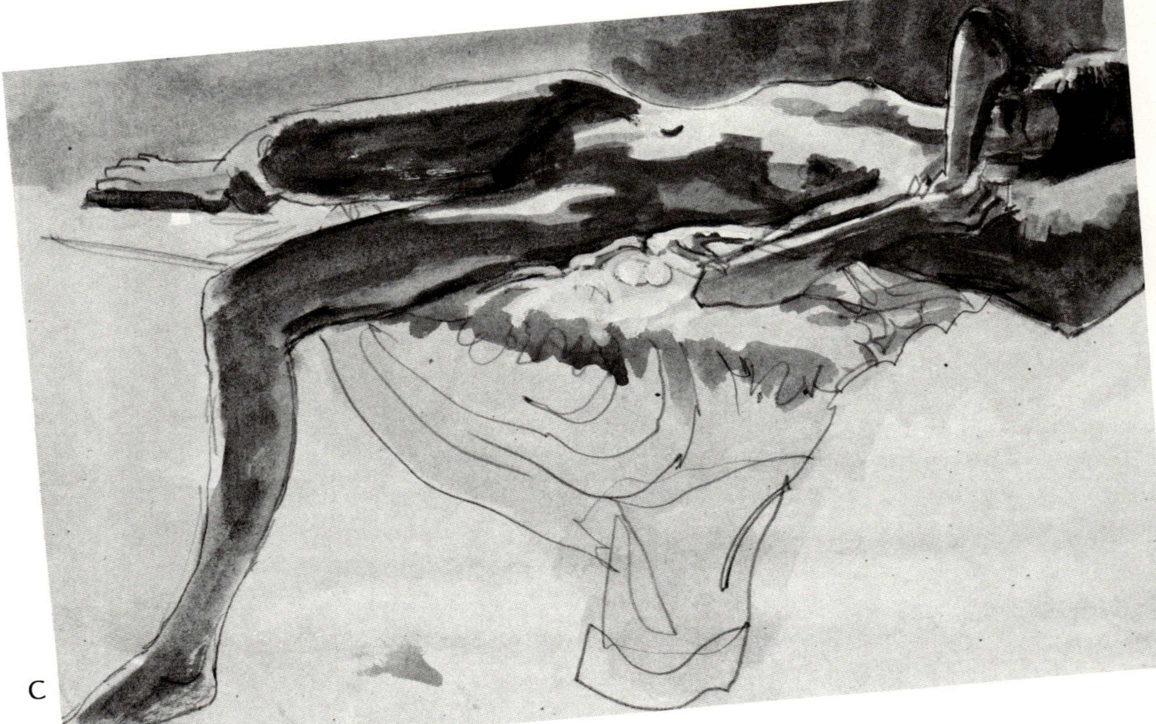

C

1

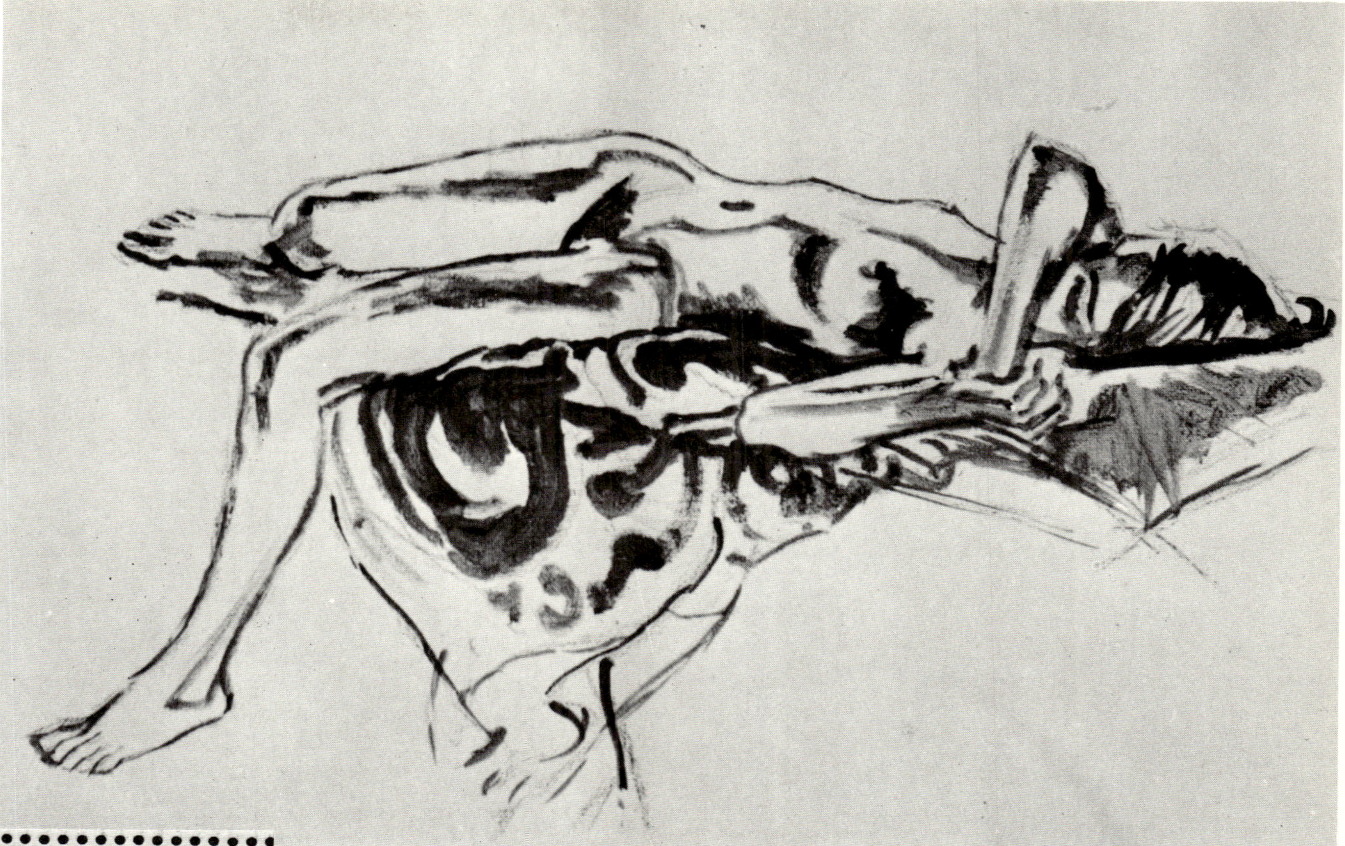

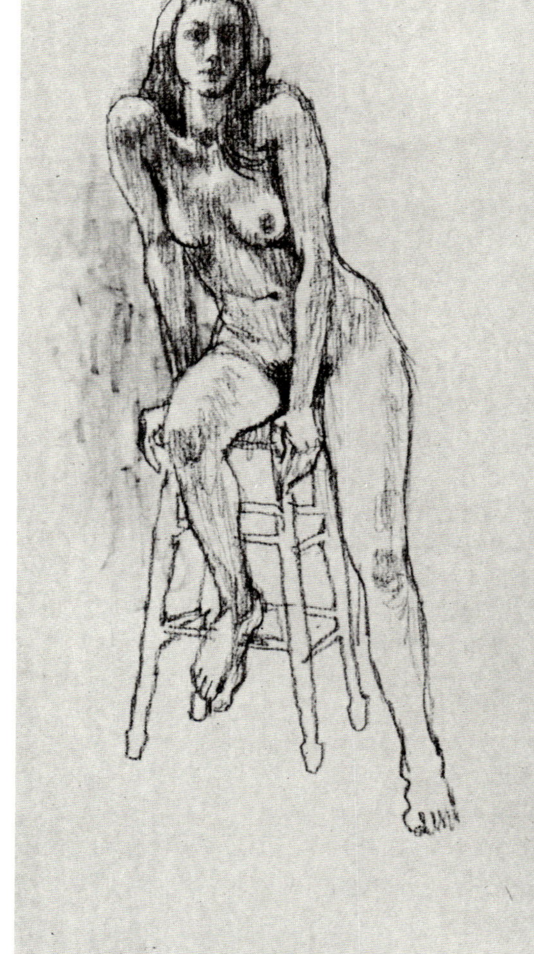

B

STAGE 1

In this demonstration let's take a formula not unlike the one used for the still life on page 73 and apply it to a nude.

Figures A, B, C, and D are drawings from my sketchbook. I'm going to take one of them, Figure C, and make a painting from it. I also took a photograph of this pose to refer to in this demonstration.

Like the still life and landscape, this will be a dark-to-light sequence, but this time I tint the panel first with a light wash of raw sienna and permanent green. Now I lay in the figure and robe with burnt umber, using a #2 bristle round. I try to keep a rhythmic, flowing action to this brushwork without bothering to follow the charcoal guidelines with complete accuracy. This stage of the painting should have plenty of dash and spirit.

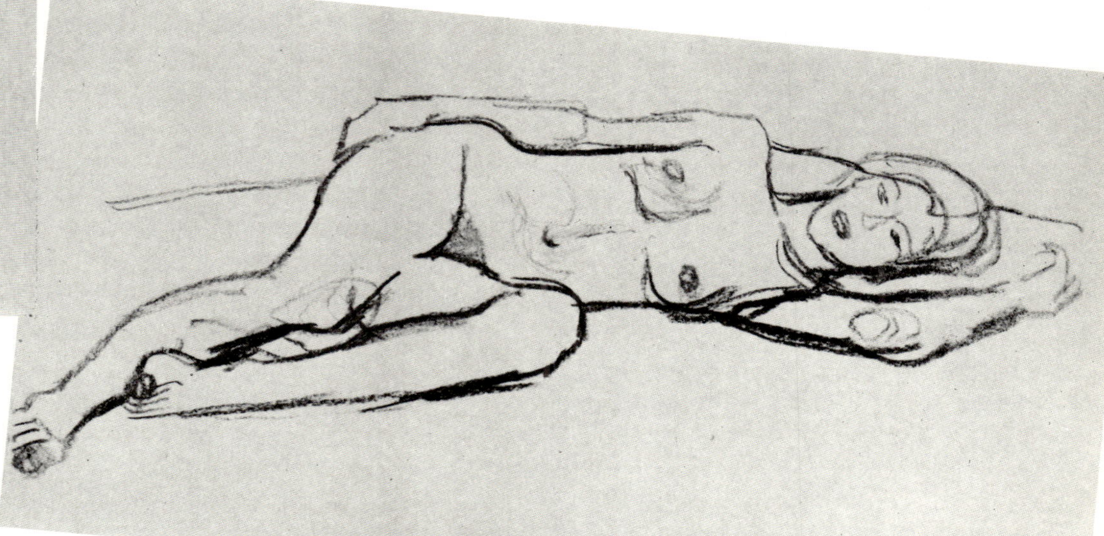

D

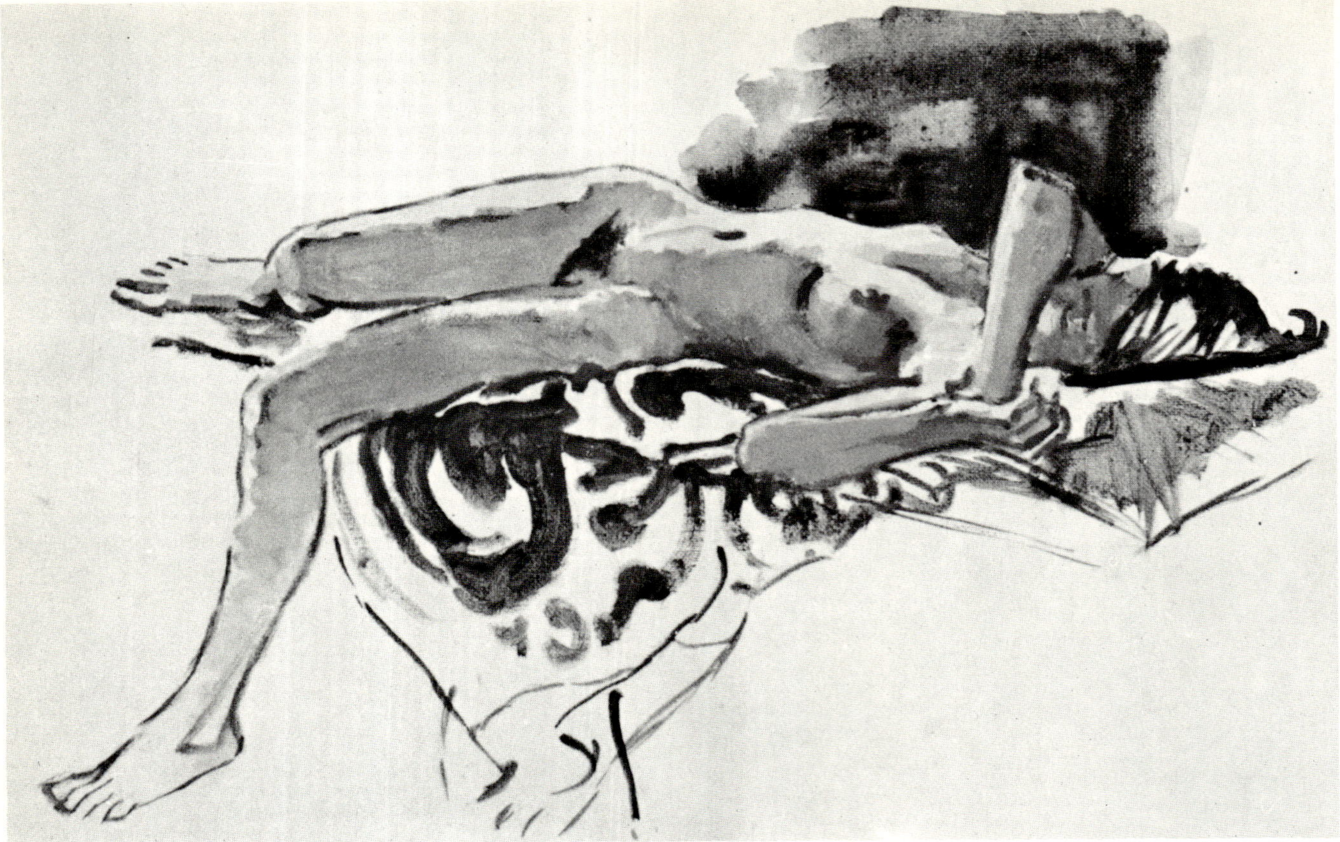

STAGE 2

The foundation is in. Now for the skin tone, starting with the shadow color. It would seem fairly simple to render this area in a single solid tone; but it would also be pretty uninteresting. Within this solid mass of color are many subtle variations and changes from warm to cool. In painting flesh I use the following colors: orange, cadmium red light, crimson, yellow oxide (ochre), raw sienna, burnt sienna, viridian, thalo blue, and a little, but very little, white. Sometimes it's hard to decide how to apply the paint — along the forms or across them. I've found that varying the direction of the brush strokes is more interesting and, in addition, seems to "knit" the painting together. However, the last thing I want to suggest is that there is any rule to this.

STAGE 3

Before doing anything more to the figure I indicate the robe in a soft pale green. Anything much stronger than this might make the figure appear to be floating in mid-air. This green, consisting of viridian, raw sienna, and just a touch of white, is mostly transparent — I want my underpainting to work for me. A word of warning about folds. Drapery is a fascinating subject in itself. If you allow your folds to become overworked or overcomplicated they are apt to upstage the figure. Keep them simple even if it means leaving them "unfinished."

In putting in the hair, I first reinforce the underpainting with burnt umber — then finish it off with burnt sienna, thalo blue and only enough white to lighten it slightly. It looks a little mousey here but I can liven it up later.

3

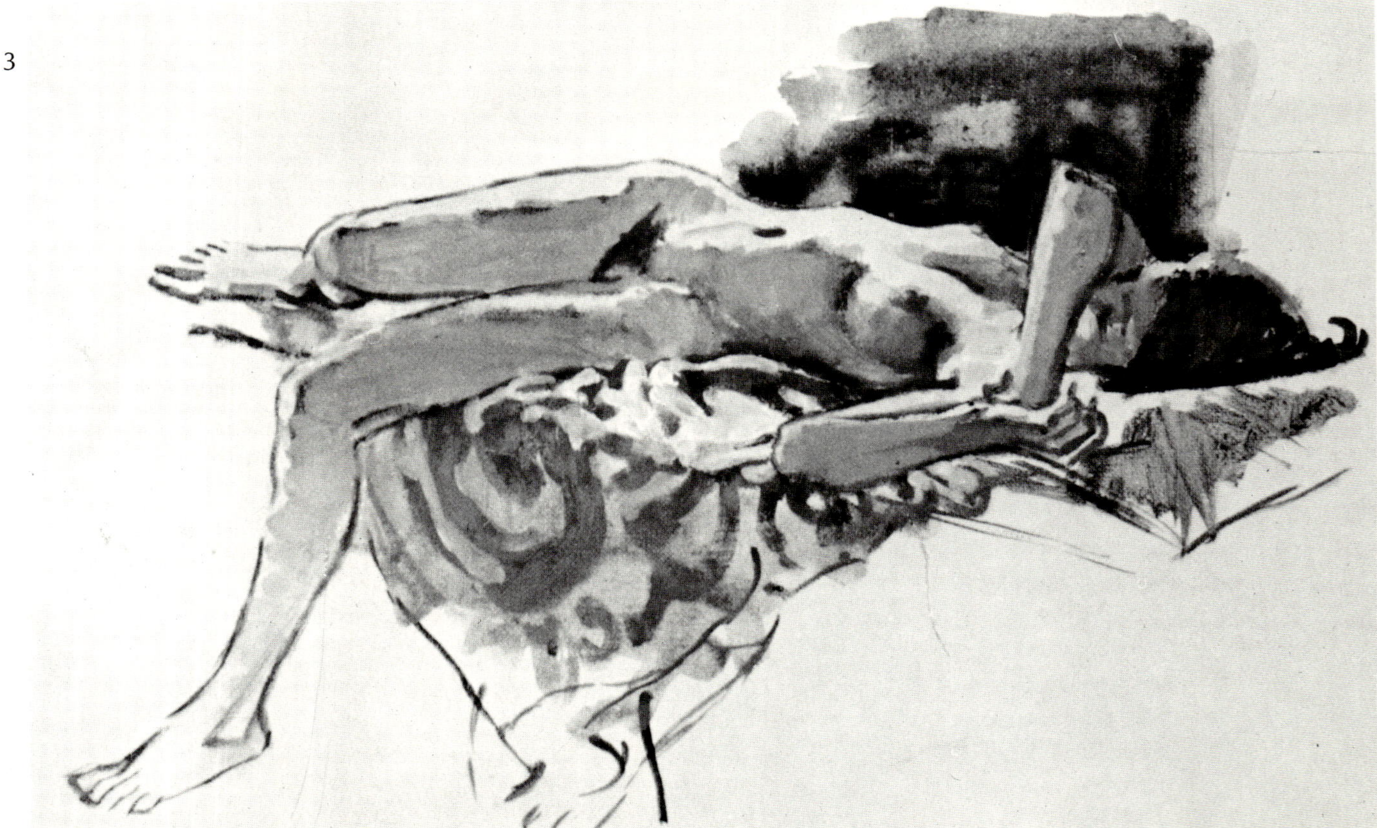

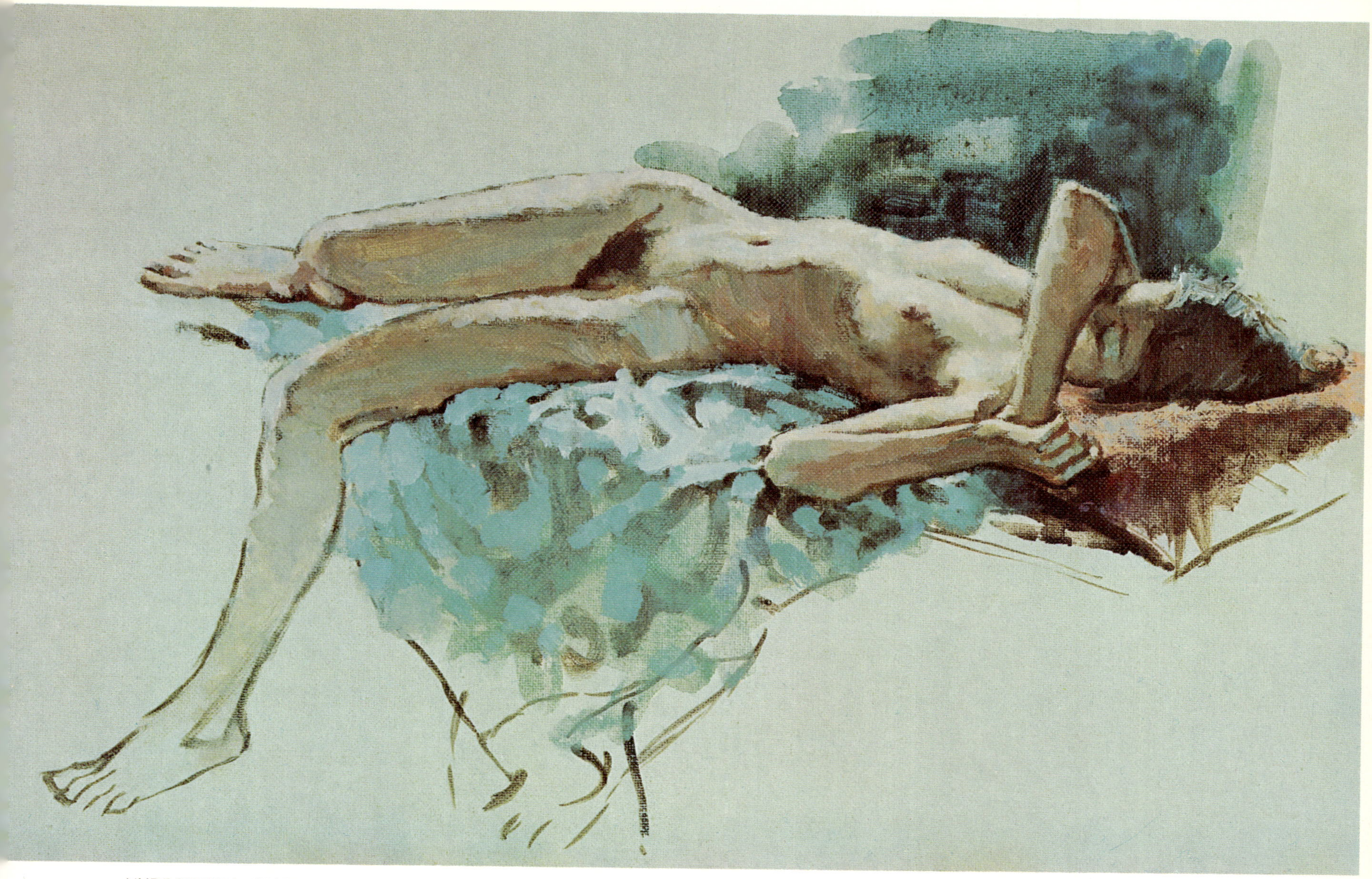

NUDE STUDY by WARD BRACKETT — acrylics

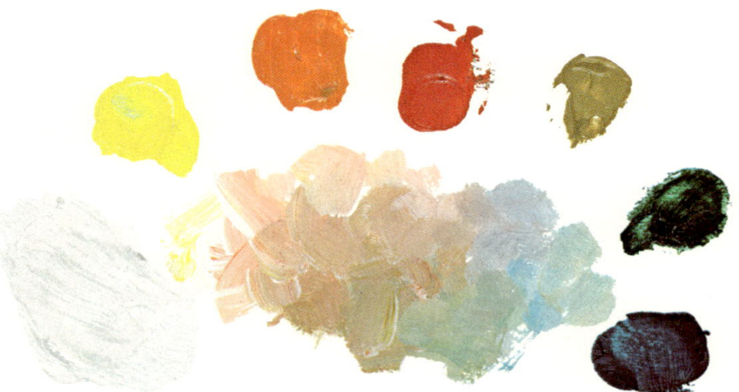

Range of flesh colors in light areas

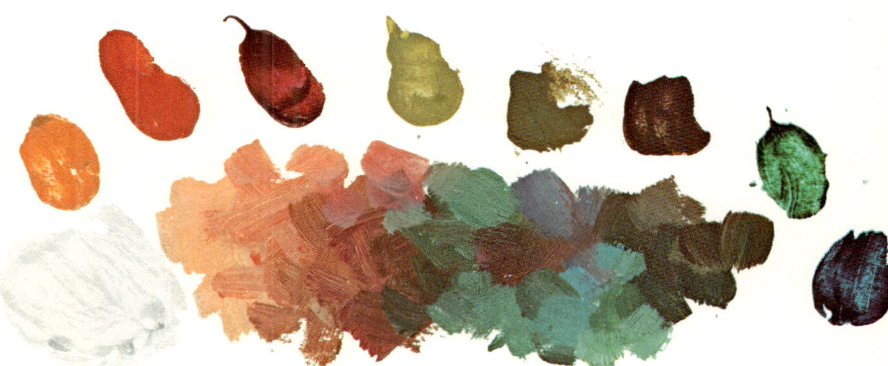

Flesh colors used in shadow areas

STAGE 4

In the final stage I get back to the light-struck areas of the figure. These areas require crisp, clear, extremely high-key colors that are very close in value. I use cadmium yellow light, orange, cadmium red light, yellow ochre, viridian and/or thalo blue for the cooler tints. And of course, plenty of white. Now I heighten the hair color a little with warm accents of burnt sienna, raw sienna, cobalt blue, and a dab of white mixed together. Then a few notes of local color are added to the robe. A touch of color in the pillow and I call it finished before I start picking at unessential details.

Learn to recognize when any one part of your painting looks right as an element of the whole design even though it may not seem to follow your original plan for it at the time. Leave it alone and develop other elements of the painting; then come back to it. Very likely, it won't need to be changed at all.

"How do you mix flesh tones?" is a question I hear about as often as any other I can think of. Aside from the obvious reasons of race and pigmentation other factors are just as important: light conditions and reflected color from surrounding areas for example. Flesh tone that appears one color in sunlight will take on an entirely different color under a cloudy gray sky. Reflected colors such as brightly colored clothing will affect skin tones considerably, especially in portraits. If I have any formula for mixing flesh color it might be the following combination, one I find myself using frequently: cadmium red light, yellow ochre, viridian green (or its equivalent, depending on the manufacturer), and white. These four colors will give a wide range of tones, from the palest blonde to rich, ruddy brunette. For cooling flesh tones there is no substitute for viridian. I'd be lost without it.

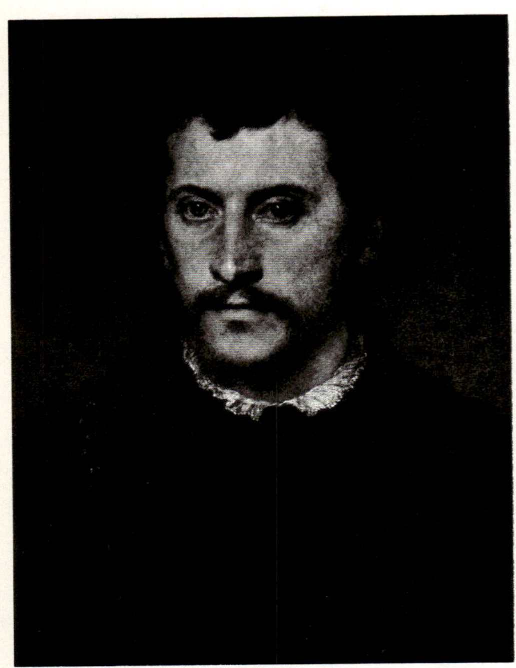

HOWARD, DUKE OF NORFOLK by TITIAN
Pitti Gallery, Florence

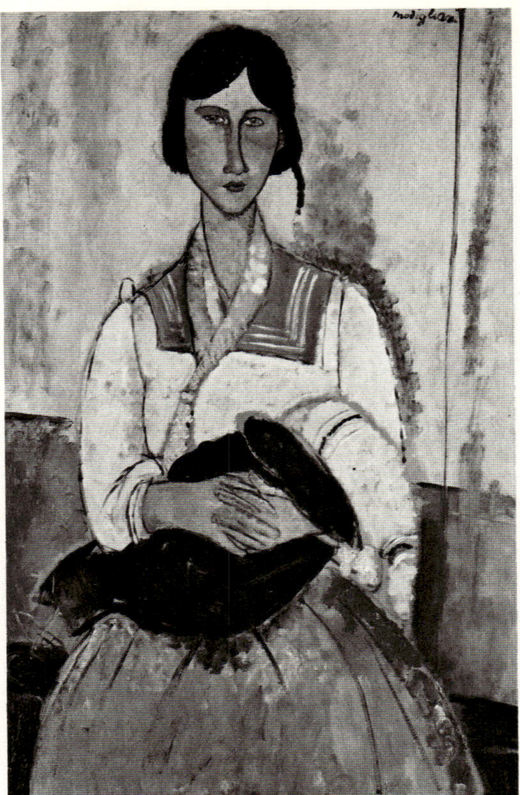

GYPSY WOMAN WITH BABY
by AMEDEO MODIGLIANI
National Gallery of Art, Washington, D.C., Chester Dale Collection

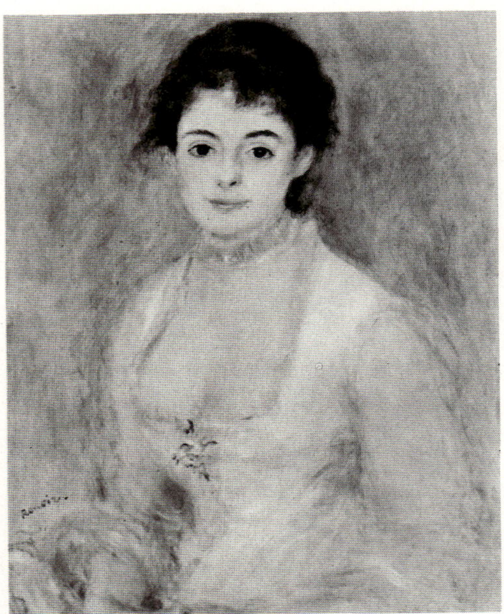

MADAME HENRIOT
by PIERRE AUGUSTE RENOIR
National Gallery of Art, Washington, D.C., Chester Dale Collection

PORTRAITURE

Portraiture is not a special kind of painting. Most of the problems of technique, color, composition and paint mixing are the same as in any other kind of painting. But there are one or two big differences.

To begin with, in accepting a portrait commission you are agreeing **in advance** to produce a painting, subject to the approval of the buyer. Conditions are similar to those encountered in taking on an advertising or editorial assignment. You are dealing with a "client" whom you must satisfy or it's no deal. And the client is rarely the subject.

Another difference, whether you work directly from the sitter or from photographs, is the person-to-person relationship that necessarily is part of painting a portrait. Your attitude toward people will be put to the test. You must be willing to seek out the best in people regardless of what personal feelings you might have about them. In many cases you will have to adapt your working time to suit their convenience. If your temperament can't take this then you had better leave portraiture alone.

One of the first problems you must cope with is the setting: where to pose the subject — in the studio, in the home, or out-of-doors. Each situation has its own advantages and disadvantages. Ideally, the perfect situation would be one in which the artist had both unlimited access to the sitter, and an outdoor setting complete with useable backgrounds, with a soft, natural light. But this sort of combination is rare. The disadvantages and restrictions imposed by weather, changing light, insects, etc., are often overwhelming. It's pretty hard to compete with a swarm of mosquitoes for your sitter's attention.

The sitter's home can make a good setting. He's at ease in his own milieu and is more apt to relax in this atmosphere. But the light is usually bad and hard to control. And, if the working area is cramped, it is sure to inhibit your approach. Moreover, people generally take a dim view of the mess the painting process makes.

This leaves the studio. Working in your home ground has obvious advantages. The climate does not vary, light is controllable, and its business-like atmosphere will allow a freer approach when it comes to slapping on the paint. I would like to stress the importance of complete freedom in applying paint in the early stages of the painting. If you have to worry about paint running down and dripping on somebody's Persian rug, you are apt to hold back some of the force that should be going into the painting, especially in the early stages.

Wherever you decide to work, have your subject move around freely to find a pose that is characteristic, interesting and natural. If he doesn't relax at first, if you sense any tension, keep him moving until he does relax. A sitter who is not at ease cannot possibly fall into a natural, un-selfconscious attitude, and will get into just about every conceivable pose but a natural one. Remember that most people never have had anyone stare at them so long and so intently in their lives. Give them plenty of time to get used to you.

Next, try to find the best possible attitude for your subject. Find out if he looks better sitting or standing. Determine which side of the face is the best side (many people will already know) and arrange the pose to favor that side.

Choose a position where the sitter is on about the same eye level with you or you will run into problems of distortion. A good rule here is to work standing if he is standing, and

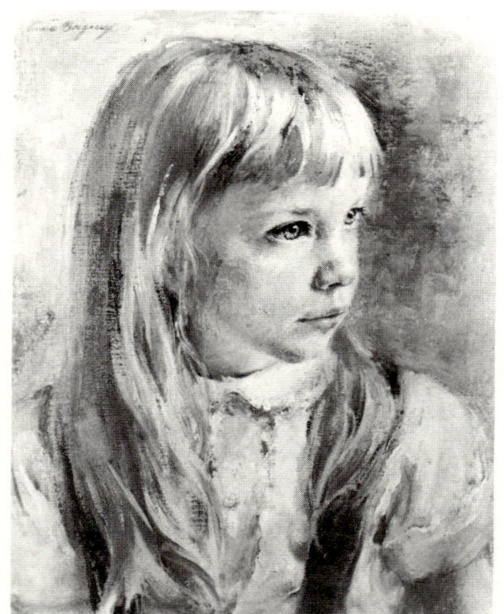

PAMELA by ARIANE BEIGNEUX

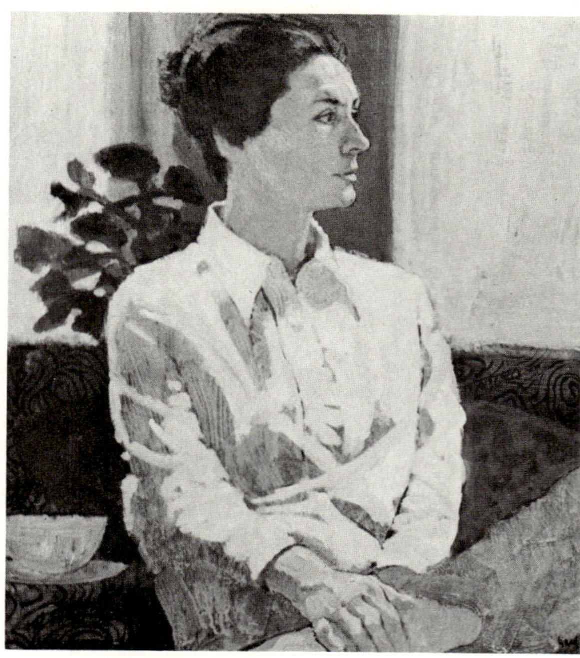

KATHY by WARD BRACKETT

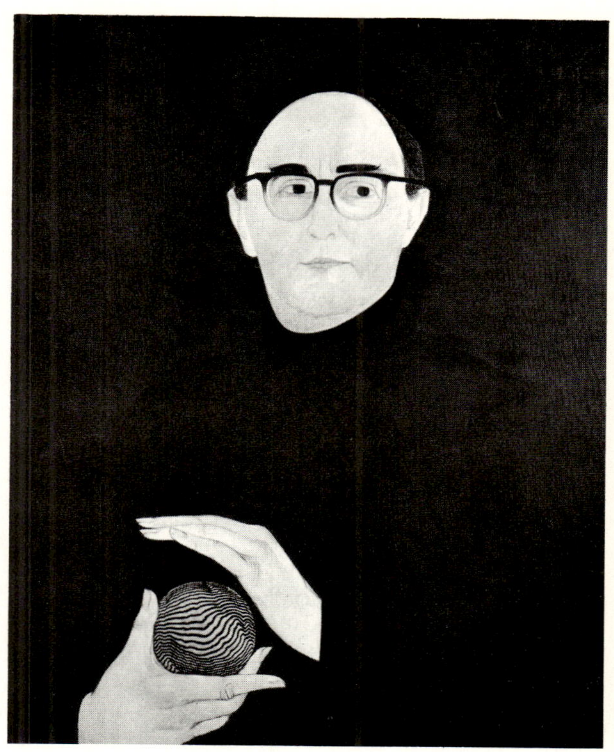

PORTRAIT OF HENRY PEARSON by WILL BARNET

to sit if he is in a sitting position. Or, if you prefer to stand when you paint, a model stand about two feet high will raise a seated model to eye level.

I rely heavily on preliminary sketches. This stage for me is the testing ground for anything that is characteristic about the model. This is the time to look for gesture and attitude that is typical of the subject. The design of the portrait emerges from this stage. Once the pose is decided, the composition will take shape as a natural outgrowth. This is one of the limitations of portraiture. The composition must be subservient to the pose, which must be directly related to the attitude of the sitter.

Do not crowd, unnecessarily, the head and hands. The detail and complexities of these areas need simple and uncomplicated space around them to set them off properly. Study Rembrandt, Velasquez and Modigliani for examples of open space and simplification. Their backgrounds usually were held to a minimum of detail which never competed with the figure. With a full-length, standing portrait, where there is more space to fill, avoid the temptation to get complicated just because there is room for more detail.

Try to fit your colors to the personality of the sitter. High key colors seem to be more characteristic and suggestive of youth. The sitter's outfit, too, has a great deal to do with this decision. Choice of costume, incidentally, should be the prerogative of the artist, although this is sure to get you into an argument sooner or later. In any event, the best costume is one that will not look dated in a short time. It also should be simple and classic in design. Discourage your sitter from wearing his "Sunday best," instead of something more comfortable. Otherwise he may never relax and is likely to have that "sitting-for-his-portrait" look.

Hands contribute eloquently to a portrait. They help to characterize the sitter by conveying some of his personality. It's the gesture that does it rather than painstaking detail. Be sure the hands are relaxed and unforced. A hand can be a very useful device in supporting the construction of the knee it is resting on, or the crook of an arm it is nestled in. Hands are particularly useful in balancing a composition, but remember never to overwork them or they will distract from the rest of the portrait. They should always remain an adjunct to the rest of the figure.

If your subject wears glasses most of the time, then he cuts a more familiar figure with them than without and should be painted wearing them. However, glasses should be suggested with a minimum of detail. Let a highlight here and a cast shadow there do the work. Don't let them look like outlines around the eyes.

It is risky to make drastic changes in the color of any dress or costume after flesh tones have been established because you can throw the color balance completely off. And always keep at least a touch of background color in the figure.

Simplify your folds. They can be seductively distracting if you don't. They should not be allowed to compete with the more important things: the face, the hands and the composition. Folds become superficial decoration if they do not convey some feeling of the figure underneath. Observe how they respond to the action and attitude of elbows, wrists and knees, for example. Practice drawing the seated figure and you will see how, anatomically, it seems to be stacked and balanced upon itself. Accenting the right folds will reflect

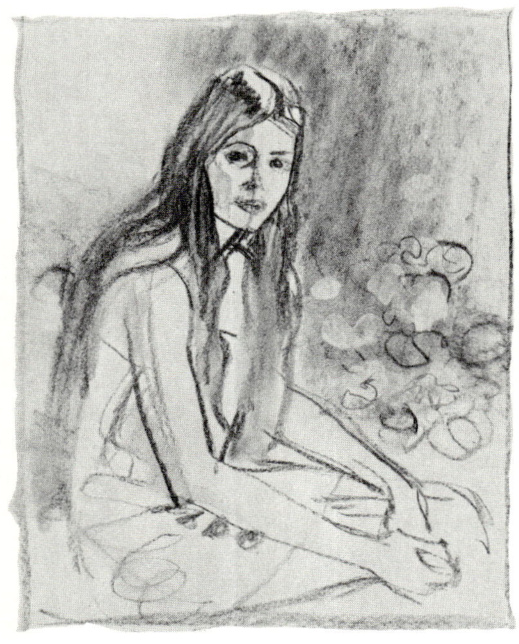
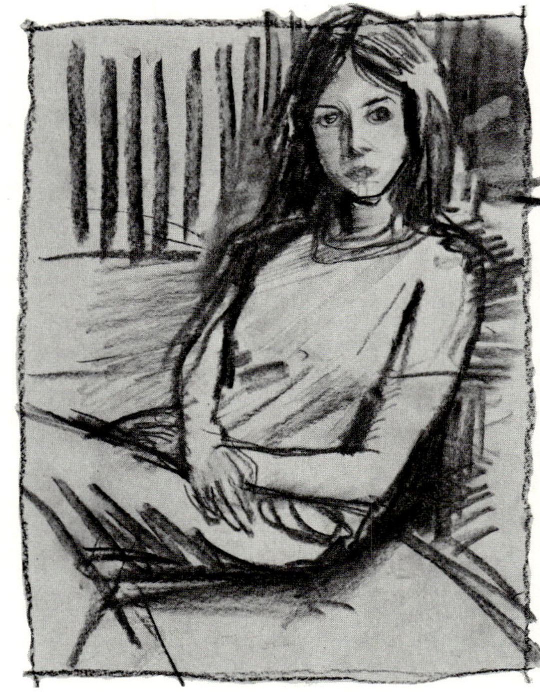
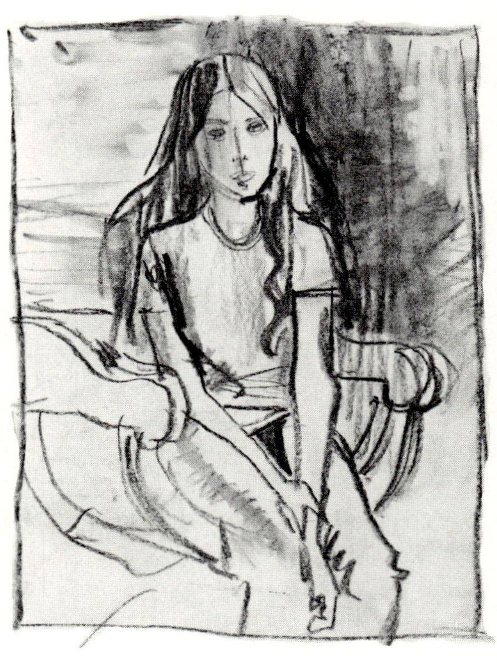

PAINTING a PORTRAIT

this action. Look for a good gesture in folds and state it simply and boldly.

Don't slight the background. Be especially careful how you "fake" any detail in this area. Unless you have a special talent for innovation, you will be better off taking what's there, if it's at all useable, and adapting it to your foreground figure. If the background is not useable, don't try to change it; move the sitter to a more sympathetic setting. Then, if you still have trouble, I would suggest you use the simplest background possible — a sheet thrown over a screen, or a blank wall. Put in the background at the same time you paint the head and the rest of the figure if you want to avoid a "pasted-in" look.

A portrait should be easily identifiable when viewed from across a room. If it is to have carrying power at this distance there has to be something characteristic about the tilt of the head, the set of the shoulders, the attitude of the hands. Look for an idiosyncrasy of expression or gesture in your sitter. If the nose is a little crooked or the mouth a bit lop-sided, don't be afraid to accent it. Some of the most compelling, personalized portraits actually border on caricature.

Establish a price before you take any commissions and stick to it. Start out with a modest price tag on your portraits; you can always go up. One suggestion is to gauge your price to the size of the portrait; most painters prefer to operate this way. They usually work in three or four different size ranges. A typical plan, starting with the smallest would be:

1. The head alone (16″ x 20″)
2. Head and shoulders (20″ x 24″)
3. Three quarter portrait (head, shoulders and hands — (24″ x 30″)
4. Full-length portrait (according to size of subject, pose and background).

These sizes, of course, should not be used inflexibly. They are merely a suggestion. You can take liberties with the proportions too. Sometimes a portrait will adapt itself better to a square shape or a horizontal one, but usually for a standing pose an elongated vertical shape is more appropriate.

The scale of a portrait is quite another matter. In checking the proportions used by the great portrait painters, from Velasquez and Rubens down to Sargent and Augustus John, I found that they usually painted heads about four/fifths life size; or in other words, somewhere between 7½ and 9 inches from the top of the head to the chin. If a portrait is scaled much smaller than this it begins to lose importance. If it is larger than life size it will appear to come forward, out of the frame. Also, I feel, there is something about an oversize portrait that is not entirely life-like and natural looking. In portraits where realism is not the goal (see Will Barnet's painting on page 89), where the whole concept is an abstraction from naturalism, scale is of little importance.

There are times when you have to be ruthless with yourself. Whenever I find I have overworked a portrait; when the features, for instance, have gotten stodgy and tight, or out of relation with the rest of the head, then I know it is time to take drastic action. One of the most futile things I could do, at this point, is to continue hacking away. It is better to make a fresh start, even if that means taking out the whole head and some good painting along with it.

A fitting title for this chapter might be, "Doing Portraits for Fun and Profit." Painting portraits of people is how I make my living. As an illustrator I have had to learn to use a camera. I've also had to learn its limitations.

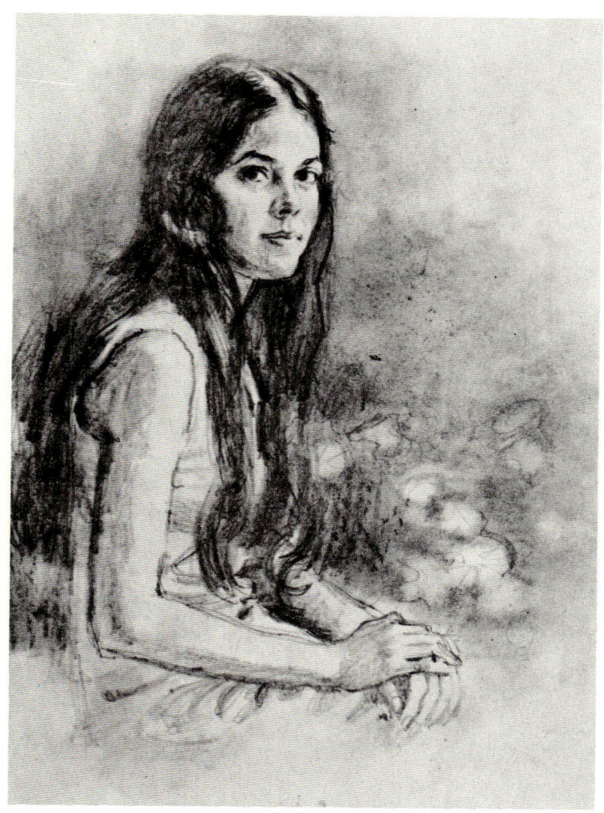

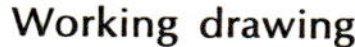

Working drawing

1

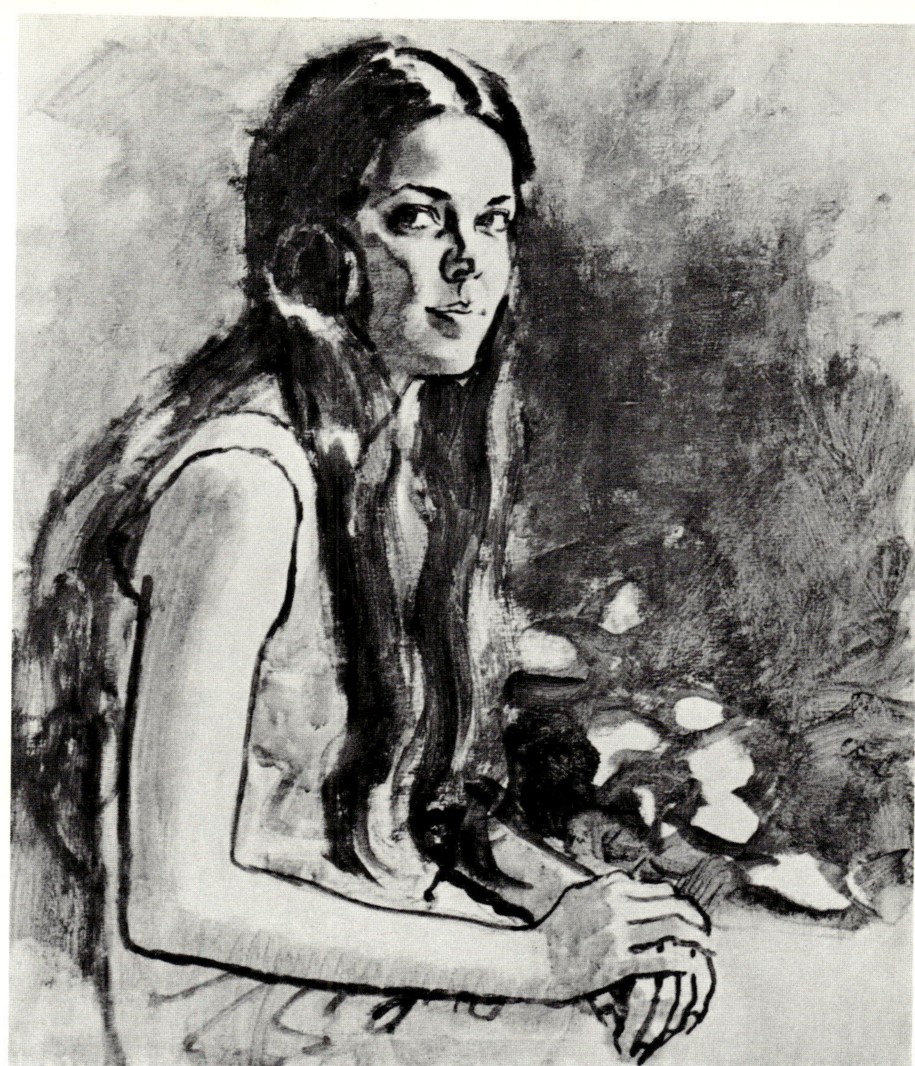

Nowhere is photography so misused as it is in portraiture. There's no doubt that the camera is a very handy labor-saving device. But too many painters use it as a means of saving themselves the trouble of drawing. It takes a lot of experience to know how to use photographs without becoming dependent on them. I would suggest that you avoid them at first and stick to the direct approach until you feel you know what you are doing. Even then, don't lose touch with direct painting. Try to get some of it into every portrait you do. Even an hour of concentrated work with the model will make a marked difference in bringing life and naturalness to a portrait that is based on a photograph.

Remember that a camera cannot "see" in three dimensions. It will interpret the turning edge of a cheek or nose as a flat plane, with no feeling of receding. The airiness and atmosphere surrounding a figure is lost to the camera. What's more, the camera cannot select what it sees nor can it emphasize what needs to be emphasized.

This is why a portrait derived entirely from a photograph will so often betray itself by a certain mechanical two-dimensional quality. The likeness may be there but the structure is lacking because it is lacking in the photograph.

I'd like to take a typical commissioned portrait and describe its development and growth, from the first exploratory studies to the final finishing touches. I would rather you didn't think of it as any kind of demonstration of method, process or technique, but rather as a chronicling of events. What I do is not necessarily what you should do! It is simply one man's way of doing a particular portrait and dealing with its particular problems.

Debbie made a very pretty subject. She has a flawless complexion, good coloring and regular features. In fact, she is so attractive I could see that it might be difficult to keep the portrait from looking like a soap ad.

Our first sitting was spent making some quick charcoal studies, three of which are reproduced here. She looked so photogenic I decided our next session would be spent taking pictures. I had her change into a very simple summer dress and move outdoors where the light was strong but shaded — not direct sunlight. Using a 35mm camera with a 105mm lens I began shooting, keeping her on the move, trying to avoid too much direction and deliberate posing. I did not want to end up with a "bridal portrait" look, if I could help it. This shooting session yielded two pictures that I used in making a composite study. This "working drawing" is the basis for the portrait. In it, drawing, modeling, and much of the tonal pattern are fairly well established. The next step is to transfer this drawing by projection (see page 121) onto a canvas of primed Belgian linen. For this I use a stick of natural vine charcoal, laying in only the guidelines.

STAGE 1

Stage 1 shows the lay-in with acrylics. It was painted freely and loosely, a brush drawing done standing up. I used a thin mixture of ultramarine and yellow ochre for this basic underpainting. This is a color that is quite neutral, one that will be compatible with the colors that follow. Gesture and drawing have to be strongly stated at this stage if they are to hold up later on when I begin the refining process. In many respects this is the most important stage in the growth of a portrait.

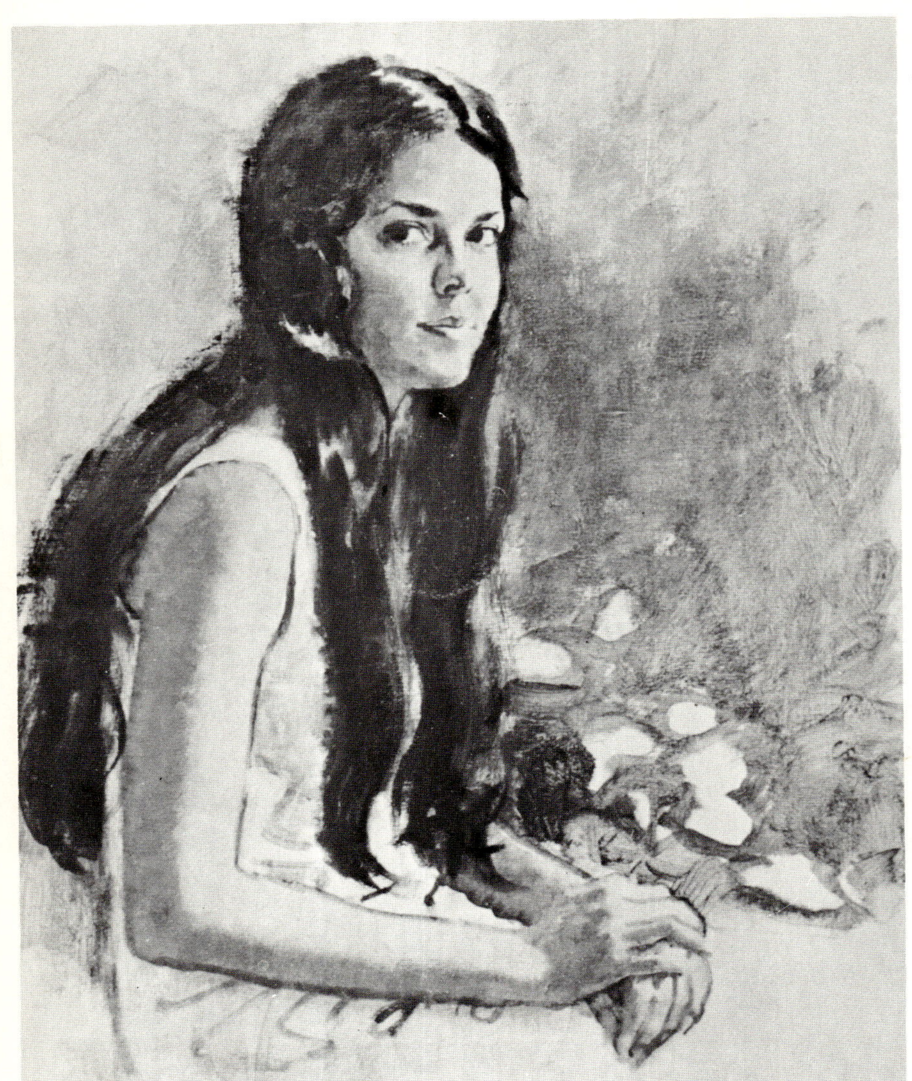

2

STAGE 2

Now, I am ready to switch to oils. This is a good time to get back to the subject. So far everything has been based on my sketches and photographs. At this sitting I establish the color of her hair and skin. I am still working broadly with fairly large brushes. First the hair. I use burnt sienna with a little yellow ochre and ultramarine for this. Next, the skin tone, starting with a thin pale undercoating "stain" of cadmium red light, yellow ochre, and a bit of viridian.

Here, using these same three colors, plus titanium white, I begin gradually to build up the flesh tones, working from **dark to light,** with increasingly thicker paint. Then some warmer, lighter notes are introduced in the hair and some indication of color in the eyes. Finally I get rid of the blank whiteness of her dress with some soft, neutral green; something like the background color but lighter and quite transparent. I do not use linseed oil; only turpentine, and I use it generously where maximum transparency is called for, as in the underpainting.

3

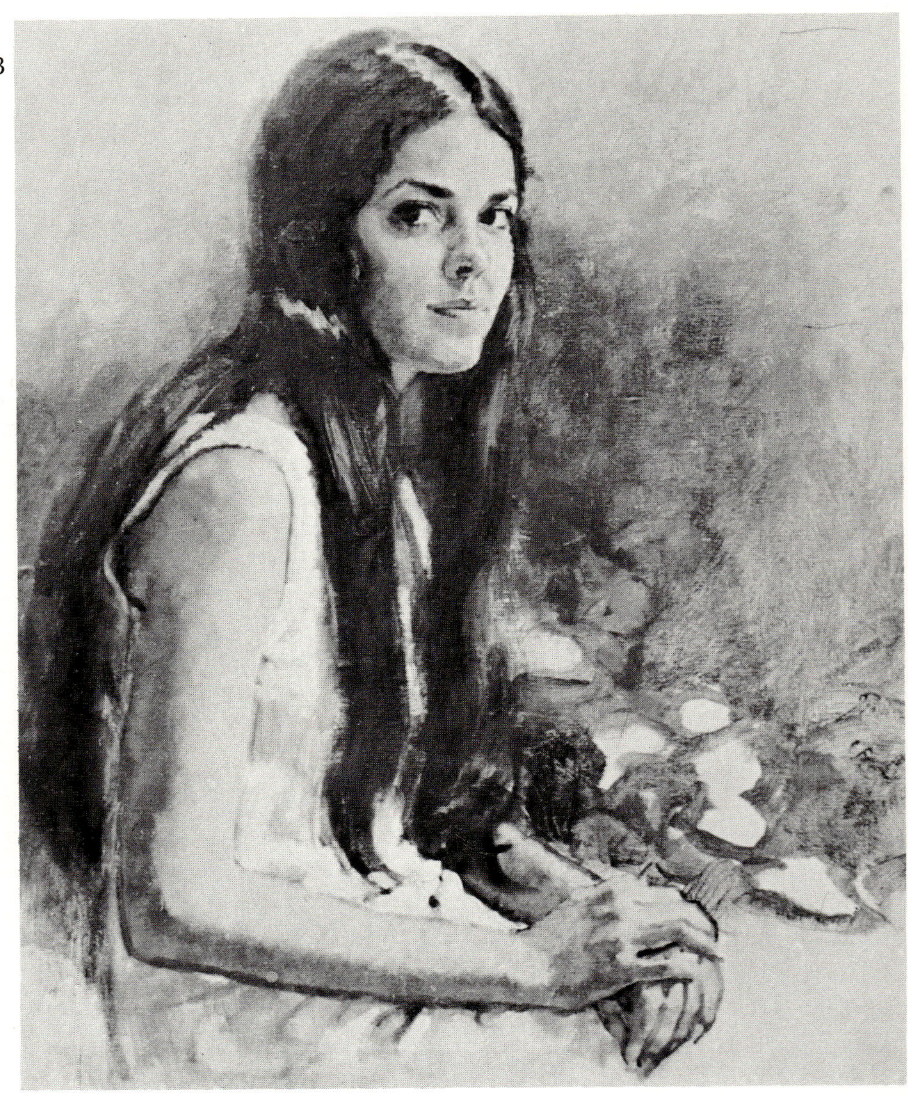

STAGE 3

The dress is now brought to a near-finish stage with off-white tints of color, consisting of cobalt, alizarin crimson, yellow ochre and white. Some of the original accents need strengthening at this point. I use the original lay-in color for most of these. Her hair is lightened with yellow ochre and cadmium orange. Now the background also needs lightening to give the head a bit more prominence.

STAGE 4

Now for a long, hard look at the painting to decide just how much more work it needs. The hair is still a bit unresolved. Hair that is soft and loosely arranged, such as this, has to be built up in layers starting with a softly defined mass of a single tone, then worked toward lighter and lighter accents.

Some final modeling around the features, highlights for the eyes and lower lip, and the figure is finished. The last things to go in are the touches of local color and some semi-transparent scumbling in the background to soften it and give it "atmosphere." Finally a little prayer that I haven't overworked it.

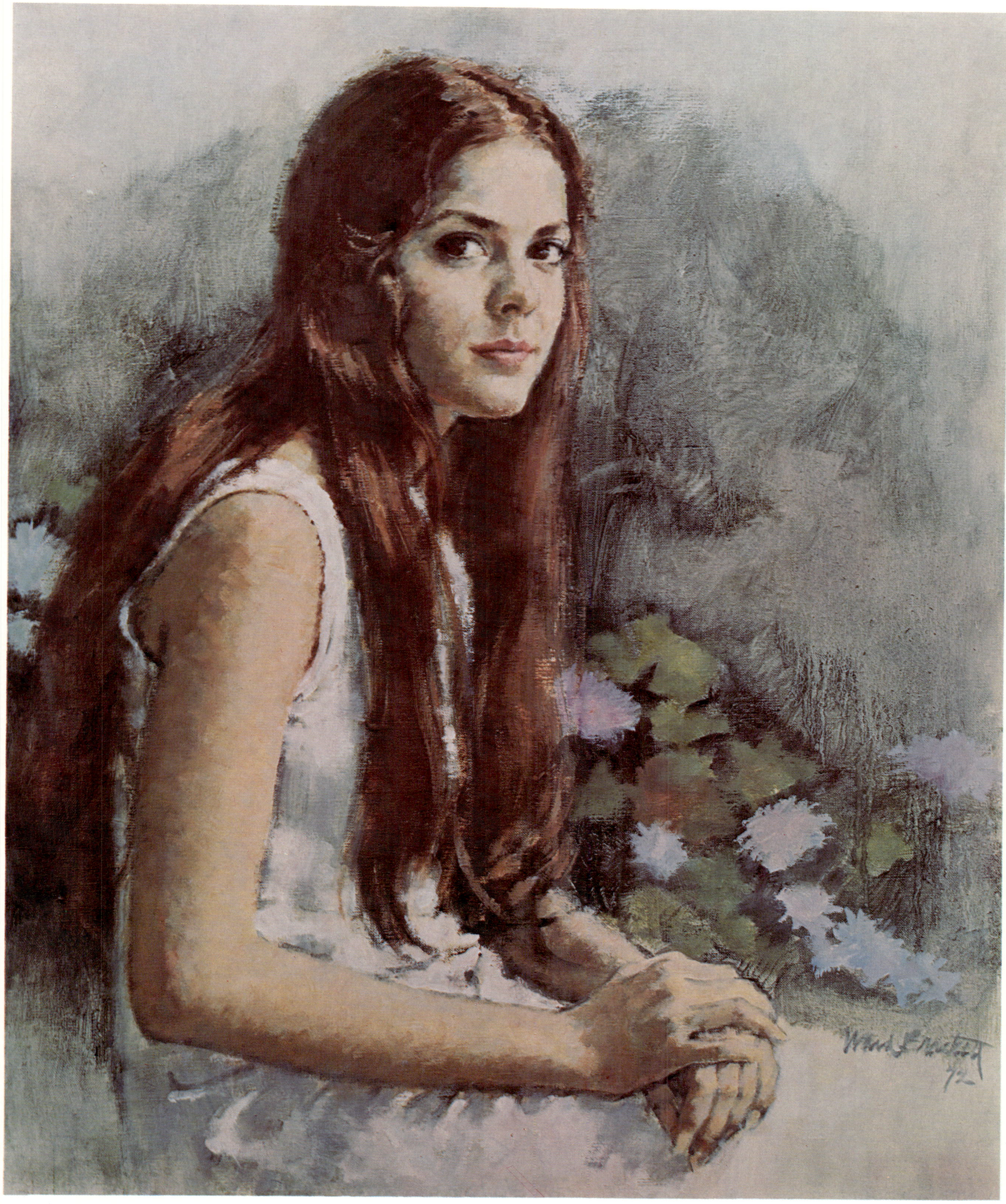

DEBBIE by WARD BRACKETT — acrylics and oil 4

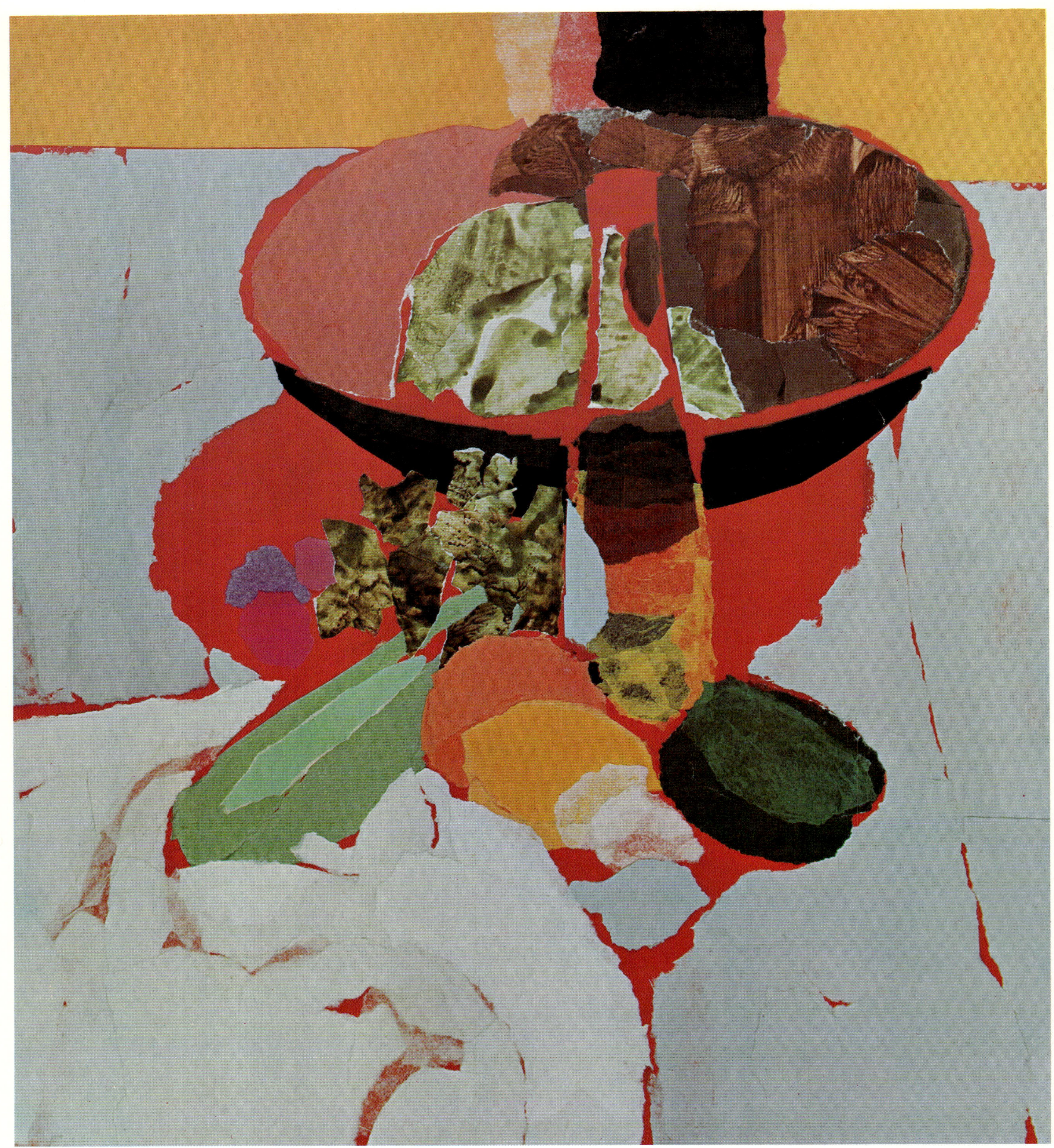

STILL LIFE IN RED by WARD BRACKETT — collage

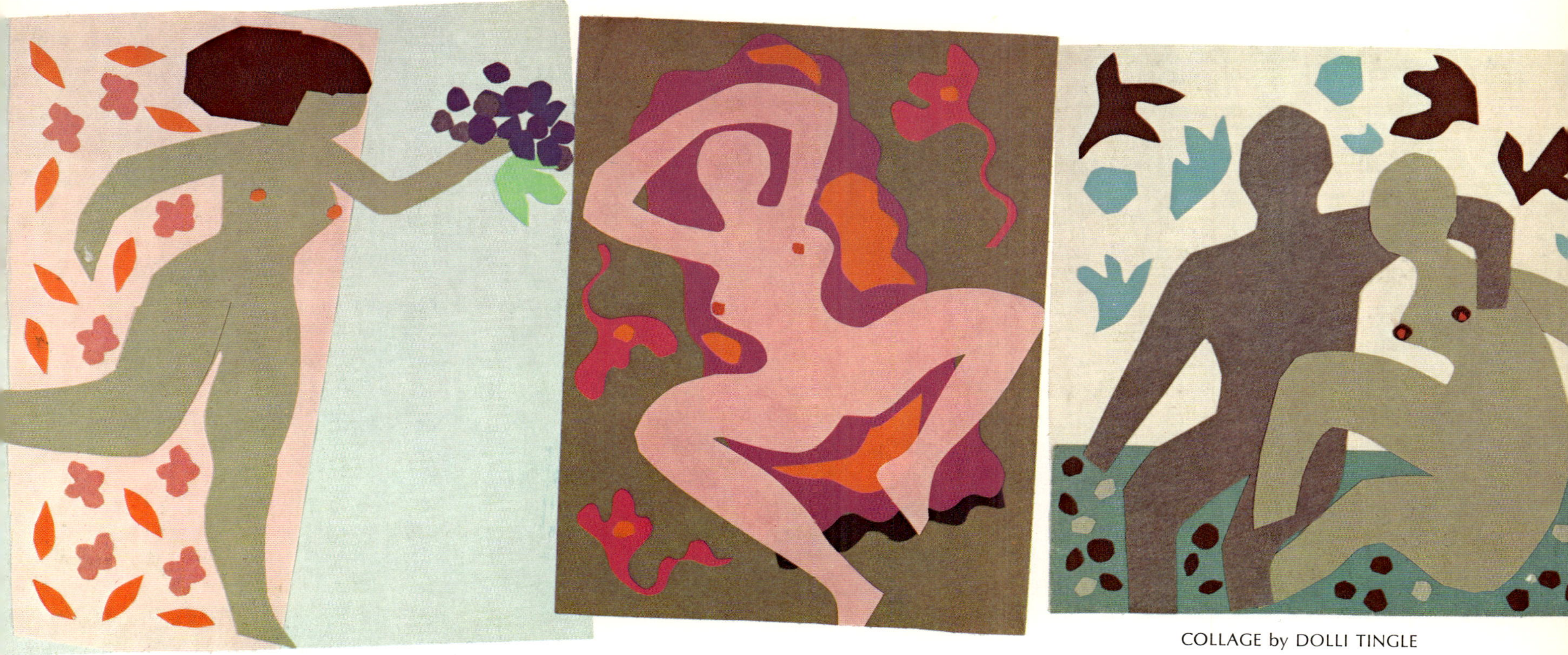

COLLAGE by DOLLI TINGLE

COLLAGE

Collage making really began hundreds of years ago as a pastime when people first started cutting and pasting bits of paper, souvenirs and other curios into scrap books. But it was not until the twentieth century that this folk art was adapted to a serious art form.

Modern collage made its debut quietly in the course of some early experiments by Braque and Picasso, wherein actual printed matter was introduced for the first time as an integral part of the design. Soon they began combining painting with unheard-of materials: metal, sand, chair caning, and oilcloth, for example. By the twenties collage had come to be accepted (by the art world at least) as a medium important enough to stand on its own, along with painting. Other movements, Cubism, Dadaism, Surrealism, Expressionism, and finally Modern Abstractionism, have all utilized collage with great success. Artists like Gris, Arp, Schwitters, and Marca-Relli, to name only four, have developed their own highly individual styles around it. Collage is the forerunner of some of today's pop art, op art, junk sculpture, kinetic art (moving mechanized contrivances), and just plain happenings.

In painting, the material (that is, the paint) is inert. But in collage, the materials are anything but inert; they demand attention — they do not become anonymous like the brush stroke, the swipe of a palette knife, or the wet-on-wet effects of water color.

With collage, the materials themselves have presence. The torn theater ticket, the snapshot, the piece of fabric, or the found object are all capable of evoking memories and experiences of their own. This is especially true of intricately detailed things like printed matter, cloth, weathered wood, pressed leaves, etc.

Working in collage for the first time was an eye-opening experience for me. I had never seen shapes quite so clearly before. If you have never done it, manipulating cutouts . . . inverting, flopping, and moving them about, can open up a whole new world of shapes to you. Collage can provide an infinite variety of possibilities in design. In fact, the effects that can be achieved are so fascinating that it's hard to know where to stop.

However, too much planning and deliberation can kill the vitality of a collage. If you are too fussy and ordered in arranging your shapes, if everything has to be just so, the result is apt to become merely ornamental. I like a collage that looks almost like a happy "accident" — like an assemblage of shapes that just happened to fall into a good design. I think the best collages are studies in artfully exploited accidental-looking patterns.

Don't be too rigidly bound by the original plan or concept. If the design is an abstract one, then of course it isn't necessary to explain anything. But even when it is figurative and realistic, don't feel that it's necessary to have a reason for everything you put in it.

Be constantly on the lookout for the unexpected. Appraise your work as it progresses. But don't get carried away and become too tricky. I have done this and things invariably ended up with an "artsy-craftsy" look.

Always keep the total design in mind. Don't allow all the intriguing little nuances, so abundant in collage, to divert you from this goal. Keep it **simple!**

One of the first things you will learn when working with papers is that all paper except the hand-made variety has a certain amount of "grain" to it. The fibers, whether they are of rag or wood pulp base, always tend to align themselves cross-wise or length-wise with the paper. This allows you to tear the paper more easily and more evenly in one direction than in another. You must first determine which way the grain runs before you can tear with any degree of control. Tearing across the grain will give you a jagged, leaf-like edge. Tearing parallel to the grain results in much straighter, more even edges. Any paper thicker than tissue can be given a "feathered" edge by laying it flat on the table and peeling it at a very flat, oblique angle.

It has been my experience that tearing and cutting quickly (with a certain amount of abandon, in fact,) will give me shapes that are more natural and more interesting. Shapes that lack individual identity are best. They do not call attention to themselves and are much more easily adapted to the overall design.

Take advantage of the many negative shapes that are created as you move pieces about. Don't overlook the left-over scraps. They are more apt to be abstract than the shapes you deliberately create. Sometimes a piece that has fallen to the floor and been walked on and scuffed a bit is exactly what is needed!

My first professional encounter with the medium of collage came about almost by accident. I had been given an assignment to illustrate a children's book dealing with the subject of relativity. Pretty abstract stuff, especially in a children's book. It was obvious that anything smart or sophisticated would not do. I racked my brain for a week. I tried every trick I knew. Finally, almost in desperation, I made some experiments with colored papers. What I was looking for was some form of expression that would be direct and clear yet naive enough in technique to communicate with and appeal to a child's awareness. It worked and I did the whole book in collage. It was a lesson I should have learned years before. An illustration from this book is reproduced on this page.

Although it is not my painting form, I still like to come back to collage from time to time as exercise and as a diversion from more conventional painting. I don't think there's a better way of providing a fresh sense of discovery in dealing with shapes. One of the greatest virtues of collage is that it allows you to change form relationships instantly, without having to touch brush and paint. It is a medium that is ideally suited to the expressionistic approach of direct attack and direct change. Matisse seems to reflect this attitude in this quote:

"I now find that the simplest and most direct way in which I can express myself is by cutouts." (1952)

Courtesy Parents' Magazine Press

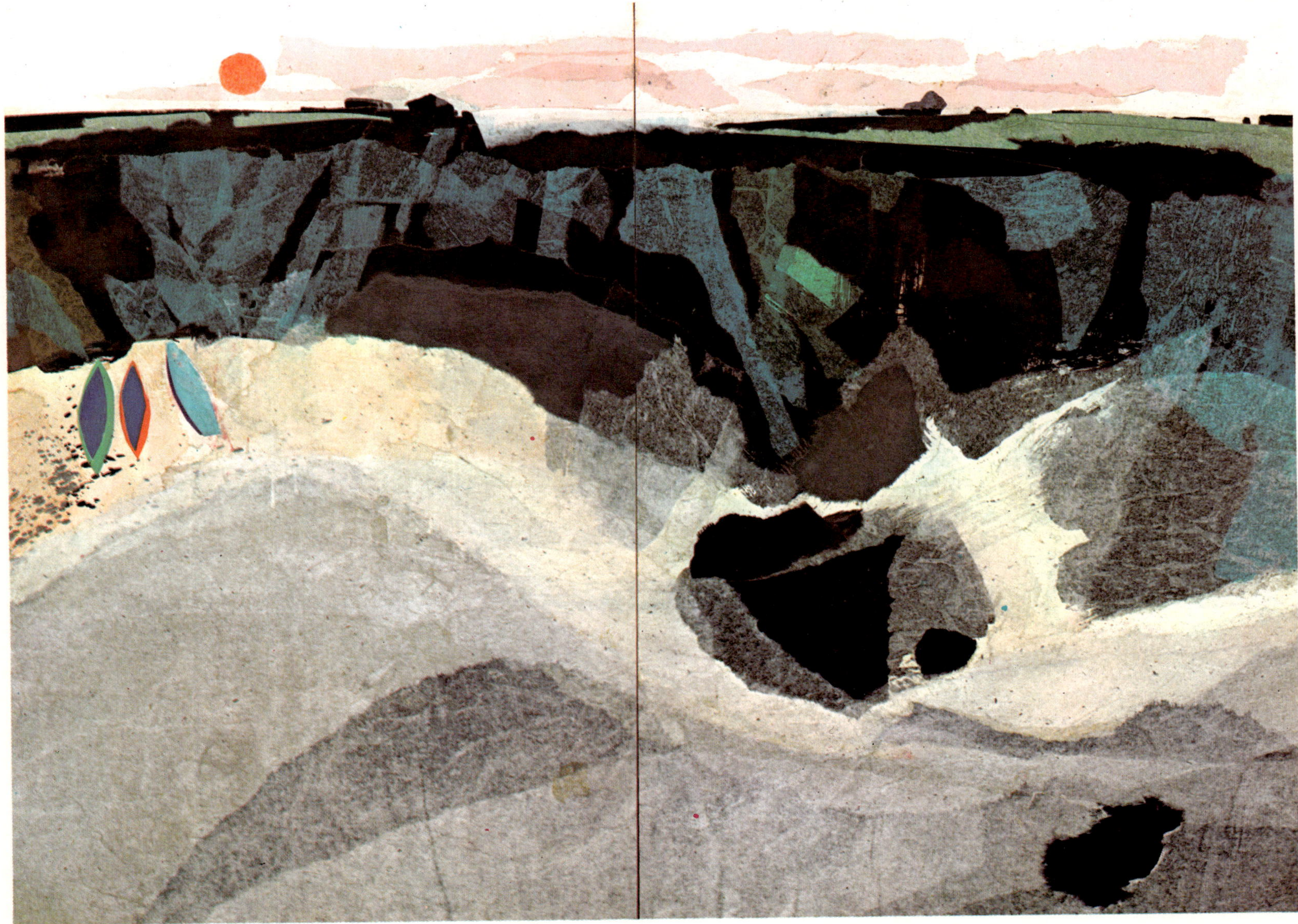

Just about any material or substance that can be induced to stick to a background base can be used in a collage. Ordinary paper, cardboard, wrapping paper, wallpaper, rice paper, cutouts from magazines, ticket stubs, printed cloth fabric, pieces of canvas, lace, straw, pressed leaves and flowers, sand, wood, oil cloth, plastic, bits of metal and string . . . all have been used.

Any kind of stable material will do as a background base as long as it will not peel, warp or otherwise deteriorate. Masonite is often used where permanency is required.

For cement, I use Elmer's glue or Acrylic medium — the former sets faster. When you don't want to wet the material, spray-on adhesive is satisfactory and fast but can be messy. Sprayed on carelessly, without using a mask around the work, it can gum up everything in the immediate area. And it's almost impossible to get off. I don't recommend rubber cement. Although it's the handiest of all, it will turn paper yellow in a few months and loses its adhesiveness in time.

Permanency and durability of materials must be primary considerations if you want your collages to last. Unfortunately, most ready-made papers are colored with dyes or inks that are far from permanent. Tests have been made with samples of colored paper to measure their light fastness. The ones found to be most fade-resistant were Color Aid and Color View papers. By contrast, Origami

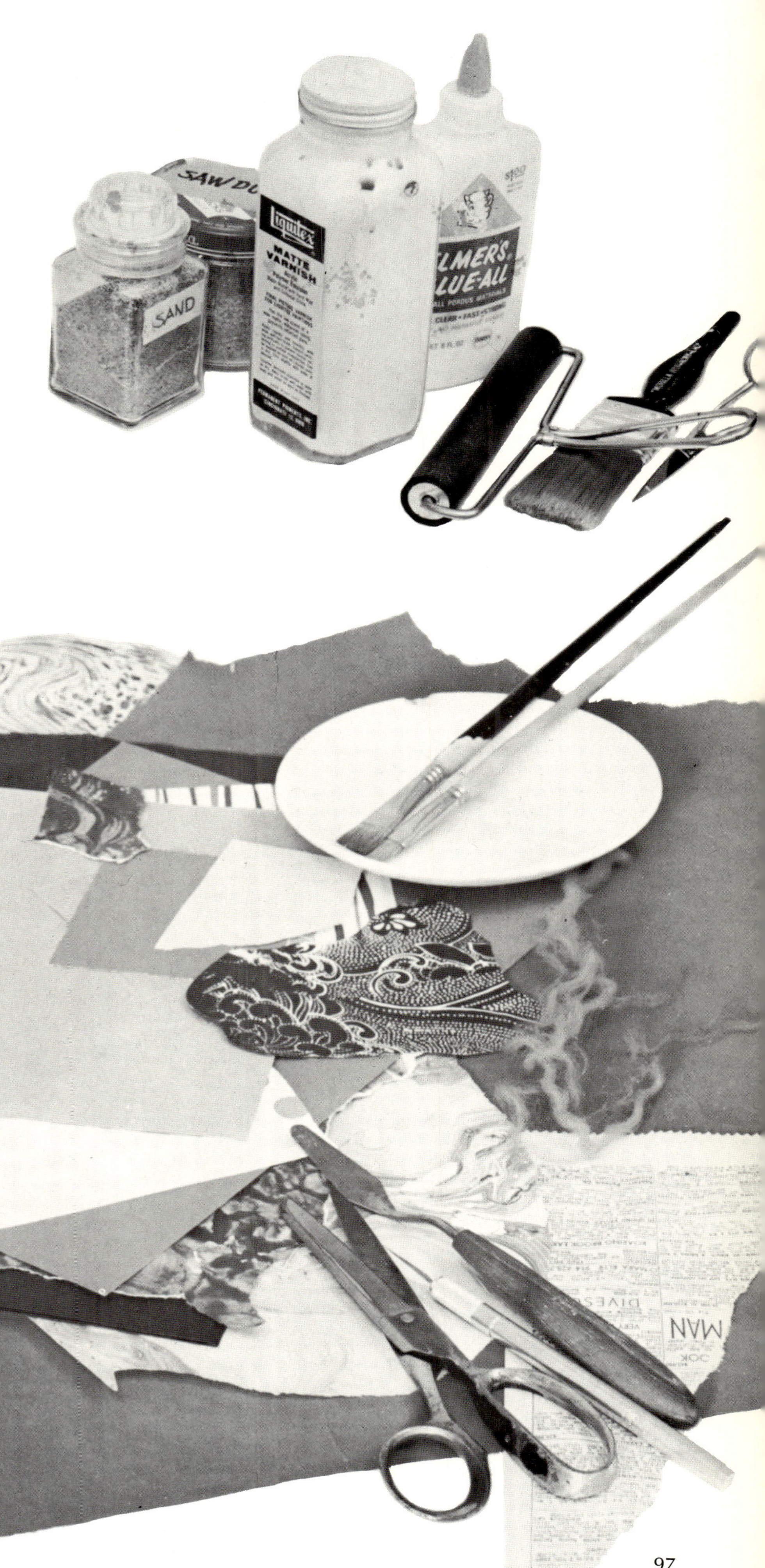

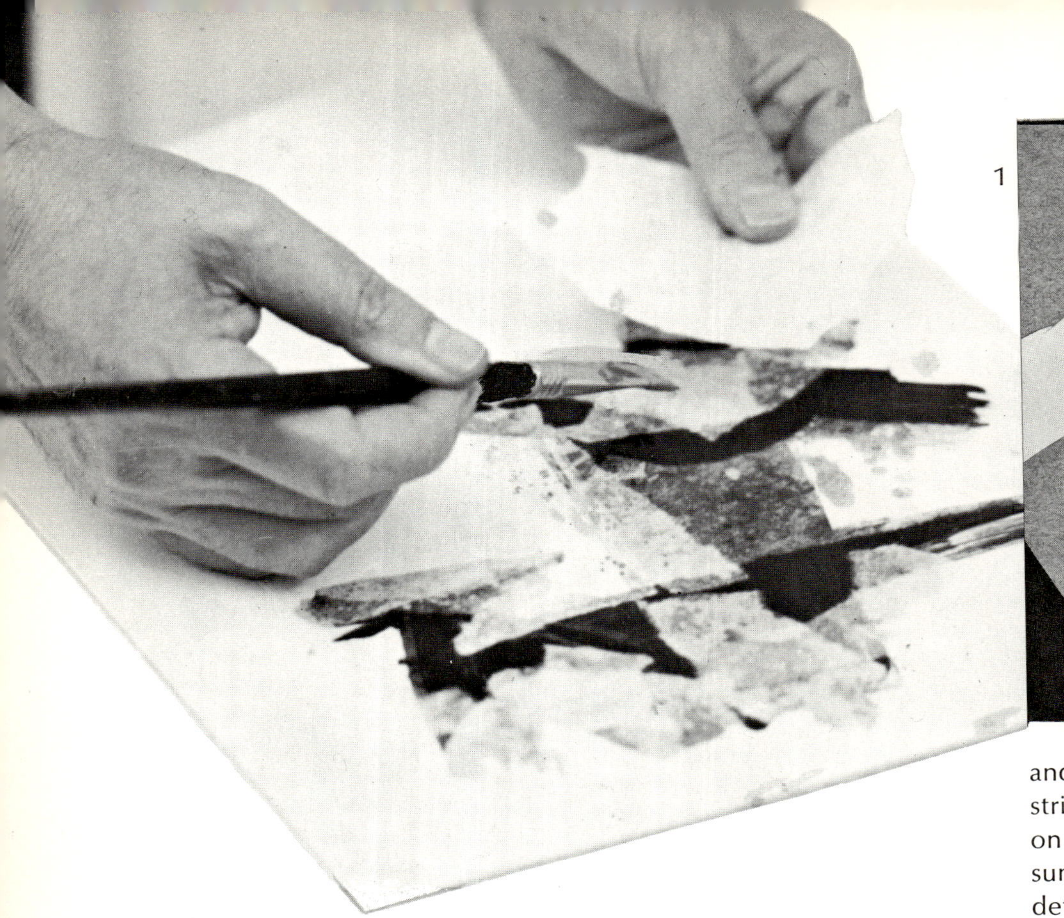

1

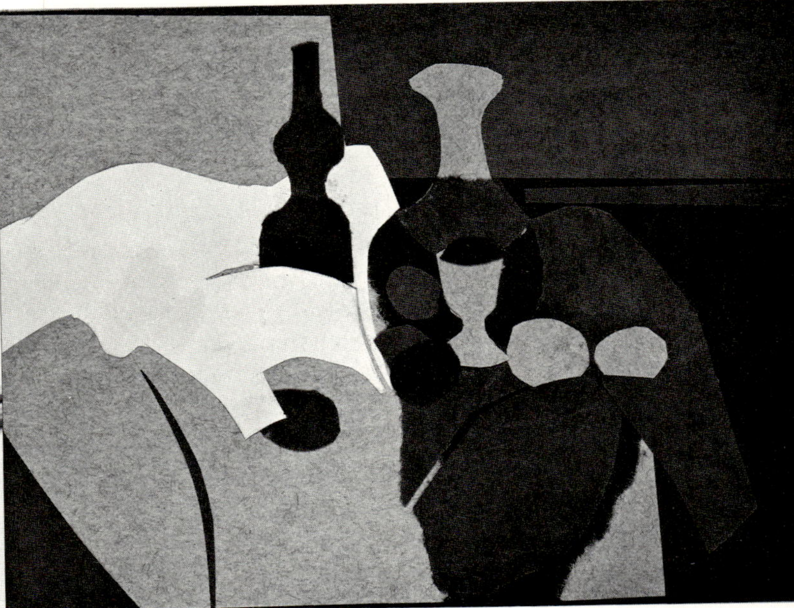

and colored tissue papers, though luscious to look at, are strictly untrustworthy. They will begin to fade in a few days on exposure to light, which doesn't even have to be direct sunlight. A sizing or spray will prevent paper or cloth from deteriorating, but when it comes to fading, light is the villain. For this reason most workers in collage prefer to color their own papers, using color fast pigments. Matisse used gouache in preparing his collage papers.

COMPOSING A COLLAGE

Without getting too complicated let's try a few experiments in collage, at the same time acquainting ourselves with some of the more commonly used terms:

First of all, the word **collage,** derived from the French word **coller** (to paste or glue), is used in a general sense and indicates the way collage began — with pasted paper.

The term **decoupage** puts it more specifically and refers to the cutting of paper. If the paper is torn we have **dechirage.** The collage on page 96 was done almost entirely by tearing, mostly with colored tissue papers and a few bits of heavy construction paper. The blacks and the sand color were painted in first with a brush.

The first exercise is a rendering in cut paper of Cézanne's

3

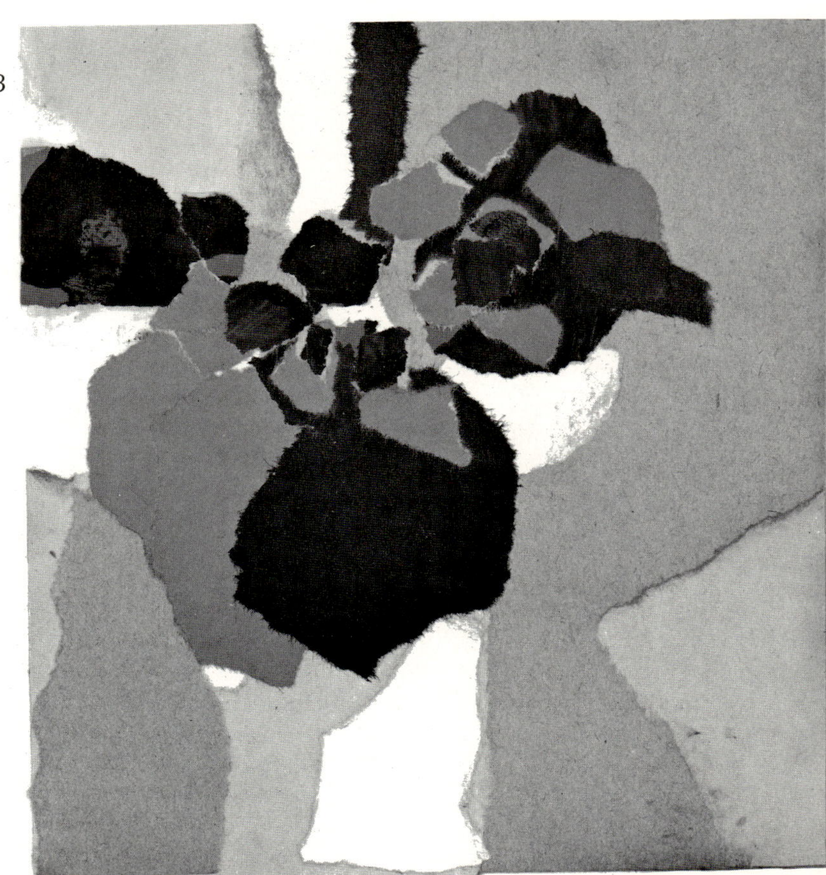

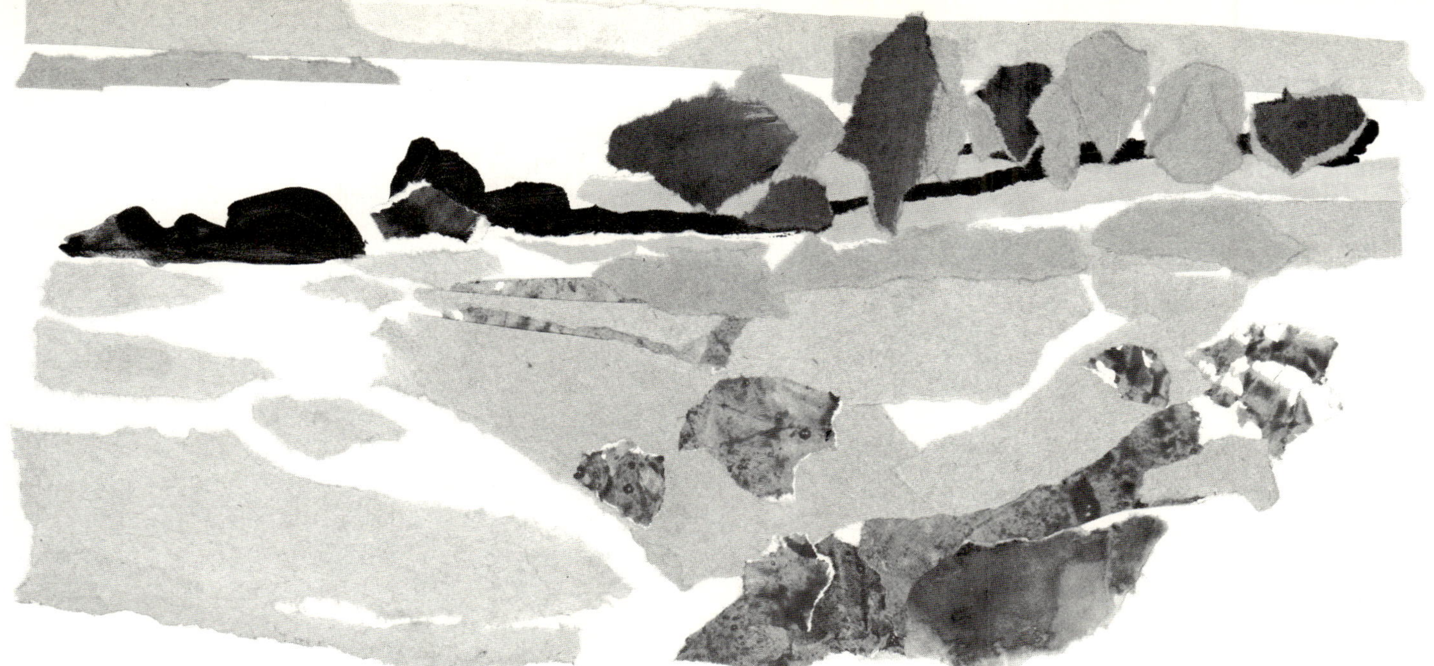

still life on page 28. I used opaque construction paper in black, white, and two grays. You can take any good composition that has well-defined shapes and a fairly wide range of tones. Do not worry about not being able to match every tone. Try to keep it as simple as possible. A collage version cannot and should not be an accurate copy. Paste in the big shapes first. I used slightly diluted Elmer's glue in a saucer, brushing it directly across the surface to be covered. Use double-weight mounting board to resist warping.

For second exercise I've taken the sketch on page 38 and used it as a jumping off point. You will notice I haven't bothered to follow any of the details of the original sketch, only the feeling or sensation of the moment. Again — construction paper was used, plus a few bits of hand-colored paper and a scrap of transparent rice paper in the sky to suggest sunlight. Try a composition of your own and approach it as freely as you can. Tear your paper quickly without trying for shapes that are realistic or recognizable in themselves.

Now let's go even more abstract. In exercise three, I've used organic shapes to develop a sort of floral motif. The same papers were used, working from the center outward.

In the first stage of exercise four, I've borrowed from Franz Kline for my basic design plan. (See page 102.) This shape was painted in with black acrylic paint using no more than four or five strokes, with a minimum of reworking. At this stage it is a "gesture painting" and the foundation on which the collage will be built. Now, using only pieces of thin rice paper I begin building up on top of the black, altering or eliminating some shapes and compounding others as I go. This same procedure was followed in the illustration on page 96. A word of caution, however. Don't get diverted by the intriguing technical effects obtainable as you proceed or you may lose sight of the overall picture. When you have found a good shape be careful not to overcomplicate it with further detail. You may ruin it. When in doubt, squint and you will see the big shapes better.

Paper can be torn and stripped from a collage after it has been pasted down, provided you do it before it sets. This technique is known as **decollage.** When a hard edge is desired, the paper should first be cut with a razor blade.

4

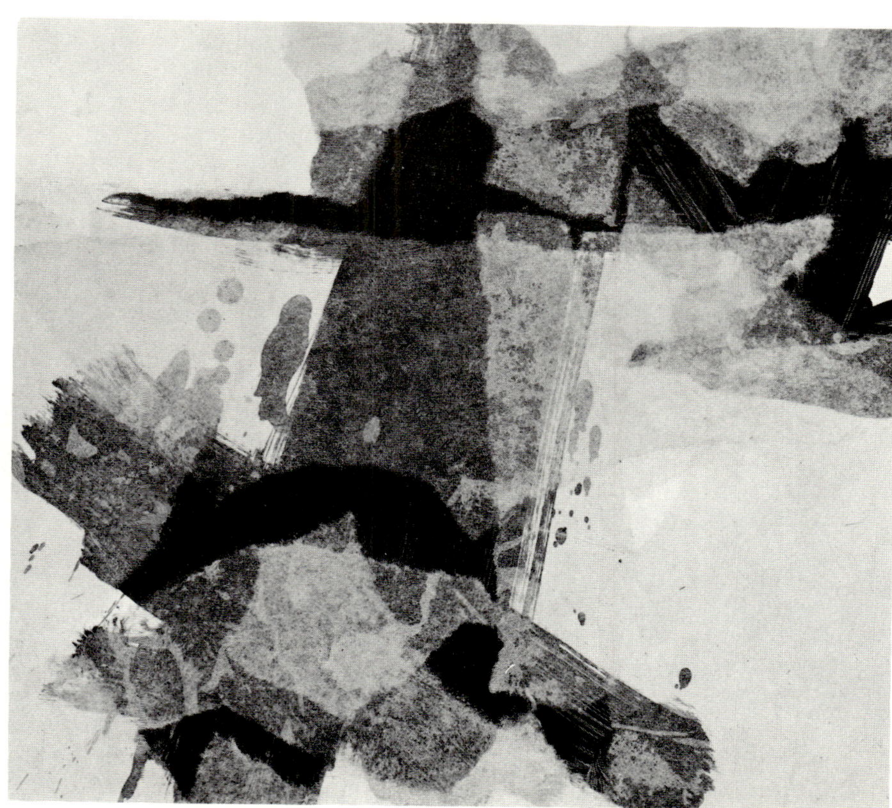

ASSEMBLAGE

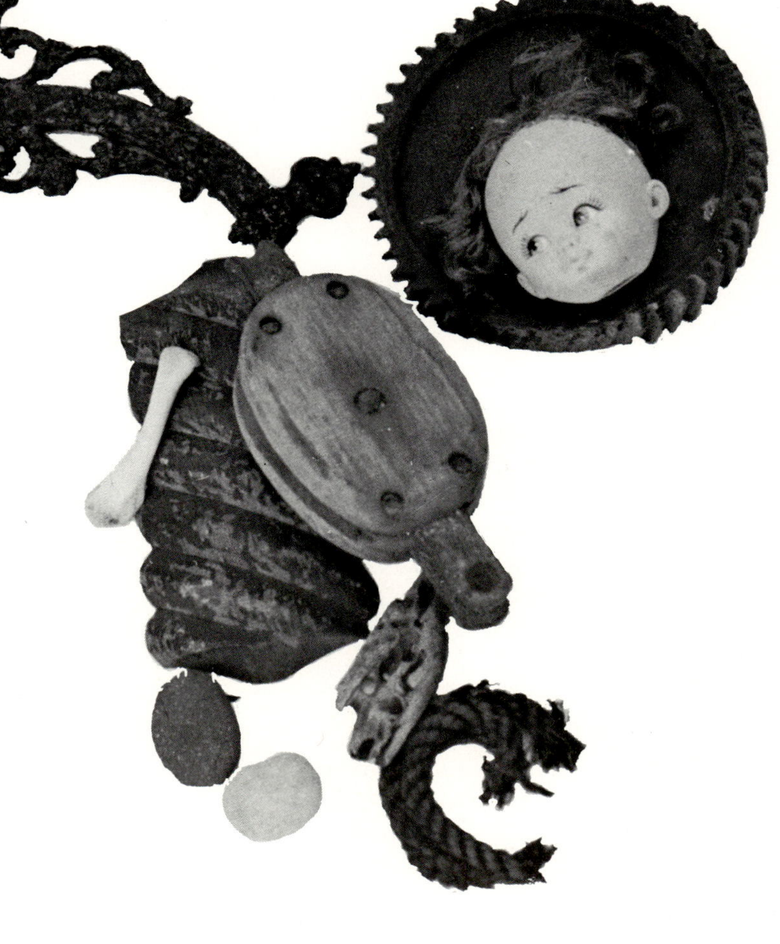

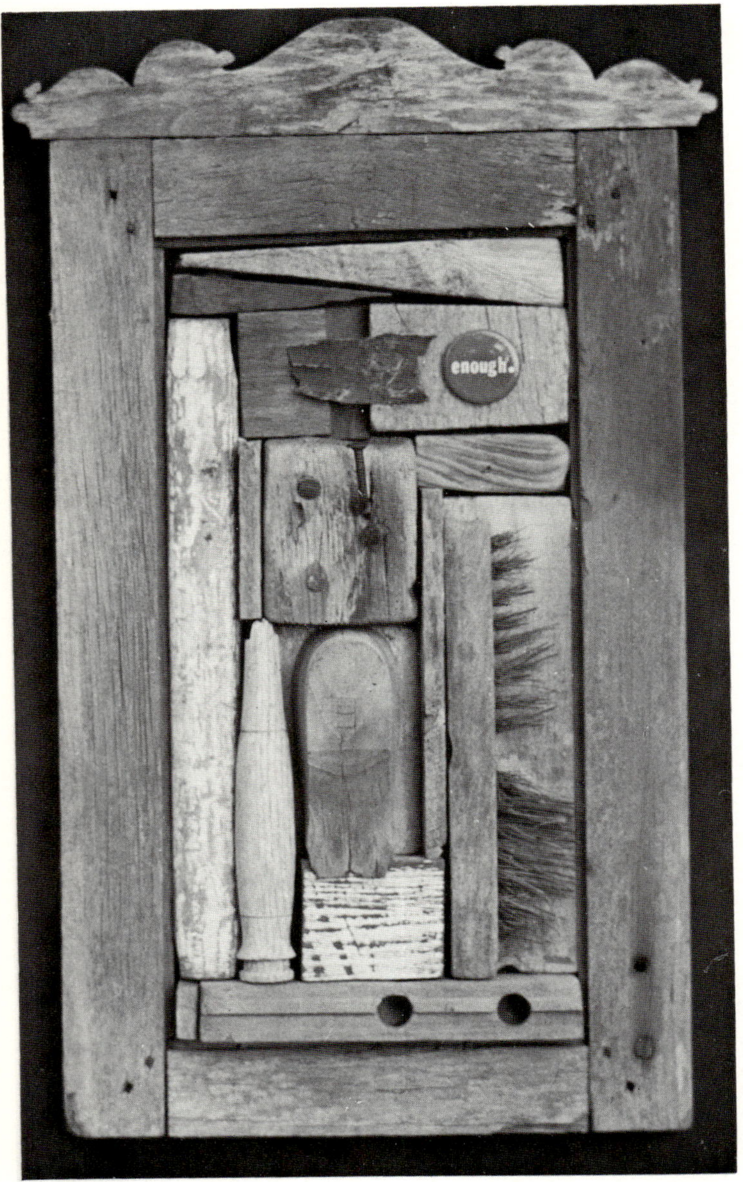

1

ASSEMBLAGE by ANN JONES SCHWARTZ

The most familiar collages are those which come under the heading of **assemblage,** a very general term for almost any collection of flat or solid objects grouped together in a two- or three-dimensional design plan. A page from the stamp collector's book or the family album is an assemblage of sorts. So is the town hall or post office bulletin board, with its mug shots of wanted people, pictures of lost dogs, auction notices and new stamp issues. Assemblage is an invaluable adjunct for the interior decorator, and the set designer.

As a beach bum with years of experience, I am partial to

WHITE, BLACK AND GRAY 1968 by ESTEBAN VICENTE — collage
Dallas Museum for Fine Arts

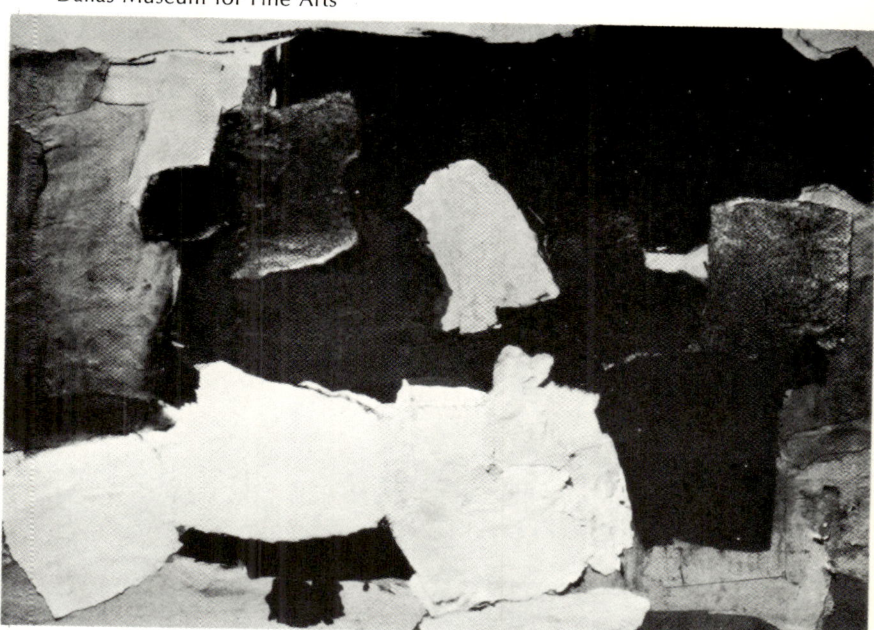

KAKAO by KURT SCHWITTERS — collage
Marlborough Gallery, N.Y.

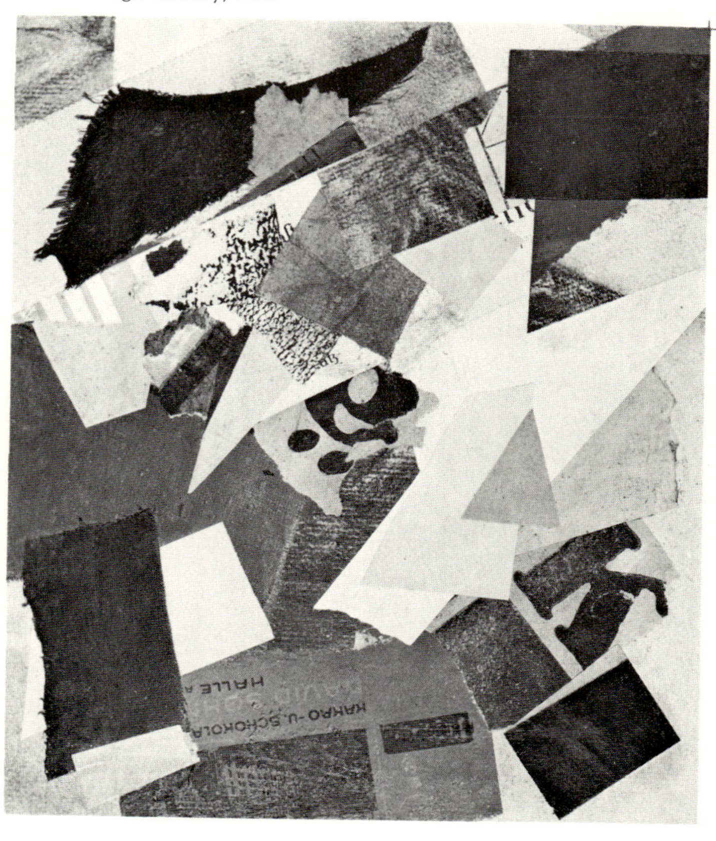

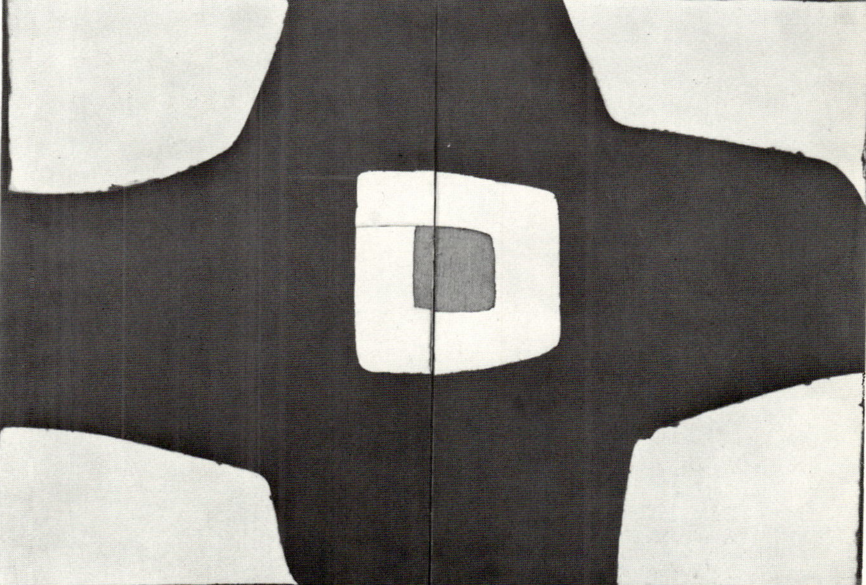

L-L-4-72 by CONRAD MARCA-RELLI — painted canvas collage
Marlborough Gallery, N.Y.

assemblages of found objects — shells, bones, pieces of driftwood, worn bits of glass, stone and metal, etc. (See Fig.1.) If you plan to use something really heavy or chunky in your assemblage it might be wise to look into the epoxy cements. These wonder adhesives will stick just about anything to anything, including the kitchen sink. When using heavy objects be sure to mount them on a surface strong and rigid enough to stand the strain. Quarter inch Masonite or plywood panels make the best base.

Creating an assemblage is so much a matter of taste, impulse, and just pure whimsy that it is useless to try to prescribe any method or plan of procedure. Experiment — plunge in, and have fun.

Montage, another very common form of collage, is the technique of mixing a variety of often unrelated pictorial elements in a composition in such a way that they blend and support each other in an integrated design. It's especially effective in advertising art and in modern cinematography where "flash-backs" and psychological impressions are wanted. The double exposure, a form of montage, is being used in modern photography in a way that approaches Expressionism.

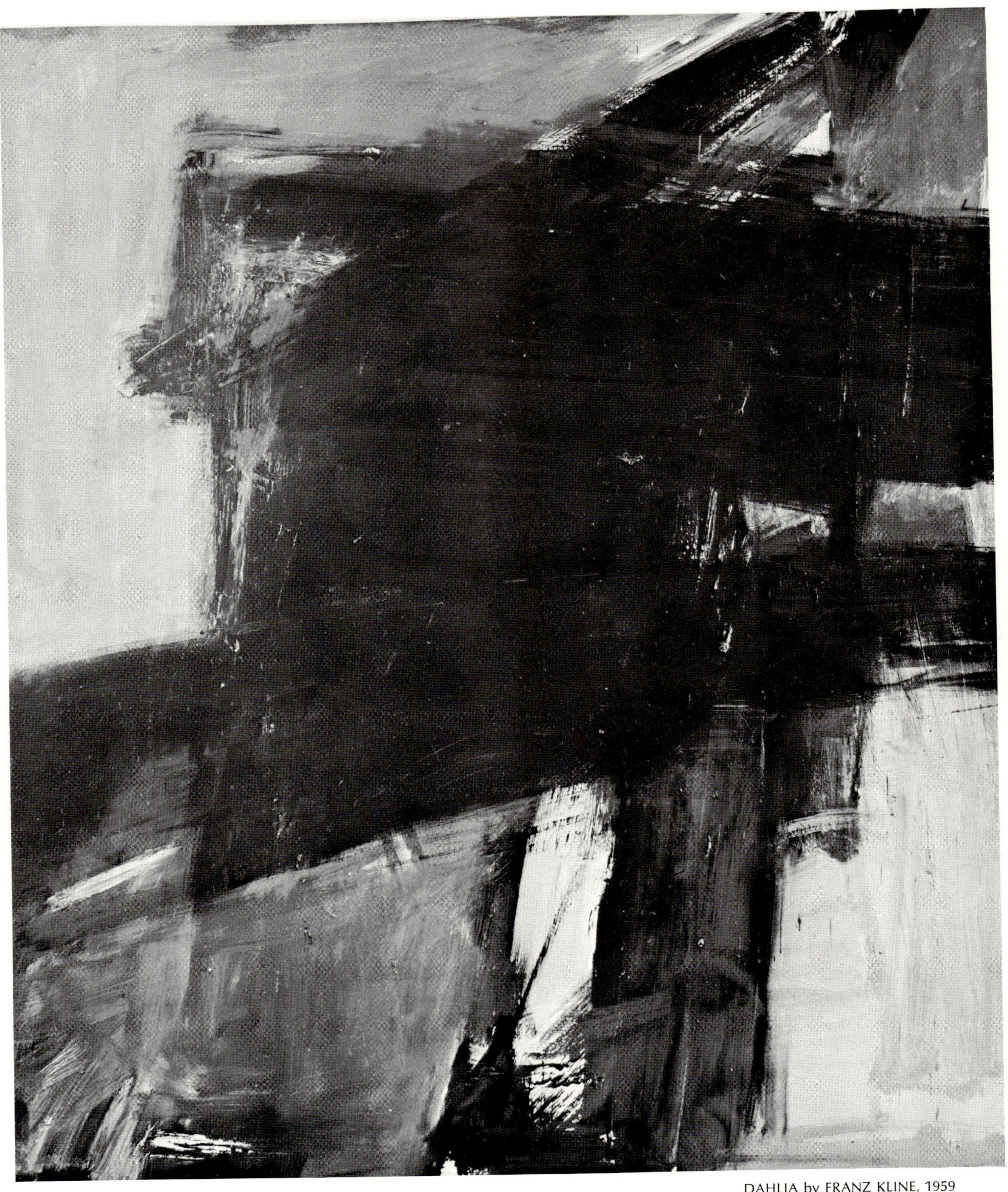

DAHLIA by FRANZ KLINE, 1959
Whitney Museum of American Art, N.Y.

I PAINT NOT THE THINGS I SEE,
BUT THE FEELINGS THEY AROUSE IN ME.
Franz Kline

ABSTRACT PAINTING

Up to now we have been dealing pretty much with tangibles, drawing and painting what we see and analyzing as we go. But all the time (I hope) we have been moving gradually in the direction of a more intuitive way of thinking. Whether or not you ever become involved with abstract, or non-figurative painting, I think this is a good time to discuss it. Even if you never paint an abstract picture you must be aware by now that there is abstraction to be found in the most faithfully detailed realistic paintings just as there may be naturalism behind the wildest abstractions.

This chapter on abstract painting, in many ways, is a summing-up of everything that has gone before. The exercises in Part I on Negative Shapes and Overlaps gave us our first taste of an abstract spatial concept. As far back as 1907 the Cubists, most notably Picasso and Braque, were turning out some of the first abstractions, getting away from the traditional representation of objects and stressing the geometric construction behind them. Which, of course, takes us even further back to Cézanne who started it all with his theory of controlled planes and geometric forms.

It was a short step then to the breaking up of recognizable forms, and multiple images (as though the artist had walked part way around his subject in the process of painting it). When this fragmented image concept was finally combined with a free use of color, it was the beginning of modern abstract painting.

All new movements are rooted in rebellion. Abstract painting is no exception. Up until a few years ago it was a generally accepted notion among painters that it doesn't matter what you paint as long as it is well painted. But the new school of abstractionists of the early forties, including Adolph Gottlieb, Mark Rothko, Willem de Kooning and Clifford Still, were not going along with this kind of academicism. They maintained that there is no such thing as good painting about nothing. They believed that art had to have a reason for being, other than that of mere decoration. Subject was crucial.

Painting was becoming more mystical, more metaphysical. In their search for new ways of expression artists were turning more and more to the use of symbols and images.

FROM REALISM to ABSTRACT

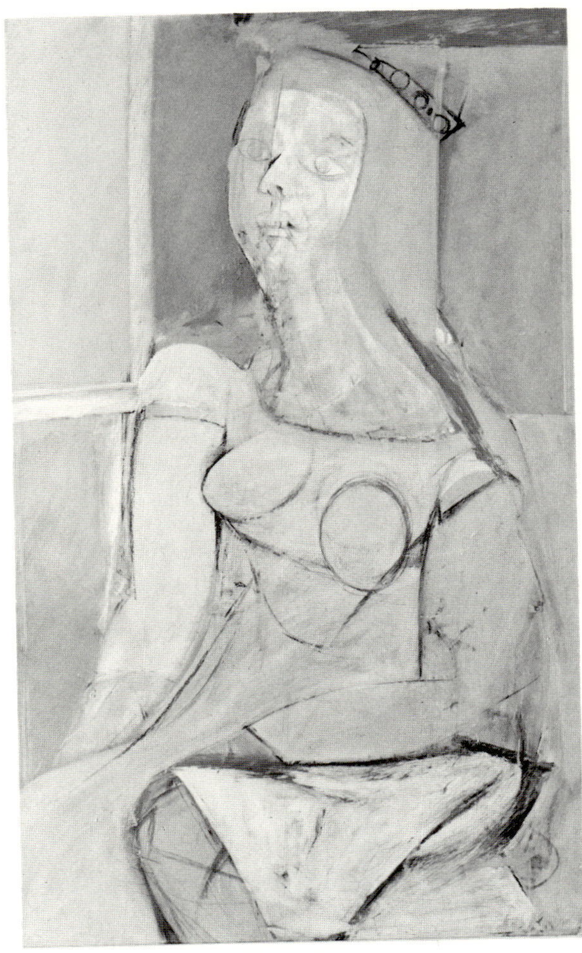

QUEEN OF HEARTS by WILLEM DE KOONING
The Hirshhorn Museum and Sculpture Garden, Smithsonian Institution

At first glance this spread looks like a random selection of picture post cards that one might pick up at the main desk of any large museum. The fact is, they were carefully selected to serve a purpose, to show as graphically as possible the process of transition from naturalism to abstraction. Implicit in these six paintings is a conflict between direct observation and imagination. In fact, in some cases this conflict seems to become the subject of the painters' art, as with Paul Klee, John Marin, and Picasso.

Most importantly, these pictures show how shapes immediately take on an added dimension and importance when they are *abstracted* and made less realistic and less recognizable. In going toward abstraction, shapes that are a result of "observed reality" give way to forms that exist only in the human mind. And these forms, to have any meaning, should reflect the artist's personal experiences and reactions to life.

Many artists have devoted half a lifetime to a more-or-less realistic, or figurative, way of painting and then turned to abstraction. Symbolism has come to be the most pervasive force in art today, both in gallery painting and illustration; and abstraction is the purest and most direct means of expressing it. Our imagination is stimulated and whetted by shapes that are symbolic and mysterious. Abstract forms and patterns such as those found in clouds, rocks and foliage, for instance, are always more exciting than any we can invent. You will find that the best abstract painters never wander too far from nature — they never completely lose touch with her influence.

A late bloomer, Milton Avery unfortunately did not hit his stride until he was in his fifties. The influence of Matisse is apparent in the early years but his later work shows a more personal conviction and an almost total dedication to form. Avery's work is deceptively simple. It never dazzles or shocks, like Picasso or de Kooning. It is more fugue-like and poetic, a good example of semi-abstract painting.

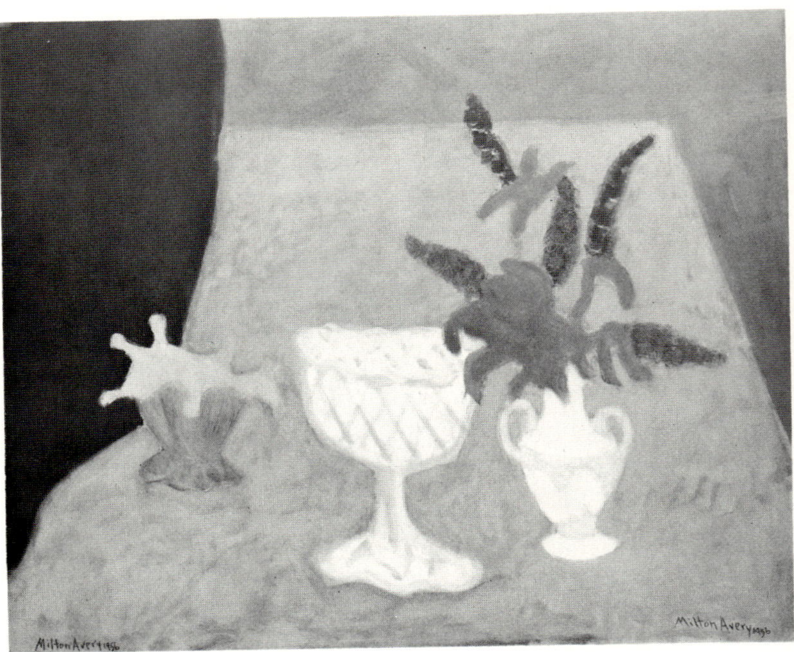

VICTORIAN STILL LIFE by MILTON AVERY
Grace Borgnicht Gallery, N.Y.

IT IS ONLY IN APPEARANCE THAT SIMPLIFICATION
LEADS AWAY FROM NATURE . . . IT LEADS BACK TO NATURE,
BECAUSE IT EXTRACTS THE ESSENCE FROM NATURE.

Marino Marini

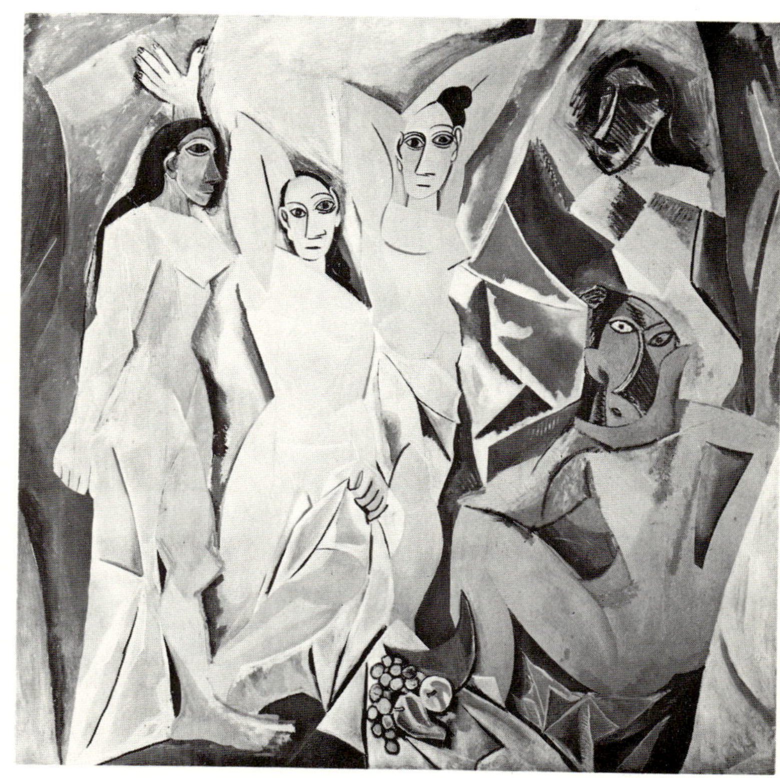

LES DEMOISELLES D'AVIGNON by PABLO PICASSO
Collection, the Museum of Modern Art. Lillie P. Bliss Bequest

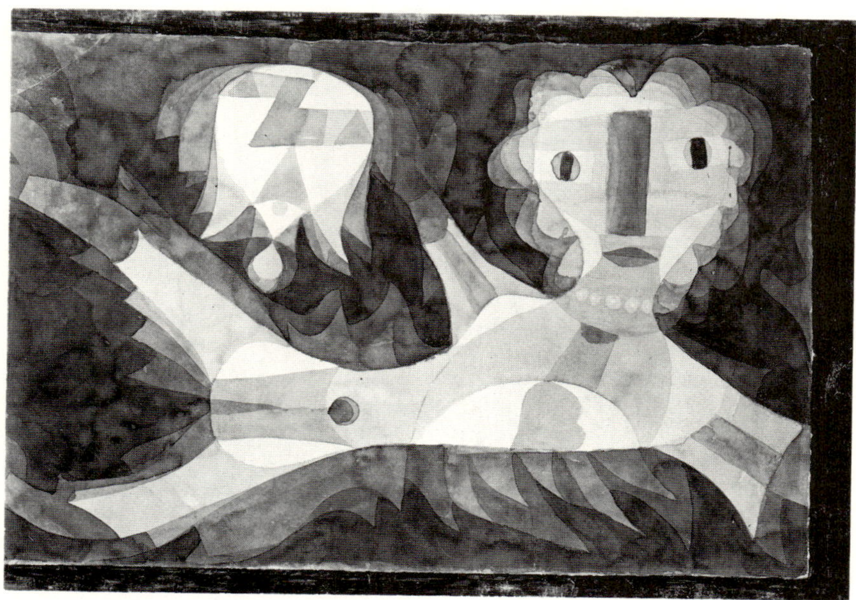

GOLDFISH WIFE, 1921 by PAUL KLEE
Philadelphia Museum of Art
Louise and Walter Arensberg Collection

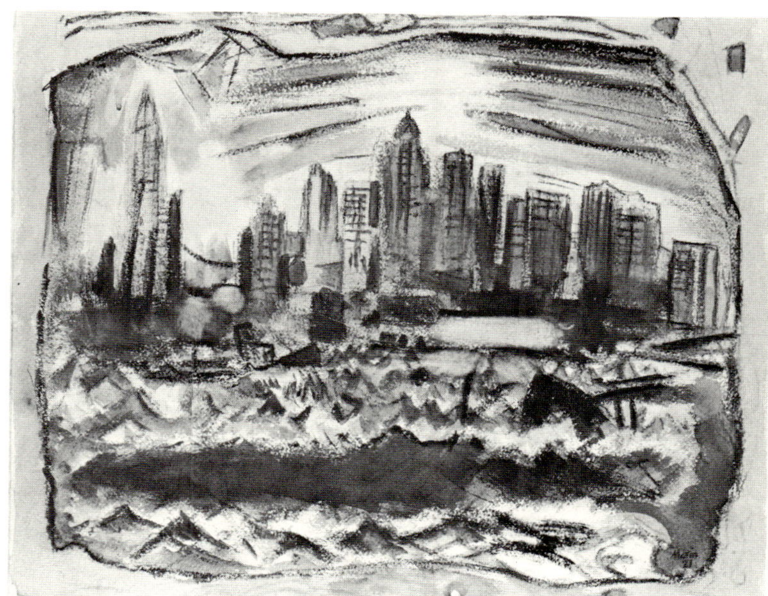

LOWER MANHATTAN FROM THE RIVER, NO. 1 by JOHN MARIN
Metropolitan Museum of Art. The Alfred Stieglitz Collection

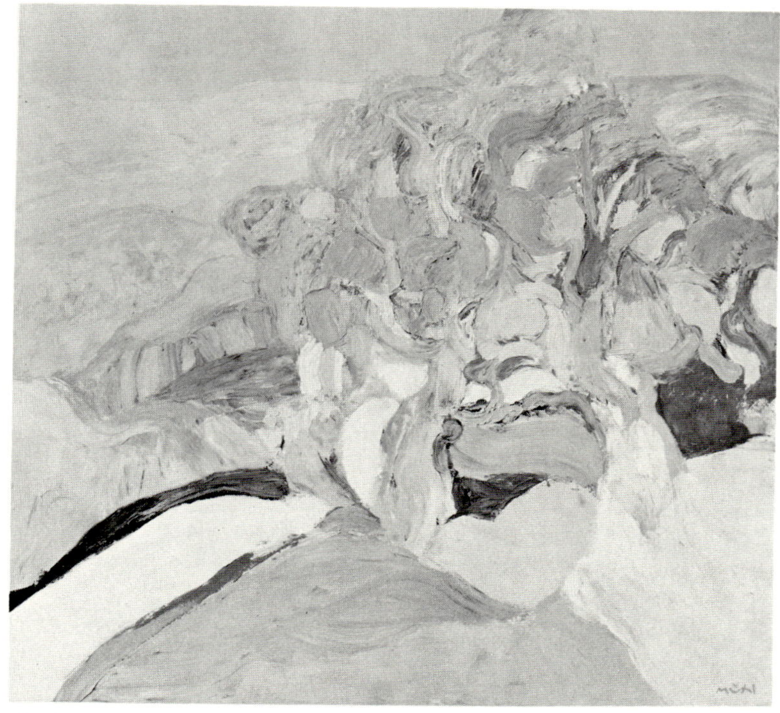

LES O'LIVIERS by ROGER MUHL
Findlay Gallery, N.Y.

THE SOURCE

Fig. 1 Lichen

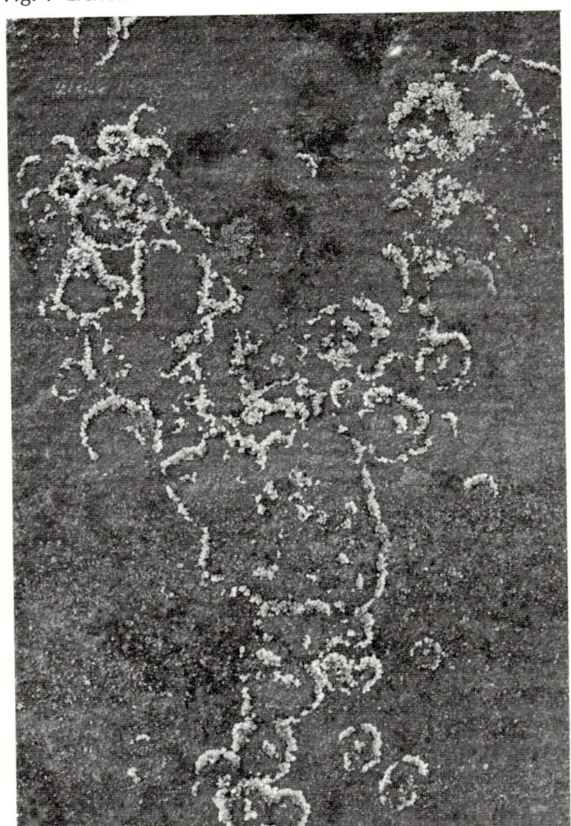

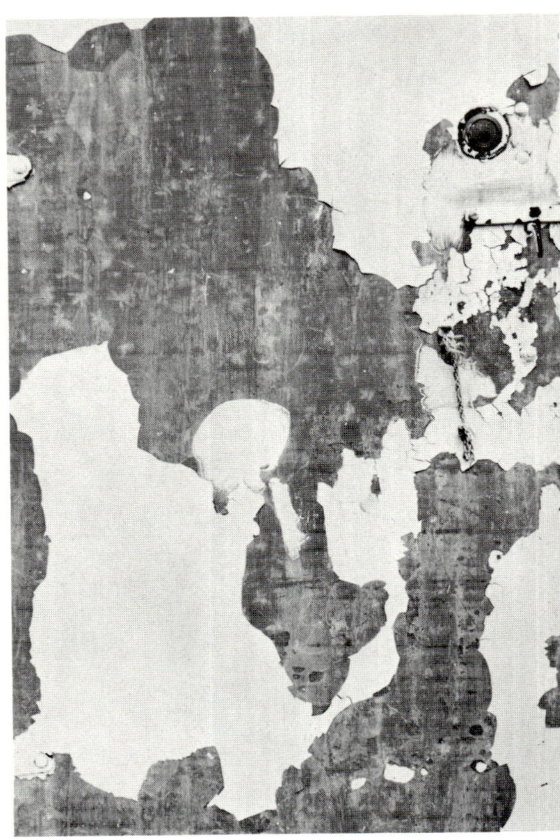

Fig. 5 Peeling paint

Fig. 2 Puddled paint

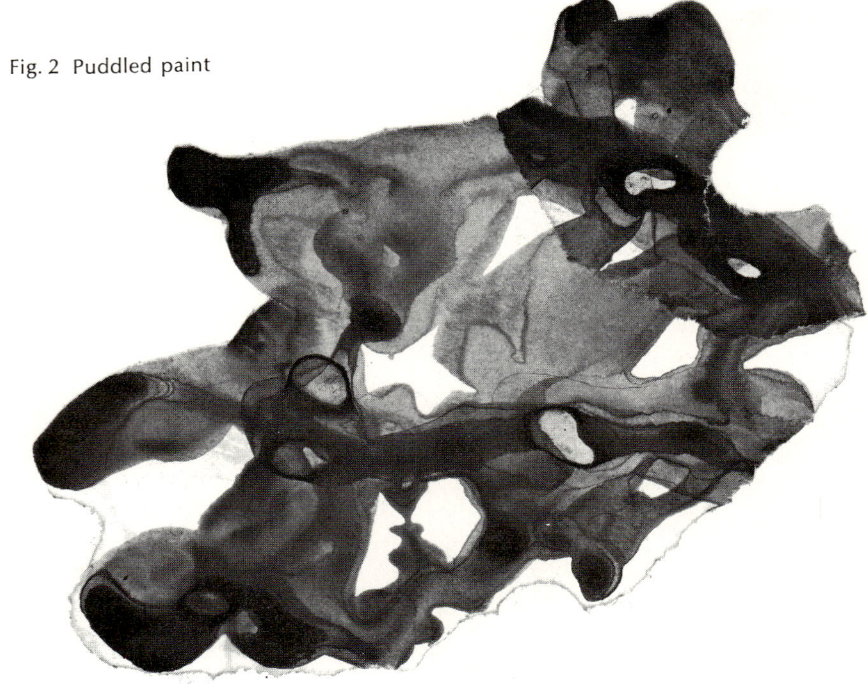

Fig. 3 Telephone "doodles"

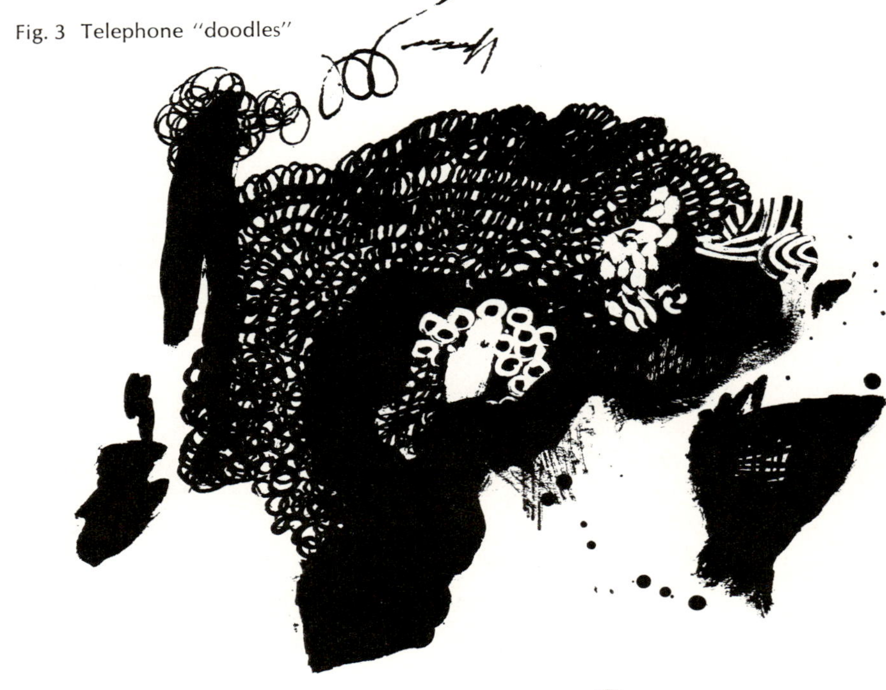

Fig. 4 Palette dabblings

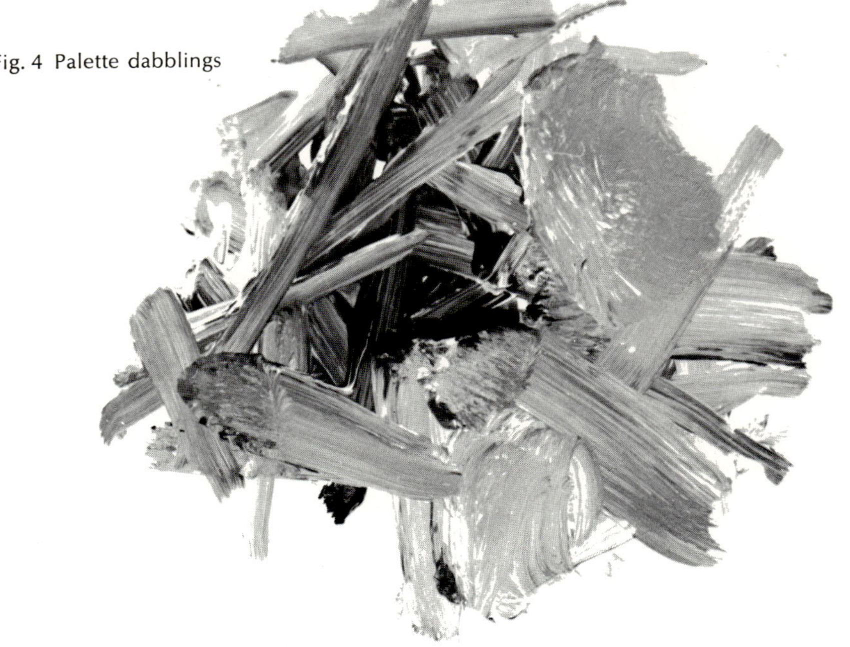

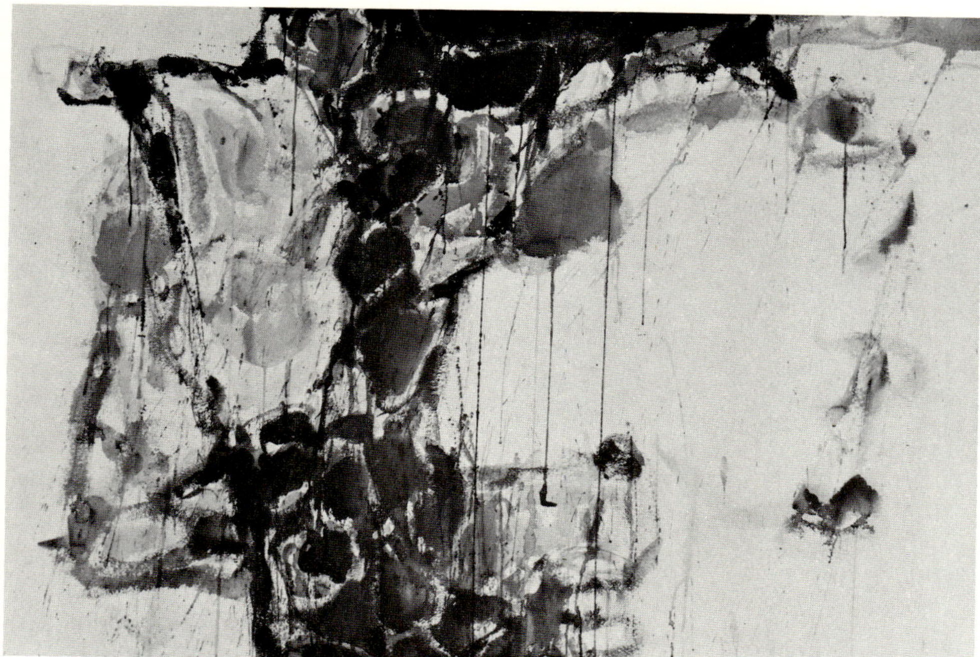

COOL VIOLET 1956-57 by SAM FRANCIS Martha Jackson Gallery, N.Y.

BLAST, I (1957) by ADOLPH GOTTLIEB
Collection, the Museum of Modern Art, N.Y., Philip C. Johnson Fund

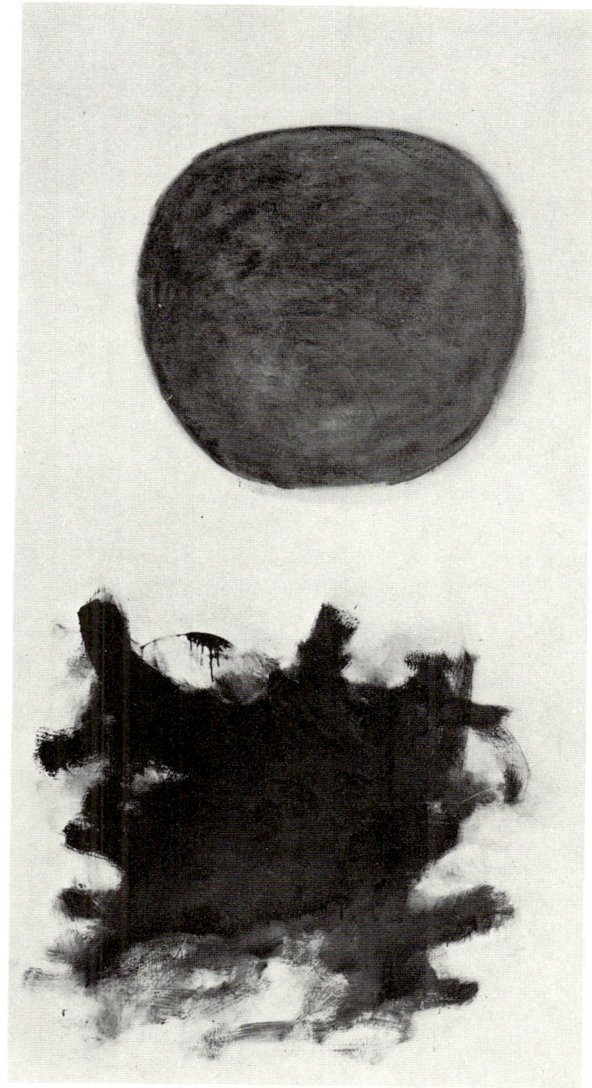

Good abstract painting starts with an idea, or at least the nucleus of one. Many modern abstractionists in fact develop their particular themes and styles right from nature with only minor alterations and rearrangement of the original visual idea. Just for the fun of it, let's explore the possibilities of a few sources. If you keep your eyes open and look around, you will find that you don't have to look very far. But you do have to look — and sometimes looking means moving in very close.

In Figure 1, lichen growing on an old gravestone looks like mystic, ancient hieroglyphics, or primitive Chinese art.

This next one, Figure 2, is full of symbolism. If you gaze at it a while, all kinds of embryonic and biological forms begin to emerge. This was done as an experiment for the abstract design on pages 12 and 13.

Figure 3 is right off my note pad, the by-product of a ten minute telephone conversation. I saved it because it mystified me a bit, like something drawn by somebody else. I think it's healthy, once in a while, to do things you don't understand. Some abstract painters attach as much importance to their telephone doodles as they do to their more deliberate constructions.

Ever since I started using acrylics and a porcelain tray for a palette I have been fascinated by the abstractions that result from the simple act of mixing daubs of paint. See Figure 4. Sometimes the effects are very much like "action painting," a fairly recent concept wherein the gesture of brushwork (or palette knife) is given meaning and significance. Action painters like Franz Kline, Willem de Kooning, Adolph Gottlieb, and Jackson Pollock developed their respective styles from this broad, slashing, often explosive manner of applying paint.

The artists represented here and on page 109 all had to go through transitional stages of development before they arrived at their present styles. We can only guess what inspired them originally and what their sources were. These random samples of peeling paint, lichen, and paint dabblings are a few things that happened to catch my eye. I had nothing in particular in mind when I found them. But, when I got them all together, the more I studied them, the more they began to suggest abstracts. Some of them even seemed to have a relationship with the styles of certain painters of today.

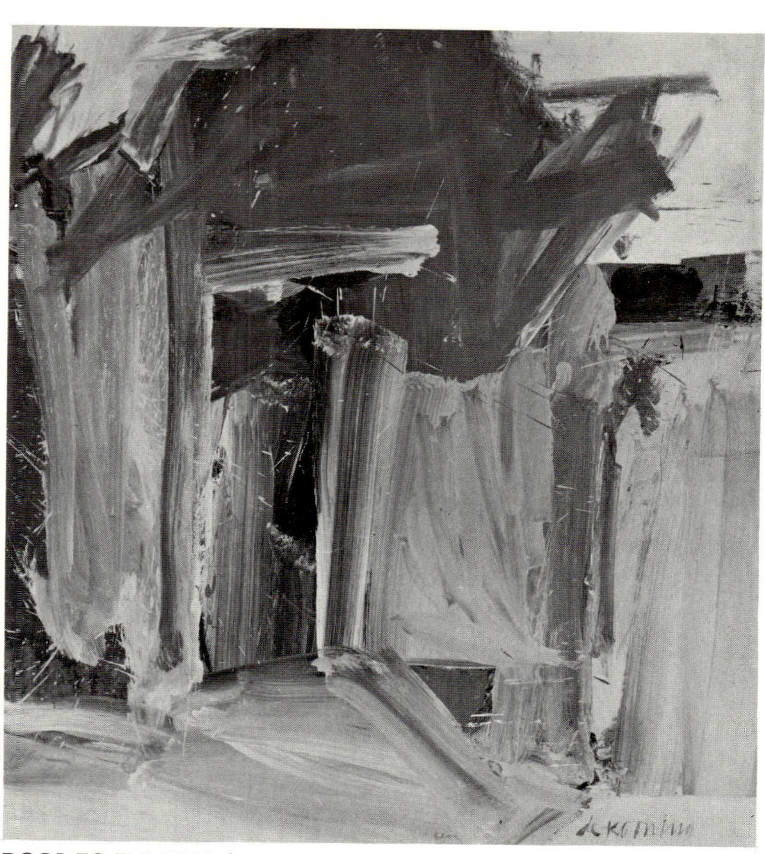

DOOR TO THE RIVER by WILLEM DE KOONING
Whitney Museum of American Art, N.Y.— Gift of the Friends of the WMAA

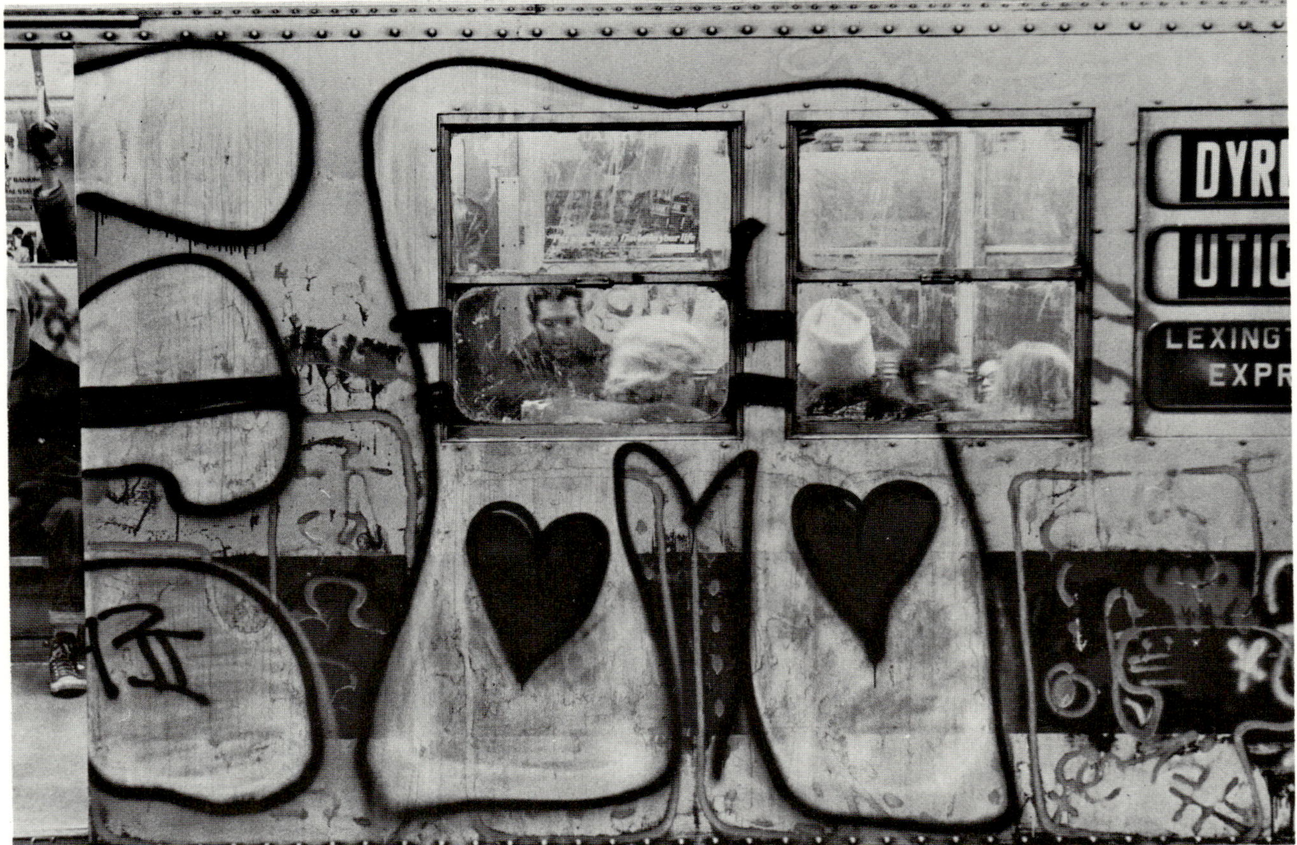

PHOTO by GEOFFREY REED

THE SIGNS OF THE PSYCHE... SYMBOLS, IMAGES and ICONS

STILL LIFE by SARAH REID (age 8)

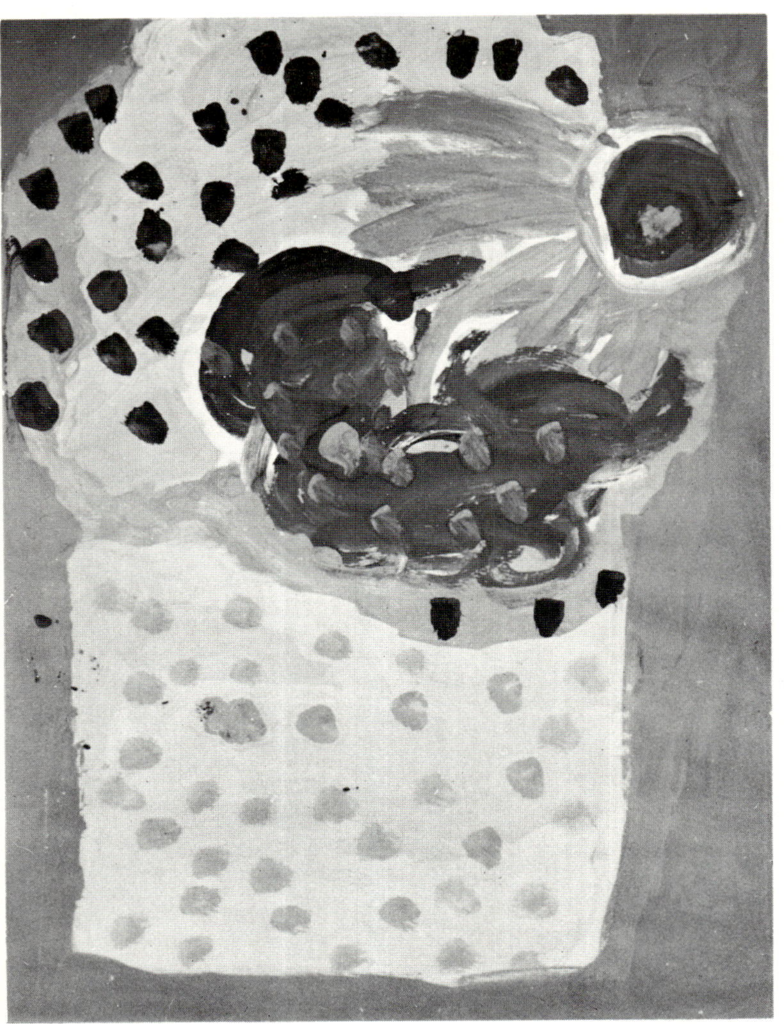

1

Symbolism can be seen in graffiti on walls and pavements. It proliferates in the incidental markings of man — the by-products of excavation, demolition, and urban decay, for example. There are symbols to be found in the aftermath of floods and erosion, fire and war.

Some of the most obvious symbolism can be found in children's paintings. (See Fig. 1.) When children paint they unconsciously use shapes and forms that are all the more direct and powerful because their use of tools and materials is inept and awkward. Craftsmanship and cleverness have not yet managed to get in the way of direct and spontaneous expression.

Fantasy and mystery play an important role in the work of the four painters on the right. They work in four distinctly different styles, yet they evoke similar sensations of space and mystery. James Brooks does it by using multi-layered forms that loom and fuse. Helen Frankenthaler achieves an effect of cataclysmic upheaval with a technique of flooding on forms that are sometimes embryonic in structure and sometimes nuclear in their image. Like Brooks, Clifford Still uses pitch black to set the stage for deep space in his paintings. Then he will shatter this void with a lightning bolt of yellow or white.

Burlesque is one of the most valuable elements in the art of the irreverent Jean Dubuffet. His work has had a marked impact on younger painters and on avant-garde illustration. Though more down-to-earth than the other three, it is nonetheless strongly directed toward imagery and fantasy.

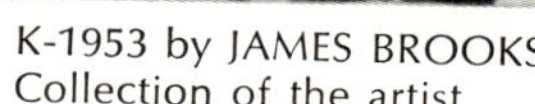

K-1953 by JAMES BROOKS
Collection of the artist

LA GARDE AUX CIMES by JEAN DUBUFFET
Marlborough Gallery, N.Y.

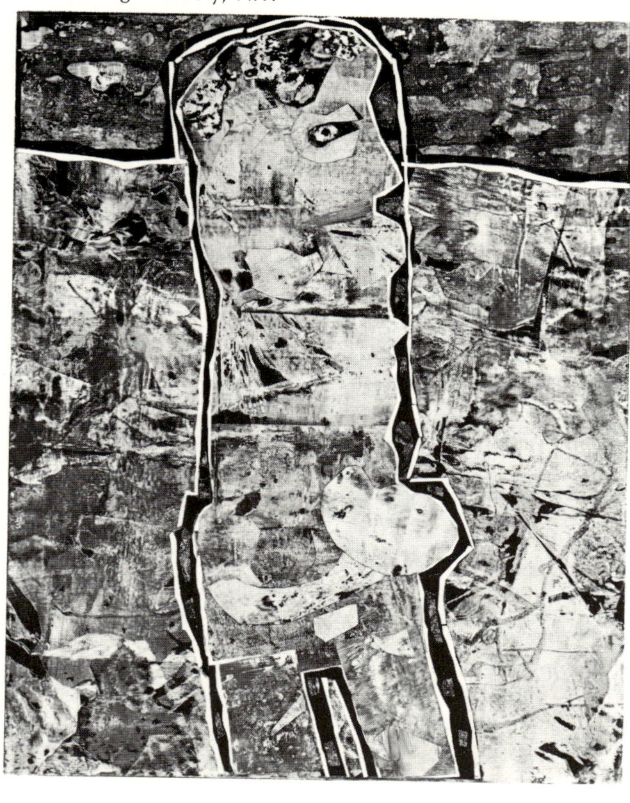

1957-D-NO. 1 by CLIFFORD STILL
Albright-Knox Art Gallery, Buffalo, N.Y.— Gift of Seymour H. Knox

FLOOD by HELEN FRANKENTHALER
Whitney Museum of American Art, N.Y.— Gift of the Friends of the WMAA

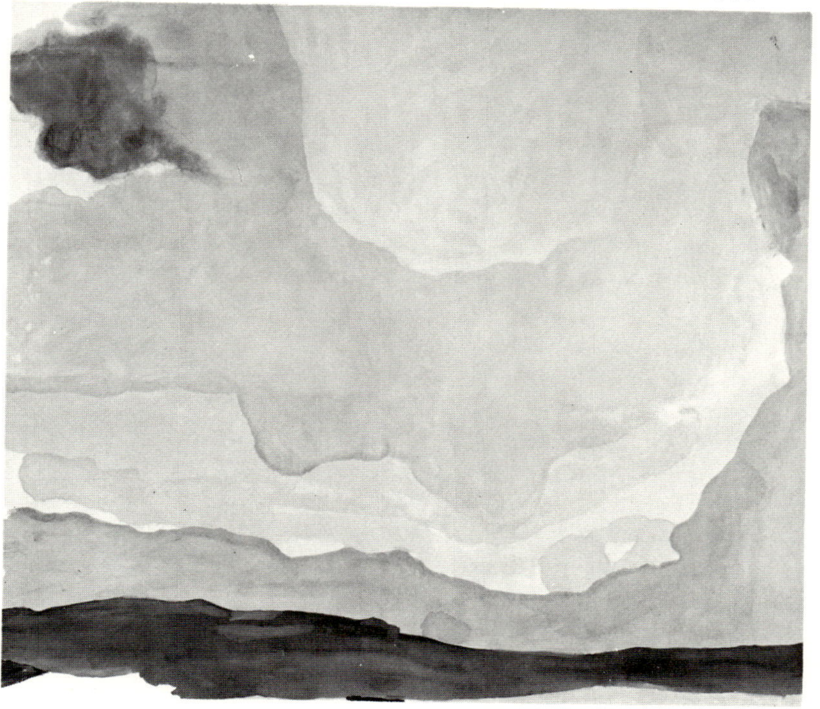

THE ROLE of the PRELIMINARY SKETCH

You've been hearing a lot about preliminary sketches — gesture drawings, thumbnail sketches, comprehensive sketches, on-the-spot color sketches, and working drawings for paintings. Here is a variety of examples of this type of preliminary design planning.

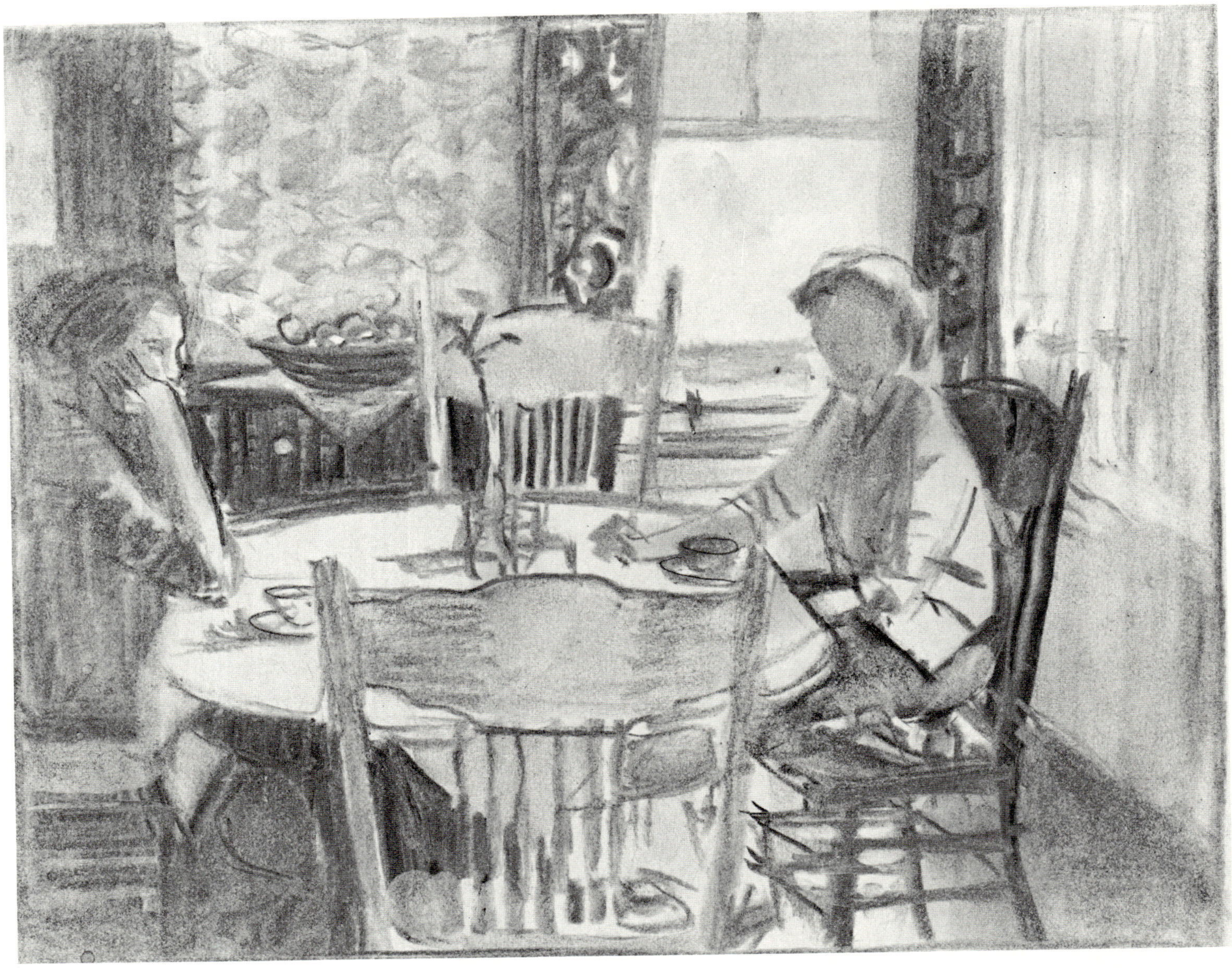

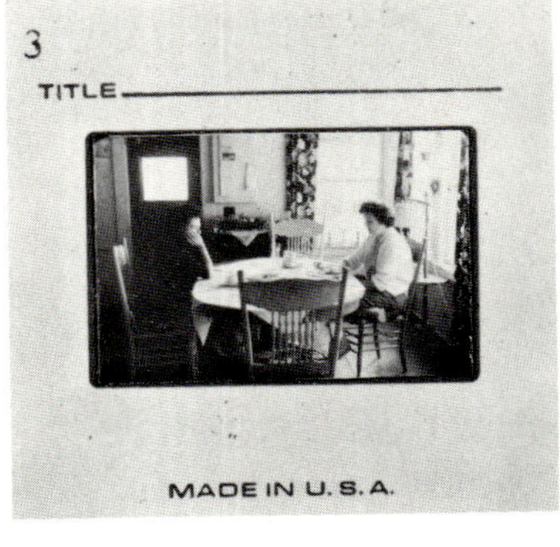

This thumbnail sketch was made from a 35 mm candid color shot — well, almost candid. Although the action was shot without posing it and with almost no warning, the composition was first worked out through the camera's view finder. Then I waited for coffee time and my two models. The dazzling morning light of Cape Cod made the use of flash or flood light unnecessary.

I use this sketch to demonstrate how it's possible to take a bad picture and transform it into a good one. The original painting was done on the spot in about an hour and a half. It is badly composed and much too crowded. Now — in the revised version I have taken most of the same elements and juggled them around a bit, redistributing and simplifying the main forms and giving the negative shapes more prominence. The design of the picture is now dominated and held by the dark row of hydrangeas running across the middle ground. There is an orchestration of horizontal and vertical connections that makes the vase of flowers the focal point and the center of interest.

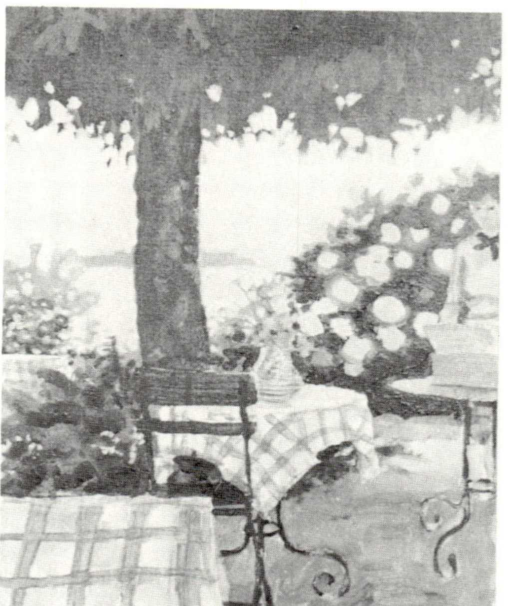

Original version

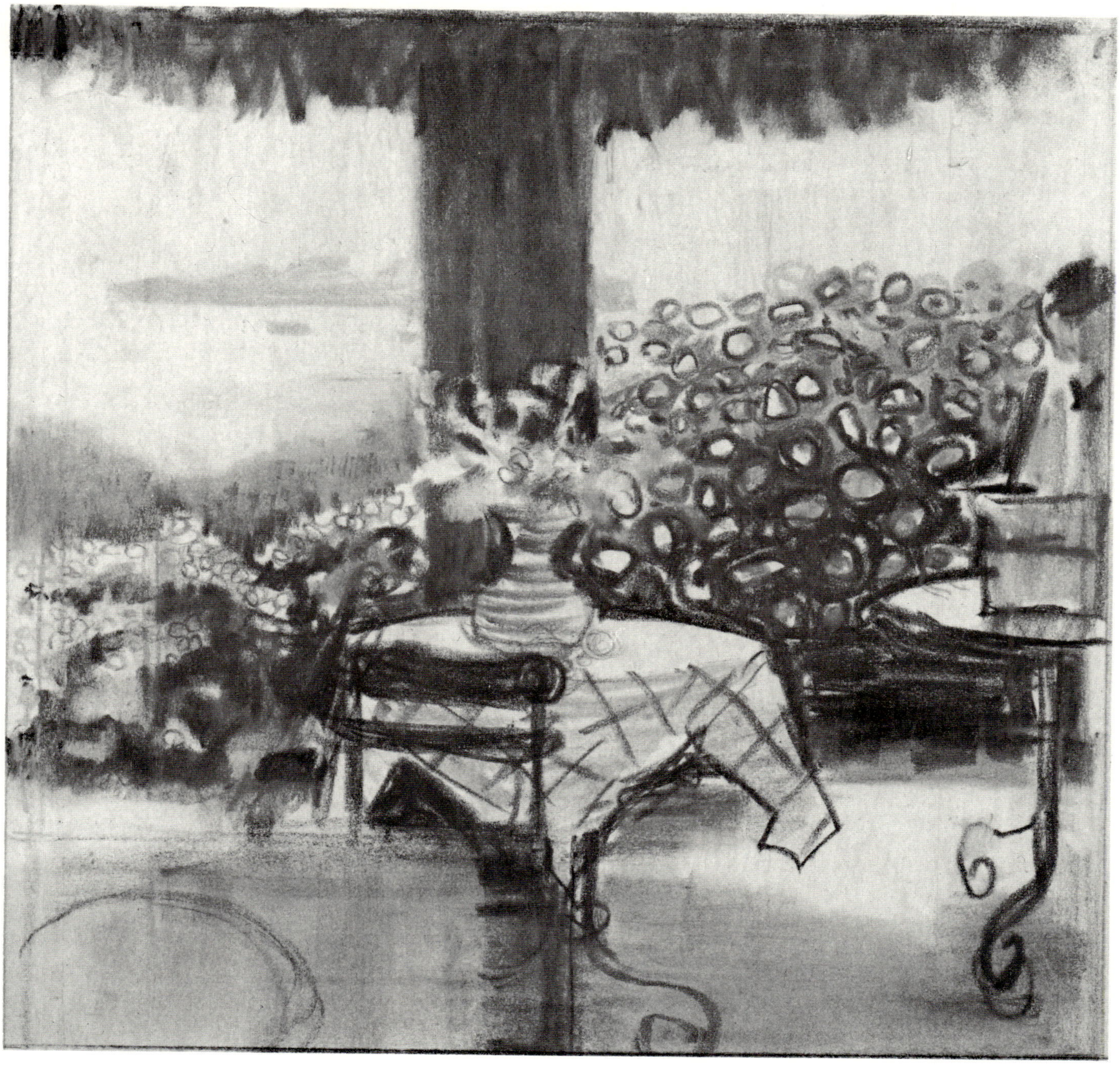

THE FIRST OUTLINES THROUGH WHICH AN ABLE MASTER INDICATES HIS THOUGHT CONTAIN THE GERM OF EVERYTHING SIGNIFICANT THE WORK WILL OFFER.

From the Journal of Eugene Delacroix

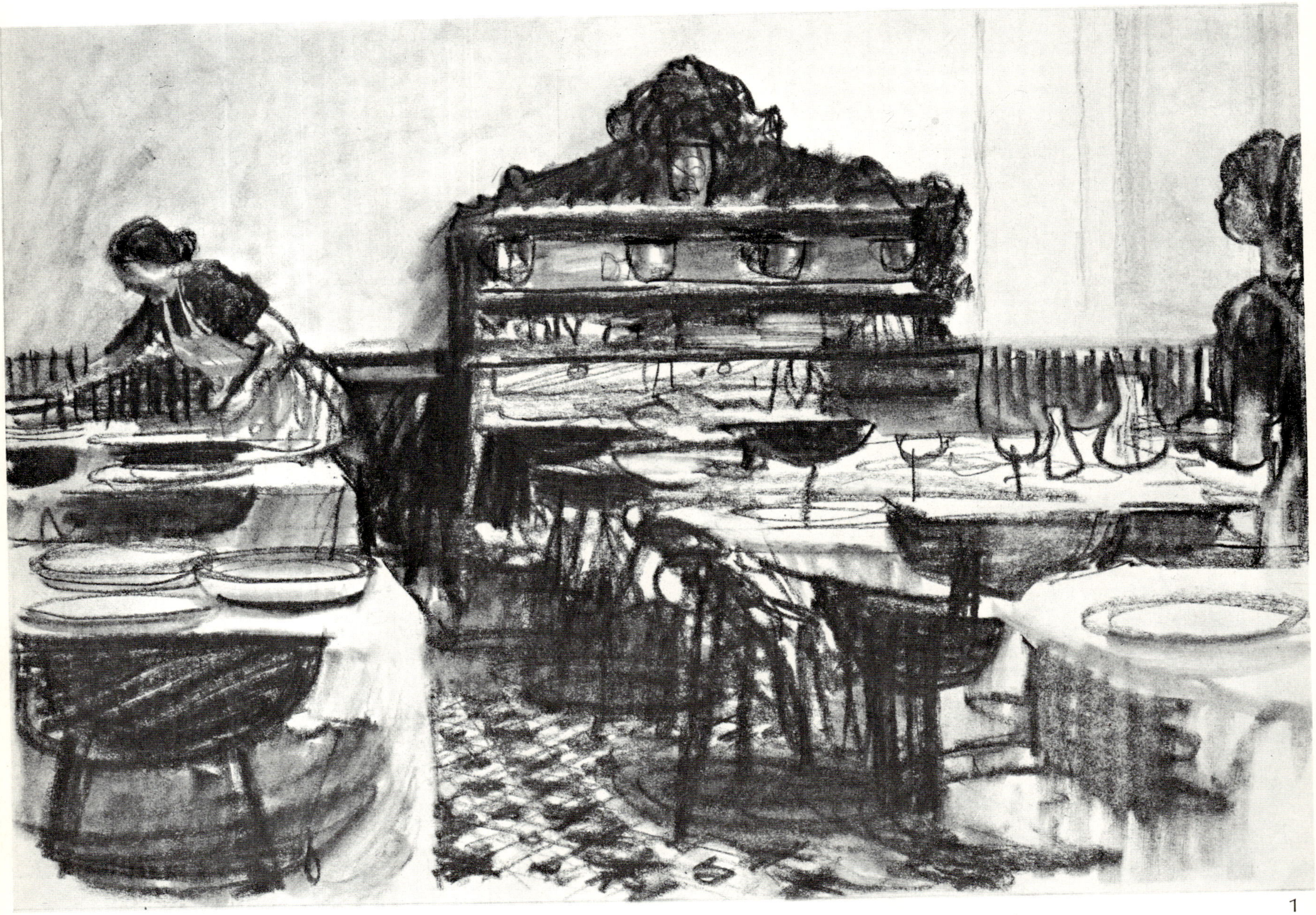

1

Dining Room, Mont Louis, France

Seeing this dining room for the first time was a little like stepping into an interior by Bonnard or Vuillard. It seemed the absolute essence of the provincial French pension (Fig. 1). I doubt if it had changed very much in a hundred years. I sketched it in the hope of catching some of this changeless atmosphere, just as the women were setting the tables for breakfast. Now I wish I had taken more color notes. It ought to make a good painting.

The big difference between a magazine illustration and a picture made to be framed and hung on a wall lies in what is expected of it. If it's a story illustration then it has a job to do; it has to sell the story — it has to make the reader want to stop and read it. Any aspirations it might have as a work of art are secondary. However, a good illustrator will try to imbue his work with those picture qualities that go beyond the limitations of the specific story.

In illustration the role of the preliminary sketch is a crucial one. This stage of development is the proving ground for the idea and the eventual finished picture. Out of the preliminaries there can only be one winner. Fig. 2 is a comprehensive sketch that was rejected in favor of one from a more unusual angle looking through the glass, into the hallway. For a short story for *Good Housekeeping* magazine, it was done from a black and white photograph using natural light. Outdoor detail, plant, and tiles I invented, as well as the color scheme.

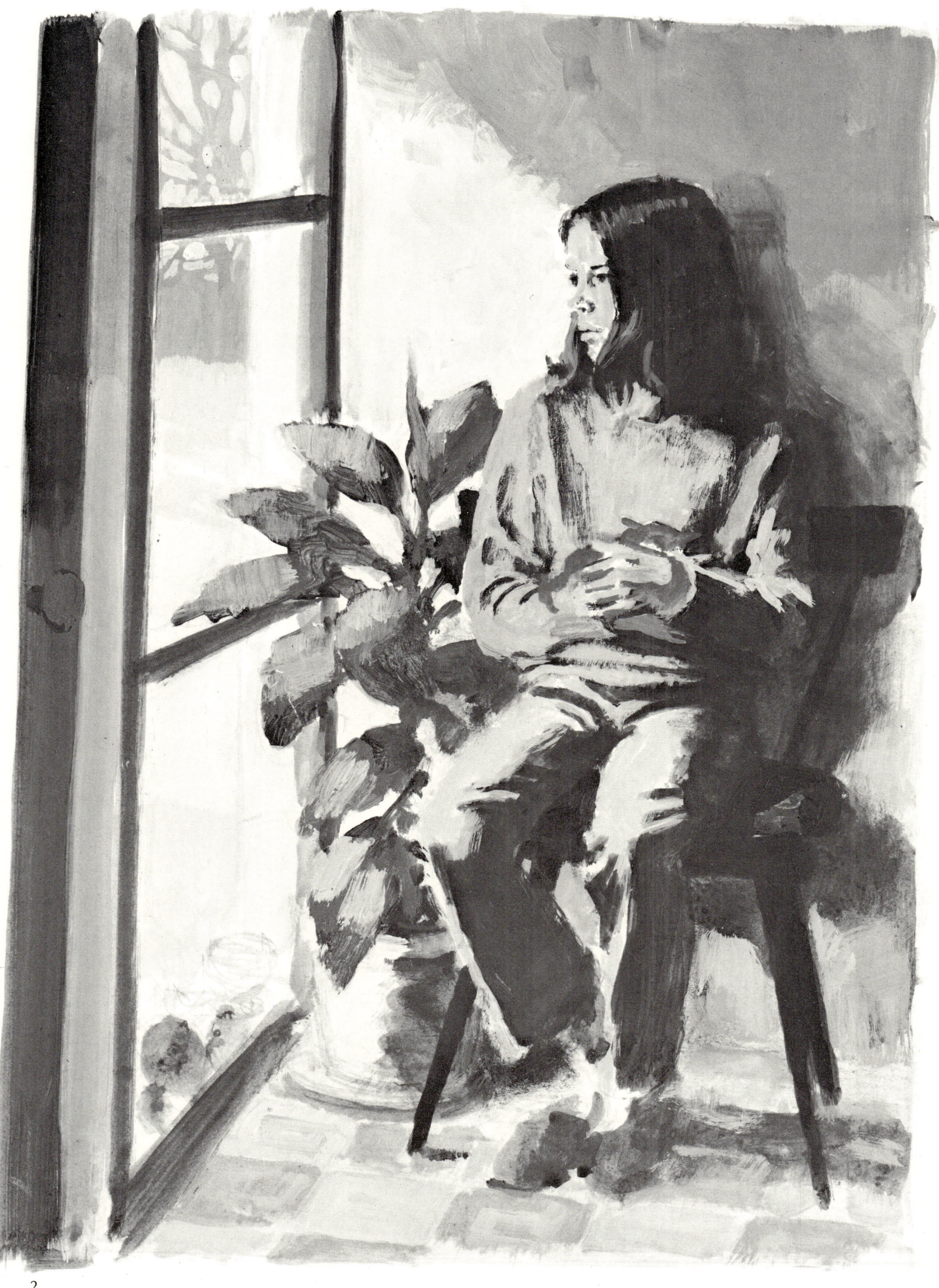

2

I tried a painting from this sketch several years ago without much success. I still like the composition and mood of it, however, and plan to have another try at it some day on the theory that I may have learned something since then. There are all kinds of interesting abstract possibilities in its strongly contrasting shapes.

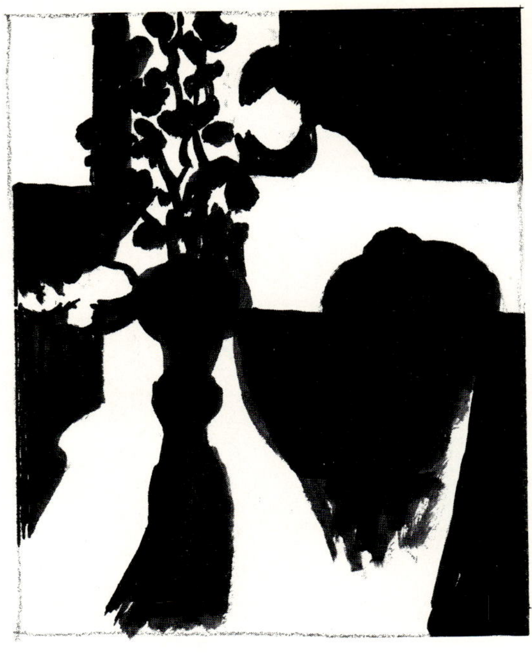

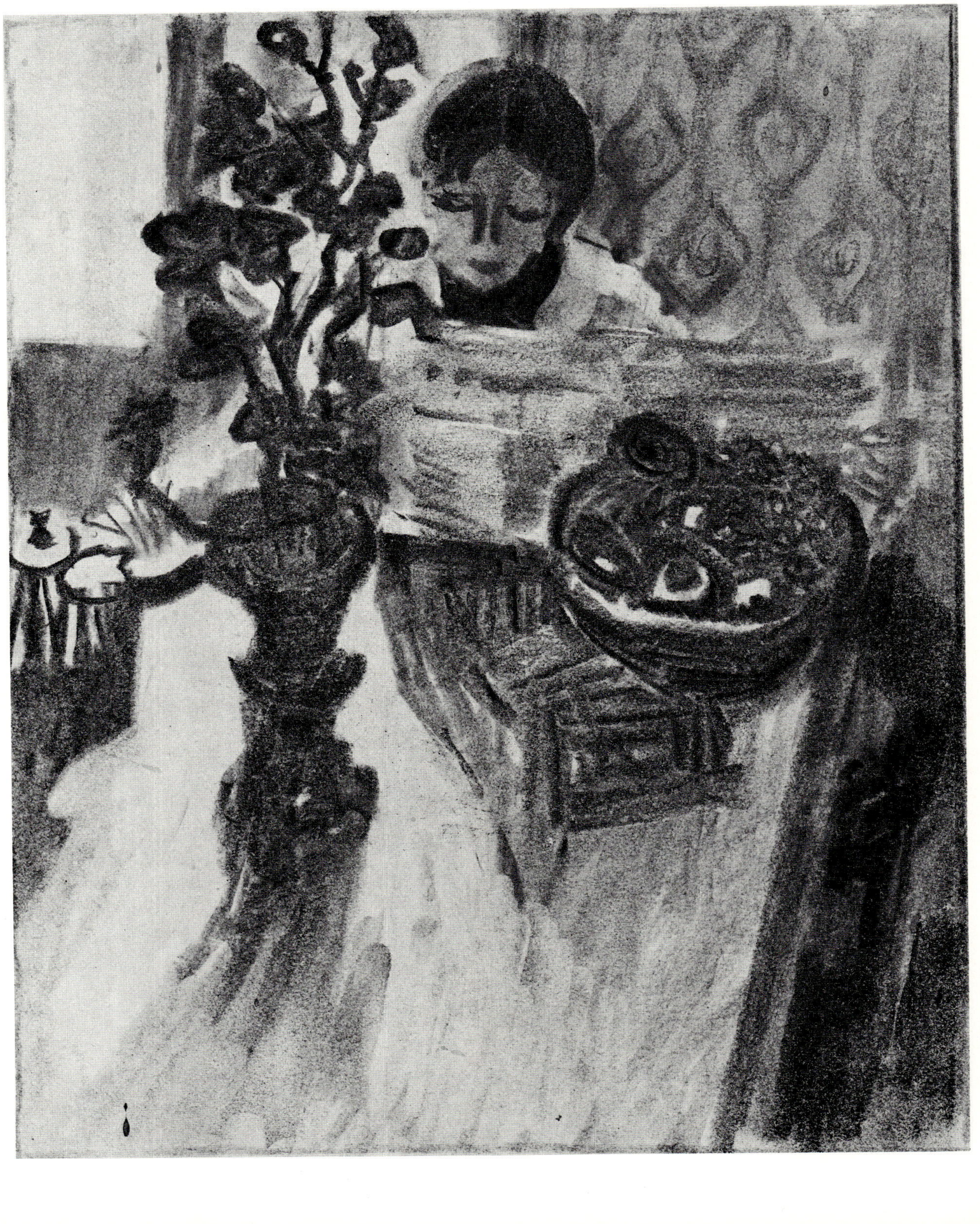

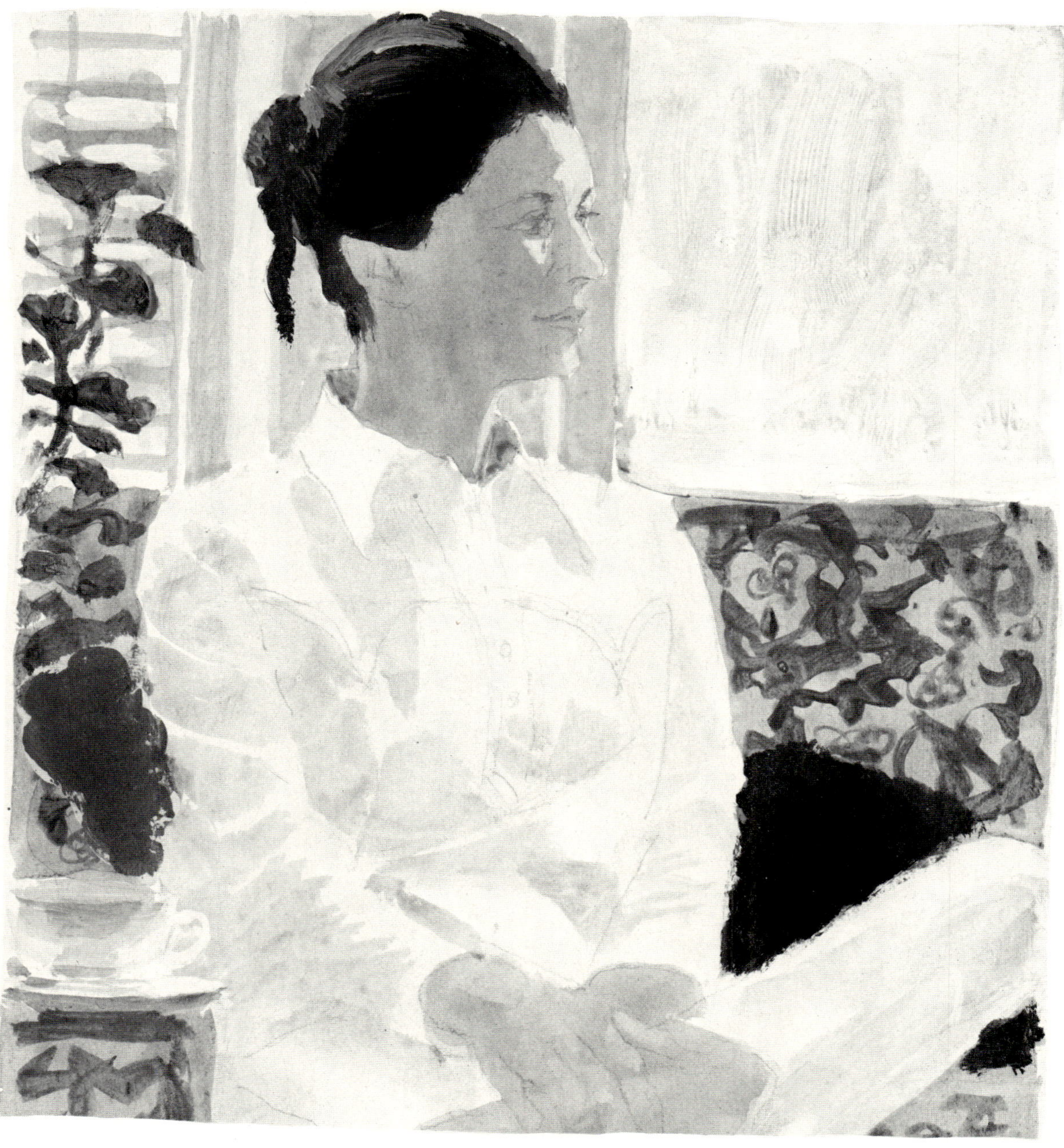

This preliminary sketch, reproduced here actual size, was done for the portrait on page 89. The finished painting was an experiment in a new (for me) underpainting technique. Since it was not a commissioned assignment I had nobody to please but myself. I needed to jar myself loose from some old and comfortable habits of working. As a successful portrait it falls a bit short but as an exploratory exercise it was a success. Both the sketch and the finished painting were rendered in acrylics.

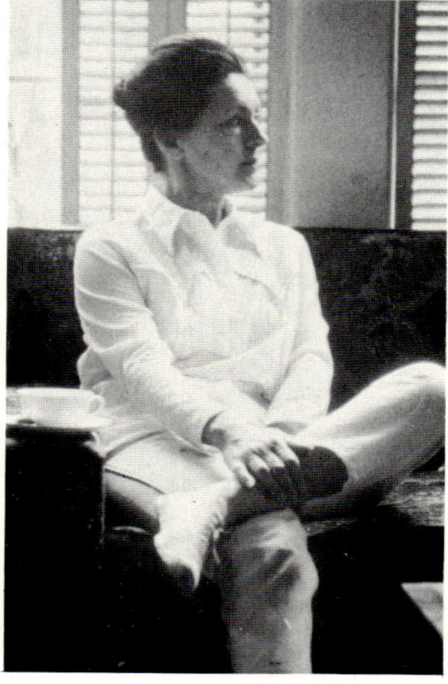

On the left is one of several reference photos taken to help me establish the pose and maintain the likeness as the painting progressed.

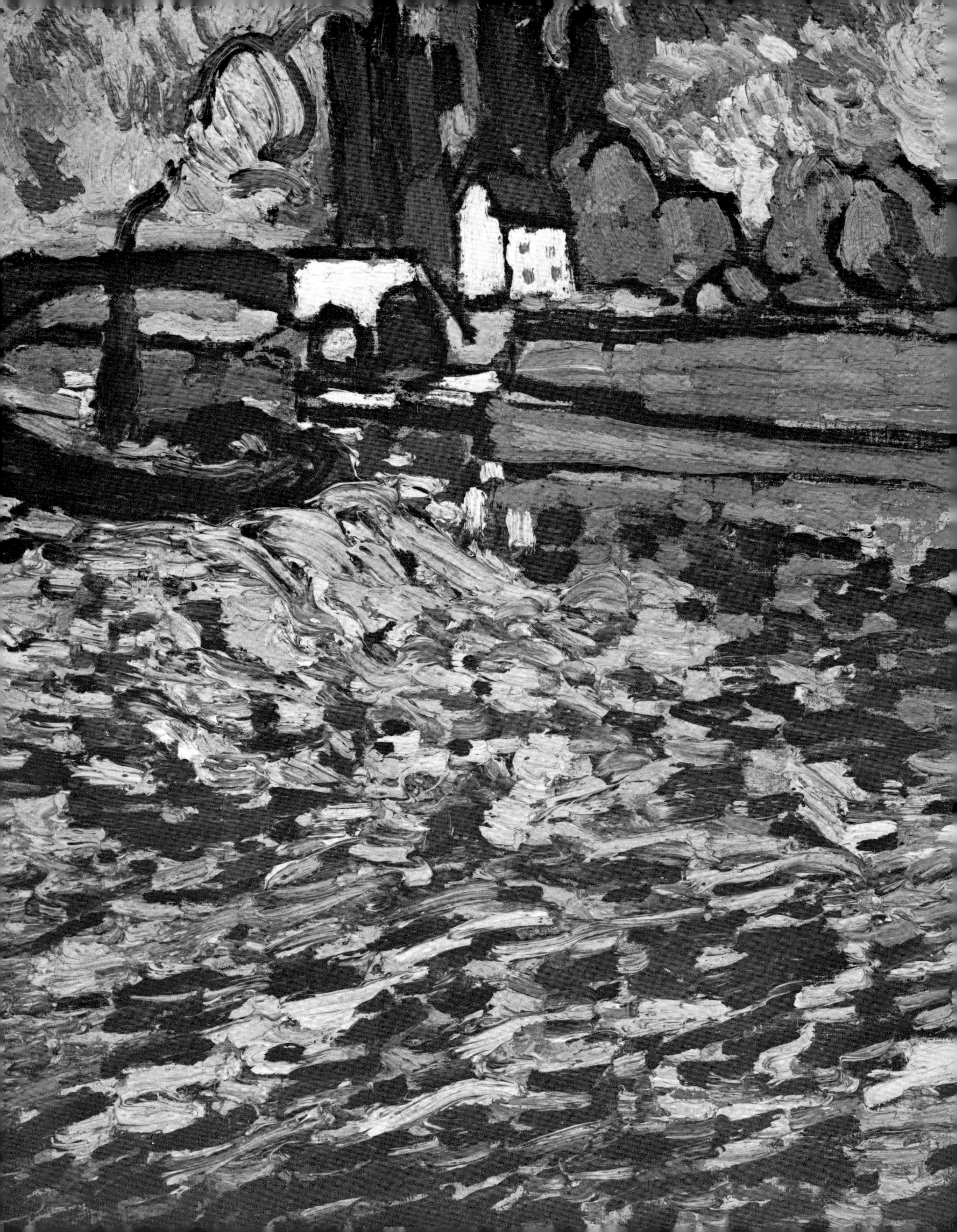

STYLE

INSTINCT WHICH NOURISHES METHOD CAN OFTEN BE SUPERIOR TO A METHOD WHICH NOURISHES INSTINCT.
Pierre Bonnard

What is style? Style is Van Gogh's squirrely brush strokes; Kokoschka's distorted, wide-angle perspective; Dubuffet's wryly ironic mud-like figures; Rembrandt's luminous use of light; Bonnard's daubs of pure vibrating color; Klee's poetic images; Dali's surrealistic dreamworld apparitions; Rothko's shimmering bars of light; Kline's or de Kooning's slashing brushwork; Corot's monumental calm.

Style is often confused with technique, which is something else. Think of style as the end result and technique as but one means of attaining it. Style is something that has to develop — it has to evolve out of a combination of things. Every artist is attracted differently by subject matter, mediums, tools, and techniques. He will be influenced by his own personal experiences and beliefs, and almost certainly by the work of other artists. Every important artist's style is a mutation of other styles.

Style is the product of a harmonious marriage of idea, tool, and medium. Without all three, style is nothing more than a transparent affectation.

A method of painting in wide use today is one that can be roughly described as a procedure of "putting everything in" and then painting out whatever is not wanted. This of course is no more than a technique, but it's a sound one that allows you to make a statement — to "try it out." Then if you don't like the effect, you can eliminate it, as in a collage. Another advantage to this procedure is in the "ghost" images that result, where forms have been painted out but are still faintly visible. These shadowy vestiges of shapes can be very effective in creating depth and dimension and that valuable but elusive quality — mystery.

There is no advantage that I can see to working with thick paint (impasto) just for the sake of piling it on, unless it is to disguise the fact that there is nothing underneath. Tons of this kind of painting are being troweled out by painters who achieve little more than tricky surface effects. The palette knife can be a sensitive and expressive tool in the hands of someone who knows how to use it interpretively. However, when it is not used skillfully the results are no more than "stylish" artifice.

About 1950 a style that could be called the "unfinished" look began to dominate abstract painting. That this style had a positive value is evident in the later works of artists such as Motherwell, de Kooning and Larry Rivers. Every professional artist, realist or abstractionist, struggles with the problem of knowing when to lay down his brush and declare a painting finished. Knowing when to quit is an art in itself, and one that many painters never learn. It is a fact that some of the best paintings — the freshest, most exciting and most stimulating — are those that were never completed; where raw canvas and pencil or charcoal line and underpainting show through.

Indecisiveness in a painting will stand out like the performance of an actor who is not sure of his lines. Decide what you want to paint and how you want to paint it — then say it loud and clear. It may not be the ultimate masterwork but it will carry weight if it is stated with authority.

RIVER SCENE WITH BRIDGE by MAURICE de VLAMINCK (detail)
Courtesy Wadsworth Atheneum, Hartford
Gift of Mr. and Mrs. Robert Montgomery

PART 4 · PHOTOGRAPHY

THE CAMERA – ENEMY or ALLY

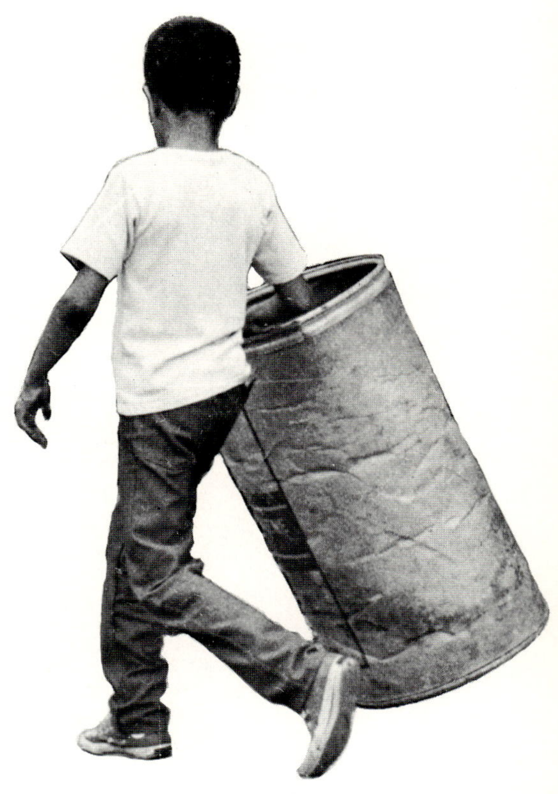

There is no reason why the camera, provided it is properly used, should not take its place alongside all the other tools and implements available to the artist. Degas used photography and Utrillo painted some of his best street scenes from picture post cards of Paris. Da Vinci tried to invent a camera and I'm sure if he had been successful his contemporaries would have put it to use long before the twentieth century.

The fact is, many modern artists use photographs in their work, some as pictorial reference; others, like Robert Rauschenberg, Andy Warhol, and Larry Rivers, actually incorporate photographs and photostats into their paintings and collages.

If you are going to use photographs as a source of reference you should be aware of their limitations. First of all — forget the old saying, "the camera does not lie." Actually the camera is shamefully untrustworthy. I have seen photographs of people I knew fairly well that bore almost no resemblance to them whatsoever. In truth, a photograph can present a highly distorted and unreal image. Be careful how you let a piece of machinery, no matter how expensive and sophisticated, do your thinking for you.

Remember that the photographer must always work within the limitations of his camera. What the camera sees it records — it cannot make judgments, it cannot arbitrarily eliminate or alter things in its field of vision like the artist can.

One thing the camera can do that the human eye cannot is record and "freeze" split-second action. This kind of suspended image is not always good. On the contrary, it frequently is anything but natural looking and the artist who uses a camera to record movement should be aware of this. The eye does not see movement at a 1/500th of a second but forms a sort of composite impression of the action — in other words, it sums it up. Ideally, a good action drawing can sometimes suggest what has just happened and what is about to happen.

The impressionistic effects of out-of-focus photography are nothing new to the professional photographer. Portrait and fashion photographers in particular have been using limited depth of focus for years to get some surprisingly unrealistic effects, simply by manipulating the camera's diaphragm. To explain: when a camera is set with diaphragm "stopped down" to its smallest opening, the "in focus" range between foreground and background is maximal. Conversely, if the diaphragm is set at "wide open" (largest aperture) then virtually everything it sees will be out of focus except that which it is optically focussed on. The result is a blurring and fusing of the background (or foreground), depending on where the focus is set (Figure 1).

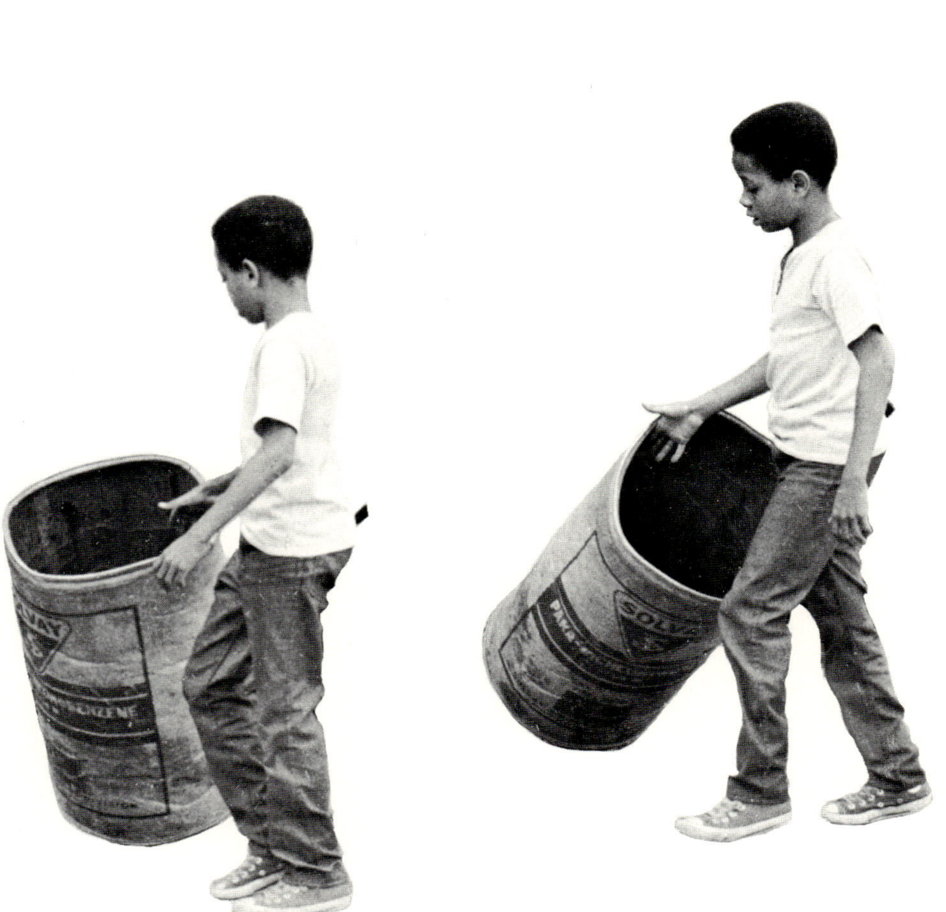

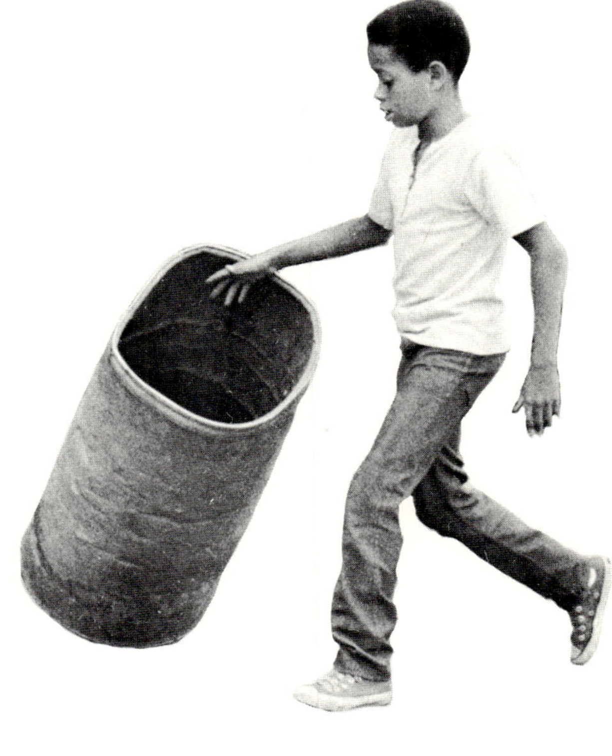

An example of unposed, "hit-or-miss" photography. Some of the action is good — some not so good. But it would take a master draftsman to come up with action this authentic without the use of a camera. In this case I panned with the action, moving from right to left, shooting at 1/500th of a second. For this kind of action a "robot" camera probably is best. It is power driven, advancing the film and cocking the shutter automatically, much faster than you can do it by hand. All you do is click the shutter.

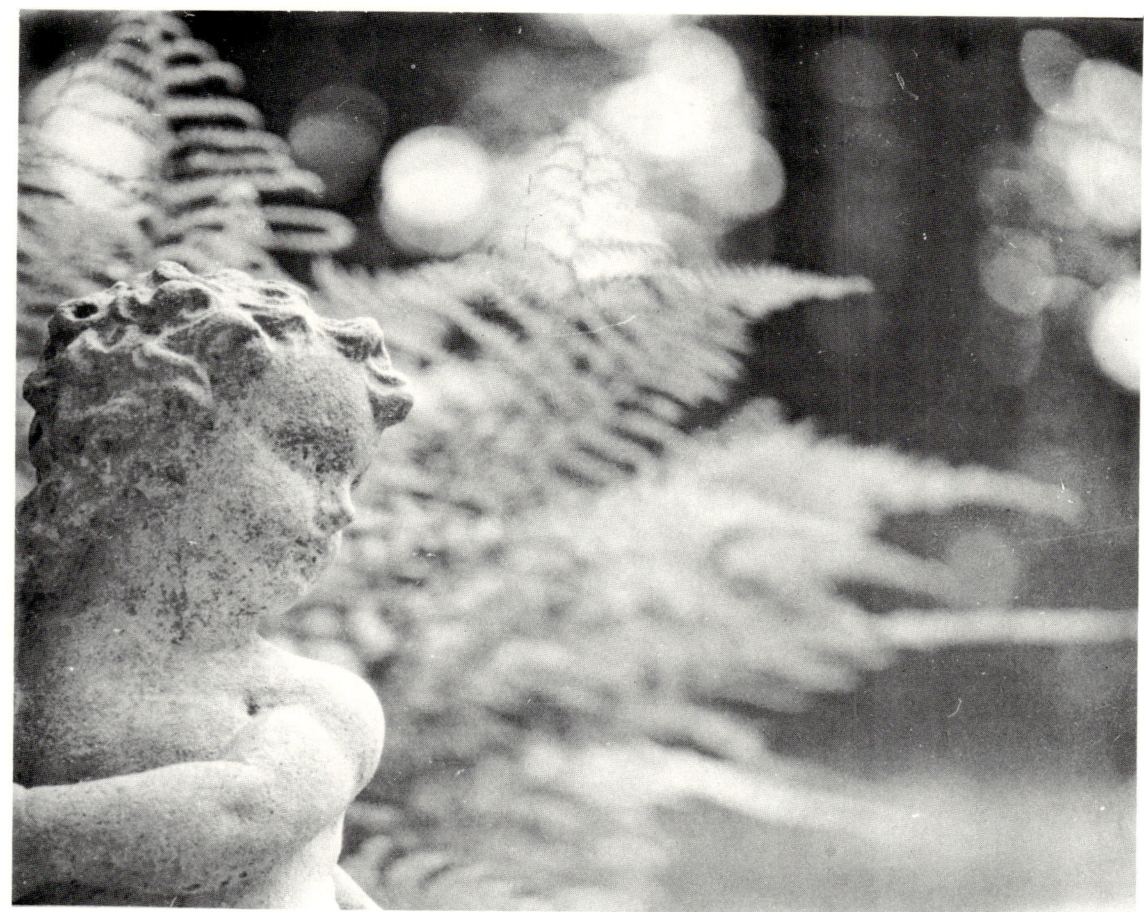

1

TELEPHOTOGRAPHY

The telephoto lens and the zoom lens have greatly broadened the scope of modern photography, and the artist might just as well take advantage of this. A telephoto lens will bring in distant objects that would otherwise be lost. It is useful in situations where getting close enough for ordinary pictures is difficult or impossible. (See Fig. 1.)

Little seems to have been written on the subject of color slides in connection with painting. Many painters still are reluctant to admit that they use photography at all. About half the illustrators I know use slides to some extent. Not a few, in fact, would be lost without them. I use color slides occasionally on commercial assignments and am now experimenting with them in landscape painting. But there are some rather obvious dangers in relying solely on slides or on any kind of photography for that matter. One of these dangers is that photographs give us total accessibility to the subject. Paradoxically, this can be unhealthy in that it allows us unlimited time to consider the subject, to intellectualize, and too often, to belabor it to death. Working from life on the other hand, whether it's a landscape or a figure, encourages a more decisive approach. When we do not have the time to deliberate, the results are

1

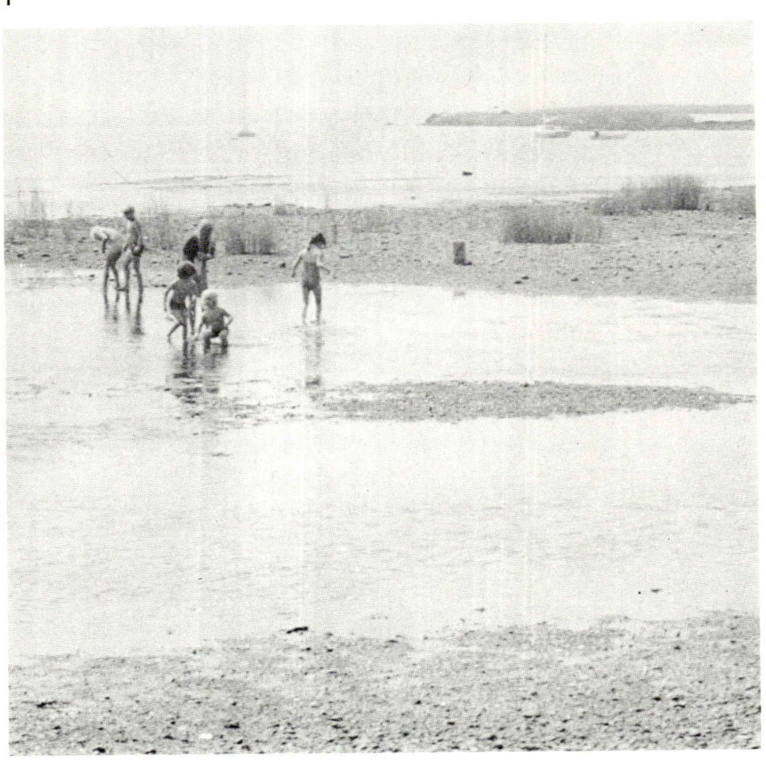

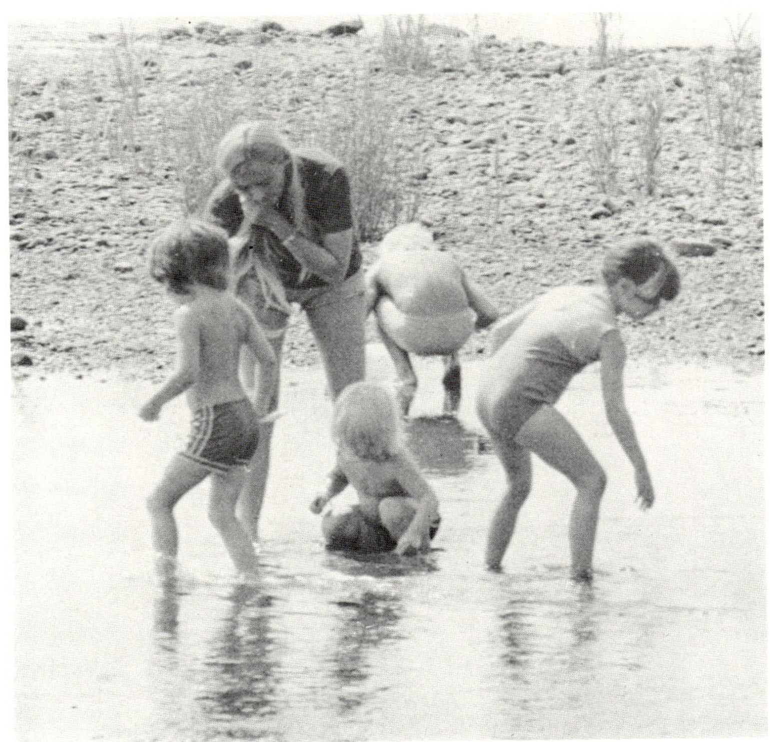

PROJECTION

often more direct and more authoritative. It depends a lot, of course, on your style and on how realistic you want to be. The painter who is striving for ambience and the feeling of "being there," is not going to work up the same enthusiasm over a two-dimensional color slide as he might, were he actually on the scene. I see no harm in using slides, however, provided that their use is augmented by plenty of experience in working from nature.

If you are going to paint from transparencies you will need a way to project them that gives a bright, clear picture in light strong enough to work by. The best answer is a projection box that uses a rear projection screen. These can be bought (they are not cheap) or you can make your own. (See Fig. 2.)

Most museums permit picture taking, although they frown on the use of tripods and flash bulbs as a public nuisance (which they are). Many European museums will make you check your camera at the door, though. They don't want any competition with their post card business, I guess. You will want to shoot color so be sure your film is right for the light if it is artificial. Your photo supply store can advise you on this (Fig. 3).

3

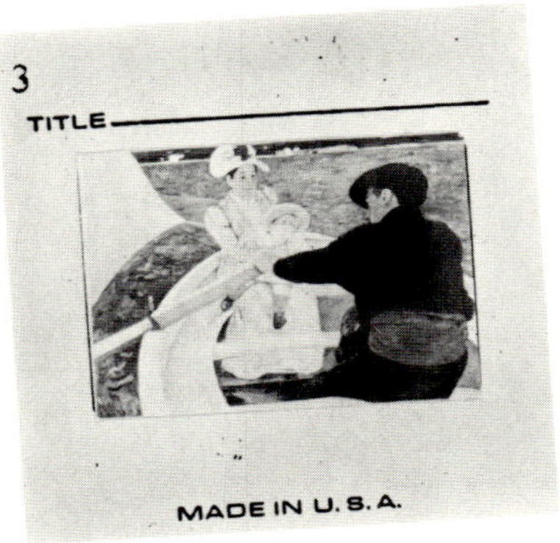

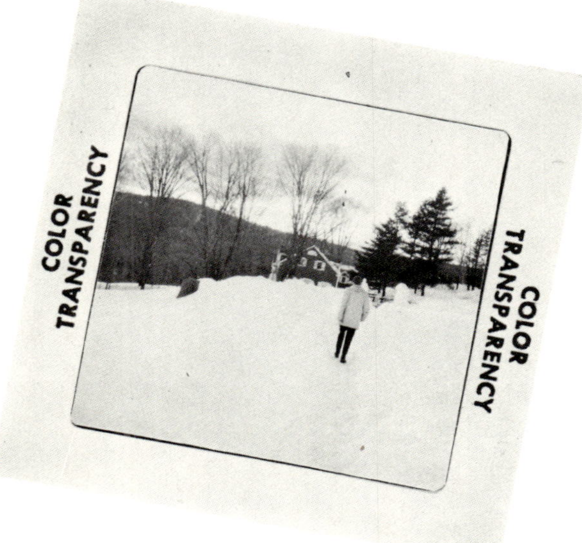

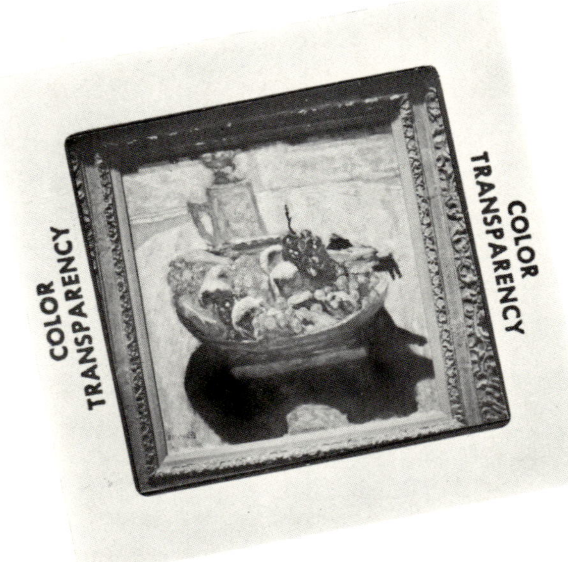

3

I use a 300 watt projector with my projection box. Anything stronger is so bright that the eye has trouble making the adjustment, back and forth, from picture screen to working surface. In working from slides, try to discipline yourself to think and paint just as you would in working from nature. Design your picture — change the colors — simplify. Don't try to use everything in the photo.

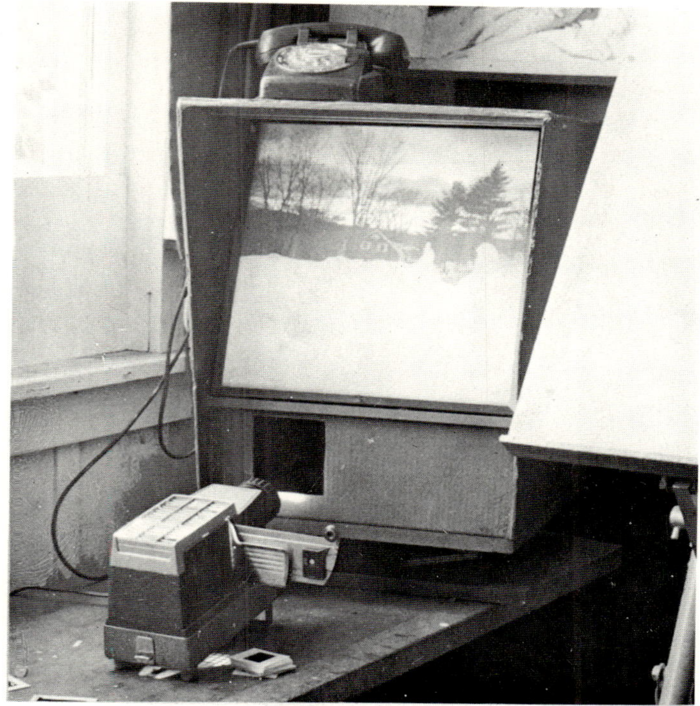

2

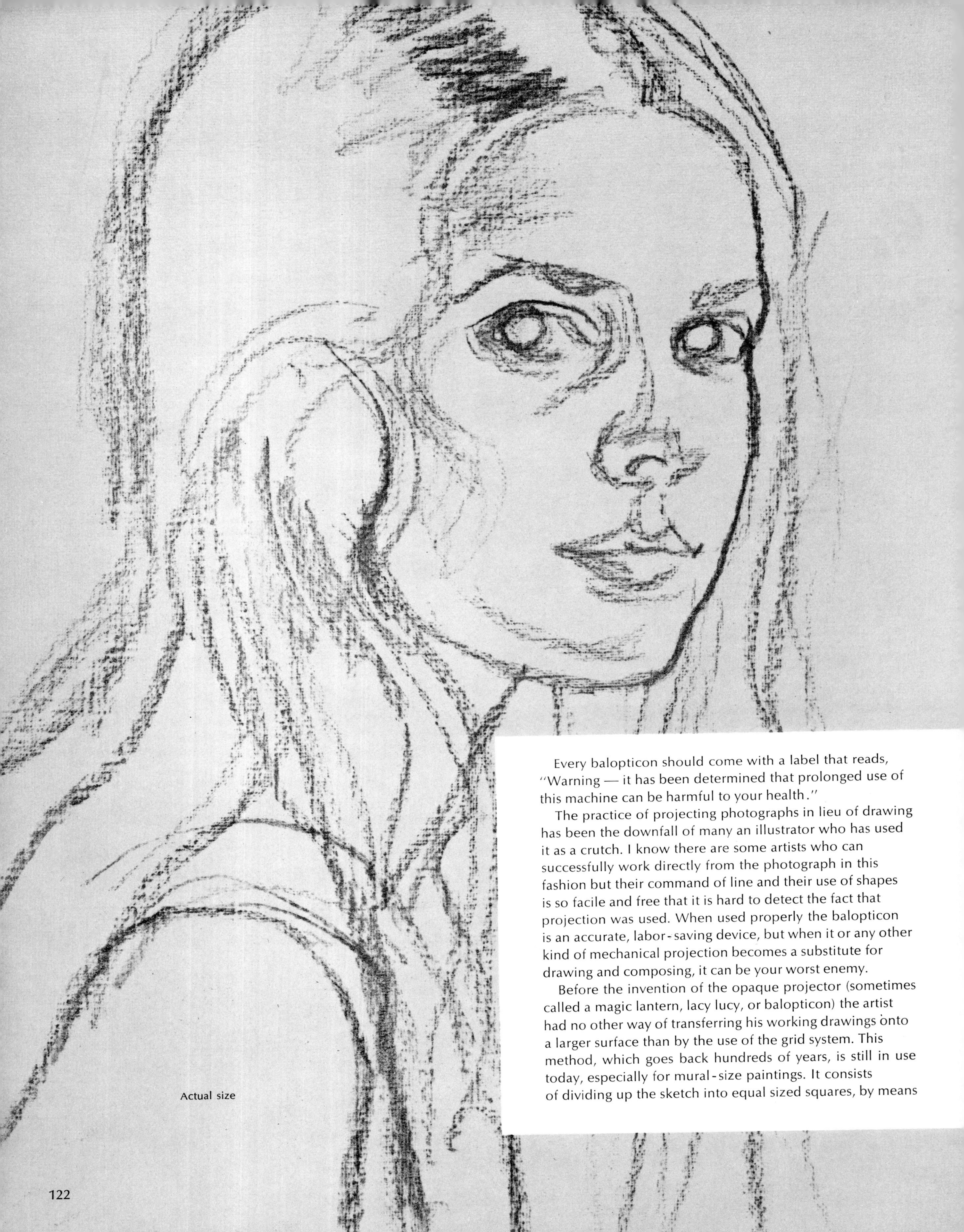

Actual size

Every balopticon should come with a label that reads, "Warning — it has been determined that prolonged use of this machine can be harmful to your health."

The practice of projecting photographs in lieu of drawing has been the downfall of many an illustrator who has used it as a crutch. I know there are some artists who can successfully work directly from the photograph in this fashion but their command of line and their use of shapes is so facile and free that it is hard to detect the fact that projection was used. When used properly the balopticon is an accurate, labor-saving device, but when it or any other kind of mechanical projection becomes a substitute for drawing and composing, it can be your worst enemy.

Before the invention of the opaque projector (sometimes called a magic lantern, lacy lucy, or balopticon) the artist had no other way of transferring his working drawings onto a larger surface than by the use of the grid system. This method, which goes back hundreds of years, is still in use today, especially for mural-size paintings. It consists of dividing up the sketch into equal sized squares, by means

Here is my venerable balopticon in operation, blowing up a 4½"X 6" pencil drawing onto a 21" X 26" canvas for the portrait on page 93. This is by far the easiest and most accurate way to transfer a small drawing to a larger working surface. There's an additional advantage in this method which allows you to visualize the effect without making a mark on the canvas.

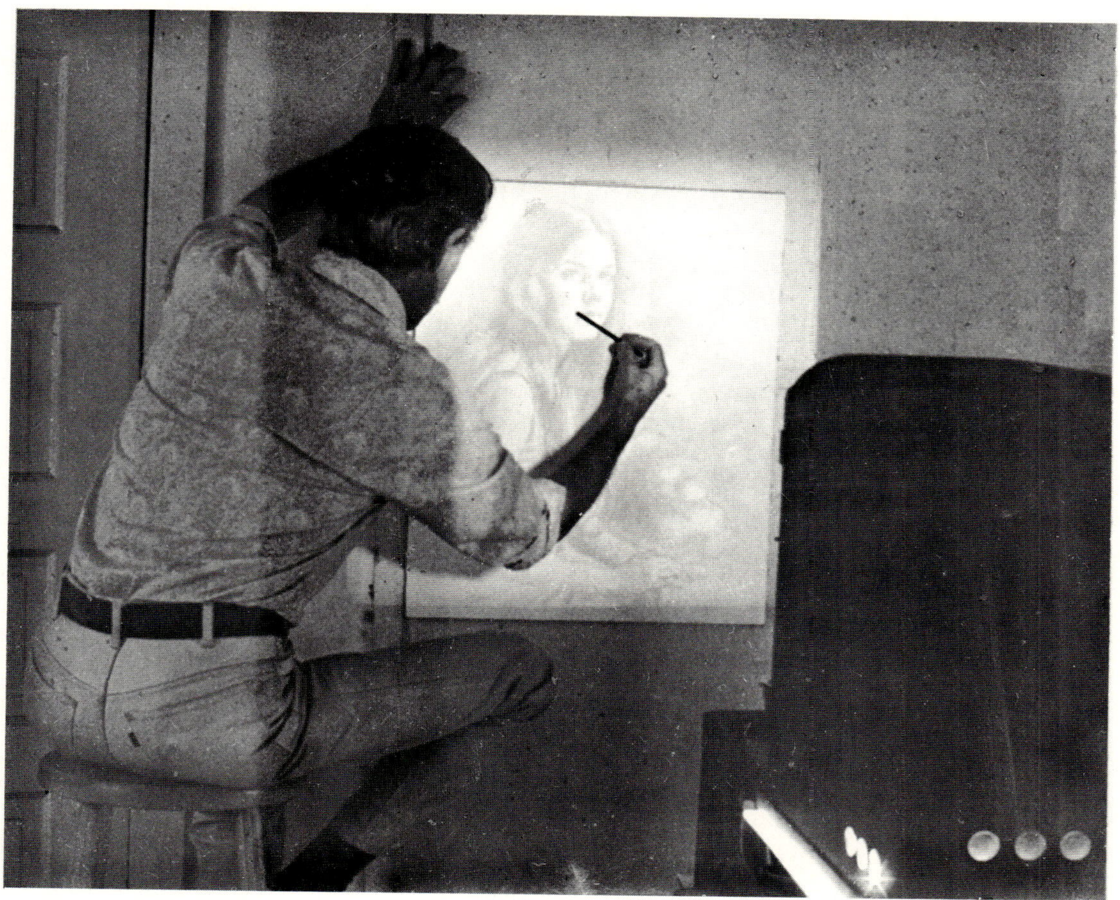

of a grid composed of vertical and horizontal lines. If further dissection is needed, as with areas of intricate detail, diagonals can be added. By placing the drawing in a corner of the painting panel or canvas and drawing diagonal lines across it from corner to corner the sketch can be scaled up to any size and always remain in proportion. I find optical projection much handier for enlarging sketches (Fig. 1) and sometimes will even project lettering and mechanical detail directly from a photograph. Either way you enlarge it, if you are going to go to the trouble of making a preliminary sketch, it should be followed closely. Arbitrarily changing or complicating a good design seldom improves it. However, and I don't know why it is, occasionally a design that looked solid enough in miniature will fall apart when it is blown up. Certain shapes seem to lose force and meaning when they are greatly enlarged. Be watchful for this when making a line-for-line enlargement of a small sketch. Check the scaled-up version carefully by stepping well back and viewing it from a distance before you start putting on paint.

1

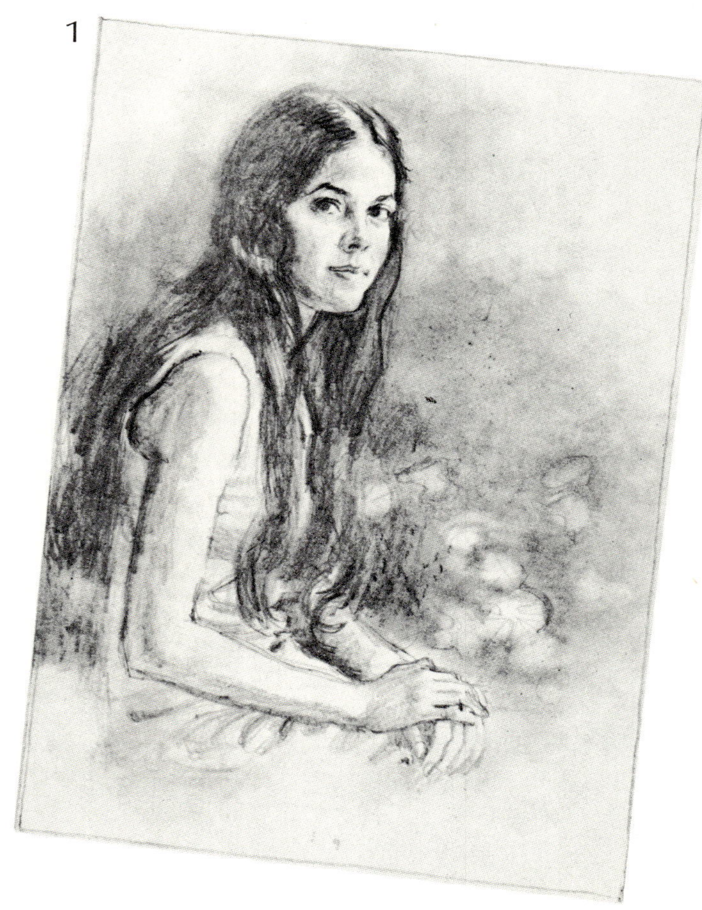

CONCLUSION

I CANNOT GIVE YOU THE FORMULA FOR SUCCESS
BUT I CAN GIVE YOU THE FORMULA FOR FAILURE.
TRY TO PLEASE EVERYBODY.

Herbert Bayard Swope

I don't think there is anything that stifles and inhibits the creative spirit quicker than a fear of the unknown. Never be afraid to experiment — to overreach yourself. And, if you will try the untried and explore the unfamiliar, you will be keeping the way open to new ideas, new concepts, and new sensations.

Art cannot stand still and survive for very long. It must continue to grow. If every new movement allowed itself to be influenced by public reaction we would never have had Impressionism, Fauvism, Cubism, or Expressionism. There would be no change — no growth. The good artist doesn't really give a damn what the public or even the critics say.

It's essential to believe in what you are doing. Work to make the viewer see things your way — not his way. As a painter you possess the means of moving others into your line of thought.

Follow your natural inclinations. While there are some proven right ways and wrong ways of using and applying craft, in the areas of concept, color, style and interpretation there are no rules, or at least none that can't be broken. No one can tell you how you were meant to work. This is something you will have to find out for yourself — by experimenting, by experiencing, and by making mistakes.

Writing this book has been good for me. It has taken me many places — mostly places I had been before and forgotten. It has also led me into new fields and introduced me to things I had always intended to explore but somehow never got around to. Bonnard said, "Every artist needs two lives. One in which to learn and the other in which to paint."

Here is a quote from Balzac. It's an afterthought — something I came across as the book was practically ready to go to press.

"The quality that above all deserves the greatest glory in art — and by that word we must include all creations of the mind — is courage; courage of a kind of which common minds have no conception, and which is perhaps described here for the first time. . . . To plan, dream, and imagine fine works is a pleasant occupation to be sure. . . . But to produce, to bring to birth, to bring up the infant work with labor, to put it to bed full-fed with milk, to take it up again every morning with inexhaustible material love, to lick it clean, to dress it a hundred times in lovely garments that it tears up again and again; never to be discouraged by the convulsions of this mad life, and to make of it a living masterpiece that speaks to all eyes in sculpture, or to all minds in literature, to all memories in painting, to all hearts in music — that is the task of execution."

— Honoré de Balzac, *Cousin Bette*

INDEX

BIBLIOGRAPHY

ARTISTS at WORK by Bernard Chaet. Webb Books

CONVERSATIONS with ARTISTS by Selden Rodman. Putnam

The ENJOYMENT and USE of COLOR by Walter Sargent. Dover

The FAUVES by Jean-Paul Crespelle. New York Graphic Society

HISTORY of ART and MUSIC by H. W. Janson & Joseph Kerman. Abrams

The JOURNAL of EUGENE DELACROIX. Grove Press

LAROUSSE ENCYCLOPEDIA of MODERN ART

MODERN ARTISTS on ART by Robert L. Herbert. Prentice-Hall, Inc.

MODERN PAINTING: CONTEMPORARY TRENDS by Nello Ponente. (Skira) World

On the ART of DRAWING by Robert Fawcett. Watson-Guptill

PAINTING and UNDERSTANDING ABSTRACT ART by Leonard Brooks. Van Nostrand-Reinhold

The TECHNIQUE of COLLAGE by Helen Hutton. Watson-Guptill

The UNKNOWN SHORE by Dore Ashton. Atlantic-Little, Brown